GW01316088

CUNARD LINE

A FLEET HISTORY

CUNARD LINE

A FLEET HISTORY

Peter Newall

Ships in Focus Publications

Published in the UK in 2012 by
Ships in Focus Publications,
18 Franklands, Longton,
Preston PR4 SPD

© 2012 Peter Newall and Ships in Focus Publications

All rights reserved. No part of this publication may be produced, stored in a retrieval system or transtmitted in any form or by any means, electronic, mechanical, photocopying, recording or otherwises without the written permission of the publisher.

The right of Peter Newall to be identified as author of this work has been asserted by him in accordance with the Copyright, Design and Patent Act 1988.

Printed by Amadeus Press Ltd., Cleckheaton.
ISBN 978-1-901703-24-5

Left: *Queen Elizabeth 2* at Lisbon on 21st April 2006. *[Louis Miguel Correira]*
Above: *Aquitania* arriving at New York at the end of her maiden voyage in June 1914. *[Russell Priest collection]*
Cover: *Queen Elizabeth* bound for Cherbourg. *[Stephen Card]*
Back cover: *Queen Mary 2* sailing from Southampton on 13th July 2012. *[Stefan and Sara Venter (upixphotography.com)]*
Endpapers: A selection of Cunard advertising material. Not all show specific ships but they depict the company's services and ports visited.

*This book is dedicated to all
those who served with Cunard Line
and its associate companies*

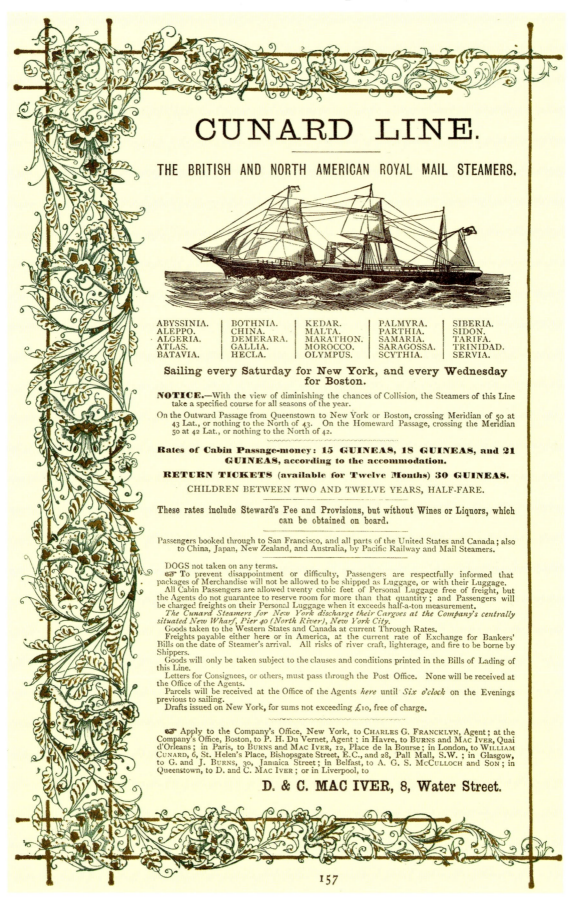

CUNARD LINE.

THE BRITISH AND NORTH AMERICAN ROYAL MAIL STEAMERS.

ABYSSINIA.	BOTHNIA.	KEDAR.	PALMYRA.	SIBERIA.
ALEPPO.	CHINA.	MALTA.	PARTHIA.	SIDON.
ALGERIA.	DEMERARA.	MARATHON.	SAMARIA.	TARIFA.
ATLAS.	GALLIA.	MOROCCO.	SARAGOSSA.	TRINIDAD.
BATAVIA.	HECLA.	OLYMPUS.	SCYTHIA.	SERVIA.

**Sailing every Saturday for New York, and every Wednesday
for Boston.**

NOTICE.—With the view of diminishing the chances of Collision, the Steamers of this Line take a specified course for all seasons of the year.

On the Outward Passage from Queenstown to New York or Boston, crossing Meridian of 50 at 43 Lat., or nothing to the North of 43. On the Homeward Passage, crossing the Meridian 50 at 42 Lat., or nothing to the North of 42.

**Rates of Cabin Passage-money: 15 GUINEAS, 18 GUINEAS, and 21
GUINEAS, according to the accommodation.**

RETURN TICKETS (available for Twelve Months) 30 GUINEAS.

CHILDREN BETWEEN TWO AND TWELVE YEARS, HALF-FARE.

These rates include Steward's Fee and Provisions, but without Wines or Liquors, which can be obtained on board.

Passengers booked through to San Francisco, and all parts of the United States and Canada; also to China, Japan, New Zealand, and Australia, by Pacific Railway and Mail Steamers.

DOGS not taken on any terms.

☞ To prevent disappointment or difficulty, Passengers are respectfully informed that packages of Merchandise will not be allowed to be shipped as Luggage, or with their Luggage.

All Cabin Passengers are allowed twenty cubic feet of Personal Luggage free of freight, but the Agents do not guarantee to reserve room for more than that quantity; and Passengers will be charged freights on their Personal Luggage when it exceeds half-a-ton measurement.

The Cunard Steamers for New York discharge their Cargoes at the Company's centrally situated New Wharf, Pier 40 (North River), New York City.

Goods taken to the Western States and Canada at current Through Rates.

Freights payable either here or in America, at the current rate of Exchange for Bankers' Bills on the date of Steamer's arrival. All risks of river craft, lighterage, and fire to be borne by Shippers.

Goods will only be taken subject to the clauses and conditions printed in the Bills of Lading of this Line.

Letters for Consignees, or others, must pass through the Post Office. None will be received at the Office of the Agents.

Parcels will be received at the Office of the Agents *here* until *Six o'clock* on the Evenings previous to sailing.

Drafts issued on New York, for sums not exceeding £10, free of charge.

☞ Apply to the Company's Office, New York, to CHARLES G. FRANCKLYN, Agent; at the Company's Office, Boston, to P. H. Du Vernet, Agent; in Havre, to BURNS and MAC IVER, Quai d'Orleans; in Paris, to BURNS and MAC IVER, 12, Place de la Bourse; in London, to WILLIAM CUNARD, 6, St. Helen's Place, Bishopsgate Street, E.C., and 28, Pall Mall, S.W.; in Glasgow, to G. and J. BURNS, 30, Jamaica Street; in Belfast, to A. G. S. McCULLOCH and SON; in Queenstown, to D. and C. MAC IVER; or in Liverpool, to

D. & C. MAC IVER, 8, Water Street.

157

CONTENTS

Scythia at Cunard's Liverpool berth, Huskisson Dock, Berth Number 1. *[Harley Crossley collection]*

INTRODUCTION

Cunard Line is the most famous shipping company in the world. However, unlike P&O, which has preserved most of its company records, archival information about Cunard's history is rather patchy. The main records for the company, held at the University of Liverpool, primarily cover the period from 1878 to 1985. Prior to the formation of the Cunard limited liability company in 1880, little information exists, other than that which can be found in the MacIver family papers. These too have been deposited at the University of Liverpool. The Cunard records for the First and Second World Wars are also incomplete, whilst those covering the cargo operations during the Trafalgar House era are virtually non-existent.

Many books have been written about Cunard's passenger ships in the 20th century but few have covered the 19th century fleet in much detail, particularly the important Mediterranean operation. Little has been written about the many ships managed by Cunard during both world wars whilst the cargo fleet has also been poorly served. During the first 150 years of Cunard's existence, transportation of cargo was as important as passenger carrying.

The main purpose of this book is to redress this imbalance and, it is hoped, correct the numerous errors which appear to have been repeated in books and on many internet sites. Every effort has been made to collect information from original sources.

The production of this Cunard fleet history has also been a great team effort and without the help of my friends and colleagues it would never have got off the ground. I would like to offer a special thank you to Fred Hawks who spent many hours at the National Archives at Kew going through registration documents and to Bill Schell, who has been a guiding light in our mission to provide ship information which is as accurate as possible. I would also like to mention Dr. Maureen Watry, Head of Special Collections and Archives at University of Liverpool, who gave me much help with information about the early years of Cunard, Malcolm McRonald who kindly searched the Liverpool Port Registers for key ship information, my good friend Stephen Card for producing the flags, funnels and a stunning cover painting for the book and to Lisa Royall, Bob Todd and Roy Fenton for meticulously proofing the finished work.

My publishers have, as always, been a pleasure to work with and many thanks also for photographs and information to: Stephen Berry, Dag Bakka, Declan Barriskill, Andrew Bell, Steve Booth, David Burrell, John Clarkson, Luis Miguel Correia, Malcolm Cranfield, Harley Crossley, Jennifer Dunn, Ian Farquhar, Heather Fenton, Michael Gallagher, Andy Hernandez, Dave Hocquard, David Hodge, Brian Ingpen, Bård Kolltveit, Robert Langois, Martin Lindenborn, Paul Louden-Brown, Louis Loughran, Steve Moore, Hisashi Noma, Paolo Piccione, David Powers, Russell Priest, Stefan and Sara Venter, Vic Young and Carlos Alfaro Zaforteza. If I have left anyone out, please accept my apologies.

Peter Newall, Blandford Forum, 2012

NOTES ON THE SHIP HISTORIES

The notation '1', '2' etc. in brackets after a ship's name indicates that she is the first, second etc. ship of that name in the fleet where the name has been used more than once. The dates following the name are those of entering and leaving the company ownership or management. Hulls are made of steel unless otherwise stated. For many 19th century ships, the type of rig is also mentioned.

On the second line is given the ship's Official Number in the British registry. This is followed by her tonnages, gross (g), net (n), at the time of acquisition. Dimensions given on the next line are the overall length x breadth x draft expressed in decimal feet. Tonnages and dimensions following any rebuild are quoted on subsequent lines.

On the next line begin descriptions of the engine at the time of acquisition with the following abbreviations: 2-cyl. two-cylinder simple, C.2-cyl. for compound two-cylinder, C-3-cyl. for compound three-cylinder, T.3-cyl. or T.5-cyl. for three- or five-cylinder triple-expansion, Q.4-cyl. quadruple expansion, 4SC four-stroke cycle, 2SC two-stroke cycle, SA single-acting and DA double-acting. Then follows the name and location of the engine builder, horse powers and speed as recorded in registration documents.

The speed is taken from registration documents or Lloyd's Register, and is usually an estimate not a trial's figure. The speeds shown also tend to be service speeds or best averages when the engines were relatively new, and during fair weather conditions. If the vessel was re-engined at some point in its career, the new engine details are given on the next line.

Subsequent lines give passenger numbers, the completion date, name and location of the builder and yard number followed by details of the ship's full career, including wherever possible dates of UK registration. The city indicated after the title of the owning company is where it was domiciled, and not necessarily the port of registry. Unless otherwise stated, the vessel flies the national flag of the owning company's domicile. Prior to the formation of the Cunard Steamship Co. Ltd. in 1879, ships were registered in the names of the various partners. For simplicity, registered ownership during this period is either The British and North American Royal Mail Steam Packet Company for Atlantic ships or The British and Foreign Steam Navigation Company for Mediterranean ships.

Apart from a few of the more recent ships, the key details for each ship under British ownership have been obtained from the registration documents in classes BT107-110 at the Public Record Office, Kew. Passenger numbers can vary considerably and where they are included they are usually when the ship was completed followed by any major changes which occurred. For some 19th century ships, the number of passengers on the ship's Board of Trade Passenger Certificate are also included.

The ships' histories have been corrected to information published in 2012.

All the illustrations are from the Newall Dunn Collection, unless otherwise specified. The Newall Dunn Collection is a combination of images collected by the author over the past 50 years and the collections of the late Laurence Dunn and Captain Emile Sigwart, both of whom started collecting in the 1920s and obtained images from a multitude of sources.

MAJOR INFORMATION SOURCES

Board of Trade Casualty Returns
Board of Trade Merchant Shipping Movement Cards 1939-1945
Board of Trade Passenger Certificates
Board of Trade Wreck Registers
Board of Trade Wreck Reports
Bonsor, Noel, notes for North Atlantic Seaway (WSS)
Bureau Veritas
Cunard Line Archives, University of Liverpool
Ellis Island Ship Database
Engineer
Fairplay
Frank Bowen notebooks, Southampton Library
Journal of Commerce
Lloyd's Register of Shipping
Lloyd's Register Wreck Books
Lloyd's War Losses - World War One
Lloyd's War Losses - World War Two
Lloyd's List
Lloyd's Confidential Index
Lloyds Weekly Casualty Reports

Lloyd's Weekly Shipping Index
MacIver Papers, University of Liverpool
Marine News
Mercantile Navy List
Mitchell's Steam Shipping Journal
New York Herald
New York Times
Port registers for Liverpool and Southampton
Rhodes Directory of Passenger Steamers
Sea Breezes
Service List: First World War
Service List: Second World War, Ministry of War Transport
Shipbuilding and Shipping Record
The Journal of Commerce
The Motorship
The Shipbuilder
The Shipbuilder and Marine Engine-Builder
The Times
White papers on Boer War transport movements

KEY REFERENCE BOOKS

Arnell, J.C. *Steam and the North Atlantic Mails*, Unitrade Press, Toronto,1986

Bonsor, N.R.P. *North Atlantic Seaway*, Brookside Publications, Jersey, 1975

Bowen, Frank C. *A Century of Atlantic Travel*, Sampson Low, Marston, and Co., London, c.1930

Brinnin, John Malcolm. *The Sway of the Grand Saloon*, Macmillan, London, 1971

Broakes, Nigel. *A Growing Concern*, Littlehampton Book Services, 1979

Cunard Line. *Official Guide of the Cunard Steamship Service 1877-1878*

Cunard Line. *History of the Cunard Steamship Co.* c.1885

Cunard Line. *Cunard Line and The World's Fair*, 1893

Cunard Line. *Cunard Line*, 1905

Cunard Line. *The Cunarders,* 1969

Cunard Line. *Triumph of a Great Tradition*, London, 1990

Dodman, Frank E. *Ships of the Cunard Line,* Adlard Coles, Southampton, 1955

Dunn, Laurence. *Passenger Liners*, Adlard Coles, Southampton, 1961

Ellery, David. *RMS Queen Mary the World's Favourite Liner*, Waterfront Publications, Blandford Forum, 1994

Farquhar, Ian. *The Tyser Legacy, A History of Port Line*, New Zealand Ship & Marine Society, 2006

Forwood, Sir William B. *Reminiscences of a Liverpool Shipowner*, Henry Young & Sons, Liverpool, 1920

Grant, Kay. *Samuel Cunard pioneer of the Atlantic Steamship*, Abelard-Schuman, Toronto, 1967

Green, E. and Moss, M. *A Business of National Importance*. Methuen, London, 1982

Hughes, Tom. *The Blue Riband of the Atlantic*, Patrick Stephens, Cambridge, 1973

Hurd, Archibald. *A Merchant Fleet at War*, Cassel and Co., London, 1920

Hutchings, David F. *Caronia Legacy of a Pretty Sister*, Shipping Books Press, Market Drayton, 2000

Hyde, Francis E. *Cunard and the North Atlantic*. Macmillan Press, 1975

Isherwood, J. *Cunard Portraits*, World Ship Society, Kendal, 1990

Johnston, Ian. *Ships for a Nation*, West Dunbartonshire Libraries and Museums, 2000

Jones, Clement. *Pioneer Shipowners*, Charles Birchall, Liverpool, 1938

Kennedy, John. *The History of Steam Navigation*, Charles Birchall, Liverpool, 1903

Kludas, A. *Great Passenger Ships of the World*, Volumes 1 to 6, Patrick Stephens, Cambridge, 1975 to 1986

Lindsay, W.S. *History of Merchant Shipping and Ancient Commerce*, Sampson Low, Marston, Low, and Searle, London, 1876

Louden Brown, Paul. *The White Star Line*, Titanic Historical Society, Herne Bay, 2001

Lyon, David John. *The Denny List*, National Maritime Museum, London, 1975

Maginnis, Arthur J. *The Atlantic Ferry*, Wittaker and Co., London, 1892

Manny, Louise. *Ships of Miramichi*, Miramichi Books, Saint John, New Brunswick, 2000

McLennan, R.S. *Anchor Line 1856-1956*, Anchor Line, Glasgow, 1956

McCart, Neil. *Atlantic Liners of the Cunard Line*, Patrick Stephens, Cambridge, 1987

Mitchell, W.H. and Sawyer, L.A. *The Oceans, The Forts and The Parks*, Sea Breezes, Liverpool, 1966

Rabson, S. and O'Donoghue, K. *P&O A Fleet History*, World Ship Society, Kendal, 1989

Smallpeice, Sir Basil. *Of Comets and Queens*, Airlife Publishing, Shrewsbury, 1981

Spargo, Owen G. and Thomason, Thomas H. *Old Time Steam Coasting*, Waine Research, Albrighton, 1982

Spratt, H. Philip. *Transatlantic Paddle Steamers*, Brown, Son and Ferguson, Glasgow, 1951

Steele, James. *Queen Mary*, Phaidon Press, London, 1995

Telford, P.J. *Donaldson Line of Glasgow*, World Ship Society, Kendal,1989

Wilkinson, H.C. *Bermuda from Sail to Steam*, Oxford University Press, London, 1973

Winchester, Clarence. *The Queen Elizabeth the World's Greatest Ship*, Winchester Publications, London, 1947

HISTORICAL OVERVIEW FROM 1839 TO THE PRESENT DAY

The beginning of the line in the 1830s and 1840s

The 1830s was a period of great change across the Atlantic. There had been a four-fold increase in the number of immigrants entering the United States from around 14,000 per annum in the 1820s to around 60,000 in the 1830s. With steam power in its infancy, many travelled in overcrowded sailing ships between Liverpool and New York, Boston or Philadelphia. Meanwhile, the mails from Britain to Canada and Bermuda were carried in armed Royal Navy packet brigs. To prevent smuggling, the Admiralty had taken control of the overseas mails from the Post Office in 1823.

The first steamship line to be established on the North Atlantic was the British and American Steam Navigation Company. It had been formed in 1835 by an ambitious London-based American entrepreneur John Junius. He saw that the future of Atlantic travel lay not in sail but in steam-powered ships which could half the average westbound crossing time of over a month. A 1,862g paddle steamer was ordered from the London shipyard, Curling and Young. Laid down as *Royal Victoria*, her maiden voyage in 1838 was delayed because the engine builders went bankrupt. This hold up meant that she would be pipped to the post by a recently completed rival, the 1,340g *Great Western*, designed by Isambard Kingdom Brunel for the Great Western Steamship Company's service from Bristol to New York. However, Brunel's new ship suffered a serious fire and her first sailing was postponed. Determined to be the first to operate to New York, British and American chartered the 703g Irish Sea passenger ship *Sirius*. This tiny ship sailed from London with twenty-two passengers on 28th March 1838 and, despite rough weather and limited coal supplies, she arrived in New York on the morning of 23rd April. A few hours later *Great Western* appeared and even though she left four days after *Sirius*, it was *Sirius* which claimed the headlines and glory for British and American.

Sirius sailed for England on 1st May with mail, newspapers and forty-nine passengers travelling for Queen Victoria's coronation. On 16th May, three days from Falmouth, she came across the becalmed Admiralty packet brig H.M. *Tyrian*, which had left Halifax twenty days earlier with mails and a group of prominent Nova Scotian dignitaries, also bound for the coronation. They included two leading lights in Halifax, the publisher and politician Joseph Howe (1804-1873) and Judge Thomas Haliburton (1796-1865). The Falmouth mails were transferred to *Sirius* and she soon departed, leaving *Tyrian* with her sails flapping idly in the breeze. This event had a profound impact on the Canadians, especially Joseph Howe who wrote 'there can be little doubt that ere long the Atlantic will be aswarm with these sea monsters and that a complete revolution will be wrought in the navigation of the ocean, as has already been witnessed on the rivers and inland seas'. How right he was. Within two years, the British postal system had been revolutionised with the introduction of the Uniform Penny Post and, more importantly, the awarding by the Admiralty of subsidised mail contracts. These led to the formation of Britain's leading shipping lines, including P&O, Royal Mail, Pacific Steam and, of course, Cunard Line. At a stroke, the world would become a smaller place with a faster and more reliable postal service. Instead of months waiting for mails and newspapers, they would arrive in a matter of weeks.

On their arrival in England, Joseph Howe and Judge Haliburton travelled to Bristol for discussions with the Great Western Steamship Company about the possibility of running a steam ship service to Halifax. The directors agreed to this proposal on condition the British Government granted a subsidy for the carriage of mails. Not long after these discussions, Joseph Howe met up in London with his good friend Samuel Cunard. Fifty-one-year-old Sam Cunard, as he was known to his friends, was one of Halifax's most successful entrepreneurs and ship owners. His family-owned business, S. Cunard and Company (see page 291), had its own wharf in Halifax and he had many interests including logging and mining and was the Halifax agent for the East India Company. He also had the Admiralty contract to carry mails from Halifax to Boston and Bermuda.

Samuel Cunard was very interested in Howe's idea, especially as he had been a shareholder in the early 1830s in *Royal William*, the first Canadian-built, deep-sea steam ship. On his return to Halifax, Cunard prepared a proposal for a regular transatlantic steamship service to Halifax, where the mails for Boston and New York would be transferred to auxiliary sailing ships. He sought investment in Boston and Halifax for his plan but, unfortunately, there was little interest as marine steam technology was still relatively new. Meanwhile pressure from the Canadian colonists paid off on 18th October when the Treasury instructed the Admiralty to advertise tenders for a monthly subsidised mail service between any one of five English ports (Bristol, Falmouth, Liverpool, Plymouth or Southampton) and Halifax and between Halifax and New York. The advertisement appeared in 'The Times' on 7th November 1838 and early in 1839, Samuel Cunard submitted his bid for the contract.

The bids from the Great Western Steamship Company and the St. George Steam Packet Company, owner of *Sirius*, were rejected and Samuel Cunard was awarded the seven-year mail contract on 4th May 1839. The £55,000 subsidy required a twice monthly, year-round sailing from Liverpool to Boston via Halifax, using three ships. The mails for Quebec were to be carried by steamer from Pictou, Nova Scotia as long as the St. Lawrence River was ice-free. The subsidy was increased on 4th July to £60,000 as it became apparent that a reliable schedule could only be operated with four ships. For the construction of his ships, Samuel Cunard turned to Robert Napier (1791-1876), the foremost Scottish marine engine builder and designer. At the time, Napier did not have his own shipyard and subcontracted the construction of the hulls to other builders on the Clyde. He also introduced Cunard to George Burns (1795-1890), who, with his brother James (1789-1871), operated a line of Irish Sea steamers from Glasgow. Burns helped Cunard raise the necessary funds for the new venture. Thirty-two subscribers, including Samuel Cunard, contributed a total of £270,000 to form The British and North American Royal Mail Steam Packet Company on 23rd July 1839. Two of the partners were the Burns' shipping associates. The brothers David (1807-1845) and Charles MacIver (1812-1885) were based in Liverpool, the homeport for the new company. Their company D. and C. MacIver became the fleet managers for British and North American, whilst in Glasgow George and James Burns managed the company finances including the

Samuel Cunard
1787-1865

Robert Napier
1791-1876

George Burns
1795-1890

Charles MacIver
1812-1885

construction of ships and negotiations for the mail contract. Until the formation of the Cunard Steamship Co. Ltd. in 1878, all the company's ships were registered in Glasgow. With Samuel Cunard and his sons managing the North American side of the business, the scene was set for the start of the first successfully managed steamship line on the North Atlantic.

In May 1840 the 649g paddle steamer *Unicorn* became the first ship owned by the British and North American Royal Mail Steam Packet Company. This tiny ship, built in 1837 for one of G. and J. Burns' Irish Sea coastal companies, was bought for the mail and passenger feeder service between Pictou and Quebec. Pictou is about 100 miles to the north east of Halifax and the mails between the two towns were carried overland by stagecoach, a journey which took two days. Because of a delay in the completion of *Britannia*, it was decided that *Unicorn* would take the inaugural sailing for the new line. She moved from Liverpool's Clarence Dock into the River Mersey on Friday 15th May 1840 and the following day embarked the

mails, newspapers and twenty-seven passengers, including Samuel Cunard's son Edward. After a rough crossing, *Unicorn* arrived at Halifax on Monday 1st June. During her brief stay in Halifax, around 3,000 people visited the ship before she sailed for Boston, arriving there on the 3rd. She berthed at the new 750-feet-long Cunard Wharf, which had been erected by the East Boston Company. The wharf on Marginal Street was also close to the depot of the Eastern Railroad and the ferry to Boston city.

Just over a month later at 2pm on Saturday 4th July, the 1,154g *Britannia*, the first of British and North American's new ships, sailed from Liverpool at the official start of the new transatlantic service. Aboard were ninety-three crew and sixty-three passengers, including Samuel Cunard, his daughter Ann and her friend Laura Haliburton, daughter of Judge Haliburton. *Britannia* arrived at Halifax in the early hours of Friday 17th July, having crossed the Atlantic in 12 days and 10 hours at an average speed of around 8.5 knots. Much to the disappointment of the people of Halifax who had prepared a great celebration for the ship,

This evocative image of *Britannia* sailing from Liverpool on her maiden voyage was painted by the well-known artist, Charles E. Turner (1883-1965) in the 1950s. From the 1920s until the 1960s many of Turner's paintings were used as official Cunard postcards.

she sailed again at 9am for Boston. Passengers for Quebec were transferred to *Unicorn*, whilst the mails for Bermuda were placed aboard Samuel Cunard's mail brig *Velocity*, which departed the following day, arriving at Bermuda on the 1st August. *Britannia* arrived at Boston at 10pm on Saturday 18th July, having made the journey from Liverpool in 14 days and 8 hours. The ship received a tremendous welcome with marching parades and a dinner attended by 2,300 people. Samuel Cunard was later presented with a magnificent two and a half feet high silver cup, which remains in pride of place aboard *Queen Mary 2,* Cunard Line's current flagship.

The mail contract stipulated that, between March and October, there would be two sailings a month, on the 4th and 19th, from Liverpool to Halifax and Boston. In the winter months these would be reduced to one departure on the 4th of each month. *Britannia's* sisters *Acadia, Caledonia* and *Columbia* were delivered at regular intervals during 1840 and the operation settled seamlessly into the planned sailing schedule.

Meanwhile the company's main rivals on the North Atlantic, British and American and Great Western, were planning increasingly large ships. British and American's *Royal Victoria*, completed in 1839, was renamed *British Queen* in honour of the new queen's ascendancy. (A smaller *British Queen* was part of the Cunard fleet from 1852-1898.) At that time she was the world's largest steamship and was joined in 1840 by an even larger running mate. The 2,366g *President* was another giant of her day. On 11th March 1841 she sailed from New York with 136 people aboard and was never seen again. This was the first major steamship disaster on the North Atlantic and spelt the end of the British and American Steam Navigation Company. Great Western's massive, iron-hulled and screw-driven 3,270g *Great Britain* was delivered in 1845 and, although a wonder of the time, was a commercial failure and, despite commencing sailings from Liverpool with *Great Western*, the Great Western company soon went into decline. The major problems for these and other companies of the time was that, unlike Cunard, their ships were not built in series and this resulted in sailing schedules which were erratic.

During its first full year of operation, running costs were higher than expected and, with a tight schedule, there was little slack when problems did occur. Another ship was needed in case one of the fleet suffered a serious mechanical failure. The annual subsidy was increased from £60,000 to £80,000 and a fifth, longer and more powerful ship was ordered. The arrival of *Hibernia* in early 1843 was perfectly timed when, later that year, the company suffered its first loss when *Columbia* was wrecked off the coast of Nova Scotia, fortunately without any loss of life or damage to her cargo and mails. A replacement was ordered for delivery in 1845. *Cambria* was a sister to *Hibernia* and both ships reduced the crossing times between Halifax and Liverpool to less than ten days. In the same year one of the founding partners, David McIver, died unexpectedly and his place was taken by his brother Charles who was to oversee the management of the fleet for the next quarter of a century.

There were two major developments in the postal system in 1845. From April the Canadian mails were landed and embarked at Boston instead of Halifax following an agreement between the United States and British governments which allowed Canadian mails to be sent via the U.S. without examination. This 'closed bag' arrangement brought about the closure in 1844 of the summer-only St. Lawrence River mail-feeder service from Halifax to Quebec via Pictou and *Unicorn* was sold in 1845. With the rapid development of rail links between the United States and Canada, it was often quicker to travel to Canadian destinations via Boston or New York than via Halifax. Thus Halifax began to lose its long-standing status as the gateway to Canada.

On 3rd March 1845 Congress also passed an act which authorised the United States Postmaster General to contract the transport of overseas-bound U.S. mail. This was because of the growing concern about subsidised foreign services, such as Cunard, carrying U.S. mail. The act also encouraged the construction of U.S.-built mail ships which could be used as naval transports at time of war. In October tenders were invited for routes out of New York to Liverpool, Bristol, Southampton and ports in France, Germany and Belgium. This led to the formation of the U.S.-owned Ocean Steam Navigation Company, which was awarded a substantially larger subsidy than that provided by the British Government to British and North American. As the formation of this new company posed a serious threat to its viability, Cunard negotiated a new contract with the Admiralty in July 1846 which agreed that it would operate in the summer months a weekly Saturday sailing, alternating direct to New York one week and to Boston via Halifax the following week. The annual subsidies were increased to £145,000 and the new contract also stipulated that, in case of war, the ships could be requisitioned as troopships and fitted with guns. In one fell swoop, The British and North American Royal Mail Steam Packet Company had moved from being simply a mail ship operator to a company of national importance to Britain's interests in North America. Samuel Cunard also managed to get his Halifax-Bermuda mail contract extended to include St. John's, Newfoundland. The Nova Scotia, Newfoundland and Bermuda Royal Mail Steam Packet Company was formed and three screw-driven steamships were ordered for the service (see page 256).

The Liverpool-New York direct service was planned to start on 1st January 1848 and four new ships were ordered for delivery during 1848. *America, Niagara, Europa* and *Canada* were enlarged versions of the earlier ships but with more powerful Napier engines. The first Cunarder to arrive in New York was *Hibernia* on the 30th December 1847. The new service was an immediate success and in 1848, the first full year of operation, the value of the cargo handled at New York was a third higher than for Boston. By the end of 1850, it was almost double Boston's cargo value. At the time the head of the cargo department was Donald Currie who later founded Castle Line, which merged with Union Line in 1900 to form Union-Castle Line.

The 1850s and even greater challenges
The British and North American Royal Mail Steam Packet Company started its second decade with a sense of great optimism. Through careful planning and gradual evolution, it had become one of the leading British shipping lines and this was epitomized by the comment in the 'Liverpool Albion' of 18th February 1850 that its ships were 'a magnificent fleet which stands pre-eminent among ocean steamers'. However, this was soon to change with the

arrival of a new company which was determined to knock Cunard off its top spot on the North Atlantic. The New York and Liverpool United States' Mail Steamship Company, better known as Collins Line, was formed after it had been awarded the U.S. mail contract between New York and Liverpool in 1847. Its owner, Edward Knight Collins, had successfully operated the Dramatic Line of sailing packets between the two ports since 1836 and proposed a fortnightly service with four large paddle-driven steam ships, which would be built in the U.S.A. After numerous construction delays, the first to arrive in Liverpool on 10th May 1850 was the 2,845g *Atlantic*. Compared with Cunard's relatively simple passenger accommodation, she was an eye-opener and started the trend for improved facilities for passengers crossing the Atlantic. Her interior was sumptuously fitted out with elegant wood panelling and decorations. The best cabins on the stern had stained-glass windows, whilst steam heating was fitted for the first time in a steam ship. There were also electric bells in cabins, a dining room and a general saloon, a barber and a separate smoking room. On Cunard ships, smoking was not allowed below decks so it had to be enjoyed in a covered shelter on the open deck.

The response to the Collins' challenge was the 2,226g *Asia*, the largest ship built to that date on the Clyde, and her sister, *Africa*. Delivered in 1850, they were the last ships to be based on the three-masted *Britannia* design. Their accommodation was a great improvement on earlier ships and included a well-lit, sixty-feet-long saloon with velvet-covered seats and papier-mâché paintings on *Asia* showing various well known locations such as Buckingham Palace and the Great Wall of China. They were also the first in the fleet with two classes of accommodation. In keeping with the company's constant focus on safety, they had a white light on the mainmast and green starboard lights and red lights on the port side, well before this became accepted practice for deep-sea vessels. Despite these improvements and the weekly sailing from Liverpool extended year round, the new ships were no match for the Collins' liners, not only for passenger comfort but also for speed. In the first half of 1852 the average crossing on a Collins ship was around four hours shorter than by Cunard. The company also carried more passengers and freight than Cunard although the latter conveyed three times more mail. However, the Collins' quartet was very expensive to operate and the company had to ask the U.S. Government for greater assistance in order to stem the losses.

Meanwhile, in 1852, Cunard again rose to the challenge with its first two-funnelled ship, the 2,393g paddle steamer *Arabia*. She was fitted with the largest and most powerful engines installed in a ship to that date. Although she achieved a speed of 15 knots on trials, it was soon apparent that her engines were too powerful for her wooden frame, which needed constant repairs. Considered a failure, she was subsequently transferred to the Boston route and it is little wonder that she became Cunard's last wooden ship. In fact, a month before *Arabia*'s introduction, the company took delivery of its first iron-hulled ship, *Andes*. She and her sister *Alps* were also the first purpose-built ships in the fleet with propeller propulsion. The second-hand *British Queen*, which entered service in July 1852, was the first screw-driven ship in the fleet although Samuel Cunard's Nova Scotia, Newfoundland and Bermuda Royal Mail Steam Packet Company had operated screw steamers since 1848.

Andes and *Alps* had considerable cargo capacity and, along with another pair with mountain names, *Jura* and *Etna*, were designed for a new service between Liverpool and Chagres on the Isthmus of Panama via New York and Jamaica. This short-lived service was thought to have been established primarily for gold miners bound for California during the 'Gold Rush', enabling them to travel overland via the Isthmus. At the time the Royal Mail Steam Packet Company was suspicious of Samuel Cunard's motives and was concerned that he was after a mail contract for the Australian mails to be sent via Chagres, especially as his Bermuda mail service had recently been extended to St. Thomas, Virgin Islands. However, technical problems with *Andes* and *Alps* delayed the start of the new route until 1853 and a year later, on 28th March 1854, Britain declared war on Russia. This was the start of the Crimean War which lasted until February 1856. Within months, thirteen Cunard ships were chartered by the British Government for use as supply and troopships, including eight of the Atlantic fleet. This not only played havoc with the schedules, it also brought to an end the plans for the Chagres route. The Atlantic ships sent to the Crimea were joined by those from the Mediterranean service run by The British and Foreign Steam Navigation Company, which had been established in 1853 (see page 164).

Although Collins Line was initially able to capitalise on Cunard's depleted fleet, on 27th September 1854 disaster struck when *Arctic* sank near Cape Race, Newfoundland in thick fog after a collision with a small French steamer. Of the 381 passengers and crew aboard, 322 drowned, including the wife, son and daughter of Edward Knight Collins. Sixteen months later, on 23rd January 1856, *Pacific* sailed from Liverpool with 45 passengers and 141 crew and was never seen again. This was a mortal blow from which Collins Line never recovered and, after a reduction of its mail subsidy, the company ceased operations in February 1858. This was a sad end for a company whose ambitious plans revolutionised the North Atlantic shipping business. However, its arrival had forced Cunard to modernise its fleet with new ships which would re-establish the company's reputation as the premier line on the North Atlantic. The first of these was the beautiful paddle steamer *Persia* of 1855. The first iron-hulled paddle ship on the Atlantic, this 3,300g vessel was the largest ship in the world at the time of her construction and also among the fastest. She sailed from Liverpool on her maiden voyage three days after the unfortunate *Pacific*. Although she suffered serious ice and storm damage to her paddle floats and bow, she arrived safely in New York.

The 1850s also saw the arrival of a number of new companies on the North Atlantic which would play a key role in the years to come. These included Anchor Line, Allan Line, Compagnie Générale Transatlantique (French Line), Norddeutscher Lloyd, Hamburg-Amerika Linie and Inman Line. The last mentioned was founded by William Inman in 1850 as the Liverpool and Philadelphia Steam Ship Company and was one of the first lines to recognise the opportunities for carrying emigrants to the United States in steam ships. Whilst Cunard and Collins were locked in battle for control of the cabin class market, William Inman ordered ships which also had ample accommodation for steerage passengers. Traditionally, these passengers had travelled in cramped conditions on sailing ships. The voyages were often hazardous, uncomfortable and usually took a long time. In a relatively short period, Inman built up an impressive fleet of screw-driven steamers on the route between Liverpool and Philadelphia. In 1857 Philadelphia was dropped in favour of New York and Inman Line became a direct competitor of Cunard.

As the decade drew to a close, Samuel Cunard was rewarded for his endeavours when he received a knighthood in March 1859 for his company's contribution to the war effort in the Crimea. A year earlier George Burns, the driving force behind the commercial running of the business, including the supervision of the shipbuilding programme and negotiations of the mail contracts, had retired. He handed over the reins to his capable son John Burns.

In November 1859 *Canada* inaugurated a fortnightly call at Queenstown (Cobh) in southern Ireland. This meant that passengers to Canada and the United States, could save up to twelve hours by travelling to Queenstown via Holyhead and Dublin. Trains from London, Birmingham, Manchester, Liverpool and Newcastle connected with an early morning steamer departure from Holyhead which was met at Kingstown (Dublin) by a special train to Cork. There, passengers and mails were transferred to the ship aboard the company's tender *Jackal*.

The 1860s, Inman Line and the death of Samuel Cunard

The 1860s started with a major change in the way mail contracts were operated and this was to have a profound impact on the way the company ran its business. The Post Office had strongly opposed the renewal of Cunard's contract in 1857 because of the lack of competitive tendering, but was overruled by the Admiralty and Treasury. A subsequent Parliamentary enquiry recommended that the power to award these mail contracts be returned to the Post Office and this came into effect in 1860.

Also in 1860, no doubt spurred on by the success of Inman Line, Cunard took its first tentative steps into the emigrant market when it announced a fortnightly service for cabin and steerage passengers to New York with *Etna*, *Jura* and its recently acquired *Australasian*, then the largest screw steamer on the Atlantic. These vessels were surplus to requirements and this was a useful means of keeping them employed although it should be noted that *Arabia* also originally had steerage space. The Liverpool agent for steerage passengers was James Baines and Company and *Etna* took the first sailing from Liverpool to New York with 67 steerage passengers aboard. However, this was a short-lived venture. In the months following the outbreak of the American Civil War in April 1861, emigrant numbers fell significantly.

In early 1862 the Robert Napier shipyard delivered two new passenger ships for Cunard. The 2,529g *China*, the first purpose-built screw steamer ordered for

the mail service, and the 3,871g *Scotia*, the last paddle steamer. Whilst *Scotia* was one of the finest ships built for the company up to that date, not only in terms of appearance but also passenger comfort, compared with *China* she was very expensive to operate with a daily coal consumption double that of the screw steamer. At the time, paddle power still had the edge over propeller-driven ships and, as Cunard was determined to have the fastest ships on the Atlantic, prestige took precedence over cost. *Scotia* did not disappoint her owners and in 1863 she broke *Persia*'s seven-year-old records in both directions. Her record from Queenstown to New York (8 days 3 hours), averaging 14.5 knots, remained unbroken until 1872 whilst her New York-Queenstown record (8 days 5 hours 42 minutes) averaging 14.2 knots, remained in place until 1867.

China was also the first in the fleet with a large steerage capacity and her success paved the way for a series of five similar ships with clipper bows, which were built between 1864 and 1868, primarily to compete with Inman Line, which also introduced five new ships during this period. The rivalry between the two lines was intense and 'races' such as the one between *Russia* and *City of Paris* in February 1868, generated much public interest. *Russia* was built by J. and G. Thomson, the shipyard which later became John Brown & Co. Ltd., and which had a long association with Cunard. Sadly, Sir Samuel Cunard was not around to witness this event as he died in London on 28th April 1865, aged 77. He had retired from the business in 1863 and his son Edward, who managed the New York office, inherited his title but he too died four years later, aged only 54. Samuel's second son William who looked after the Halifax end of the business replaced him as a senior partner in the line and also became the company's London agent.

The 1867 mail contract negotiations were a turning point for the company. The Admiralty contract expired on 31st December 1867 and the Post Office was determined to reduce Cunard's £170,000 annual subsidy by basing it

Samuel Cunard is buried alongside the eastern wall of the Brompton Cemetery, Fulham Road, London. Given the importance of his name to the multi-million pound Cunard brand, it is a shame to see the grave of this great man in such a neglected state.

on the amount of mail carried rather than offering a fixed subsidy. Competitive tenders were sought but Cunard refused to bid for the contract. The Post Office eventually reduced its demands and agreed to a much reduced annual fixed subsidy of £70,000 per annum for the new Liverpool, New York and Boston contract which was due to commence in 1869. Meanwhile, the Liverpool to Halifax mail contract was awarded to Inman Line and, as if to protest its feelings about the new deal, on 1st July 1867 Royal Mail was dropped from the company name, which became The British and North American Steam Packet Company. *Cuba* took the final sailing from Liverpool to Halifax and Boston on 21st December 1867, bringing to a close a route which had been served by the company since its inception in 1840. The Inman Liverpool-Halifax-New York contract commenced on 1st January 1868.

The 1870s

The decade following the death of Samuel Cunard was another time of great change for The British and North American Steam Packet Company. Not only did it have to face up to a major new rival across the Atlantic, it also had to accept the fact that, unless it modernised, its very existence would be threatened. The ultra-conservative management, personified by the autocratic Charles MacIver, had undoubtedly held back the progress of the company and a contemporary journal noted that 'for 30 years they have never altered the saloons, the state rooms, the bill of fare, the meal hours, or any detail of their vessels. They had no bath or smoking rooms, no piano and only an apology for a ladies' cabin.' The same publication also related the story of Charles MacIver's appearance before the Royal Commission on Unseaworthy Ships in 1874, when he stated that as far as he was concerned, both the company's ships and management were 'perfect'. The Duke of Somerset, the Chairman of the Commission, responded with the cutting remark 'We are quite right to admit, Sir, that there is only one Charles MacIver in the world'. At the time, Cunard's fleet consisted of a series of old-fashioned ships, including one of the last paddle steamers to operate across the Atlantic.

The development of the compound engine for screw-driven ships in the 1850s was one of the great advances in 19th century marine engineering. Although the single-expansion engine was easy to operate, it was a very inefficient use of steam power. The compound engine, on the other hand, allowed the steam to be passed through two cylinders of differing sizes without much loss of temperature and this not only provided better power, it also saved on the amount of coal used. Whilst coal was cheap and in plentiful supply, lower coal consumption meant smaller coal bunkers and thus more space for revenue-earning cargo. Regular use of compound engines started in the late 1860s after Alfred Holt's pioneering installation of these engines on his China-bound Blue Funnel Line freighters. Although the first ship on the North Atlantic with a compound engine was the small steamer *Brandon* in 1854, the first Atlantic liner constructed with a compound engine was Anchor Line's 2,290g *India* in 1869. Interestingly, these advances in marine engineering coincided with the arrival of the professional marine engineer. The Merchant Shipping Act of 1862 required that all ocean-going steamships of upwards of 100 nominal horse power had to carry two certified marine engineers, a first and second engineer.

Batavia was British and North American's first ship with a compound engine. Delivered in May 1870, she was bought on the stocks from the Denny shipyard and was the last ship in the fleet to be completed with a clipper bow and figurehead, which ironically was torn off by heavy seas on her maiden voyage. *Abyssinia* and *Algeria*, the first of a new series of flush-deck vessels, were also delivered in 1870 but with simple engines. This under-powered pair not only had accommodation for large numbers of emigrants, they were also the first in the fleet with a straight stem. The maiden voyages of *Abyssinia* and *Batavia* both took place in May and the company was able to make a direct comparison between the performances of the two engine types. *Batavia*'s coal consumption was about half that of *Abyssinia* and, as a result, the decision was taken to install compound engines on the new *Parthia*, which was under construction at Denny.

Powerful compound engines also played a key role in the phenomenal success of Thomas Ismay's Oceanic Steam Navigation Co. Ltd., commonly known as White Star Line, which commenced operations across the Atlantic in 1871 with the 3,707g *Oceanic*, the first of a quartet of elegant ships built at Belfast by Harland and Wolff. These four-masted ships were a revelation on the Atlantic with their extreme length and accommodation extended to the full width of the hull instead of the traditional narrow amidships deckhouse. The main dining saloon was also placed amidships where there was least motion and noise from the propellers. From the very beginning, White Star Line focussed on constant improvements in passenger comfort such as gas lighting and larger cabins. What a contrast to the attitude of Charles MacIver when replying to a passenger who dared to complain about the service 'Going to sea is a hardship and the company did not make anything else out of it'.

The new White Star liners soon broke the Atlantic crossing records and, during 1873, the average time for a Cunard Liverpool to New York voyage (10 days 16 hours 54 minutes) was almost a day slower than with White Star (9 days 19 hours 48 minutes). Inman Line had also been spurred into action with the arrival of the new company and ordered a number of new ships, including the record breaker *City of Berlin*. Meanwhile, the Cunard response to these new vessels were *Bothnia* (1874) and *Scythia* (1875), the first Cunarders with a saloon amidships. Although they had a large cargo capacity, they were simply enlarged versions of *Abyssinia* and *Algeria* with more powerful engines.

The transportation of European immigrants was the mainstay of the transatlantic lines. In 1870 Cunard was in fifth place behind Inman, National, Guion and Anchor Line for numbers of passengers carried, although its ships had the most cabin class passengers. In an attempt to capture more of the lucrative emigrant market, especially after the rise in numbers wishing to escape from Europe in the period after the Franco-Prussian war of 1870-1871, Cunard sent four of the 1860-built Mediterranean ships to Belfast to be lengthened by Harland and Wolff. These ships were transformed into North Atlantic emigrant carriers and were given compound engines. However, the 'panic of 1873' led to a run on the banks in the United States and the start of a severe economic depression on both sides of the Atlantic which lasted until 1879. Immigrant numbers fell sharply and the leading emigrant lines soon found themselves financially exposed. Cunard, on the other hand, was able to switch ships to the Mediterranean trades and was also less affected by the downturn because of the mail contract and its greater share of the cabin class market.

In 1877 the subsidised mail contract was replaced with one which paid by weight of letter (4 shillings per pound) and newspapers (3 pence per pound) carried. During this period, the company also disposed of a number of older ships, including the last paddler *Scotia*. The economic crisis also meant that it was four years before another new Cunarder appeared on the Atlantic run. That was *Gallia* in 1879, the final and largest ship in the flush-deck group of the 1870s.

Servia was completed with a full sail rig. This was later removed.

There was a sense of déjà vu for Cunard when, a month after *Gallia*'s maiden voyage to New York in May 1879, Guion Line's *Arizona* entered service. Built by John Elder and designed to be the fastest ship on the Atlantic, this 17-knot ship was the first of the so-called 'Atlantic greyhounds'. Her maiden crossing from Queenstown to New York took only 7 days 11 hours 32 minutes, almost a full day less than Cunard's newest and largest ship.

Once again, Cunard's management had been shown to be lacking in progressive thinking. Something had to be done to regain the former glory of the company. A year earlier the main shareholders in the privately-owned The British and North American Steam Packet Company decided to form a limited liability company with a capital of £2 million. £1,200,000 in shares was held by the MacIver, Burns and Cunard families, whilst the remainder would be offered to the public in 1880 in order to raise capital for new ships. The new company was called the Cunard Steamship Co. Ltd., and the first Chairman was John Burns, George's son, who later became the first Lord Inverclyde. Cunard also had a new flag. The old Burns and MacIver flags were replaced by one with a crowned standing lion holding a globe. This iconic emblem was designed as the crest of the new company. It was also adopted, after the dissolution of the Burns and MacIver partnership in 1881, by G. and J.Burns as its house flag but with a blue background instead of red.

The 1880s and the first express liners
With the retirement of the old guard, in particular Charles MacIver (D. and C. MacIver ceased to be managers in 1883), the new Cunard Line was ready to take on the challenges of what was to be the start of the modern era of Atlantic travel. It also saw the arrival of Cunard's first purpose-built intermediate second-line ships on the Boston route. The story of these intermediate liners from 1881 onwards can be found on page 81.

The company announced in November 1879 that it had placed an order with J. and G. Thomson, for a 'screw steamship, the size of which will only be exceeded by *Great Eastern*, while the speed will be greater than that of any ocean steamship afloat'. In November 1881 it took delivery of the 7,392g *Servia*. Not only was she a major break with the past, she was Cunard's first ship built from steel. (The first steel ocean-going ship, Union Steam Ship Company of New Zealand's *Rotomahana* (1,727g), entered service two

years earlier, the same year as the first steel ship to operate on the North Atlantic which was Allan Line's 4,820g *Buenos Ayrean*.) Like the Belfast-built White Star liners, *Servia* was a long narrow ship. She also had a long, full-height forecastle in place of the usual transatlantic turtleback forecastle and was the first Cunarder to have electric lighting and remote-controlled watertight doors. However, although she was a relatively fast ship, she was not a record-breaker and, with her tall twin funnels, looked somewhat ungainly, certainly in comparison with White Star's crack ships. Despite this, when she arrived for the first time at New York, she was thrown open to the public and a reported 10,000 people visited the ship.

The battle for the Atlantic speed record intensified in the early 1880s with the arrival of two more fast ships for Guion, *Alaska* and the magnificent *Oregon* of 1883, which reduced the crossing time to around six and a half days in each direction. In the same year, Cunard introduced *Aurania* as a running mate to *Servia*. Although similar looking to *Servia*, she had a shorter and more beamy hull. This hull design was developed by the Thomson yard as an answer to the speedier ships produced by its arch rival, John Elder. It was termed a 'fine-ended model' where the increased beam amidships tapered to fine lines fore and aft. This reduced the resistance of the hull through water and therefore made the ship more fuel efficient. *Aurania* was also the first Cunard ship to have her main dining saloon forward of the engine room and the first with 'exclusive cabins'. These were four larger cabins on the promenade deck which shared a small lounge-cum-smoking room.

The success of the Elder-built Guion ships was another watershed for Cunard Line and it began discussion with their designer William Pearce about building a pair of express liners, which would re-establish Cunard as the dominant force on the Atlantic. The company also turned its back on J. and G. Thomson and ordered *Umbria* and *Etruria* from John Elder and Company. These 7,718g vessels were in 1884 the largest, excluding *Great Eastern*, and most powerful ships in the world. They were designed to compete with *Oregon* and continued the twin-funnel, three-mast Cunard-look of the 1880s. Despite their size, they were fitted with auxiliary sails in case of emergency as single-screw ships continued to be prone to broken propeller shafts and other mechanical failures. Their compound engines were among the most powerful yet built and were capable of producing speeds in excess of 20 knots. The pair also held the transatlantic record for four years, with *Etruria* reducing the westbound

Umbria was once the world's largest and most powerful ship.

and eastbound crossing times to 6 days 1 hour 55 minutes and 6 days 4 hours 50 minutes respectively. With superior and spacious accommodation for first class passengers, they were in their day among the most luxurious liners on the Atlantic run.

In 1884, the same year the new Cunard 'giants' entered service, Guion Line was unable to pay the instalments for *Oregon* and she was handed back to the yard which then sold her to Cunard. The plan was to operate a three-ship express service between Liverpool and New York and to use her as a running mate for the similar-sized *Umbria* and *Etruria*. Sadly, this only lasted a short while as *Oregon* was sunk two years later in a collision. Fortunately there was no loss of life and the claim that Cunard had never lost a passenger in peace time endured well into the 20th century. In fact, four passengers had drowned aboard *Sidon* when she was wrecked off the coast of Spain in 1885. Despite her short career with Cunard, *Oregon* regained the eastbound crossing record, which had been lost in 1869.

During the 'Russian scare' of 1885, a Russian invasion of Afghanistan almost triggered a war between Britain and Russia, and sixteen British liners, including *Oregon* and *Umbria*, were requisitioned as armed merchant cruisers. Up to that point liners tended to be requisitioned in times of war as troopships or transports. Although *Umbria* was not used, *Oregon* was commissioned by the Admiralty after undergoing major modifications, which included strengthened decks for guns and increased bunker capacity to increase her cruising range. She took part in an exercise to demonstrate the effectiveness of using fast liners as armed merchant cruisers. The success of this led to an agreement in 1887 between the Admiralty and Cunard and White Star whereby an annual payment would be made for each ship made available to the Admiralty in times of crisis. The first liners built under the terms of the auxiliary cruiser scheme were White Star's *Teutonic* (1889) and *Majestic* (1890).

After *Oregon*'s loss, *Umbria*, *Etruria*, *Aurania* and *Servia* operated the New York express service, whilst the outdated *Gallia*, *Bothnia* and *Scythia* were transferred to the Boston run. In the meantime, foreign competition intensified as Compagnie Générale Transatlantique (French Line) and the two German rivals, Hamburg-Amerika Linie and Norddeutscher Lloyd, introduced their first express transatlantic liners. The German lines also called at Southampton on their way to and from New York. Inman Line, meanwhile, had become U.S. owned in 1886 after it got into serious financial difficulties. The new company, which was later known as American Line, placed an order with J. and G. Thomson for a pair of handsome three-funnelled ships with clipper bows, *City of New York* and *City of Paris*, which entered service in 1888 and 1889. Not only did these ships have the latest triple-expansion engines, they also had twin screws. They soon reduced the New York crossing time to less than six days and, once again, Cunard faced a new decade with fresh challenges to its supremacy.

The 1890s and the start of the new century
With four ships operating the New York express service, Cunard adopted a wait-and-see strategy before reacting to the arrival of the new White Star and Inman liners. On 11th August 1891, Cunard signed a contract with Fairfield Shipbuilding and Engineering Co. Ltd., successors to John Elder and Company, for another pair of powerful ships, which would also be record breakers in terms of speed and size. The 12,952g *Campania* and *Lucania* entered service in 1893 and, because they had twin screws, were the first in the fleet to dispense with sails. Their five-cylinder, 47-feet-high triple-expansion engines, another first for Cunard, were so immense that the cylinder tops reached the promenade deck. As the first Cunarders to be built to Admiralty specifications under the armed auxiliary cruiser scheme, many safety features were incorporated into their design.

The passenger accommodation, especially first class, was superb with red velvet curtains and rich mahogany panelling much in evidence. There was also a fully-stocked library, an impressive three-deck-high dining saloon and, for the first time on a Cunard ship, large suites with a parlour and attached bedroom. They were popular ships and *Lucania*, the faster of the two, went on to shatter the westbound record to 6 days 4 hours 50 minutes with an average speed of over 21 knots. *Lucania*'s record remained in place until 1898

Campania of 1893. [J. and M. Clarkson collection]

15

when it was taken by Norddeutscher Lloyd's *Kaiser Wilhelm der Grosse*, which had claimed the eastbound record the previous year. Germany had started to flex its muscles on the international stage and this was reinforced by the German liners of Hamburg-Amerika Linie and Norddeutscher Lloyd, which introduced increasingly larger and faster ships. Until the arrival of *Lusitania* in 1907, Germany held the transatlantic speed record in both directions.

Whilst Cunard built vessels designed to break speed records, White Star had decided to concentrate its effort on liners with high quality passenger accommodation. In 1899 White Star's 17,274g *Oceanic* entered service as the world's largest ship. With a length of over 700 feet, she was the first to exceed the length of *Great Eastern*, which had been broken up in 1889. *Oceanic* was a beautifully proportioned liner with three tall masts, two funnels and a narrow beam. In 1901 *Great Eastern*'s 18,915g tonnage was surpassed by the 20,904g *Celtic*, the first of four intermediate liners of this size ordered by White Star Line. These huge ships not only offered new standards of comfort for passengers, they also had large cargo capacities and were able to carry over 2,000 passengers in steerage. With more than a half million emigrants annually seeking a new life in the United States, this lucrative trade continued to play an important role in the transformation of the transatlantic liner business. There was also a marked shift in the origin of immigrants in the late 1890s with the majority emanating from southern and eastern Europe instead of northern and western Europe. In 1904, despite German opposition, Cunard was awarded a contract by the Hungarian government to carry immigrants from Trieste to the United States. The Cunard Hungarian-American Line was formed to run a fortnightly service between Trieste-Fiume-Palermo-Naples and New York (see page 81).

The strategic importance of Cunard Line to Britain was re-emphasised during the Second Boer War (1899-1902) when eight Cunard ships were requisitioned as troopships and transports. However, once again the company saw its reputation as the premier transatlantic line eroded with the arrival of larger and faster ships. The express liners of the early 1890s, *Lucania* and *Campania*, were now looking decidedly outdated. To add to Cunard's concerns, in April 1902 John Pierpoint Morgan (1837-1913), the U.S. financier and banker, announced the formation of the International Mercantile Marine Corporation of New Jersey (IMM). This company was created to take over a number of key transatlantic lines including White Star Line. IMM also had a working relationship with Cunard's German rivals, Hamburg-Amerika Linie and Norddeutscher Lloyd. The formation of IMM threatened not only Cunard Line's position on the Atlantic but also the independence of British shipping on this important trade route. With national prestige at stake, the British Government was persuaded to loan Cunard Line £2.6 million to build two of the largest, fastest and most luxurious liners ever seen. A key condition of this agreement was that Cunard Line would remain in British ownership. The official announcement about this low-interest loan was made by Prime Minister Arthur Balfour on the 30th September 1902. In October 1902 four shipyards were asked to tender for two 700-feet-long liners able to carry 2,000 passengers, powered by reciprocating engines and capable of speeds of 23-24 knots. These liners would also need to meet the requirements of the Admiralty's armed auxiliary cruiser scheme. In May 1903 John Brown &

Co. Ltd., Clydebank, formerly J. and G. Thomson, and the Newcastle-based Swan, Hunter and Wigham Richardson Ltd. were awarded the contracts to build respectively *Lusitania* and *Mauretania*.

Six years earlier on 26th June 1897, the Cunard directors aboard *Lucania* unknowingly faced the future when Charles Parson's *Turbinia* dashed uninvited through the line of ships taking part in the great Diamond Jubilee Fleet Review at Spithead. Travelling at over 30 knots, this tiny vessel gave a spectacular demonstration to the world of the superiority of the new turbine engine. In 1901 the first merchant ship fitted with a turbine was the Clyde steamer *King Edward*. Having initially turned down the use of this relatively untried type of engine, Cunard was persuaded by the Admiralty to set up a committee of marine professionals to look at its possible use on the new liners. The relative merits of turbines and reciprocating engines were investigated in a series of trials between Newhaven and Dieppe using the turbine-driven cross-Channel ferry *Brighton* and the similarly-designed *Arundel*, which had reciprocating engines. The Turbine Committee was convinced by these and other tests that turbines were the way forward and recommended on 24th March 1904 that they should be used on the new express liners. In order to gain some experience of these new engines, Cunard asked John Brown to fit turbines on *Carmania*, the second of a pair of 19,500g-intermediate liners under construction at the yard. *Carmania* was completed in 1905 and this gave Cunard almost two years of experience before the introduction of

Turbinia's engines revolutionised marine engineering in the 20th century.

their new super liners in 1907.

The 31,550g *Lusitania* made her maiden voyage in September 1907 and was followed by the slightly larger *Mauretania* two months later. By far the largest ships in the world, these vessels were the first over 30,000 gross tons, the first on the Atlantic with quadruple screws and the first British liners with four funnels. They were fast ships and soon reduced the crossing time to less than five days in each direction. *Mauretania*'s average speed was over 25 knots and her transatlantic record remained unbeaten for twenty years. They also offered 50% more light, air space and deck promenade per passenger than any other liner afloat. The accommodation for first class passengers was indeed spacious and no expense was spared in the decoration and

Mauretania ready for launching. *[J. and M. Clarkson collection]*

panelling of their magnificent public rooms. On *Mauretania* just under a quarter of a million square feet of fancy hardwoods was used to fit out her interiors.

In 1909 it was decided that the express liners would stop at Fishguard on the south west coast of Wales. This small port was the main departure point for the short sea crossing to Ireland via the Great Western Railway's London Paddington service. The Fishguard call meant that passengers and the mails could reach London at least half a day earlier than travelling via Liverpool. In 1912 Queenstown was dropped from the eastbound schedule with passengers leaving New York on Wednesday morning able to reach London on Monday afternoon and Paris the same evening. In 1914 Queenstown was dropped in both directions for the express service.

The 1910s and the First World War
In 1908 White Star Line responded to the Cunard challenge by placing an order with Harland and Wolff for three immense 45,000-ton, 882-feet ships. These ships would not only be floating palaces for the super-rich, they would also accommodate over 1,000 steerage passengers. *Olympic*, the first in the series, was completed in 1911. She was a revelation with an à la carte restaurant in addition to her first class dining saloon, a gymnasium, plunge pool, Turkish bath and a squash court. The first class staterooms were outstanding with cot beds and decorated in various designs from French Empire to Adam style. Size of ship now became the new mantra and in 1910 Hamburg-Amerika

Linie, led by the dynamic Albert Ballin, ordered three even larger ships, the 52,000g *Imperator* class, for delivery between 1913 and 1915. In 1907 White Star Line had moved its main transatlantic mail service from Liverpool to Southampton and with HAPAG also calling at Southampton, the new giant ships would compete head-to-head.

As it owned the fastest liners in the world and not wishing to take part in another expensive race to beat the competition, Cunard decided to consolidate its position on the Atlantic. In December 1909, it started to plan for a new liner, which would be a running mate to *Lusitania* and *Mauretania* and, once again, enable the company to offer a weekly, three-ship express service between Liverpool and New York. Although not as fast as the current record breakers, the new liner would be bigger than White Star's *Olympic* trio. On 31st January 1911 John Brown & Co. Ltd. was awarded the contract to build the 45,646-ton *Aquitania*. This magnificent liner was undoubtedly one of Cunard's finest ships. She also signalled the end of an era with her 18th century country-house-style interiors. Her maiden voyage to New York was in May 1914 but, after only two months, Cunard's dream of a three-ship express service was again in tatters following Britain's declaration of war on Germany on the 4th August. All three of the express liners were requisitioned by the Admiralty as armed merchant cruisers but were considered too large for naval service. *Mauretania* and *Aquitania* became troopships whilst *Lusitania* remained on the New York run as the sole express liner.

In the years leading up to the start of the First World War, Cunard had been busy with a series of major acquisitions. In 1911 it bought the Thomson Line and its London to Canada route. The Thomson ships were given *A*-names and, in May, Cunard made its first commercial sailing to the St. Lawrence River and the first to any Canadian port since December 1867. The return to the Canadian route led to a new building programme for the service and the purchase in 1916 of Canadian Northern Steamships (see page 82).

In November 1911 Cunard acquired an interest in the Glasgow-based Anchor Line (Henderson Brothers Ltd.), one of its oldest competitors on the Atlantic, which also had ships with names ending in *ia*. By 31st March 1912 Cunard had secured all the ordinary shares of Anchor Line but not the 32,500 preference shares. This meant that it did not have financial or operating control over the company. However, the two companies worked closely together not only with joint services across the Atlantic but also in the building of similar ships, especially in the 1920s (see page 82). Anchor-Donaldson Line was formed in 1916 to operate joint liner services between Glasgow and Canada. Badly hit by poor trading results and the 1930s slump, Anchor Line (Henderson Brothers Ltd.) went into liquidation in April 1935 and a new company, Anchor Line (1935) Ltd., was formed in which Cunard had no involvement and subsequently wrote off its initial investment, apart from some financial dispersements in 1940. It also brought to an end Anchor-Donaldson Line, which became Donaldson Atlantic Line. Despite this change, Donaldson Atlantic Line's two passenger ships, *Athenia* and *Letitia*, continued to operate jointly with Cunard.

For Cunard, the most significant outcome of the Anchor Line deal was a shareholding in the Anchor-Brocklebank services between Glasgow, Liverpool and

Calcutta. This came about when the long-established Liverpool firm Thos. and Jno. Brocklebank Ltd., bought Anchor Line's Calcutta conference rights and four Anchor ships in 1912. In return, Anchor Line acquired shares in Thos. and Jno. Brocklebank. This complex arrangement concluded on 27th April 1921 when the final shares in Thos. and Jno. Brocklebank were purchased (a controlling interest had been obtained in 1919) and the company became a wholly-owned subsidiary of Cunard Line. It also meant a close involvement in Cunard's affairs with the Brocklebank and Bates families. The Bates had been major shareholders in Brocklebanks and the formidable Sir Percy Bates (1879-1946) was the Chairman of Cunard from 1930 until 1946. His wife was the granddaughter of Charles MacIver and he played a key role in the formation of Cunard White Star Line and the building of *Queen Elizabeth* and *Queen Mary*. Sir John Brocklebank (1915-1974) was Chairman from 1959 to 1965 and was in charge during the contract negotiations for *Queen Elizabeth 2*, whilst Sir Percy's nephew Philip Bates became Chairman of Atlantic Container Line in 1969.

An equally good investment occurred on 8th June 1916 when the company bought the Commonwealth and Dominion Line. This was a large private cargo concern which was primarily involved in the transportation of refrigerated produce and general cargo between the United Kingdom and Australia and New Zealand. Its ships had *Port* names and in November 1937 the company name was changed to Port Line Ltd. Although the vessels had Cunard funnel colours since 1919, Port Line, like Thos. and Jno. Brocklebank, was allowed to trade in its own right and both companies contributed significantly to the Cunard balance sheet, especially during the lean years of the 1930s.

Cunard played an important role during the First World War and made available its shore establishments for the war effort. It assisted in the construction of an aeroplane factory near Liverpool's Aintree race course and established the Cunard National Shell Factory at Bootle, which employed 1,000 people, mainly women. It also provided the Admiralty with three armed merchant cruisers, the most famous being *Carmania*, whilst its passenger liners became troopships and hospital ships and carried over 900,000 officers and men during the

war years. It operated a number of freighters with *V*-names, most of which were sunk, and managed sixteen ships for The Shipping Controller between 1915 and 1921(see page 259). At war's end Cunard had lost twenty ships, totalling 205,460 gross tons or 56% of its total tonnage. One of the most infamous casualties was the unarmed *Lusitania* on 7th May 1915 off the Old Head of Kinsale, Ireland when she was torpedoed by a German submarine whilst nearing the end

Carmania's battle with the *Cap Trafalgar* (above) and *Volodia*, the first of three V-ships to be sunk by submarine during the First World War (below).

Valeria survived a submarine attack but was lost the following year in the River Mersey.

Lusitania was lost with almost 1,200 lives. *[J. and M. Clarkson collection]*

of a commercial voyage from New York. The loss of 1,198 lives was condemned on both sides of the Atlantic and also showed the vulnerability of large liners to the ever-increasing danger from submarines. With all their vital equipment below the waterline, *Lusitania* and her sister had of course been designed to resist attack from surface gunfire and not torpedoes.

The 1920s and the post-war reconstruction

Cunard embarked on an extensive rebuilding programme to replace war losses. Thirteen ships totalling 214,000 tons were ordered, including five 20,000-ton intermediate liners for the

New York and Boston service and six 14,000-ton A-class intermediate liners for the Canadian route. This scheme to double the passenger capacity was financed mainly through the issue in 1921 of £4,000,000 in debenture stock. Unable to run a full transatlantic service during the immediate post-war years, a number of liners were chartered for the Liverpool to New York route. Among these were Union-Castle Line's *Saxon*, *Balmoral Castle*, *Walmer Castle* and *Dunvegan Castle*, Netherland Line's *Prinses Juliana*, Pacific Steam Navigation's *Orca*, *Ortega* and *Oriana* and Lamport and Holt's *Byron*, *Tennyson*, *Vestris*, *Vauban*, *Vasari* and *Vandyck*. Meanwhile, the three HAPAG *Imperator*-class had been allocated as war reparations to the Allies in 1919 and the first in the series, *Imperator*, was handed over to Cunard as a replacement for the lost *Lusitania*. She became the popular *Berengaria* and, until 1934, was Cunard's largest ship. The other two in the trio, *Vaterland* and *Bismarck*, were allocated to United States Lines and White Star Line and renamed *Leviathan* and *Majestic* respectively. In 1919 Cunard moved its New York express liner passenger-mail service from Liverpool to Southampton and *Mauretania* inaugurated the new Southampton and Cherbourg to New York service on 18th November 1919. A company-owned tender operation was also established at Cherbourg (see page 250).

(see page 250).

Although the express service had transferred to Southampton, Cunard's headquarters remained in Liverpool. Its status as one of Liverpool's leading companies was greatly enhanced in 1917 when the company moved from its long-established offices at 8 Water Street to the magnificent Cunard Building on the Pier Head, which is close to the Princes Landing Stage. Designed to resemble an Italian renaissance palace, it is situated between the Royal Liver Building and the Port of Liverpool (formerly the Mersey Docks and Harbour Board) Building. Known as Liverpool's 'Three Graces', this group of buildings has been designated a World Heritage Site by UNESCO. The Cunard War Memorial is also located on the river side of the building and was erected in 1921 in memory of the employees killed during the First World War. Across the Atlantic in New York, Cunard's new North American headquarters at 25 Broadway was completed in May 1921. The imposing Cunard Building, with its immense, groin-vaulted ticketing hall, remained Cunard's New York office until 1968, when the office moved uptown to 555 Fifth Avenue.

In the early 1920s Cunard's big three liners, *Mauretania*, *Aquitania* and *Berengaria*, were converted from coal-burning to oil-firing and operated the weekly Southampton-Cherbourg-New York express service. In

For most of late 19th century, Cunard's head office in Liverpool was 8 Water Street.

The magnificent Italian renaissance-style Cunard Building on the Pier Head is one of Liverpool's 'Three Graces'. The Cunard War Memorial in front of the building consists of a Doric-style column and a large bronze classical statue of a naked man holding a shield and a victory wreath. The exterior of the building is ornate and features the Cunard lion in the top right hand corner (left). The interior, which also includes the ticketing office and first class waiting room, is well preserved. The ground floor has a coffered roof, classical columns and pilasters with a large letter C in the capital (right).

1926 Cunard started planning for replacements for this trio, especially *Mauretania*. With advances in marine engineering, it would now be possible to operate a two-ship express liner service. In fact, Norddeutscher Lloyd did just that with its 50,000-ton *Bremen* and *Europa* at the end of the decade. With top speeds of over 28 knots, both ships won the Blue Riband, as the Atlantic speed record had become known. Once again, Cunard had lost its top spot for speed to a German competitor and the company's position was clearly stated in the 1931 Shareholders Report: 'The Cunard Company has been striving for some ninety years to keep its flag in the forefront on the Atlantic, and it is a race which has no end. It is its business to be in that race. If it had not kept that object always before it, the Cunard Company would not be afloat today.'

The 1930s and the formation of Cunard White Star
The planning for the new liners was exhaustive and Cunard stressed that the need for these ships had to be 'commercially driven and not designed merely to win trophies'. Like it had done twenty five years earlier for *Lusitania* and *Mauretania*, in 1928 the company formed a committee of marine experts

to decide what machinery would be most suitable, i.e. turbo-electric, diesel or steam turbine. It recommended steam turbines whilst White Star revealed that its new 60,000-ton liner *Oceanic* would be driven by diesel-electric power. Although the *Oceanic* project was cancelled in 1929 because of the financial problems within the Kylsant group which owned White Star, it is interesting to note that diesel-electric is commonplace on today's cruise ships whilst steam turbines are definitely a thing of the past. Despite the Wall Street Crash of 1929 and the onset of the Great Depression, on 28th May 1930 it was announced that John Brown had won the contract to build the first 80,773g, 28.5-knot ship. Work began in December 1930 on the unnamed liner, known only by its 534 yard number. Because of the high cost of insurance for the new ship and a possible second vessel, Cunard secured an agreement from the Board of Trade to provide insurance cover. This was done in the Cunard (Insurance) Agreement Act of 1930.

In July 1931 interest rates more than doubled and, because Cunard relied on money raised on the money market to pay for construction, it had no option but to suspend all work on the ship in December. This was a major blow, not only to the shipyard but also to the thousands of Clydebank workers who were laid off. However, help came from the most unlikely source, White Star Line. In July 1930 the British Government stepped in to rescue Lord Kylsant's huge shipping empire which had collapsed. At the time, it controlled a sixth of British shipping interests, including White Star Line, which had been purchased in 1927. Discussions between Cunard's Chairman Sir Percy Bates and the key stakeholders in White Star Line started soon afterwards about what Cunard could do to assist in rescuing the company. Because it was not interested in a complete purchase of the line, nothing was resolved. However, after the cessation of work on 534, Sir Percy proposed in February 1932 that Cunard would purchase White Star if the government would guarantee funds for the unfinished 534 and the second ship. This was initially rejected but after lengthy and convoluted negotiations it was agreed that Cunard and White Star would amalgamate to form a new company Cunard White Star Ltd. The control of the company would be 62:38 in Cunard's favour, i.e. Cunard would own 62% of the shares. In exchange, the government agreed to a £9.5 million loan to complete 534 and to build a running mate. The Cunard Steam Ship Co. Ltd. (Steamship became Steam Ship in the early part of the 20th century) continued as a holding company with the four B-class Mediterranean cargo ships, the only ships registered to it.

Cunard White Star Ltd. came into being on the 1st January 1934 and soon after the loan legislation was passed by Parliament in the North Atlantic Shipping (Advances) Bill on 27th March 1934, work recommenced on Cunard's idle giant. Number 534 was launched as *Queen Mary* in September and completed in March 1936. As it wanted to signal a complete break with the past, she was the first Cunard express liner not to be given a name ending in *-ia*. This was a company decision which was taken before Royal approval was sought from Buckingham Palace. Despite her outdated appearance, certainly in comparison with French Line's streamlined *Normandie*, *Queen Mary*'s maiden voyage received an extraordinary amount of publicity world-wide. She also claimed the Blue Riband record from her French rival and her 1938 record crossing in both directions of just under four days at an average speed of around 31 knots remained unbeaten for fourteen years.

Soon after the formal transfer of Cunard and White Star assets to Cunard White Star Ltd. on 19th May 1934, the clear-out of older tonnage started, including *Mauretania* and *Olympic*. Joint operations for the two fleets commenced on the 1st July. By 1936 the White Star fleet was reduced to three ships (see page 134). However, the smart White Star livery continued to be used for the surviving liners until the 1960s. On these ships the White Star flag was hoisted above the Cunard flag. On Cunard liners, the flags were reversed.

Meanwhile, with the Cunard Insurance Agreement Act about to expire in 1936, Cunard had to make a decision about a running mate for *Queen Mary*. After discussions with a number of shipyards, the company turned once again to John Brown

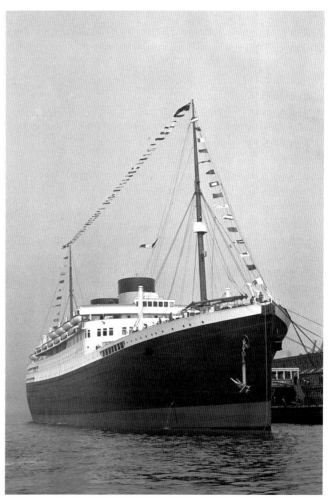

Georgic, the last ship built for the White Star Line, at Liverpool prior to her maiden voyage. *[John McRoberts]*

and on 28th July 1936 the Chancellor of the Exchequer announced to Parliament that John Brown had won the order for the new ship. The contract was signed on 6th October and the keel for *Queen Elizabeth* was laid on 4th December. Although not to be as fast as *Queen Mary*, she was to be the largest ship in the world and her record size as a passenger ship remained unchallenged for 56 years. She also turned her back on the Art Deco excesses of *Normandie*. Designed in an understated British modern style, her comfortable public rooms were elegant but not brash, with soft colour schemes and restrained hidden lighting. She was described at the time

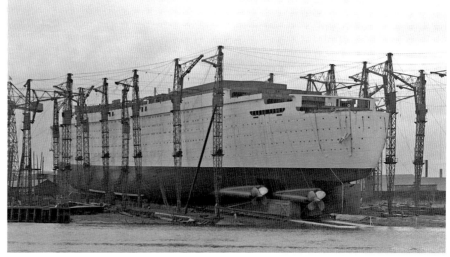

Queen Mary shortly before her launch. *[B. and A. Feilden/J. and M. Clarkson collection]*

as being a 'vast show-palace of all the best in contemporary techniques of interior decoration. An extraordinary variety of materials has been used for her furnishings from traditional leathers and wood panelling to the newest wonders of metal alloys and plastics.' In 1939 Cunard took delivery of a new 35,738-ton *Mauretania*. With a large cargo capacity, this intermediate liner, which looked like a small *Queen Elizabeth*, was designed for the London-New York route but also as a substitute for the *Queen*s during annual overhauls.

Mauretania of 1939 in the Mersey shortly after her completion. [J. and M. Clarkson collection]

The Second World War and post-war reconstruction

On 1st September 1939 Germany invaded Poland and two days later at 11.15am on Sunday 3rd September the British Prime Minister Neville Chamberlain announced to the nation that Britain was at war with Germany. Later that day, the unarmed and unescorted Donaldson Atlantic liner *Athenia* (13,465/1923) was torpedoed west of Ireland without warning by a German submarine. She was bound for Quebec on the joint Cunard service out of Liverpool. Two days later *Bosnia* became the second British merchantman to be sunk by U-boat. She was the first of many in the Cunard group to be lost during the Second World War. Unfortunately, the declaration of war also meant the cancellation of plans to celebrate the triumphant arrival of *Queen Elizabeth* as the world's largest ship during Cunard's 100th anniversary year in 1940. Instead, she slipped out of the Clyde and sailed to New York and was subsequently fitted out as a troopship at Singapore. *Queen Mary* was also converted into a trooper, as were many other Cunard liners, including *Aquitania*, which was due to be scrapped. She was given a new lease of life and became the only Cunarder to take part in both world wars.

During the Second World War the Cunard group lost thirty six ships: Brocklebank sixteen; Port Line fourteen; Cunard White Star five and the Cunard Steam Ship Company

one. This excludes the ships managed on behalf of the Ministry of War Transport. For example, Cunard White Star managed over 30 ships and five were lost through enemy action. It also suffered one of the largest single losses of life in the war when *Lancastria* was bombed during the evacuation of St. Nazaire in 1940 and over 3,000 people lost their lives. However, the company also loaded over nine million tons of freight in the war years and up to the 31st May 1945 Cunard liners had carried a staggering 2,473,040 personnel around the globe. 1,243,538 of these were carried on *Queen Elizabeth* and *Queen Mary* and on the Atlantic these two ships alone transported 869,694 eastbound and 213,008 westbound, a total of 1,082,702. In his address to the Cunard White Star annual general meeting in July 1945, Sir Percy Bates commented: 'I like to believe that these two ships shortened the war in Europe by a whole year'.

Planning for the post-war era began soon after the June 1944 D-Day landings, when Cunard had discussions with John Brown about the return of *Queen Mary* to commercial service and the building of a new 10,000-ton passenger-cargo liner after the war had ended. This was *Media*, the first of two large intermediate passenger-cargo liners. Cunard's transatlantic freight operation was very important and, before the war, the dozen 1920s-built intermediate liners, with their large cargo capacities, played a key role in this sector of the business. However, only four returned to the post-war fleet and the company bought a number of wartime standard freighters as a stop gap until a new series of purpose-built cargo ships were built (see page 196).

Queen Elizabeth and *Queen Mary* were handed back to their owners in March and September 1946 respectively. As she was six years old and had still not carried a fare-paying passenger, *Queen Elizabeth* was given a priority refit by John Brown. Her maiden voyage on 16th October 1946 was eagerly awaited and among those travelling to New York were Sir Percy Bates and his wife. Unfortunately he died suddenly on the day of departure

Aquitania at Southampton after the Second World War. She is still in wartime grey.

Parthia, sister of Media, on the Princes Landing Stage preparing to sail for New York. [Harley Crossley collection]

from Southampton. The loss of this dynamic man who had transformed Cunard was a great blow the company. On 31st July 1947 his dream of a weekly, two ship express service was at last realised when *Queen Mary* sailed on her first post-war voyage to New York. The day before, the Cunard Steam Ship Co. Ltd. took full control of Cunard White Star Ltd. when it bought the 38% share in the company owned by the Oceanic Steam Navigation Realisation Co. Ltd., H.M. Treasury and the Government of Northern Ireland. The assets of Cunard White Star Ltd. were transferred to the Cunard Steam Ship Co. Ltd. on the 31st December 1949 and the following day the company started the second half of the 20th Century as the Cunard Steam-Ship Co. Ltd. The hyphen may have been inserted as a sign of a new stage in the company's history. Despite the demise of Cunard White Star, the Cunard and White Star flags continued to be used until the 1960s on the large passenger liners.

The 1950s and airline competition
Between 1947 and 1957 Cunard took delivery of seven intermediate ships, including the 22,000-ton *Saxonia* quartet for the Canadian run and *Caronia*, the dual-purpose transatlantic liner and cruise ship. These were heydays for Cunard as sea travel numbers across the Atlantic continued to rise. In 1957 a million passengers crossed by sea. However, this was also the start of the jet age. The British-designed De Havilland Comet was the world's first passenger jet aircraft and had been operating commercial flights with the British Overseas Airways Corporation (BOAC) since May 1952. On 4th October 1958 BOAC Comet 4s flying between London and New York started the first passenger jet service across the Atlantic. 1958 was also the year in which transatlantic sea travel numbers started to fall. By 1965, these numbers had dropped to 650,000 whilst, at the same time, the numbers of air travellers rose to four million.

Interestingly, Cunard had anticipated the arrival of transatlantic air travel as early as 1934. During the formation of Cunard White Star, the company articles encompassed the operation of air services. In the early 1940s Cunard hoped to handle BOAC bookings in the United States and to take a stake in BOAC's first air services across the Atlantic. This did not happen as the Labour Government, which came to power in 1945, forbad Cunard's commercial involvement with BOAC. However, in 1959 Cunard took the plunge and bought Eagle Airways Ltd., which had obtained a licence to operate between London and Nassau, Bahamas. Cunard Eagle Airways was formed and two Boeing 707s were purchased for a potential service between London and New York. A licence was granted in July 1961 but was revoked after an appeal by BOAC. Facing mounting costs, Cunard turned to BOAC and on 24th June 1962, BOAC-Cunard Ltd. was formed. Cunard had a 30% shareholding in the company and transferred its two 707s to the operation whilst Eagle Airways was sold to its founder, Harold Bamberg. In September 1966, partially because of the national seamen's strike, Cunard's financial position was dire and it decided to pull out of air travel and sold its share of BOAC-Cunard to BOAC. In 1977 Transmeridian Air Cargo was acquired and in 1978, HeavyLift Cargo Airlines, a specialised air freighter company based at Southend Airport, was formed. In later years, Cunard also worked closely with British Airways and produced the ultimate in transatlantic travel - a five-day voyage on *Queen Elizabeth 2*, returning by Concorde in less than four hours.

The 1960s and a new Queen
Although its main threat in the 1950s and 1960s was from air travel, Cunard also faced serious competition from its transatlantic rivals. In 1952, United States Lines's *United States* had reduced *Queen Mary*'s fourteen year-old record westbound crossing to 3 days 10 hours 40 minutes, with an average speed of over 34 knots whilst French Line, Holland America Line and Italia Line introduced beautiful streamlined flagships such as *France, Rotterdam, Michelangelo* and *Raffaello*. The Cunard pre-war liners on the New York run were looking decidedly old-fashioned and out of date and, once again, the company had to face up to a major fleet renewal programme. In 1957 it reserved a

A Cunard Eagle Airways Boeing 707. Cunard Eagle was the first independent British airline to carry passengers in a jet aircraft.

berth at John Brown for a replacement vessel for the 33-year-old *Britannic*, which was reaching the end of her life. Although this order was not confirmed, the company announced in April 1959 that it intended to replace *Queen Mary* with a new ship. Once again Cunard would have to go cap in hand to the British Government for financial assistance. In September 1959 a special committee, under the chairmanship of Lord Chandos, was set up by the Ministry of Transport to investigate how to maintain Britain's traditional supremacy on the weekly transatlantic service. In June 1960 the Chandos Report was published and it recommended that the *Queen Mary* replacement should be a 75,000g, 29.5-knot, 990-feet, 2,270-capacity liner. The cost was estimated to be up to £28 million, of which Cunard would contribute £12 million and the rest would come from government loans. The 'Q3' project, as it became known, evoked mixed reactions. A leading shipping journal summed up the opinion of those against the project as being 'a thoroughly retrograde step and a relic of the 'status symbol' days of the early '30s which brought into being the first two *Queens*'. Nevertheless, the major British shipyards were asked to tender for the job and in July 1961 the tenders were received by Cunard. A joint Vickers Armstrongs/Swan Hunter bid offered not only the lowest price, but also offered two designs: one for an all-steel, four-screw ship and the other, a smaller, twin-screw vessel made from a mixture of aluminium alloy and steel. However, because of a continuing decline in transatlantic traffic, Cunard decided on 19th October 1961 to postpone the 'Q3' project although Vickers Armstrongs was given a contract to develop a concept proposal for the smaller, twin-screw liner, which later became known as 'Q4'. The Chairman of Cunard, Sir John Brocklebank commented that the new Cunarder should be 'a top flight cruise ship and a revolutionary North Atlantic unit with a concept in advance of any existing ship'. So it was that *Queen Elizabeth 2* was conceived. On the 19th August 1964, five yards were invited to tender and on 30th December 1964 the contract was signed with John Brown for the new liner, which was due for delivery in 1968. A £24 million loan was obtained from the British Government.

In November 1965 Sir Basil Smallpeice (1906-1992) became Chairman of Cunard and found a company teetering on the brink of bankruptcy. The passenger ships were losing over £3 million a year whilst the cargo side only earned £2 million in profit. In fact, the cargo operations had grown from 46% of the business in 1956 to 60% in 1964. Half the cargo revenue came from Port Line, whilst Cunard's transatlantic cargo services had overtaken those of Brocklebank, which faced a serious downturn in its Indian trades. Drastic measures

Mauretania in the 1950s with the Blue Ensign at the gaff, and Cunard and White Star flags on her mainmast.

Mauretania was painted 'cruising green' in 1962. *[Malcolm Cranfield collection]*

were needed if Cunard was to survive. A new management team was brought in and the head office was moved from Liverpool to London in 1967. The Cunard buildings in Liverpool and New York were also sold as were unprofitable ships, and the number of staff reduced by a third. Cunard's future lay in diversification. It entered the tanker business in 1964 with the purchase of Moss Tankers (see page 230) and in December 1966 joined the Atlantic Container Line consortium and ordered two roll-on-roll-off/container ships. In April 1968 it also bought Offshore Marine Ltd., a Great Yarmouth-based company servicing oil rigs in the North Sea. Meanwhile, the move from traditional passenger liner services to cruise ships started in 1962 with the conversion of two of the Canadian intermediate liners into the full-time cruise ships *Carmania* and *Franconia*. Around the same time, *Mauretania* also became a year-round cruise ship. *Queen Elizabeth* and *Caronia* were given new lido decks in the mid-1960s but this did not improve their profitability and they were both taken out of service in 1968, a year after *Queen Mary* had retired. Also in 1968 the remaining passenger ships were transferred into Cunard Line Ltd., a management company set up in 1962, and all the Cunard-owned and chartered cargo ships together with those owned by Thos. and Jno. Brocklebank and Moss Tankers were

Atlantic Causeway was Cunard's first container ship. [J. and M. Clarkson collection]

Caronia at Southampton in July 1968, shortly before her sale. [Stephen Berry]

Queen Elizabeth arriving at Southampton in 1968. Her last sailing from Southampton to New York was in October of that year. [Stephen Berry]

managed by a new company, Cunard Brocklebank Ltd. By 1969, the company profits were £3 million, the best result for over twelve years.

After a spectacular launch by Her Majesty Queen Elizabeth in September 1967, the completion of *Queen Elizabeth 2* in late 1968 was an embarrassment not just for Britain but British shipbuilding in particular. During her final acceptance trials and shake-down cruise, she developed a major technical problem with her starboard turbine. On her arrival back at Southampton in January 1969, Cunard refused to accept the ship and there was a five-month delay before her maiden voyage. Despite these teething problems, *Queen Elizabeth 2* went on to become one of the best-loved passenger ships of the 20th century.

The 1970s and 1980s and the Trafalgar House takeover

Cunard's return to profitability was short lived. The start of the 1970s heralded yet another downturn in the cyclical shipping business. Although the fall in trade also impacted on other lines, their larger profits meant that they were better prepared than Cunard to ride out the storm. The company was ripe for a takeover and, when it came in June 1971, it was from an organisation with no links to shipping. Trafalgar House, the construction and engineering conglomerate, had been founded by the ambitious entrepreneur Nigel Broackes (1934-1999) in 1962 and was seeking to diversify its widening portfolio, which would later include Beaverbrook Newspapers, the London Ritz Hotel and John Brown Engineering. In August 1971 the bid of £2.10 per share from Trafalgar House Investments Ltd. was accepted. Although this was considerably higher than Cunard's share price of only 70 pence in November 1965, it was a bitter blow for Cunard and, for the first time since the formation of the company in 1839, it lost its independence. Many predicted that Trafalgar House would asset strip the company. How wrong they were as most of the next two decades would prove to be a renaissance for Cunard, especially for its passenger fleet.

In 1971 and 1972, the company took delivery of its first purpose-built cruise ships, *Cunard Adventurer* and *Cunard Ambassador*. This pair had been ordered for a joint venture with the United States airline,

Overseas National Airways but, when the carrier pulled out of the deal, they were registered with a new company, Cunard-ONA Ltd., which in 1973 became Cunard Cruise Ships Ltd. 1975 and 1977 saw the arrival of two more ships for Cunard Cruise Ships. The 17,586g *Cunard Countess* and *Cunard Princess* were built as replacements for *Carmania* and *Franconia*. Whilst the new cruise ships were aimed at the mass market, the company wanted to achieve a greater share of the lucrative luxury market, which had once been its preserve on the Atlantic. On 11th May 1983 Cunard Line announced that it had acquired the Norwegian American Cruises operation and its two ships, *Vistafjord* and *Sagafjord*. These top-rated ships were in the same de-luxe category as *Queen Elizabeth 2* and Trafalgar House's Ritz Hotel, London. Cunard's commitment to the top end of the market was re-emphasised three years later, when it chartered the 4,260-ton yacht-like cruise ships *Sea Goddess I* and *Sea Goddess II* and operated them under the Cunard name. Meanwhile, *Queen Elizabeth 2* was re-engined in the winter of 1986/1987 and given diesels in place of her expensive steam turbines. The new engines were designed to halve her fuel costs and extend the ship's life by 20 years.

In the late 1980s Cunard started planning a replacement for *QE2*. Code-named 'Q5', the vessel would have been a triple-screw, 2,500-capacity, 90,000g dual-purpose transatlantic liner-cum-cruise ship. Designed to enter service in 1991, with a speed of 40 knots she would have crossed the Atlantic in just under four days. Working with the Finnish engineering and consultancy firm Deltamarin, the proposals reached an advance stage before they were cancelled because of the huge investment required to build the ship.

Cargo operations expanded rapidly in the 1970s with new tankers, bulk carriers and reefers joining the fleet. With the move to containerisation, the conventional cargo ships within the Cunard group were also reduced to a handful and by 1983 all had been sold. That year Trafalgar House made an unsuccessful bid for P&O and by the mid-1980s the cargo division faced another downturn in worldwide trade. When Trafalgar House bought Ellerman Lines plc in July 1987 and formed Cunard Ellerman Shipping Services Ltd.

Cunard Adventurer, delivered in 1971, at Bermuda in 1972. *[Stephen Berry]*

Carmania and *Franconia* laid up in the River Fal, Cornwall. Both were sold to Russian buyers in 1973. *[Malcolm Cranfield collection]*

Queen Elizabeth 2 in 1983 with her short-lived grey colour scheme. *[Stephen Berry]*

to manage the company's cargo operations, the cargo fleet was down to three tankers, two large container ships and five small container vessels.

The 1990s and the start of a new era

1990 was a milestone year for Cunard when it celebrated its 150th anniversary. However, for Trafalgar House the 1990s started badly with major losses starting to accrue. On 18th July 1991 Cunard Ellerman was sold to P&O, leaving the company with a single container ship, *Atlantic Conveyor*. The following year, Sir Nigel Broackes resigned from the company he founded twenty years earlier. Cunard meanwhile, despite the purchase of the world's highest-rated cruise ship, *Royal Viking Sun*, had problems of its own with poor profitability and a public relations disaster in December 1994 when *Queen Elizabeth 2* sailed from Southampton for New York with refit work incomplete. This fiasco generated much negative publicity for Cunard and a firm of consultants subsequently described it as 'the worst-managed company we have ever looked at'. Things got worse the following year when it posted a £16.5 million loss. However, this was nothing compared with Trafalgar House's staggering £321 million loss in 1995. Two years earlier on 27th January 1993, Cunard and Crown Cruise Line, a subsidiary of the Effjohn Group, signed a ten year marketing agreement whereby Cunard would take over the sales and marketing of the three Crown ships (*Crown Monarch*, *Crown Dynasty* and *Crown Jewel*) and market them under the Cunard Crown name. However, this venture lasted only two years.

On 4th April 1996 the Norwegian shipbuilding and engineering company Kværner acquired Trafalgar House and became the world's largest engineering and construction firm. As Kværner was only interested in Trafalgar's engineering, oil and gas and shipbuilding operations, it let it be known that the loss-making Cunard was up for sale. Despite being such a famous name, Cunard's image had been further tarnished by a series of incidents, including an engine room fire on *Sagafjord*, which caused the ship to abandon a world cruise. In 1997, the company's North American headquarters moved from New York to Miami.

In May 1998, Cunard was sold to a consortium of Norwegian investors and the Miami-based Carnival Corporation, the world's largest cruise company. In the deal, Carnival bought 68% of the company and, the following year, it took full control when it purchased the remaining 32% of the shares. In order to re-establish Cunard as a leading cruise line, the new owner started planning a replacement programme for the rather disparate fleet. Seabourn Cruise Line also became a subsidiary of Cunard in 1998. In 2002 P&O Princess Cruises plc, the world's third largest cruise company, was taken over by the Carnival Corporation and Cunard's headquarters was moved to the offices of Princess Cruises in Santa Clarita, California. As part of the Carnival-P&O Princess merger, P&O Princess was relisted on the London Stock Exchange as Carnival plc. The British end of the business operates as Carnival UK, a separate company with headquarters in Southampton. In 2009 executive control of Cunard Line was transferred to Carnival UK.

In the meantime, the first ship in the new Cunard fleet was the French-built 148,528g *Queen Mary 2*, which entered service in January 2004. At the time she was the largest passenger ship in the world and was designed not only for transatlantic crossings but also for world-wide cruising. She was joined in 2007 and 2010 by the 90,000-ton *Queen Victoria* and *Queen Elizabeth*, a pair of ships built in Italy to a standard Carnival company design known as the Vista-class. Meanwhile, *Queen Elizabeth 2* was sold in 2008 to Dubai for use as a floating hotel.

By December 2011, after it moved its three cruise ships to the Bermuda register, for the first time in its 172-year history Cunard Line had no ships registered in Britain. However, because Bermuda is Red Ensign Group 1, the ships still fly an undefaced Red Ensign or a Blue Ensign if the master is an officer in the Royal Navy Reserve.

Queen Elizabeth (2) at Lisbon. *[Luis Miguel Correia]*

TRANSATLANTIC PADDLE STEAMERS

Between 1840 and 1856, The British and North American Royal Mail Steam Packet Company ordered fifteen paddle steamers for the transatlantic service. They were fitted with engines built by Robert Napier, the foremost Scottish engine builder and designer. Napier designed the company's first ships.

The company also placed two small paddle steamers, *Unicorn* and *Margaret*, on the Pictou to Quebec passenger and mail feeder service.

UNICORN 1840-1845 Wooden barque rigged paddle
O.N. 32708   649g 390n
162.9 x 23.5 x 17.3 feet.
2-cyl. side-lever engine by Caird and Co., Greenock; 260 HP, 8 knots.
Passengers: *1849*: 45 after cabin, 28 fore cabin, 28 steerage; *1852*: 56 cabin, 200 second.
4.7.1836: Completed by Robert Steele and Co., Greenock for the Glasgow and Liverpool Steam Shipping Company, Glasgow (one of the G. and J. Burns' companies) as UNICORN.
8.5.1840: Registered at Glasgow under the ownership of The British and North American Royal Mail Steam Packet Company, Glasgow.
16.5.1840: Sailed from Liverpool to Halifax, Nova Scotia.
1.6.1840: Arrived with 27 passengers and proceeded to Boston, arriving *3.6.1840*. She then made a series of voyages between Halifax and Boston prior to BRITANNIA's arrival on *17.7.1840*.
29.6.1840: Maiden call at Quebec.

1840-1844: During the summer months she operated a feeder service between Pictou, Nova Scotia and Quebec. Mail and passengers went overland by stagecoach between Halifax and Pictou. In winter she was laid up in Halifax.
11.11.1843: Rescued survivors from the transport PREMIER, which was wrecked near the mouth of the St. Lawrence River.
11.10.1845: Registered under the ownership of James Whitney, St. John, New Brunswick.
6.1.1847: Registered at St. John, New Brunswick.
1-4.1848: Reboilered by Caird and Co., Greenock.
23.1.1849: Registered at Halifax, Nova Scotia under the ownership of Samuel Cunard.
1.2.1849: Transferred to Edward Cunard, New York, USA.
1.2.1849: Final sailing from Halifax. Arrived New York *5.2*.
31.10.1849: Arrived at San Francisco and sold to the Pacific Mail Steam Ship Co., San

Francisco, U.S.A. Used to carry passengers and mail between Panama and California.
7.1.1850: British register closed.
22.8.1853: Arrived at Sydney, Australia and offered for sale.
25.2.1854: Re-registered at Sydney under the ownership of Edye Manning, Sydney.
26.1.1855: Arrived in Hong Kong and again offered for sale. Operated in the Chinese coastal trade.
7.1855: Badly damaged during a typhoon, towed to Hong Kong and beached for repairs at Whampoa.
3.10.1856: Sold at auction in Hong Kong to Thomas Hunt and Co., a local U.S.-owned company and placed under the U.S. flag.
1857: Renamed E.H. GREEN although taken over by the Chinese during the Anglo-Chinese War.
18.7.1858: Arrived at Whampoa and laid up.
19.5.1859: Final listing for the ship in the 'China Mail' newspaper.
16.5.1872: British register closed.

Unicorn, the former Glasgow to Liverpool steamer, was bought for the Pictou to Quebec feeder service. She was the first Cunard ship to cross the Atlantic and the first to arrive at Halifax and Boston. This is the only known image of the ship. She is depicted in November 1843 at Cape Chatte, in the Gulf of St. Lawrence, rescuing troops and crew from the wrecked transport *Premier*.

Britannia was the lead ship of four paddle steamers delivered at regular intervals during 1840. Her hull narrowed forward of the engines and, like a sailing ship, her steering position was on the poop. The passenger staterooms were situated below the saloon, which had two

long, green-baize tables and continuous leather covered settees. Although her interior was relatively plain, this model in the Science Museum, London shows that she had fancy scrollwork on her stern and paddle boxes. She also had a 225 ton cargo capacity.

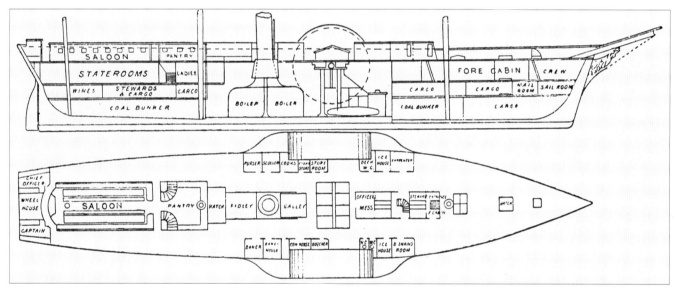

BRITANNIA 1840-1849 Wooden barque rigged paddle
1,154g 619n
203.7 x 31.8 x 22.2 feet.
2-cyl. side-lever engine by Robert Napier, Glasgow; 423 HP, 8.5 knots.
Passengers: 115 cabin.
5.2.1840: Launched by Robert Duncan and Co., Greenock as BRITANNIA.
18.6.1840: Registered at Glasgow under the ownership of The British and North American Royal Mail Steam Packet Company, Glasgow.
4.7.1840: Left Liverpool on maiden voyage to Halifax and Boston.
17.7.1840: Maiden arrival at Halifax. Passengers and mails for Quebec were transferred to UNICORN whilst mails for Bermuda were transferred to VELOCITY (see page 256).

18.7.1840: Maiden arrival at Boston.
3.2.1844: Sailed from Boston after being trapped in the harbour by ice. She was freed after Boston merchants raised $1,500 to have a seven-mile channel cut to release her.
14.10.1847: In thick fog, on a voyage from Liverpool to New York, sustained hull damage after briefly going on rocks near Cape Race, Newfoundland. During four days of repairs at New York, received a new keel and forefoot.
18.12.1848: Final departure from Boston.
1849: Sold with ACADIA to the Central German Confederation for use in the first German navy (Deutsche Reichsflotte), which had been formed in 1848 to protect German merchant ships from attack during the war with Denmark.
28.2.1849: British register closed.
11.3.1849: Sailed from Liverpool to

Bremerhaven.
15.3.1849: Converted into a steam frigate, renamed BARBAROSSA and became the flagship for Karl Rudolf Brommy, the Commander-in-Chief.
1.5.1852: After the Deutsche Reichsflotte was disbanded, became part of the Prussian Navy and converted at the Royal Dockyard, Danzig into an accommodation and guard ship for Danzig. At some stage became a brig with the removal of her mizzen mast.
1865: Machinery removed and became an accommodation ship at Kiel.
5.5.1880: Decommissioned.
28.7.1880: Torpedoed and sunk as a target ship at Kiel by SMS ZIETEN.
10.11.1880: Refloated and subsequently broken up in the Imperial Dockyard at Kiel.

**ACADIA 1840-1849 Wooden barque
rigged paddle**

O.N. 20841 (*1858*) 1,136g 613n
202.9 x 30.7 x 22.4 feet.
2-cyl. side-lever engine by Robert Napier,
Glasgow; 425 HP, 8.5 knots.
Passengers: 115 cabin; *1852*: 50 cabin,
second, 450 steerage.
4.1840: Launched by John Wood and Co.,
Port Glasgow as ACADIA.
21.7.1840: Registered at Glasgow under
the ownership of The British and North
American Royal Mail Steam Packet
Company, Glasgow.
4.8.1840: Left Liverpool on maiden voyage
to Halifax and Boston.
29.11.1848: Final departure from Boston.
12.12.1848: Arrived Liverpool.
1849: Sold with BRITANNIA to the Central
German Confederation for use in the first
German navy (Deutsche Reichsflotte), which
had been formed in 1848 to protect German
merchant ships from attack during the war
with Denmark.
28.2.1849: British register closed.
9.3.1849: Sailed from Liverpool for
Bremerhaven after work in the Coburg
Docks to strengthen her decks to carry heavy
guns.
12.3.1849: Ran ashore near Terschelling,
Netherlands.
20.3.1849: Refloated and arrived at
Bremerhaven.
1849-1851: Converted at Brake into a
steam frigate and renamed ERZHERZOG
JOHANN. Never used by the navy.
4.1852: Deutsche Bundesflotte disbanded.
16.3.1853: Sold to W.A. Fritze and Co.,
Bremen, Germany. Reverted to a passenger/
cargo ship and renamed GERMANIA.
2.8.1853: Inaugurated a new service from
Bremerhaven to New York operated by W.A.
Fritze and Co. and Bremen merchant Carl
Lehmkuhl.
3.1855: Chartered by the British Government
as Crimean War Transport No. 207.
10.1857: Arrived at Southampton for
possible use as an Indian Mutiny transport.
29.1.1858: Registered at London under the
ownership of I. Marks, Greenwich
19.12.1863: Register closed after being
broken up.

**CALEDONIA 1840-1850 Wooden
barque rigged paddle**

1,138g 615n
202.5 x 31.0 x 22.5 feet.
2-cyl. side-lever engine by Robert Napier,
Glasgow; 425 HP, 8.5 knots.
Passengers: 115 cabin.
1840: Launched by Charles Wood,
Dumbarton as CALEDONIA.
6.8.1840: Registered at Glasgow under
the ownership of The British and North
American Royal Mail Steam Packet
Company, Glasgow.
19.9.1840: Left on maiden voyage from
Liverpool to Halifax and Boston.
18.12.1849: Arrived at Liverpool after final
Atlantic crossing.

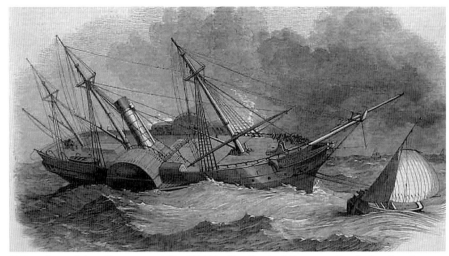

Britannia and *Acadia* were sold in 1849 to the Central German Confederation for
use in the first German navy, the Deutsche Reichsflotte. On her delivery voyage
to Bremerhaven *Acadia* ran ashore near Terschelling, Holland. She was refloated
eight days later.

Caledonia was the third of the *Britannia*-class and was sold with *Hibernia* in 1850 to
the Spanish Government for use as a troopship. This illustration shows her flying
the Burns and MacIver pennants on her foremast. G. and J. Burns managed the
company's finances in Glasgow, whilst D. and C. MacIver managed the ships at
Liverpool.

8.1850: Sold with HIBERNIA to the Spanish
Government (via its London agent Pedro
Juan de Zulueta) for use as troopships to
Cuba.
11.9.1850: British register closed.
8.7.1852: Renamed CONDE DE REGLA
and used on the Cadiz to Cuba mail service
operated by the Spanish Navy.
25.4.1855: Carried the first mails from Cuba
to Spain with prepaid stamps.
1857-1860: Used as a troopship.
1860: Decommissioned.

**COLUMBIA 1840-1843 Wooden barque
rigged paddle**

1,138g 642n
205.9 x 31.6 x 22.7 feet.
2-cyl. side-lever engine by Robert Napier,
Glasgow; 425 HP, 8.5 knots.
Passengers: 115 cabin.
14.9.1840: Launched by Robert Steele and
Company, Greenock as COLUMBIA.
23.10.1840: Registered at Glasgow under
the ownership of The British and North
American Royal Mail Steam Packet

Company, Glasgow.
5.1.1841: Left on maiden voyage from
Liverpool to Halifax and Boston.
2.7.1843: Wrecked in thick fog on
Black Ledges about one mile off Seal
Island, on the south west coast of Nova
Scotia, whilst on a voyage from Boston
to Halifax. The 168 passengers and
crew were landed on Seal Island and
transferred to the company's feeder ship
MARGARET, which sailed to Halifax and
onwards to Liverpool, where she arrived
on *23.7.1843*. This was The British and
North American Royal Mail Steam Packet
Company's first loss.
19.3.1844: Register closed.

**MARGARET (2) 1842-1872 Wooden
paddle**

O.N. 1306 632g 370n
185.0 x 26.1 x 18.0 feet.
2-cyl. side-lever engine by G. Forrester and
Co., Liverpool; 230 HP.
1.10.1835: Completed by Humble and
Milcrest, Liverpool.

Columbia was The British and North American Royal Mail Steam Packet Company's first loss when she was wrecked on the south west coast of Nova Scotia in 1843, fortunately with no loss of life.

Cambria was ordered as a replacement for the lost *Columbia*. She and her sister *Hibernia* were slightly larger than the original quartet and were fitted with more powerful Napier engines. In 1861 she became a transport in the newly-formed Italian Royal Navy, Regia Marina. Her figurehead, depicting a bard with a long flowing beard (below), can be found in the Museo Tecnico Navale di La Spezia, La Spezia, Italy.

31.10.1835: Registered at Liverpool under the ownership of J. Tobin, Liverpool as MARGARET.
14.6.1837: Sold to H. Littledale, Liverpool.
26.7.1842: Registered at Glasgow under the ownership of The British and North American Royal Mail Steam Packet Company. Bought to complement UNICORN on the Halifax-Pictou-Quebec feeder service.
22.8.1842: Sailed on first voyage from Liverpool to Halifax.
1850s: Operated on the Liverpool to Havre route and between Liverpool and the Mediterranean.
9.1856: Engines removed and converted into a barque rigged sailing ship.
1.7.1867: Company restyled the British and North American Steam Packet Company, Glasgow.
9.12.1872: Register closed after being broken up.

HIBERNIA 1843-1850 Wooden barque rigged paddle
1,422g 791n
217.6 x 33.8 x 24.2 feet.
2-cyl. side-lever engine by Robert Napier, Glasgow; 500 HP, 9.25 knots.
Passengers: 120 cabin.
8.9.1842: Launched by Robert Steele and Company, Greenock as HIBERNIA.
6.2.1843: Registered at Glasgow under the ownership of The British and North American Royal Mail Steam Packet Company, Glasgow.
19.4.1843: Left on maiden voyage from Liverpool to Halifax and Boston.
27.8.1847: Arrived at Liverpool after record transatlantic crossing: Halifax-Liverpool in 9 days 1 hour 30 minutes.
30.12.1847: The first Cunarder to arrive at New York.
1.1.1848: Inaugurated the first eastbound sailing from New York to Liverpool.
29.9.1850: Arrived at Liverpool after final Atlantic crossing.
1850: Sold with CALEDONIA to the Spanish Government (via its London agent Pedro Juan de Zulueta) for use as troopships to Cuba.
18.10.1850: British register closed.
2.1852: Hull and machinery overhauled by Robert Napier and Sons, Glasgow and given new boiler
8.7.1852: Renamed VELASCO and used on the Cadiz to Cuba mail service, operated by the Spanish Navy.
1857-1865: Used as a troopship.
1865: Decommissioned.
1869: Broken up.

CAMBRIA* 1844-1860 Wooden barque rigged paddle
O.N. 22346 1,422g 663n
217.4 x 33.8 x 24.2 feet.
2-cyl. side-lever engine by Robert Napier, Glasgow; 500 HP, 9.25 knots.
Passengers: 120 cabin.
1.8.1844: Launched by Robert Steele and Company, Greenock as CAMBRIA.
1.1.1845: Registered at Glasgow under the ownership of The British and North American Royal Mail Steam Packet Company, Glasgow.
4.1.1845: Left on maiden voyage from Liverpool to Halifax and Boston.
18.8.1845: Arrived at Boston after the fastest passage across the Atlantic from Liverpool to Boston via Halifax: 11 days 9 hours.
11.1853: Mizzen mast removed.
31.12.1853: First voyage Havre-Southampton-Halifax-New York.
2.1854: Chartered by the British Government as a troopship during the Crimean War becoming Transport No. 101. On first voyage, carried men from the 50th Regiment.
3.1856: Returned to North Atlantic service.
4.10.1856: Arrived at Liverpool after final Atlantic crossing.
2.1857: Chartered by the European and Australian Royal Mail Steam Packet Company to carry passengers and mail

Shown outbound to the United States, *America* and *Europa* were two of four ships delivered in 1848 for the new Liverpool to New York service. They were enlarged and more powerful versions of the *Britannia* class with a significantly greater (450 ton) cargo capacity.

initially between Marseilles and Malta and later Southampton to Alexandria.
1859: Returned to her owners and laid up.
6.1860: Purchased by Agostino Bertani for the Marina Dittatoriale Siciliana. Made the voyage from England to Genoa under a British master and flying the British flag, arriving *7. 1860*. Bought for use as a troopship during Giuseppe Garibaldi's conquest of the Kingdom of the Two Sicilys.
11.1860: Transferred to Marina Militare Sarda upon dissolution of the provisional government in Sicily.
10.1.1861: British register closed.
17.3.1861: Absorbed into the newly-formed Regia Marina (Italian Royal Navy) as a transport.
31.3.1875: Demolished.

* In case of war, could be fitted with eight 32 pounder and two 8-inch guns (bow and stern).

AMERICA* 1848-1866 Wooden barque rigged paddle
O.N. 1609 1,826g 984n
249.0 x 35.1 x 25.3 feet.
2-cyl. side-lever engine by Robert Napier, Glasgow; 680 HP, 10.25 knots.
Passengers: 140 cabin.
13.5.1847: Launched by Robert Steele and Company, Greenock as AMERICA.
28.2.1848: Registered at Glasgow under the ownership of The British and North American Royal Mail Steam Packet Company, Glasgow.
15.4.1848: Left on maiden voyage from Liverpool to Halifax and New York.
2.5.1863: Left Liverpool on final voyage to Halifax and Boston.
7.1863: Chartered to Allan Line for four voyages Liverpool-Quebec-Montreal.

1866: Ran between Liverpool and Havre.
3.12.1866: Sold to J. and G. Thomson with EUROPA and NIAGARA as part exchange for SIBERIA.
13.11.1868: Register closed after being broken up.

NIAGARA* 1848-1866 Wooden barque rigged paddle
O.N. 7074 1,824g 1,008n;
1867: 1,592g 1,592n
249.1 x 35.1 x 25.2 feet;
1867: 260.5 x 46.0 x 22.8 feet.
2-cyl. side-lever engine by Robert Napier, Glasgow; 680 HP, 10.25 knots.
Passengers: 140 cabin.
28.7.1847: Launched by Robert Steele and Company, Greenock as NIAGARA.
25.4.1848: Registered at Glasgow under the ownership of The British and North American Royal Mail Steam Packet Company, Glasgow.
20.5.1848: Left on maiden voyage from Liverpool to Halifax and Boston.
19.8.1848: First voyage from Liverpool to Halifax and New York.
2.1854: Chartered by the British Government as a troopship becoming Crimean War Transport No. 48.
23.2.1854: Left Liverpool for Malta with about one thousand men from the 28th Regiment.
9.6.1862: Arrived at Liverpool on final voyage from Boston.
1866: Ran between Liverpool and Havre.
24.11.1866: Sold to J. and G. Thomson with AMERICA and EUROPA as part exchange for SIBERIA.
28.12.1866: Sold to J. Birkmyre and R. Duncan, Glasgow.
1867: Engines removed and converted into a ship-rigged sailing vessel by Robert

Duncan and Company, Port Glasgow. The same company owned and converted ASIA in 1869.
23.8.1867: Registered at Port Glasgow under the ownership of J. Birkmyre, R. Duncan and P. McFarlane.
6.6.1875: Wrecked in thick fog two miles south of South Stack, Anglesey whilst on a voyage New York to Liverpool with 120 tons of general cargo and 5,350 bales of cotton. The crew of 31 escaped in boats.
13.10.1875: Register closed.

Niagara, the second in the series, was used as a troopship during the Crimean War and later became a sailing ship.

Europa's collision with the barque *Charles Bartlett* in 1849 led to the loss of 136 lives.

EUROPA* 1848-1866 Wooden barque rigged paddle

O.N. 25943 1,834g 1,010n

249.5 x 35.2 x 25.4 feet.

2-cyl. side-lever engine by Robert Napier, Glasgow; 680 HP, 10.25 knots.

Passengers: 140 cabin.

22.9.1847: Launched by John Wood and Co., Port Glasgow as EUROPA.

28.6.1848: Registered at Glasgow under the ownership of The British and North American Royal Mail Steam Packet Company, Glasgow.

15.7.1848: Left on maiden voyage from Liverpool to Halifax and Boston.

2.9.1848: First voyage from Liverpool to Halifax and New York.

27.6.1849: Collided in thick fog with the 400-ton U.S. barque CHARLES BARTLETT in mid-Atlantic in position 50°48′N, 29°30′W whilst on a homeward voyage from Boston. The sailing ship was on a voyage from London to New York with 162 passengers and 14 crew, amongst whom 136 lives were lost.

11.1854: Chartered by the British Government as a troopship becoming Crimean War Transport No. 55.

14.8.1858: At 23:00, off Cape Race, struck on the port bow by ARABIA (2), which was bound for New York. EUROPA lost her bowsprit and forward curve of her stem and put into St. John's, Newfoundland for repairs.

3.2.1866: Left Liverpool on final voyage to Halifax and Boston.

1867: Sold to J. and G. Thomson with AMERICA and NIAGARA as part exchange for SIBERIA.

13.11.1868: Register closed after being broken up.

CANADA* 1848-1867 Wooden barque rigged paddle

O.N. 1285 1,831g 1,002n;

1869: 1,769g 1,693n

249.0 x 35.1 x 25.7 feet;

1869: 254.5 x 44.0 x 25.1 feet.

2-cyl. side-lever engine by Robert Napier, Glasgow; 680 HP, 10.25 knots.

Passengers: 140 cabin.

2.6.1848: Launched by Robert Steele and Company, Greenock as CANADA.

21.10.1848: Registered at Glasgow under the ownership of The British and North American Royal Mail Steam Packet Company, Glasgow.

25.11.1848: Left on maiden voyage from Liverpool to Halifax and New York.

28.7.1849: Arrived at Liverpool after the fastest passage across the Atlantic from Boston via Halifax: 9 days 22 hours.

29.4.1850: On a voyage from Halifax to Boston collided with the brig BELLE, which sank with the loss of two lives.

11.1859: Inaugurated calls at Queenstown (Cobh), Ireland.

23.12.1865: Left Liverpool on final voyage to Halifax and Boston.

14.6.1867: Registered under the ownership of Wm. McArthur and M. Wilson, Glasgow, who also bought PERSIA in 1868.

1869: Engines removed and converted into a ship-rigged sailing vessel.

24.2.1871: Registered at London.

19.5.1873: Registered under the ownership of J.W. Adamson and T. Ronaldson, London.

31.12.1875: Register closed after being condemned at Mauritius.

12.4.1876: Re-registered at Port Louis, Mauritius under the ownership of Ayoob Aboo Taleb, Port Louis.

9.1.1878: Registered at Calcutta under the ownership of Hadjee Vydanna Jonns, Calcutta, India.

27.11.1882: Register closed after being broken up.

Canada, the last of the 1848 quartet, was sold in 1867 and was converted to a sailing ship.

ASIA** 1850-1867 Wooden barque rigged paddle
O.N. 1284 2,226g 1,214n;
1869: 2,134g 2,054n
265.2 x 37.2 x 27.2 feet;
1869: 268.0 x 45.0 x 24.1 feet.
2-cyl. side-lever engine by Robert Napier, Glasgow; 800 HP, 12.5 knots.
Passengers: 130 cabin, 30 second.
31.1.1850: Launched by Robert Steele and Company, Greenock (Yard No. 114) as ASIA. She was the largest steam ship yet built on the Clyde.
23.4.1850: Registered at Glasgow under the ownership of The British and North American Royal Mail Steam Packet Company, Glasgow.
18.5.1850: Left on maiden voyage from Liverpool to Halifax and Boston.
28.7.1850: Arrived at Liverpool after the fastest passage across the Atlantic from Boston via Halifax: 9 days and 18 hours.
31.8.1850: First voyage from Liverpool to New York.
11.5.1865: Left Liverpool on final voyage to Halifax and Boston.
15.8.1867: Registered under the ownership of J. and G. Thomson, Govan. Taken with PERSIA and AFRICA as part exchange for SAMARIA.
25.2.1868: Registered under the ownership of Robert Duncan, Glasgow.
1869: Engines removed and converted into a ship-rigged sailing vessel by Robert Duncan and Company, Port Glasgow. The same company owned and converted NIAGARA in 1867.
23.10.1869: Registered at Port Glasgow.
3.12.1876: Destroyed by fire at Calcutta.
31.1.1877: Register closed.

AFRICA** 1850-1868 Wooden barque rigged paddle
O.N. 1821 2,226g 1,216n
265.2 x 37.2 x 27.2 feet.
2-cyl. side-lever engine by Robert Napier, Glasgow; 800 HP, 12.5 knots.
Passengers: 130 cabin, 30 second.
7.1850: Launched by Robert Steele and Company, Greenock as AFRICA.
17.9.1850: Registered at Glasgow under the ownership of The British and North American Royal Mail Steam Packet Company, Glasgow.
26.10.1850: Left on maiden voyage from Liverpool to New York.
15.2.1854: Stranded on mud flats off Jersey City. After a week, refloated and docked at Jersey City with no damage.
20.7.1855: First voyage from Liverpool to Halifax and Boston.
3.1867: Used as accommodation ship at Liverpool for troops during the Fenian uprising in Ireland.
1.7.1867: Company restyled The British and North American Steam Packet Company, Glasgow.
7.12.1867: Left Liverpool on final voyage to Halifax and Boston, the last Cunard sailing by a wooden paddle steamer.
17.1.1868: Registered under the ownership

Asia and *Africa* were built to compete with the new Collins Line ships. The largest yet built on the Clyde, they were also the last to be based on the three-masted *Britannia* design. The illustration below shows the exposed promenade space on *Asia*'s paddle boxes.

In December 1867 *Africa* made Cunard's final sailing by a wooden paddle steamer.

of J. and G. Thomson, Govan. Taken with
PERSIA and ASIA as part exchange for
SAMARIA.
16.7.1868: Registered under the ownership
of H. Moore, Glasgow.
23.9.1869: Register closed after being
broken up.

**ARABIA (1) 1852 Wooden brig rigged
paddle**
O.N. 13832 2,826g 1,758n
280.5 x 37.4 x 27.6 feet.
2-cyl. side-lever engine by Robert Napier,
Glasgow; 1,000 NHP, 13 knots.
Passengers: 116 first, 20 second.
24.12.1851: Launched by Robert Steele and
Company, Greenock as ARABIA.
1.1852: Bought on the stocks by the
Royal Mail Steam Packet Company as a
replacement for AMAZON, which had
been lost by fire on *4.1.1852*. Renamed LA
PLATA. The largest ship yet built on the
Clyde.
13.8.1852: Registered at London under the
ownership of the Royal Mail Steam Packet
Company.
17.8.1852: Left on maiden voyage from
Southampton to West Indies.
24.11.1860: Caught fire at Southampton but
later repaired.
9.5.1865: First voyage from Southampton
to Brazil
9.6.1871: Last voyage from Southampton to
Brazil
12.1871: Sold to William Denny and
Brothers, Dumbarton as part payment for
BOYNE.
16.12.1871: Registered under the ownership
of Thompson Aikman, Glasgow.
1.4.1872: Registered under the ownership of
J. Sloane, Glasgow.
22.1.1873: Register closed after being
broken up.

** In case of war, could be fitted with eight
32 and two 68 pounder guns.

ARABIA (2) ** 1852-1865 Wooden brig
rigged paddle**
O.N. 22347 2,393g 1,359n
284.2 x 37.3 x 27.6 feet.
2-cyl. side-lever engine by Robert Napier,
Glasgow; 938 HP, 13 knots.
Passengers: 180 cabin, steerage.
21.6.1852: Launched by Robert Steele and
Company, Greenock as ARABIA. Laid
down as PERSIA but was renamed after the
sale of her sister ARABIA (1) to the Royal
Mail Steam Packet Company.
9.12.1852: Registered at Glasgow under
the ownership of The British and North
American Royal Mail Steam Packet
Company, Glasgow. The last in the fleet to
be built of wood.
1.1.1853: Left on maiden voyage from
Liverpool to New York.
21.1.1854: First voyage from Liverpool to
Halifax and Boston.
5.1854: Chartered by the British Government
during the Crimean War as Transport No. 83.

Royal Mail Steam Packet Company's *La Plata* started life as *Arabia*.

Arabia (2) was Cunard's last wooden-hulled ship and the first in the transatlantic
fleet designed with two funnels and two masts. She was also fitted with the largest
and most powerful engines installed in a ship to that date. However, she was
considered a failure as her engines were too powerful for her wooden frames and,
after a year, was transferred to the Boston route.

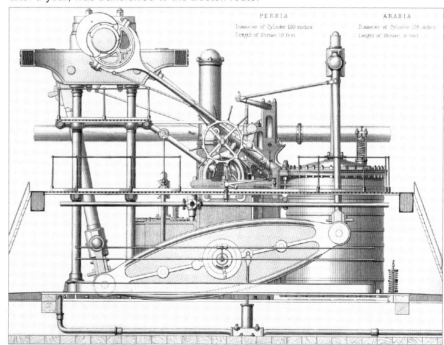

20.5.1854: Left Liverpool with the 1st Royal
Dragoons. Later also carried French troops
from Marseilles to the Black Sea.
14.8.1858: Struck the port bow of EUROPA
off Cape Race whilst bound for New

York but suffered only minor damage and
continued her voyage.
3.9.1864: Left Liverpool on final voyage to
Halifax and Boston
31.10.1865: Registered under the ownership

of Robert Duncan, Port Glasgow. Unlike NIAGARA and ASIA, there is no evidence that she was converted into a sailing ship by Robert Duncan and Company. Laid up at Greenock.

10.7.1866: Registered at London under the ownership of the Anglo-Egyptian Navigation Co. Ltd., London.

11.7.1866: Reported that she was about to be towed to Liverpool by the Clyde Shipping Company's tug CONQUEROR (199/1865).

15.6.1867: Register closed after being broken up.

PERSIA 1856-1868 Iron brig rigged paddle

O.N. 11523 3,300g 2,079n
376.0 x 45.3 x 30.0 feet.
2-cyl. side-lever engine by Robert Napier and Sons, Glasgow; 950 HP, 13 knots.
Passengers: 200 cabin, 50 second.

3.7.1855: Launched by Robert Napier and Sons, Glasgow (Yard No. 60) as PERSIA. The contract for her construction had originally been signed on *14.8.1853* with William Denny and Brothers, Dumbarton but, probably because the price was too low, Denny withdrew from the project shortly afterwards.

7.1.1856: Registered at Glasgow under the ownership of The British and North American Royal Mail Steam Packet Company, Glasgow.

26.1.1856: Left on maiden voyage from Liverpool to New York. Arrived at New York with damaged paddle floats and bowsprit after encountering heavy gales and ice. Record crossings: April, May and August.

5.1856: Mizzen mast removed.

14.12.1861: Sailed from Liverpool to Halifax with 1,270 troops during tension between Britain and the United States.

1.7.1867: Company restyled The British and North American Steam Packet Company, Glasgow.

28.12.1867: Left Liverpool on final voyage to New York.

10.2.1868: Registered under the ownership of J. and G. Thomson, Govan. Taken with ASIA and AFRICA in part exchange for SAMARIA.

11.7.1868: Registered under the ownership of Wm. McArthur and M. Wilson, Glasgow, who also bought CANADA in 1867.

18.12.1871: Registered at Liverpool under the ownership of W. Moss, G. Harding, and W.H. Shirley, Liverpool.

16.5.1873: Registered under the ownership of the breakers Sidney and Abercrombie Castle, London.

16.5.1873: Register closed after being broken up at Glasgow.

The beautifully-proportioned record breaker *Persia* was the first iron-hulled paddle steamer on the Atlantic. She was ordered to re-establish the company's reputation as the premier line on the North Atlantic. At the time, she was the largest ship in the world. This photograph from 1855 shows her under construction. *[T. & R. Annan & Sons Ltd.]*

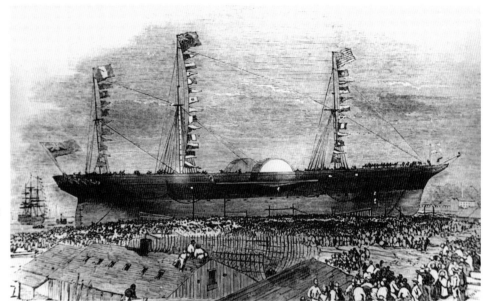

Persia was launched with three masts (above). A few months after she entered service, her mizzen mast was removed. This considerably enhanced her appearance, especially under full sail (below).

Although *Scotia* was one of the finest paddle ships ever built, compared with screw-driven ships she was expensive to operate. However, with a maximum speed of over 16 knots she was the fastest ship on the Atlantic from 1863 to 1869. She also had space for 1,400 tons of cargo. At the time of her withdrawal in 1878 she was one of the last paddle steamers to operate across the Atlantic. This fine model of *Scotia* is in the Science Museum, London.

SCOTIA 1862-1878 Iron brig rigged paddle

O.N. 43711 3,871g 2,358n;
1879: 4,667g 2,931n
379.0 x 47.8 x 30.5 feet.
2-cyl. side-lever engine by Robert Napier and Sons, Glasgow; 1,000 HP, 13.5 knots;
1879: Two 2-cyl compound engines by Laird Brothers, Birkenhead; 1,100 HP, 10 knots.
Passengers: 573 cabin, 1,500 troops in case of war; *later*: 300 cabin.
25.6.1861: Launched by Robert Napier and Sons, Glasgow (Yard No. 99) as SCOTIA. Cunard's last paddle steamer.
7.2.1862: Registered at Glasgow under the ownership of The British and North American Royal Mail Steam Packet Company, Glasgow.
10.5.1862: Left on maiden voyage from Liverpool to New York via Queenstown. Record crossings: December 1863 and July 1866.
1.7.1867: Company restyled The British and North American Steam Packet Company, Glasgow.
29.4.1876: Left Liverpool on final voyage to New York.
21.3.1878: Registered under the ownership of the Telegraph Construction and Maintenance Co. Ltd., London.
25.3.1878: Registered at London.
1879: Rebuilt and re-engined as a twin-screw, single funnel, cable ship by Laird Brothers, Birkenhead.
11.9.1903: Registered under the ownership George G. Ward, London, the nominee of the Commercial Pacific Cable Company, a U.S. company.
11.3.1904: Wrecked on Calalan Bank, at the entrance to Apra harbour, Guam and broke her back. This was close to the spot where CARONIA (2) was wrecked on *12.8.1974*. SCOTIA was on a voyage from Singapore to Guam
29.3.1904: Register closed.

In 1863 *Scotia* broke *Persia*'s seven-year-old records in both directions. Her record from Queenstown to New York (8 days 3 hours), averaging 14.5 knots, remained unbroken until 1872.

Converted to a twin-screw cable ship, *Scotia* played a major role in the laying of telegraph cables between Britain and the Mediterranean. She was fitted with twin bow and single stern cable sheaves whilst her forward cable machinery was installed on the main deck, with its drums protruding through the deck above.

EARLY TRANSATLANTIC SCREW SHIPS

ANDES 1852-1859 Iron barque rigged
O.N. 25759 1,275g 867n
236.6 x 33.2 x 24.0 feet.
2-cyl. geared beam engine by Tulloch and
Denny, Dumbarton; 300 HP, 9 knots.
Passengers: 62 cabin, 122 second.
18.8.1852: Launched by William Denny
and Brothers, Dumbarton (Yard No. 34) as
ANDES.
11.11.1852: Registered at Glasgow under
the ownership of The British and North
American Royal Mail Steam Packet
Company, Glasgow. The company's first
purpose-built screw steamer with iron hull
(the second-hand BRITISH QUEEN was the
first screw-driven ship in the fleet although
Samuel Cunard's Halifax-Bermuda mail
service had operated screw steamers since
1848), she was one of a quartet designed
for a new service between Liverpool and
Chagres on the Isthmus of Panama via New
York and Jamaica. This short-lived (until
1854) route was established primarily for
gold miners bound for California to travel
overland via the isthmus. Her sisters were
ALPS and a pair, BALBEK and MELITA,
which were completed as AUSTRALIAN
and SYDNEY respectively for the Australian
Royal Mail Steam Navigation Company in
which George Burns had a shareholding.
8.12.1852: Left Liverpool on maiden voyage
and the inaugural sailing to Chagres via New
York but returned with storm damage.
1.1.1853: Recommenced maiden voyage
from Liverpool to New York.
6.1853: She and her sister ALPS underwent
extensive alterations by McNab and Clarke.
4.1854: Chartered by the British Government
during Crimean War as Transport No. 100.
Used as a troop and hospital ship.
25.9.1854: Arrived at Constantinople from
Crimea with 300 wounded troops.
6.1856: End of Crimean charter.
1858: Operating on Liverpool to Eastern
Mediterranean service.
16.5.1859: Sold to Spanish Government.
London broker was J.S. de Zulueta.
2.7.1859: Renamed SAN QUINTIN after
conversion to an armed transport.
2.8.1859: British register closed.
11.1860: Engines overhauled on the Clyde.
1894: Decommissioned.

ALPS 1852-1859 Iron barque rigged
O.N. 1286 1,373g 818n
235.9 x 33.2 x 24.0 feet.
2-cyl. geared beam engine by Tulloch and
Denny, Dumbarton; 300 HP, 9 knots.
Passengers: 62 cabin, 122 second.
28.9.1852: Launched by William Denny
and Brothers, Dumbarton (Yard No. 35) as
ALPS. Designed for the Liverpool-Chagres
service via New York and Jamaica.
9.12.1852: Registered at Glasgow under
the ownership of The British and North
American Royal Mail Steam Packet
Company, Glasgow.

Andes was not only the company's first iron-hulled ship, she was also the first purpose-built ship in the fleet with screw propulsion. She was the first of four passenger-cargo ships with mountain names, designed for a new but short-lived service between Liverpool and Chagres on the Isthmus of Panama, via New York and Jamaica.

2.2.1853: Left on maiden voyage from
Liverpool to New York, arriving *17.2*.
6.1853: She and her sister ANDES
underwent extensive alterations by Caird
and Co., Greenock.
4.1854: Chartered by the British
Government during Crimean War as
Transport No. 82. First voyage was from
Plymouth to Malta.
9.12.1854: Departed Marseilles with French
troops for Crimea. Also used as a hospital
ship.
19.3.1856: Returned to Liverpool.
7.1856: Placed on Havre to New York
service.
1858: Operating on Liverpool to Eastern
Mediterranean service.

12.3.1859: Left Liverpool on last voyage to
New York via Halifax.
16.5.1859: Sold to Spanish Government.
2.7.1859: Renamed SAN FRANCISCO DE
BORJA after conversion to a troopship.
25.7.1859: British register closed.
1882: Decommissioned.
1885: Stricken from Spanish Navy List.

JURA 1854-1861 Iron barque rigged
O.N. 26053 2,240g 1,068n
313.8 x 35.8 x 27.6 feet.
2-cyl. geared beam engine by J. and G.
Thomson, Govan 450 HP, 11 knots.
Passengers: cabin and second; *c.1860*:
Steerage added.
27.6.1854: Launched by J. and G. Thomson,

Jura aground at the entrance to the River Mersey.

38

Govan (Yard No. 11) as JURA. Designed for the Liverpool to Chagres service via New York and Jamaica.
21.9.1854: Registered at Glasgow under the ownership of The British and North American Royal Mail Steam Packet Company, Glasgow.
10.1854: Chartered by the British Government during Crimean War as the 1,200-capacity Transport No. 14.
3-8.1857: Chartered by European and Australian Royal Mail Steam Packet Company for Southampton to Alexandria mail service.
16.9.1857: Left on first voyage from Liverpool to New York.
9.1860: Chartered by Allan Line for Liverpool-Quebec-Montreal service.
31.7.1861: Sold to James and Alexander Allan, Glasgow.
3.11.1864: At about 01:00 with a pilot aboard, ran aground on Waterloo Bank, Crosby Point whilst entering the River Mersey. She was on a voyage from Quebec to Liverpool with 95 crew and 69 passengers and all were rescued. Broke her back at 07:00 and was later declared a constructive total loss.
10.5.1865: Register closed.

EMEU 1854-1858 Iron barque rigged
O.N. 25663 1,537g 908n;
1876: 1,626g 1,584n
268.9 x 34.5 x 27.6 feet.
1876: 268.2 x 36.6 x 19.3 feet.
2-cyl. geared beam engine by Robert Napier and Sons, Glasgow; 300 IHP, 10 knots.
Passengers: 80 cabin, 130 second; *1859*: 80 first.
22.8.1853: Launched by Robert Napier and Sons, Glasgow (Yard No. 54) as EMEU. One of five ships ordered for a new passenger-mail service to Australia via Panama.
21.2.1854: Registered at London under the ownership of the Australian Pacific Mail Steam Packet Company, London. The new service was soon abandoned and she was chartered by the British Government as Crimean War Transport No.74.
1.3.1854: Embarked at Kingstown, Ireland the 33rd Regiment bound for the Crimea.
30.11.1854: Registered at Glasgow under the ownership of the The British and North American Royal Mail Steam Packet Company, Glasgow.
6.1857: Chartered by the European and Australian Royal Mail Steam Packet Company as a replacement for ONEIDA (2,293/1855) on the Sydney to Suez mail service.
30.10.1858: Sold to the Peninsular and Oriental Steam Navigation Company, London and delivered at Sydney in *2.1859*.
8.4.1859: Registered at London. Used on Bombay to Hong Kong service.
5.11.1873: Sold at auction to William McArthur, London.
8.1876: Engines removed, converted into ship-rigged sailing vessel and renamed WINCHESTER.

8.1878: Sold to G. Crowshaw and Co., London.
14.7.1880: Lost in the Macassar Straits in position 02°58′S, 117°34′E whilst on a voyage from Manila to Montreal with a cargo of sugar. No lives were lost from the 24 crew.
23.9.1880: Register closed.

ETNA 1855-1860 Iron barque rigged
O.N. 10565 1,538g 992n;
1861: 2,121g 1,494n;
1870: 2,611g 1,775n
304.9 x 36.0 x 27.0 feet;
1861: 308.6 x 37.4 x 19.0 feet;
1870: 349.4 x 37.6 x 18.9 feet.
2-cyl. geared beam engine by Caird and Co., Greenock; 450 HP, 11 knots;
1870: C.2-cyl engine by Laird Brothers, Birkenhead; 350 HP.
Passengers: cabin and second; *c.1860*: Steerage added.
26.8.1854: Launched by Caird and Co., Greenock (Yard No. 32) as ETNA. Designed for the Liverpool to Chagres service via New York and Jamaica.
13.1.1855: Registered at Glasgow under the ownership of The British and North American Royal Mail Steam Packet Company, Glasgow.
6.3.1855: Sailed from Liverpool for the Crimea with 191 Royal Artillery horses and 178 officers and men having been chartered by the British Government as Crimean War Transport No. 186.
5.2.1856: Left on first voyage from Havre to Halifax and New York.
2-8.1857: Chartered to the European and Australian Royal Mail Steam Packet Company for a Southampton to Alexandria service.
15.1.1859: Sailed on first voyage from Liverpool to New York.
26.6.1860: Inaugural Cunard sailing from Liverpool to New York with emigrants.

10.11.1860: Registered under the ownership of William Inman, Liverpool.
5.12.1860: Left Liverpool for New York on first voyage for Inman Line.
24.9.1861: Registered at Liverpool.
10.1870: Lengthened and rebuilt with new compound engine and boilers by Laird Brothers, Birkenhead.
31.12.1870: Register closed having been 'sold to foreigners' and renamed CITY OF BRISTOL. Such a sale was often the only way in which a British ship could be renamed.
7.8.1871: Re-registered at Liverpool under the ownership of William Inman, Liverpool.
5.11.1875: Transferred to the Inman Steam Ship Co. Ltd., Liverpool.
1.5.1878: Registered under the ownership of J.T. Davies, Liverpool and continued to operate between Liverpool and New York.
13.12.1880: Final sailing from Liverpool to New York.
9.12.1881: British register closed.
12.12.1881: Sold to Dufour e Bruzzo, Genoa, Italy and renamed MESSICO.
20.1.1882: First sailing from Genoa to Montevideo and Buenos Aires.
31.7.1883: Renamed SEMPIONE.
28.4.1884: Sold to Erasmo Piaggio fu Rocco, Genoa and named ADRIA.
28.5.1884: Sailed from Genoa to Montevideo and Buenos Aires under management of Società Rocco Piaggio e Figli, Genoa.
10.9.1885: Piaggio fleet merged into Navigazione Generale Italiana (NGI), Genoa. Piaggio later became Director General of NGI.
12.7.1895: Delivered to Vado Ligure, Savona for demolition. Bought by Giulio Rohmer, a French entrepreneur from Lyon, who purchased several ships and had the metal sent to France.
13.3.1896: Demolition complete.

Emeu in P&O colours. [P&O Archives]

AUSTRALASIAN 1859-1869/CALABRIA 1869-1876 Iron barque rigged

O.N. 19492 2,761g 1,513n;
1869: 2,902g 1,730n;
1879: 2,902g 2,034n
331.7 x 42.1 x 20.5 feet;
1879: 338.5 x 42.1 x 20.9 feet.
2-cyl. vertical direct acting engine by J. and
G. Thomson, Govan; 700 HP, 13 knots;
1869: 2-cyl. vertical direct acting engine by
J. and G. Thomson, Govan; 409 HP;
1879: C. 2-cyl by J. and G. Thomson,
Govan; 220 HP.
Passengers: 200 cabin, 60 second; *c.1860*:
steerage added; *1870*: 80 cabin, 900
steerage.
10.6.1857: Launched by J. and G. Thomson,
Govan (Yard No. 33) as AUSTRALASIAN
(laid down as AUSTRALIAN).
9.10.1857: Registered at Glasgow under the
ownership of W. Buchanan, W. Connal and
P. White (European and Australian Royal
Mail Company), Glasgow.
12.10.1857: Sailed on maiden voyage from
Southampton to Alexandria. Subsequently
placed on Sydney to Suez mail service.
1.7.1858: Following the collapse of the
European and Australian Royal Mail Co.
Ltd., Royal Mail Steam Packet Company
took over the Sydney to Suez mail contract
and its ships.
17.12.1859: Registered under the ownership
of The British and North American Royal
Mail Steam Packet Company, Glasgow.
25.2.1860: First voyage from Liverpool to
New York.
11.12.1861: During tensions between Britain
and the United States, sailed from Liverpool
to Halifax with troops from the 60th Rifles.
3.1867: Used as accommodation ship at
Liverpool for troops during the Fenian
uprising in Ireland.
1.7.1867: Company restyled The British and
North American Steam Packet Company,
Glasgow.

The second-hand *Australasian* had an interesting career and was the company's first screw-driven transatlantic steamer with two funnels (top).   In 1869 she was rebuilt with a single funnel and renamed *Calabria*. She and *Scotia* (1) were bought by the Telegraph Construction and Maintenance Co. Ltd. and converted into cable ships. *Calabria* laid numerous cables, including one linking Hong Kong and the Philippines. She is shown here (bottom) as a cable ship.

19.8.1869: Register closed having been 'sold
to foreigners' and renamed CALABRIA.
Such a sale was often the only way in which
a British ship could be renamed.
1869: Rebuilt with a new engine and a single
funnel.
20.12.1869: Re-registered at Glasgow.
29.1.1876: Final transatlantic sailing.
28.11.1876: Registered under the ownership
of the Telegraph Construction and
Maintenance Co. Ltd., London.
1879: Converted into a cable ship and given
a new compound engine.
7.6.1879: Registered at London.
19.4.1898: Left London for Dordrecht for
demolition in tow of tug NOORDZEE
(298/1892), having been bought by F.
Rijsdijk, Hendrik-Ido-Ambacht.
15.4.1898: Register closed.

CHINA 1862-1880 Iron barque rigged

O.N. 43705 2,529g 1,540n;
1889: 2,439g
326.2 x 40.4 x 19.3 feet.
2-cyl. geared oscillating engines by Robert
Napier and Sons, Glasgow; 550 HP, 13.9
knots;
1873: C.2-cyl. by Barclay, Curle and Co.,
Glasgow; 420 HP.
Passengers: 286 cabin, 771 steerage or 1,500
troops.
18.10.1861: Launched by Robert Napier and
Sons, Glasgow (Yard No. 102) as CHINA.
18.1.1862: Registered at Glasgow under
the ownership of The British and North
American Royal Mail Steam Packet
Company, Glasgow.
15.3.1862: Left on maiden voyage from
Liverpool to New York.

China was the first purpose-built screw steamer ordered for the mail service and the first in the fleet with a large steerage capacity. Although she was not as fast as the paddle steamer *Scotia*, which also was completed in 1862, she was far more economical to operate, with a daily coal consumption half that of the paddle ship.

1.7.1867: Company restyled The British and North American Steam Packet Company, Glasgow.
1873: New compound engine fitted.
1.7.1878: Transferred to the Cunard Steamship Co. Ltd., Liverpool.
5.8.1879: Final transatlantic sailing from Liverpool.
1879: Chartered as a Zulu War transport.
20.2.1880: Registered under the ownership of D. Hine, London.
3.1880: Sold to Don José Campo, Marqués de Campo, Cartagena, Spain for the Cádiz to Manila mail and passenger service and renamed MAGALLANES.
22.6.1880: Register closed.
1889: Sold to J.D. Bischoff, Bremen, Germany, engines removed, converted into a four-masted barque and renamed THEODOR.
1898: Sold to C.A. Bunnemann, Bremen.
4.1901: Sold to Akt. Theodor (J. Johanson og Co.), Moss, Norway
2.3.1906: Reported missing after leaving Tampa for Yokohama with a cargo of phosphates.

The success of *China* paved the way for a series of five similar ships with clipper bows and considerable space for steerage passengers, which were built between 1864 and 1868. They were ordered primarily to compete with Inman Line, which also introduced five new ships during this period. William Inman was one the first ship owners to recognise the opportunities for carrying emigrants to the United States in steam ships.

CUBA 1864-1876 Iron barque rigged
O.N. 50357 2,668g 1,535n;
1877: 2,668g 2,499n
338.2 x 42.4 x 19.4 feet.
2-cyl. geared oscillating engines by Tod and MacGregor, Glasgow; 560 HP, 12 knots.
Passengers: 268 cabin, 771 steerage or 1,500 troops.

21.7.1864: Launched by Tod and MacGregor, Glasgow (Yard No. 129) as CUBA.
17.11.1864: Registered at Glasgow under the ownership of The British and North American Royal Mail Steam Packet Company, Glasgow.
3.12.1864: Left on maiden voyage from Liverpool to New York.
1.7.1867: Company restyled The British and North American Steam Packet Company, Glasgow.
21.12.1867: Left Liverpool on the company's final sailing to Halifax.

17.4.1875: Final transatlantic sailing from Liverpool.
4.10.1876: Registered under the ownership of David Brown, London.
1876-1877: Engines removed and converted into a four-masted, ship-rigged, sailing vessel.
4.9.1877: Registered at London.
25.4.1883: Transferred to the Earl of Beaconsfield Ship Co. Ltd., London.
1.6.1883: Renamed EARL OF BEACONSFIELD.
6.11.1887: Wrecked 2.5 miles south of Aldbrough, Yorkshire whilst on a voyage from Calcutta to Hull with a cargo of wheat and linseed. There was no loss of life among the 34 crew.
14.12.1887: Register closed.

JAVA 1865-1877 Iron barque rigged
O.N. 52626 2,696g 1,761n;
1892: 2,475g 2,463n
337.1 x 42.9 x 19.4 feet.
2-cyl. vertical direct acting engine by J. and G. Thomson, Govan; 600 HP, 14 knots;
1877: C.2-cyl engine by Fawcett, Preston and Co., Liverpool; 350 HP.
Passengers: 300 first, 800 steerage.
24.6.1865: Launched by J. and G. Thomson, Govan (Yard No. 80) as JAVA.
11.9.1865: Registered at Glasgow under the ownership of The British and North American Royal Mail Steam Packet Company, Glasgow.

In 1867 *Cuba* took the company's final sailing from Liverpool to Halifax.

Java was the third of the *Cuba* class.

41

3.12.1864: Left on maiden voyage from Liverpool to New York.
1.7.1867: Company restyled The British and North American Steam Packet Company, Glasgow.
11.3.1876: Final sailing from Liverpool to New York.
2.1877: Sold to G. Palmer, Hampshire.
1877: Fitted with new compound engine.
10.1877-4.1878: Chartered to the Warren Line and ran between Liverpool and Boston.
4-8.1878: Chartered to Red Star Line and ran between Antwerp, New York and Philadelphia.
10.1878: Sold to Société Anonyme de Navigation Belge-Américaine (Red Star Line), Antwerp, Belgium and renamed ZEELAND.
26.10.1878: British register closed.
23.2.1889: Final sailing from Antwerp to New York.
3.1889: Sold to Bossière Frères, Havre, France and renamed ÉLECTRIQUE.
10.1892: Sold to John Herron, Liverpool, engines removed, converted into a ship-rigged sailing vessel and renamed LORD SPENCER.
15.10.1892: Re-registered at Liverpool.
7.11.1892: Transferred to Sailing Vessel 'Lord Spencer' Co. Ltd., Liverpool.
9.4.1895: Sailed from San Francisco for Queenstown with a cargo of wheat, 28 crew and two passengers.
13.7.1895: Thought to have collided with the British ship-rigged iron sailing ship PRINCE OSCAR (1,292/1864) in the South Atlantic in position 9°30′S, 28°20′W and was never seen again. PRINCE OSCAR was on a voyage from South Shields to Iquique, Chile with a cargo of coal. She sank with the loss of six crew. Sixteen survivors were later found in a boat with neither food nor water by a British ship, reported to be DHAMAN, which was on a voyage from Melbourne to London.
23.12.1895: Register closed.

RUSSIA 1867-1879 Iron barque rigged
O.N. 58312 2,960g 1,710n;
1879: 4,667g 2,931n
358.0 x 43.0 x 19.4 feet;
1879: 435.2 feet x 43.0 x 19.4 feet.
2-cyl. vertical direct acting engine by J. and G. Thomson, Govan; 600 HP, 14.4 knots;
1879: C.2-cyl. by J. and G. Thomson, Glasgow; 500 HP;
1889: T.3-cyl. by J. and G. Thomson, Glasgow; 582 HP.
Passengers: 300 (later reduced to 235) cabin, 1,500 steerage.
20.3.1867: Launched by J. and G. Thomson, Govan (Yard No. 93) as RUSSIA.
9.5.1867: Registered at Glasgow under the ownership of The British and North American Royal Mail Steam Packet Company, Glasgow.
15.6.1867: Left on maiden voyage from Liverpool to New York.
1.7.1867: Company restyled The British and North American Steam Packet Company, Glasgow.
11.1867: Record crossing New York to Queenstown: 8 days 28 minutes.

The progress of screw-driven ships was highlighted by *Russia* (above) in 1867 when she broke *Scotia*'s eastbound record. The rivalry between Cunard and Inman Line was also intense and 'races', such as the one between *Russia* and *City of Paris* in February 1868, generated much public interest.
Russia was considered at the time to be a comfortable ship, although the amount of deck space on this narrow-beam ship was fairly limited (below). *[Paul Louden-Brown collection]*

1.7.1878: Transferred to the Cunard Steamship Co. Ltd., Liverpool.
2.11.1878: Final sailing from Liverpool to New York.
1879: Chartered as a Zulu War transport.
9.1879: Sold to Société Anonyme de Navigation Belge-Américaine (Red Star Line), Antwerp, Belgium and renamed WAESLAND.
22.9.1879: British register closed.
1879: Lengthened and rebuilt by J. and

G. Thomson, Govan with additional mast. Engine was compounded.
1.12.1880: First sailing from Antwerp to New York.
1889: Fitted with new triple-expansion engine.
17.8.1895: Final sailing from Antwerp to New York.
11.9.1895: First sailing from Philadelphia to Liverpool for American Line which was part of the International Navigation Company, owners of Red Star Line.

6.3.1902: Sank after being hit by the steamer HARMONIDES (3,521/1891) in thick fog, 40 miles south west of Holyhead whilst on a voyage from Liverpool to Philadelphia with general cargo and 114 passengers, two of whom were lost.

SIBERIA 1867-1880 Iron brig rigged

O.N. 58336 2,498g 1,698n
320.0 x 39.2 x 26.3 feet.
2-cyl. vertical direct acting engine by J. and G. Thomson, Govan; 300 HP, 12 knots.
Passengers: 100 cabin, 800 steerage.
2.7.1867: Launched by J. and G. Thomson, Govan (Yard No. 95) as SIBERIA. She had been laid down as SUMATRA but name changed because this name had been chosen by P&O for a Denny-built vessel then under construction.
23.8.1867: Registered at Glasgow under the ownership of The British and North American Steam Packet Company, Glasgow.
24.9.1867: Left on maiden voyage from Liverpool to New York.
1.7.1878: Transferred to the Cunard Steamship Co. Ltd., Liverpool
9.1878: Final transatlantic crossing.
24.3.1880: Registered under the ownership of J. and G. Thomson, Govan and probably taken in part exchange for CATALONIA or SERVIA.
1880: Sold to Don José Campo, Marqués de Campo, Cartagena, Spain for the Cádiz to Manila mail and passenger service and renamed MANILA.
19.1.1881: British register closed.
11.5.1882: Wrecked at San Juan, Puerto Rico whilst on a voyage from Liverpool to Vera Cruz.

SAMARIA (1) 1868-1902 Iron brig rigged

O.N. 60370 2,605g 1,695n
320.6 x 39.5 x 26.6 feet.
2-cyl. vertical direct acting engine by J. and G. Thomson, Govan; 300 HP, 12 knots;
1878: C. 2-cyl by James Jack and Co., Liverpool; 288 HP.
Passengers: 130 cabin; 800 steerage.
4.7.1868: Launched by J. and G. Thomson, Govan (Yard No. 100) as SAMARIA.
12.9.1868: Registered at Glasgow under the ownership of The British and North American Steam Packet Company, Glasgow.
29.9.1868: Left on maiden voyage from Liverpool to New York.
18.4.1871: First voyage on Liverpool to Boston route.
1878: Compound engine fitted.
1.7.1878: Transferred to the Cunard Steamship Co. Ltd., Liverpool.
30.1.1896: Final transatlantic crossing from Liverpool to Boston.
19.5.1898: Registered at Liverpool.
1.8.1902: Register closed on sale to Italian breakers for demolition at Genoa.
11.8.1902: Sailed from Liverpool to Genoa under the Italian flag.
23.8.1902: Arrived Genoa.
11.1902: Broken up at Genoa.

Siberia (above) and *Samaria* (below) were smaller, emigrant-carrier versions of the *China* class ships. They were also the company's first purpose-built, brig rigged, transatlantic ships.

Samaria (1) spent most of her career on the intermediate second line service between Liverpool and Boston. *[J. and M. Clarkson collection]*

BATAVIA 1870-1888 Iron brig rigged

O.N. 63756 2,553g 1,628n
327.4 x 39.3 x 18.6 feet.
2-cyl. compound engine by Denny and Co.,
Dumbarton; 450 HP, 12.4 knots;
1885: T.4-cyl. by John Elder and Co.,
Glasgow; 500 HP.
Passengers: 150 cabin, 800 steerage.
18.1.1870: Launched by William Denny
and Brothers, Dumbarton (Yard No. 136)
as BATAVIA. Bought on the stocks by
Cunard. Whilst she was being constructed,
the Denny-owned, ex-P&O NEMESIS
(2,717/1857) was loaned to British and
North American for transatlantic service
from *10.1869* to *5.1870*.
2.5.1870: Registered at Glasgow under
the ownership of The British and North
American Steam Packet Company, Glasgow.
10.5.1870: Left on maiden voyage from
Liverpool to New York.
1.7.1878: Transferred to the Cunard
Steamship Co. Ltd., Liverpool.
12.2.1880: Advertised as sailing on a new
experimental route from Liverpool to
Bombay via the Suez Canal.
2.1884: Final transatlantic crossing.
24.7-17.11.1884: Chartered by the British
Government as transport during the Egyptian
Campaign.
22.11.1884: Registered under the ownership
of John Elder and Co., Glasgow, having been
sold with PARTHIA in part payment for
UMBRIA and ETRURIA.
1885: New four-cylinder triple expansion
engine fitted.
1887-1891: Chartered with ABYSSINIA and
PARTHIA for Canadian Pacific Railway's
first transpacific services between Vancouver
and the Far East.
5.1888: Sold with ABYSSINIA and PARTHIA
to the Guion Steamship Co. Ltd., London. Sir
William Pearce, owner of John Elder and Co.,
was also the Chairman of Guion Line.
14.6.1888: Registered at London.
1891: At end of the Canadian Pacific Railway
charter, chartered to the newly-formed Upton
Line for a Portland-Victoria-Far East service.
27.5.1892: Following failure of Upton Line,
chartered with VICTORIA (ex-PARTHIA)
to Northern Pacific Steamship Company,
Tacoma, U.S.A. for a new Tacoma-Victoria-
Far East service and renamed TACOMA.
17.7.1892: Registered at Liverpool under the
ownership of the Guion Steamship Co. Ltd.,
Liverpool.
10.1898: Sold with VICTORIA to North
American Mail Steamship Company, Tacoma
for same service.
15.10.1898: Register closed.
1899: Requisitioned as a U.S. transport
during Spanish-American War.
1901: Sold to a new Northern Pacific
Steamship Company, Tacoma, which had
been established by the Northern Pacific
Railway.
2.1904: Sold to Northwestern Steamship
Company, Seattle, U.S.A. and placed on
Seattle to Alaska service but also used on
voyages to Siberia where owners had mining

Batavia was the first in the fleet to be fitted with compound engines and the last to be built with a clipper stem and figurehead. *[J. and M. Clarkson collection]*

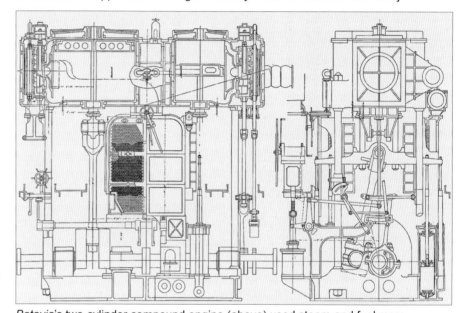

Batavia's two-cylinder compound engine (above) used steam and fuel more efficiently than a simple two-cylinder engine. *Batavia* remained afloat for 54 years until 1924 when, as *Shikotan Maru* (below) she was wrecked off the Chinese coast. *[Hisashi Noma collection]*

interests.
3.2.1905: Trapped in ice off Kunashir Strait,
Kurile Islands whilst on voyage from San
Francisco to Vladivostok with provisions
during the Russo-Japanese War.
14.3.05: Intercepted by Japanese protected
cruiser TAKACHIHO and later condemned
by prize court.
1905: Registered as the Japanese merchant
vessel SHIKOTAN MARU under the
ownership of Reizo Yamashina, Tokyo.

Ownership was subsequently changed to
Yamashina Kaisen.
1923: Sold to Momosuke Miyata, Kobe,
Japan.
23.10.1924: Stranded 12 miles north west
of Shaiweishan near Shanghai, whilst on
a voyage from Tsingtao to Shanghai, with
cargo of coal.
7.11.1924: Refloated and towed to Shanghai
but later declared a constructive total loss
and broken up locally.

ABYSSINIA 1870-1880 Iron barque rigged

O.N. 63765 3,253g 2,076n
363.5 x 42.2 x 18.9 feet.
2-cyl. vertical direct acting engine by J. and G. Thomson, Govan; 500 HP, 13 knots; *1882*: C. 2-cyl. by J. Jones and Sons, Liverpool; 500 HP.
Passengers: 176 cabin, 1,000 steerage.
3.3.1870: Launched by J. and G. Thomson, Govan (Yard No. 110) as ABYSSINIA. The first ship in the fleet with a straight stem.
13.5.1870: Registered at Glasgow under the ownership of The British and North American Steam Packet Company, Glasgow.
24.5.1870: Left on maiden voyage from Liverpool to New York.
1.7.1878: Transferred to the Cunard Steamship Co. Ltd., Liverpool.
11.1880: Sold to J. and G. Thomson in part payment for SERVIA and CATALONIA.
13.11.1880: Registered under the ownership of Stephen Guion, Liverpool.
20.11.1880: First voyage from Liverpool to New York for Guion Line.
1882: New compound engine fitted.
23.2.1885: Transferred to William Pearce, Govan (on behalf of John Elder and Co., Glasgow).
1887-1891: Chartered with BATAVIA and PARTHIA for Canadian Pacific Railway's first transpacific services between Vancouver and the Far East.
6.1888: Sold with BATAVIA and PARTHIA to the Guion Steamship Co. Ltd., London. Sir William Pearce, owner of John Elder and Co., was also the chairman of Guion Line.
14.6.1888: Registered at London under the ownership of the Guion Steamship Co. Ltd., London.
28.11.1891: At end of the Canadian Pacific Railway charter, resumed Liverpool to New York service.
18.12.1891: Destroyed by fire which broke out in a cargo of cotton in position 47°N, 44°W whilst on a voyage from New York to Liverpool. All 147 passengers and crew were rescued by the Norddeutscher Lloyd steamer SPREE (6,966/1890).
19.3.1892: Register closed.

Abyssinia (top) and *Algeria* were the first of a series of flush-deck vessels which were also delivered in 1870 but with simple engines. This under-powered pair not only had accommodation for large numbers of emigrants, they were also the first in the fleet with a straight stem. The maiden voyages of *Abyssinia* and *Batavia* both took place in May and the company was able to make a direct comparison between the performances of the two engine types. *Batavia*'s coal consumption was about half that of *Abyssinia* and, as a result, the decision was taken to install compound engines in *Parthia*, which was under construction by Denny.

From 1887 to 1891, *Abyssinia*, *Batavia* and *Parthia* were chartered by the Canadian Pacific Railway for its first transpacific services between Vancouver and the Far East. Above *Abyssinia* is seen arriving at Vancouver.

ALGERIA 1870-1881 Iron barque rigged

O.N. 63784 3,298g 2,105n
363.8 x 42.3 x 18.7 feet.
2-cyl. vertical direct acting engine by J. and
G. Thomson, Govan; 500 HP, 13 knots;
1882: C. 2-cyl. by James Jack and Co.,
Liverpool; 500 HP.
Passengers: 176 cabin; 1,000 steerage; *1902*:
steerage only.
12.7.1870: Launched by J. and G. Thomson,
Govan (Yard No. 111) as ALGERIA.
12.9.1870: Registered at Glasgow under the
ownership of The British and North American
Steam Packet Company, Glasgow.
27.9.1870: Left on maiden voyage from
Liverpool to New York.
1.7.1878: Transferred to the Cunard
Steamship Co. Ltd., Liverpool.
22.10.1881: Last voyage from Liverpool to
New York
26.11.1881: Registered under the ownership
of J. and G. Thomson having been sold in part
payment for SERVIA and CATALONIA.
1882: Sold to Société Anonyme de
Navigation Belge-Américaine (Red
Star Line), Antwerp, Belgium, renamed
PENNLAND and fitted with new compound
engine.
27.4.1882: British register closed.
13.5.1882: First voyage from Antwerp to
New York for Red Star Line.
5.1887-4.1901: Placed on the Philadelphia
to Liverpool route for American Line, which
was part of the International Navigation
Company, owners of Red Star Line.
4.5.1901: Resumed Red Star Line's Antwerp
to New York service.
1902: Steerage-only service.
23.9.1903: Last voyage from Philadelphia to
Antwerp.
4.11.1903: Arrived at Genoa for demolition
by L. Lavarello di G.B. and G.B. Bertorello
fu A., Genoa.

**PARTHIA (1) 1870-1884 Iron barque
rigged**

O.N. 63797 3,431g 2,214n
360.5 x 40.4 x 19.0 feet.
C.2-cyl. by Denny and Co., Dumbarton; 450
HP, 13 knots;
1885: T.4-cyl. by John Elder and Co.,
Glasgow; 500 HP.
Passengers: 199 cabin, 850 steerage; *1920s*:
163 first, 89 second, 242 third: *1941*: cargo
only.
10.9.1870: Launched by William Denny
and Brothers, Dumbarton (Yard No. 148) as
PARTHIA.
12.12.1870: Registered at Glasgow under the
ownership of The British and North American
Steam Packet Company, Glasgow.
17.12.1870: Left on maiden voyage from
Liverpool to New York.
1.7.1878: Transferred to the Cunard
Steamship Co. Ltd., Liverpool.
14.11.1883: Left on final voyage Liverpool-
Boston-New York.
31.12.1884: Registered under the ownership
of John Elder and Co., Glasgow, having
been sold with BATAVIA in part payment for

Algeria was in the fleet for only 11 years. In 1882 she became Red Star Line's
Pennland.

UMBRIA and ETRURIA.
1885: New triple-expansion engine fitted.
1887-1891: Chartered with ABYSSINIA and
BATAVIA for Canadian Pacific Railway's
first transpacific services between Vancouver
and the Far East.
6.1888: Sold with BATAVIA and ABYSSINIA
to the Guion Steamship Co. Ltd., London.

Sir William Pearce, owner of John Elder and
Co., was also the Chairman of Guion Line.
14.6.1888: Registered at London.
8.1891: At end of the Canadian Pacific
Railway charter, returned to Guion Line.
Modernised by Fairfield Shipbuilding and
Engineering Co. Ltd., Glasgow and given two
pole masts. The height of her funnel was also

Parthia alongside the quay at Vancouver during her Canadian Pacific Railway
charter. On her starboard side is the coal hulk *Robert Kerr*.

raised sometime in the late 1890s.

5.1892: Chartered with TACOMA (ex BATAVIA) to Northern Pacific Steamship Company, Tacoma for a new Portland-Victoria-Far East service and renamed VICTORIA

1892: Registered at Liverpool under the ownership of the Guion Steamship Co. Ltd., Liverpool.

10.1898: Sold with TACOMA to North American Mail Steamship Company, Tacoma and used on same route.

1898: British register closed.

9.1899-3.1900: Requisitioned as a U.S. transport during Spanish-American War.

1901: Sold to the Northern Pacific Steamship Company, Tacoma, U.S.A., a new company established by the Northern Pacific Railway.

2.1904: Sold to Northwestern Steamship Company, Seattle., U.S.A. Placed on Seattle to Alaska service but also used on voyages to Siberia where owners had mining interests.

1.1.1908: Northwestern Steamship Company merged with Alaska Steamship Company, Seattle to form the Alaska Steamship Company. Placed on San Francisco-Seattle-Nome service.

1912: New oil-fired boilers. Around this time her bridge deck was extended aft.

1920s: Modernisation included enclosed bridge, bulwarks forward and plated-in boat deck amidships.

1937: Laid up in Lake Union, Seattle.

1940: Passenger accommodation removed and converted into a freighter for the United States War Shipping Administration. Painted grey, she had guns mounted fore and aft.

1947: Returned to owners.

8.1952: Laid up at Kirkland, Lake Washington, Seattle.

1954: Sold to Dulien Steel Products Company, Seattle who stripped out the engines and cut the hull down to a barge.

1955: Sold to Straits Towing Ltd., Vancouver, Canada and renamed STRAITS No. 27.

1956: Sold to Japanese shipbreakers, renamed STRAITS MARU, registered at Osaka and loaded with scrap, she was towed from Victoria to Osaka by the Canadian tug SUDBURY (1,892/1941).

16.10.1956: Arrived Osaka.

Parthia had an extraordinary career and was demolished only in 1956. At 86, she was the second-longest surviving Cunard ship after *Hecla*.

Middle and bottom: From 1940 *Victoria* (ex-*Parthia*) carried only cargo and here she is in the late 1940s or early 1950s with cars on deck.

Left: *Parthia*'s bell was presented to Cunard by the Alaska Steamship Company and was displayed aboard the 1948-built *Parthia*.

In the early 1870s, Cunard's response to the new White Star Line and Inman Line record breakers were *Bothnia* and *Scythia*, the first Cunarders with an amidships saloon. Although they had a large cargo capacity, they were simply enlarged versions of *Abyssinia* and *Algeria*, but with more powerful engines.

Because of the economic crisis in the 1870s, there was a four-year gap before another new Cunarder appeared on the Atlantic run. That was *Gallia* in 1879, the final and largest ship in the flush-deck group of the 1870s. All three became intermediate ships in the mid 1880s.

BOTHNIA (1) 1874-1899 Iron barque rigged
O.N. 68094 4,535g 2,923n
422.3 x 42.2 x 18.9 feet.
C.2-cyl. by J. and G. Thomson, Clydebank; 600 HP, 13.8 knots.
Passengers: 300 cabin, 900 steerage.
4.3.1874: Launched by J. and G. Thomson, Clydebank (Yard No. 128) as BOTHNIA. Her keel had been the first to be laid at Thomson's new Clydebank yard.
5.5.1874: Registered at Glasgow under the ownership of The British and North American Steam Packet Company, Glasgow.
8.8.1874: Left on maiden voyage from Liverpool to New York.
1.7.1878: Transferred to the Cunard Steamship Co. Ltd., Liverpool.
15.4.1885: First voyage from Liverpool to Boston.
8.10.1896: Final transatlantic crossing.
19.5.1898: Registered at Liverpool.
21.2.1899: Arrived at Marseilles from Barcelona for demolition and register closed. Her last voyage was probably a charter for

Bothnia was transferred to the Boston route in 1885. *[J. and M. Clarkson]*

the Spanish Government from Cienfuegos, Cuba to Barcelona, presumably repatriating Spanish troops or other personnel from Cuba.
1899: Broken up in the third quarter.

SCYTHIA (1) 1875-1899 Iron barque rigged
O.N. 71693 4,557g 2,907n
420.8 x 42.2 x 18.9 feet.
C. 2-cyl. by J. and G. Thomson, Clydebank; 600 HP, 13.8 knots.
Passengers: 300 cabin, 900 steerage.
28.10.1874: Launched by J. and G. Thomson, Clydebank (Yard No. 129) as SCYTHIA.

2.2.1875: Registered at Glasgow under the ownership of The British and North American Steam Packet Company, Glasgow.
1.5.1875: Left on maiden voyage from Liverpool to New York.
1.7.1878: Transferred to the Cunard Steamship Co. Ltd., Liverpool.
9.7.1884: Left on first voyage from Liverpool to Boston.
19.5.1898: Registered at Liverpool.
20.9.1898: Final transatlantic crossing.
9.3.1899: Register closed on sale to Italian breakers.
22.3.1899: Sailed from Liverpool to Genoa under the Italian flag.
2.4.1899: Arrived Genoa.

Scythia remained in Cunard service for 24 years. *[J. and M. Clarkson collection]*

GALLIA 1879-1897 Iron barque rigged
O.N. 78837 4,809g 3,082n
430.1 x 44.6 x 26.8 feet.
C. 3-cyl. by J. and G. Thomson, Clydebank; 700 HP, 15.5 knots.
Passengers: 276 first, 1,100 steerage; *1897*: 300 first, 95 second.
12.11.1878: Launched by J. and G. Thomson, Clydebank (Yard No. 163) as GALLIA.
12.2.1879: Registered at Liverpool in ownership of the Cunard Steamship Co. Ltd., Liverpool.
5.4.1879: Left on maiden voyage from Liverpool to New York.
23.6.1885: Broke her shaft in mid-Atlantic during a homeward voyage.

25.6 to *28.6.1885*: Towed 300 miles east of ice fields by the steamer RIVER AVON (1,092/1883). Repairs were made and she arrived at Queenstown under own steam on *5.7.1885*.
20.4.1886: Left on first voyage from Liverpool to Boston.
1896: Bareboat chartered to Compañía Transatlántica, Barcelona, Spain and used as troopship to Cuba during Spanish-American War. Renamed DON ALVARO DE BAZAN and placed under Spanish registry.
29.8.1896: British register closed.
1.4.1897: Re-registered at Liverpool in the ownership of the Cunard Steamship Co. Ltd., Liverpool and reverted to GALLIA.
17.11.1897: Registered under the ownership

of the Beaver Line Associated Steamers Ltd., Liverpool.
5.1899: Chartered to Allan Line for Liverpool-Quebec-Montreal route.
14.5.1899: Stranded near Sorel Point, Quebec. She took a month to refloat and then sailed for Montreal and Quebec. Despite minimal hull damage, Allan Line cancelled her charter.
10.8.1899: Arrived at Liverpool and laid up.
19.12.1899: Registered under the ownership of the Salvage Association Ltd., London.
8.2.1900: Registered under the ownership of the Marine Association Ltd., Port Talbot.
17.2.1900: Arrived Cherbourg from Liverpool for demolition.
23.2.1900: Register closed.

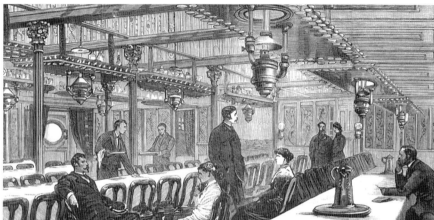

Gallia's weather deck forward of the foremast (above) featured a look-out bridge between the lighthouse-shaped port and starboard navigation lights.

Like her running mates, *Gallia*'s saloon (top right) was amidships and featured long tables.

By the time *Gallia* (middle and bottom) entered service in 1879, she was totally outclassed by Guion Line's 17-knot *Arizona,* the first of the so-called 'Atlantic greyhounds'.   *[Bottom: J. and M. Clarkson collection]*

A year after the formation of the Cunard Steamship Co. Ltd., the company took delivery of *Servia*, the first of its express Atlantic liners. The largest ship in the world at that time, excluding *Great Eastern*, she was also the first Cunarder to have a steel hull, electric lighting and remote controlled watertight doors.

Like the Belfast-built White Star liners, *Servia* was a long narrow ship with a long, full-height forecastle in place of the usual transatlantic turtleback forecastle. However, although she was a relatively fast ship, she was not a record breaker and with her tall twin funnels, looked somewhat ungainly, certainly in comparison with White Star Line's crack ships.

SERVIA (1) 1881-1902 Barque rigged
O.N. 84172 7,392g 3,971n
515.0 x 52.1 x 20.5 feet.
C.3-cyl. by J. and G. Thomson, Clydebank; 1,472 HP, 16.7 knots.
Passengers: 404 cabin, 750 steerage; *1890s*: 462 first, 160 second, 200 steerage
1.3.1881: Launched by J. and G. Thomson, Clydebank (Yard No. 179) as SERVIA.
18.4.1881: A fire in the yard's joinery shop caused the loss of many fittings, and delivery was further delayed by a broken propellor shaft.
18.11.1881: Registered at Liverpool under the ownership of the Cunard Steamship Co. Ltd., Liverpool.
26.11.1881: Left on maiden voyage from Liverpool to New York.
4.7.1891: Broke down after a fracture in the crank pin of the high-pressure cylinder 217 miles east of Sandy Hook whilst homeward bound from New York. Towed back to

Sandy Hook by the Dutch-registered tanker CHESTER (2,834/1888).
2.10.1899-11.5.1900: Chartered by the British Government during Boer War as Transport No. 31.
17.9.1901: Final transatlantic crossing.

1902: Sold to Thos. W. Ward Ltd., Sheffield for demolition.
9.4.1902: After being partially stripped at Barrow-in-Furness, arrived at Preston for demolition.
18.9.1902: Register closed.

Servia was completed with a full sail rig (above) which was later removed (top).

Partially stripped at Preston in 1902, awaiting demolition.

Although similar looking to *Servia*, *Aurania* had a shorter and more beamy hull. This hull design was developed by the Thomson yard as an answer to the speedier ships produced by its arch rival, John Elder. It was termed a 'fine ended model' where the increased beam amidships tapered to fine lines fore and aft. This reduced the resistance of the hull through water and therefore made the ship more fuel efficient.

    Aurania was also the first Cunard ship to have her main dining saloon forward of the engine room and the first with 'exclusive cabins'. These were four larger cabins on the promenade deck which shared a small lounge-cum-smoking room.

Aurania as built.

AURANIA (1) 1883-1905 Barque rigged
O.N. 87839 7,269g 4,030n
470.0 x 57.2 x 20.9 feet.
C.3-cyl. by J. and G. Thomson, Clydebank; 1,170 HP, 17 knots.
Passengers: 363 cabin, 700 steerage; *1890s*: 432 first, 160 second, 1,200 steerage; *1903*: first and steerage.
26.12.1882: Launched by J. and G. Thomson, Clydebank (Yard No. 187) as AURANIA.
13.6.1883: Registered at Liverpool under the ownership of the Cunard Steamship Co. Ltd., Liverpool.
23.6.1883: Left on maiden voyage from Liverpool to New York. Broke down mid Atlantic after the high-pressure connecting rod broke and smashed the cylinder and arrived at New York under sail. Towed back to Glasgow for repairs. This mechanical failure and the delays building SERVIA, CATALONIA and PAVONIA were major reasons for Cunard switching builders to John Elder and Co.
12.4.1884: Resumed Liverpool to New York service.
1.10.1899-2.1903: Chartered by the British

Leaving Cape Town as a Boer War troopship.

Government as Boer War Transport No. 20.
14.4.1903: Resumed Liverpool to New York service as an intermediate liner.
20.10.1903: Inaugurated the Cunard Hungarian-American Line service. First

voyage from New York toTrieste.
2.1905: Sold at Fiume to L. Pittaluga fu F., Genoa, Italy.
27.2.1905: Register closed.
13.3.1905: Arrived at Genoa for demolition.

Aurania in the River Mersey. Her mizzen mast was further aft than that of *Servia*.

Cunard acquired Guion Line's year-old record-breaker *Oregon* after its owner was unable to keep up payments to the shipyard. The plan was to operate her as part of a three-ship express service between Liverpool and New York with the similar-sized *Umbria* and *Etruria*.

During her short career with Cunard, *Oregon* regained the eastbound crossing record, lost by Cunard in 1869.

OREGON 1884-1886 Iron ship-rigged
O.N. 87887 7,374g 3,129n
501.0 x 54.2 x 21.3 feet.
C.3-cyl. by John Elder and Co., Glasgow; 2,000 HP, 18.5 knots.
Passengers: 338 first, 76 second, 1,000 steerage
23.6.1883: Launched by John Elder and Co., Glasgow (Yard No. 274) as OREGON.

26.9.1883: Registered at Liverpool under the ownership of Stephen Barker Guion (Liverpool and Great Western Steamship Co. Ltd., Liverpool, trading as Guion Line).
6.10.1883: Maiden voyage from Liverpool to New York.
13-19.4.1884: Record voyage from Queenstown to Sandy Hook: 6 days10 hours 30 minutes.
3.6.1884: Because Guion Line was unable to complete the payments for the ship, returned to the builders and acquired by Cunard Steamship Co. Ltd., Liverpool. Cunard's first four-masted ship.
6.6.1884: Registered at Liverpool under the ownership of the Cunard Steamship Co. Ltd., Liverpool.
7.6.1884: First voyage from Liverpool to New York for Cunard.
6.8.1884: End of record voyage from Sandy

Hook to Queenstown: 6 days12 hours 54 minutes.
28.3.1885: During a Russian 'war scare', requisitioned by the British Government and fitted out at Liverpool as an armed merchant cruiser.
3.6.1885: Commisioned until *11.1885*.
14.3.1886: Sunk after collision with an unknown U.S. schooner 26 miles south east of Fire Island Light, near Long Island whilst on a voyage from Liverpool to New York. The other vessel was probably the three-masted schooner CHARLES H. MORSE (535/1880) which went missing around this time on a coastal voyage with cargo of coal. All the OREGON's passengers and crew were rescued by the Norddeutscher Lloyd steamer FULDA (4,814/1883). Her wreck remains a popular site for divers.
2.4.1886: Register closed.

With her four masts and raked twin funnels, *Oregon* was the most powerful ship in the world in 1883.

Because of the success of the Elder-built Guion ships and building delays, Cunard turned its back on J. and G. Thomson, and ordered *Umbria* and *Etruria* from John Elder and Company.

These ships were the largest, excluding *Great Eastern*, and most powerful ships in the world, with maximum speeds in excess of 20 knots. Although designed to compete with *Oregon*, they continued the Cunard-look of the 1880s, i.e. twin funnels and three masts.

The pair also held the transatlantic record for four years and were, at that time, among the most luxurious liners on the Atlantic.

UMBRIA 1884-1910 Barque rigged
O.N. 91159 7,718g 3,245n
501.6 x 57.2 x 21.4 feet.
C.3-cyl. by John Elder and Co., Glasgow; 2,500 HP, 19.5 knots.
Passengers: 478 first, 800 steerage; *1890s*: 650 first, 160 second, 250 steerage
25.6.1884: Launched by John Elder and Co., Glasgow (Yard No. 285) as UMBRIA.
8.10.1884: Registered at Liverpool under the ownership of the Cunard Steamship Co. Ltd., Liverpool.
1.11.1884: Maiden voyage from Liverpool to New York.
30.3.1885: During a Russian 'war scare', requisitioned by the British Government for six months as an armed merchant cruiser. Fitted out at Liverpool but never used.

4.6.1887: Arrived at New York after record voyage: 6 days 4 hours 12 minutes from Queenstown to Sandy Hook.
10.11.1888: Collided with the French steamer IBERIA (1,331/1881) off Long Island in fog whilst on a voyage to Liverpool. UMBRIA sustained only slight damage whilst IBERIA lost her stern and sank.
23.12.1892: Shaft broke in position 42°48´N, 57°17´W on a westbound voyage.
31.12.1892: Arrived at New York following temporary repairs.
20.12.1899-27.6.1900: Chartered by the British Government as the Boer War Transport No. 77.
12.2.1910: Final transatlantic crossing.
9.5.1910: Arrived Bo'ness for demolition by the Forth Shipbreaking Company.
22.11.1910: Register closed.

Umbria in the River Mersey dressed overall for Queen Victoria's birthday.

ETRURIA 1885-1909 Barque rigged

O.N. 91187 7,718g 3,258n

501.6 x 57.2 x 21.4 feet.

C.3-cyl. by John Elder and Co., Glasgow;
2,500 HP, 19.5 knots.

Passengers: 478 first, 160 second, 800
steerage; *1890s*: 650 first, 160 second, 250
steerage

20.9.1884: Launched by John Elder and Co.,
Glasgow (Yard No. 286) as ETRURIA.

10.3.1885: Registered at Liverpool under
the ownership of the Cunard Steamship Co.
Ltd., Liverpool.

25.4.1885: Maiden voyage from Liverpool
to New York.

5.1885 (westbound); *3.1887* (eastbound) and
5.1888 (westbound) record voyages.

26.2.1902: Lost propeller and rudder in mid
Atlantic.

9.3.1902: Arrived at Azores under jury rig.
Towed home by two tugs.

20.10.1906: Rammed in the stern by Atlantic
Transport Line's steamer MINNEHAHA
(13,714/1900) whilst anchored off New York
in fog. Sustained only minor damage and
continued on voyage to Liverpool.

26.8.1908: Collided with a lighter as she
proceeded to the landing stage at Liverpool
to embark passengers for New York. The
three crew members of the lighter were
thrown into the water and one drowned.
The wreckage of the lighter was entangled
in ETRURIA's rudder and propellers.
Repaired, she was laid up in reserve but
never re-entered service.

11.1909: Sold to Thos. W. Ward Ltd.,
Sheffield for demolition.

10.4.1910: After being partially stripped at
Birkenhead, arrived at Preston under tow of
BLACK COCK (254/1886) and HANNAH
JOLIFFE (178/1900).

15.4.1910: Register closed.

Despite their size, *Etruria*, seen here, and *Umbria* were fitted with auxiliary sails in case of emergency as single-screw ships continued to be prone to broken propeller shafts and other mechanical failures.

After 20 years service, *Etruria* still managed to cross the Atlantic at an average speed of 18.3 knots.

·:· ABSTRACT OF LOG ·:·				
OF THE				
CUNARD ROYAL MAIL STEAMSHIP "ETRURIA"				
(Captain T. POTTER).				
FROM LIVERPOOL TO NEW YORK.				

Date 1905.	Distance.	Latitude.	Longitude.	Winds.
Saturday Sept. 2		Left L'pool 4·32 p.m.		West
Sunday ,, 3	228	Arrived at Queenstown 6·43 a.m.		West
	53	Left Daunt's Rock at 10·25 a.m.		
Monday ,, 4	439	51·22 N.	20·50 W.	N. W. to W. N. W.
Tuesday ,, 5	416	50·16 ,,	31·36 ,,	W. N. W. to West
Wednesday ,, 6	429	48·10 ,,	42·06 ,,	N. N. W. to N. W. by W
Thursday ,, 7	456	45·12 ,,	52·15 ,,	N. W. by W. to West
Friday ,, 8	475	42·25 ,,	62·40 ,,	West to N. E.
Saturday ,, 9	484			N. E. to N. N. E.
,, ,, ,,	44	To Sandy Hook L'ship		At 2·09 p.m., Sandy Hook Lightship abeam.
From Liverpool Bar to S. H. L'ship...	3,024			PASSAGE
				Daunt's Rock to Sandy Hook Lightship
From Daunt's Rock to S. H. L'ship ...	2,796			6 days, 8 hours, 44 minutes.
				Average speed per hour 18·30 knots.

" Lucania," " Campania," " Etruria," " Umbria," " Saxonia," " Ivernia" " Caronia," & " Carpathia" are fitted with " Marconi" System of Wireless Telegraphy.

Etruria being taken to her final berth at Preston in 1910. *[J. and M. Clarkson collection]*

Fairfield Shipbuilding and Engineering Co. Ltd., successors to John Elder and Company, built a second pair of record breakers in 1893.

As *Great Eastern* had been broken up in 1891, *Campania* and *Lucania* were the world's largest ships. They were also the fastest and, because they had twin screws, were the first in the fleet to dispense with sails. Built to Admiralty specifications under the new armed auxiliary cruiser scheme, they also were the first Cunard ships with triple-expansion engines.

CAMPANIA 1893-1914 Twin screw
O.N. 102086 12,950g 4,974n
601.0 x 65.2 x 28.1 feet.
Two T.5-cyl. by Fairfield Shipbuilding and Engineering Co. Ltd., Glasgow; 2,500 HP, 21 knots.
Passengers: 600 first, 400 second, 1,000 steerage; *late 1890s*: 400 first, 300 second, steerage.
8.9.1892: Launched by Fairfield Shipbuilding and Engineering Co. Ltd., Glasgow (Yard No. 364) as CAMPANIA.
10.4.1893: Registered at Liverpool under the ownership of the Cunard Steamship Co. Ltd., Liverpool.
22.4.1893: Maiden voyage from Liverpool to New York.
5.1893 (eastbound), *6.1893* (westbound) and *8.1894* (westbound) record voyages.
Winter 1893-1894: Promenade well decks filled in and plating extended fore and aft.
15.10.1894: Record eastbound crossing: 5 days 9 hours 13 minutes.
15.10.1894: Record westbound crossing: 5 days 9 hours 6 minutes.
26.7.1897: Took part in the Diamond Jubilee Naval Review at Spithead.
21.7.1900: Collided with the British barque EMBLETON (1,196/1881) in thick fog 27 miles north east of Tuskar Rock, St. George's Channel whilst on a voyage from Queenstown to Liverpool. The sailing ship, which was on a voyage from Liverpool to Wellington, New Zealand with general cargo was hit amidships and sliced in two with the loss of eleven lives.
11.10.1905: Hit by a massive wave in mid-Atlantic whilst on voyage from Liverpool to New York. Five steerage passengers were washed overboard and drowned.
23.5. to 19.7.1914: Chartered to Anchor Line for Glasgow to New York service.
15.10.1914: Final arrival at Liverpool from New York.
10.1914: Sold to Thos. W. Ward Ltd., Sheffield for demolition.
27.11.1914: Sold to the Admiralty and converted by Cammell Laird and Co. Ltd., Birkenhead into a seaplane carrier with a ramp over the forecastle deck and parallel to the waterline.
17.4.1915: Commissioned as HMS CAMPANIA.
10.9.1915: Register closed.
12.1915: As original ramp was not satisfactory, returned to Cammell Laird for a further refit, which included a downward-sloping launching platform and the fore funnel being split.
5.4.1916: Conversion work complete.
5.11.1918: Dragged anchor during a heavy squall and sank in Firth of Forth after collision with the light battlecruiser HMS GLORIOUS and battleship HMS ROYAL OAK.
1947: Wreck demolished with explosives.

Campania, with the Cunard baggage and fresh water carrier *Otter*, alongside the Princes Landing Stage, Liverpool.

The original level ramp fitted to *HMS Campania* (middle) was not a success. She was then fitted with a downward sloping ramp (bottom) to assist her aircraft when taking off. At the same time the original forward funnel was removed and replaced with a split funnel. *[Middle: J. and M. Clarkson collection]*

LUCANIA 1893-1909 Twin screw
O.N. 102105 12,952g 4,975n
601.0 x 65.2 x 28.1 feet.
Two T.5-cyl. by Fairfield Shipbuilding and
Engineering Co. Ltd., Glasgow; 2,500 HP,
21 knots.
Passengers: 600 first, 400 second, 1,000
steerage; *late 1890s*: 400 first, 300 second,
steerage
2.2.1893: Launched by Fairfield
Shipbuilding and Engineering Co. Ltd.,

Glasgow (Yard No. 365) as LUCANIA.
8.8.1893: Registered at Liverpool under the
ownership of the Cunard Steamship Co.
Ltd., Liverpool.
2.9.1893: Maiden voyage from Liverpool to
New York.
10.1893 and 8-10.1894: Record westbound
voyages.
5.1894 and 5.1895: Record eastbound voyages.
15.6.1901: Left Liverpool with the first
Marconi wireless telegraph system installed

aboard a Cunard ship.
3-10.10.1903: On a voyage from New
York to Liverpool with Guglielmo Marconi
aboard, the 'Cunard Bulletin' was published,
the first Cunard daily newspaper at sea.
26.6.1909: Final transatlantic crossing.
14.8.1909: Destroyed by fire in the
Huskisson Dock, Liverpool.
1910: Broken up at Swansea by Thos. W.
Ward Ltd., Sheffield.
10.10.1910: Register closed.

The funnels on *Campania* and *Lucania* (above) were widely spaced because the first class drawing room and dining saloon were situated between the uptakes – see page 292. The tender *Skirmisher* is alongside. *[A.Green/Russell Priest collection]*

Lusitania and Mauretania

These liners were built to re-establish Cunard's reputation as the premier transatlantic line. They were the company's answer not only to White Star Line's new ships but also to the record breakers of its German rivals, Hamburg-Amerika Linie and Norddeutscher Lloyd.

Almost three times larger than *Campania* and *Lucania*, they were by far the largest ships in the world, the first on the Atlantic with quadruple screws and the first British liners with four funnels. Turbine-driven, they reduced the crossing time to less than five days in each direction. They also offered 50% more light, air space and deck promenade per passenger than any other liner afloat and no expense was spared in the decoration and panelling of their magnificent public rooms.

During her trials, *Lusitania* steamed at over 26 knots on the measured mile.

LUSITANIA 1907-1915 Quadruple screw

O.N. 124082 31,550g 9,145n
762.2 x 87.8 x 61.7 feet.
Four steam turbines by John Brown & Co. Ltd., Clydebank; 70,000 SHP, 25 knots.
Passengers: 552 first, 460 second, 1,168 third.
7.6.1906: Launched by John Brown & Co. Ltd., Clydebank (Yard No. 367) as LUSITANIA.
30.8.1907: Registered at Liverpool under the ownership of the Cunard Steam Ship Co. Ltd., Liverpool. The largest ship in the world at the time.
7.9.1907: Maiden voyage from Liverpool to New York.
6-11.10.1907: Record westbound crossing: 4 days 19 hours 52 minutes from Daunt's Rock (Queenstown) to Sandy Hook.
10.8.1914: Requisitioned by the British Government as an armed merchant cruiser but released as being unsuitable.
7.5.1915: Torpedoed and sunk by the German submarine U 20 fifteen miles south of the Old Head of Kinsale, Ireland, in position 51°24′N, 08°31′W, whilst on a voyage from New York to Liverpool, with the loss of 1,198 lives.
21.5.1915: Register closed.

Top: *Lusitania* in the River Mersey.
Middle: *Lusitania*'s superstructure was dominated by her four huge funnels.
Bottom: *Lusitania* alongside the Princes Landing Stage. The Mersey Docks and Harbour Board building had recently been completed whilst the Royal Liver Building, under construction, was finished in 1911.

Mauretania fitting out at Swan, Hunter and Wigham Richardson's Wallsend yard on the River Tyne.

MAURETANIA (1) 1907-1935 Quadruple screw

O.N. 124093 31,938g 8,948n;
1922: 30,696g 12,542n
762.2 x 88.0 x 61.3 feet.
Four steam turbines by Wallsend Slipway and Engineering Co. Ltd., Wallsend; 70,000 SHP, 25 knots.
Passengers: 563 first, 475 second, 1,138 third; *1922*: 589 first, 392 second, 767 third.
20.9.1906: Launched by Swan, Hunter and Wigham Richardson Ltd., Wallsend (Yard No. 735) as MAURETANIA.
14.11.1907: Registered at Liverpool under the ownership of the Cunard Steam Ship Co. Ltd., Liverpool. The largest ship in the world at that time.
16.11.1907: Maiden voyage from Liverpool to New York.
30.11.1907: Sailed from New York to make record eastbound crossing: 4 days 22 hours 29 minutes from Ambrose Light Vessel to Daunt's Rock (Queenstown). This was the first of numerous transatlantic records claimed by the ship. From September 1909 until July 1929 she was the fastest merchant ship in the world.
24.1.1909: First voyage from Liverpool to New York with new propellers.
30.8.1909: Made Cunard's first call at Fishguard (instead of Queenstown) for eastbound express liner sailings.
17.8.1914: Requisitioned by the British Government as an armed merchant cruiser but released as being unsuitable.
10.1914: Laid up at Liverpool.
11.5.1915 to 1.3.1916: Requisitioned by British Government, initially as a troopship for the Gallipoli campaign and from *22.10.1915-25.1.1916* as a hospital ship home-based at Southampton.
9.1916: Requisitioned by the British Government as a troopship until *7.1919*.
18.11.1919: Inaugurated Cunard's Southampton-Cherbourg-New York service.

In November 1916 *Mauretania* embarked troops at Halifax, Nova Scotia (above) and was later 'dazzle painted' (below).

9.1921-11.3.1922: Converted to oil-firing by her builders.

7.2.1923: Left New York on first cruise which was to the Mediterranean. Chartered by American Express.

11.1923-5.1924: Refit included the plating in of the forward end of the first class promenade deck with sliding windows.

5.1933: Converted at Southampton into a full-time cruise ship and painted white.

5.7.1934: Transferred to Cunard White Star Ltd., Liverpool.

2.10.1934: Laid up on final arrival at Southampton.

2.4.1935: Sold to Metal Industries Ltd. for demolition.

14-23.5.1935: Auction at Southampton of fixtures and fittings by Hampton and Sons.

4.7.1935: Arrived Rosyth for demolition.

13.10.1936: Register closed.

Mauretania after 1924, when the forward end of the first class promenade was plated in and fitted with sliding windows (top and middle)
Mauretania at Southampton in her final guise as a full-time cruise ship (below). Her transatlantic record had remained unbeaten for twenty years.

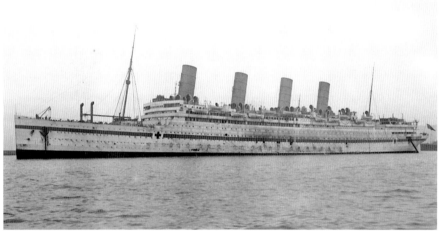

Above: *Aquitania* was over 100 feet longer than *Lusitania* and *Mauretania*. Left; Fitted out as a hospital ship during the First World War. *[J. and M. Clarkson collection]*

Below: *Aquitania* as a Second World War troopship at the Tail of the Bank, River Clyde.

Opposite page, top left: *Aquitania* showing off her slim lines as she sails from Southampton in the 1930s, bound for New York.

Opposite page, top right: A contrast in stern designs: *Aquitania* and *Queen Mary* at Southampton.

Aquitania was designed to run with *Lusitania* and *Mauretania* on a weekly, three-ship express service between Liverpool and New York. Although not as fast as the 1907 record breakers, she was larger than White Star Line's *Olympic* trio.

This magnificent liner was undoubtedly one of Cunard's finest ships and the only liner in the fleet to serve in two world wars. With her elegant 18th century English country-house-style interiors, she also represented the end of a way of life, which was destroyed by the First World War.

AQUITANIA 1914-1950 Quadruple screw
O.N. 135583 45,646g 21,992n;
1938: 44,786g 19,296n
868.7 x 97.0 x 49.7 feet.
Four steam turbines by John Brown & Co. Ltd., Clydebank; 60,000 SHP, 23.5 knots.
Passengers: 618 first, 614 second, 1,998 third; *1926*: 610 cabin, 950 second, 650 tourist (third); *1948*: 650 first, 1,100 tourist.
21.4.1913: Launched by John Brown & Co. Ltd., Clydebank (Yard No. 409) as AQUITANIA.
12.5.1914: Completed.
26.5.1914: Registered at Liverpool under the ownership of the Cunard Steam Ship Co. Ltd., Liverpool.
30.5.1914: Maiden voyage from Liverpool to New York.
2.8.-5.9.1914: Requisitioned by the British Government as an armed merchant cruiser and fitted with twelve six-inch guns. Considered too large for naval service and laid up.
5.1915-1919: Requisitioned by the British Government as a troopship and hospital ship.

In February 1950, *Aquitania* is seen approaching the Narrows at Rosneath at the entrance to the Gareloch. This was five miles from her destination, the breakers yard at Faslane.

14.6.1919: First voyage Southampton-Halifax-New York.
7.1920: Converted to oil-firing.
17.7.1920: Resumed Liverpool to New York service.
14.8.1920: First voyage Southampton-Cherbourg-New York.
1926: Accommodation altered to cabin, second and tourist class. Passenger accommodation underwent many changes during the 1920s and 1930s.
3.2.1932: Sailed from New York on first Mediterranean cruise.
5.7.1934: Transferred to Cunard White Star Ltd., Liverpool.
12.11.1939: Requisitioned by the Ministry of Shipping, London as a troopship. The company code name for the ship was ATLAS.

31.3.1948: Returned to owners and refitted at Southampton.
25.5.1948: First voyage from Southampton to Halifax as an emigrant ship chartered by the Canadian Government.
1.12.1949: Arrived Southampton from Halifax on last transatlantic voyage.
22.12.1949: Transferred to the Cunard Steam Ship Co. Ltd., Liverpool.
1.1.1950: Owners restyled as the Cunard Steam-Ship Co. Ltd., Liverpool.
18.2.1950: Sold to British Iron and Steel Corporation (BISCO). Fixtures and fittings auctioned in Southampton by Hampton and Sons.
21.2.1950: Arrived at Faslane for demolition by Metal Industries Ltd.
11.3.1952: Register closed

Imperator coaling in preparation for her maiden voyage. Her bow featured a huge crowned eagle clutching a globe with the words 'Mein Feld ist die Welt ', literally, 'The world is my field', but in English might be 'The world is our oyster', as used by HAPAG for a promotional book.

In 1910, Albert Ballin's Hamburg-Amerika Linie ordered three massive liners of just over 52,000g. The first to be delivered in 1913 was *Imperator*. She had a giant eagle on her bow and the first full-size swimming pool at sea. Her public rooms were also vast. She was followed a year later by *Vaterland*.

Unfortunately, war intervened and the final ship, *Bismarck,* was only completed after the conflict, by which time all three had been allocated as war reparations to the Allies. *Vaterland* became United States Lines' *Leviathan, Bismarck* was renamed *Majestic* for White Star Line, whilst *Imperator* was handed over to Cunard as a replacement for *Lusitania*, and renamed *Berengaria*. These ships remained the world's largest until 1935.

IMPERATOR 1919-1921/BERENGARIA 1921-1938 Quadruple screw
O.N. 144301 52,021g 23,229 n;
1922: 52,226g 22,016n
882.9 x 98.3 x 57.1 feet.
Four steam turbines by Vulcan-Werke, Hamburg, Germany; 62,000 SHP, 22.5 knots.
Passengers: 908 first, 972 second, 942 third, 1,772 steerage; *1922*: 972 first, 630 second, 515 tourist, 606 third
23.5.1912: Launched by Vulcan-Werke, Hamburg (Yard No. 314) as IMPERATOR.
24.5.1913: Completed for Hamburg-Amerikanische-Packetfahrt-Actien-Gesellschaft (HAPAG), Hamburg. The name originally chosen was EUROPA.
10.6.1913: Left on maiden voyage from Cuxhaven to New York.
11.1913: Returned to builders because of problems with stability. Funnels shortened by nine feet and heavy fittings replaced with lighter items.
3.1914: Work complete.
8.1914: Laid up for duration of the war.

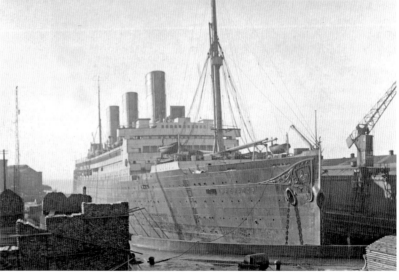

From 1918 until 1934, when *Majestic* entered the fleet, *Berengaria* was Cunard's largest ship. Here she is after 1924 when all her lifeboats had been moved to the boat deck.

5.5.1919: Allocated to the U.S. as war reparations, handed over in New York to U.S. Navy for use as a troopship and renamed U.S.S. IMPERATOR.

10.8.1919: Handed over to the U.S. Shipping Board and laid up in New York.

29.9.1919: Allocated to Great Britain.

24.11.1919: Handed over in New York to The Shipping Controller, London under the management of the Cunard Steam Ship Co. Ltd., Liverpool. Painted in Cunard colours.

11.12.1919: First voyage from New York to Southampton.

24.12.1919: Registered at London under the ownership of The Shipping Controller, London.

21.2.1920: Left on first voyage from Liverpool to New York.

3-5.1920: Refitted at Southampton.

6.6.1920: Left on first voyage Southampton-Cherbourg-New York.

25.2.1921: Acquired by the Cunard Steam Ship Co. Ltd., Liverpool.

9.3.1921: Registered at Liverpool under the ownership of the Cunard Steam Ship Co. Ltd., Liverpool.

26.3.1921: Renamed BERENGARIA.

31.10.1921-26.4.1922: Converted to oil-firing by Armstrong, Whitworth and Co. Ltd., Walker-on-Tyne. Passenger accommodation was also altered whilst aft lifeboats on promenade deck were moved to the boat deck.

1923/4: Remaining three lifeboats either side of the promenade deck moved.

5.7.1934: Transferred to Cunard White Star Ltd., Liverpool.

3.3.1938: Seriously damaged by fire in first class lounge area whilst in New York. U.S. marine safety authority refused to allow her to sail with passengers.

10.3.1938: Arrived at Southampton for the final time and laid up.

7.12.1938: Arrived Jarrow for demolition at the former Palmer Shipbuilding and Iron Co. Ltd. yard, having been bought by Sir John Jarvis to provide work for people in Jarrow.

6.1941: Remains sold to Shipbreaking Industries Ltd., a subsidiary of Metal Industries Ltd.

23.7.1946: Remains towed to Rosyth for demolition.

20.11.1947: Register closed.

Middle: *Berengaria* at Southampton. *[B. and A. Feilden/J. and M. Clarkson collection]*

Bottom: *Berengaria* at Jarrow awaiting demolition. *[Andy Hernandez collection]*

On her trials *Queen Mary* achieved a record speed of 32.84 knots. Opposite: Arriving at Cunard's Pier 90, New York.

Queen Mary is Cunard's best-known liner. In comparison with French Line's streamlined *Normandie*, she had an old-fashioned and rather bulky appearance.

However, from her maiden voyage onwards, she received an extraordinary amount of publicity world-wide and remained a popular ship for her entire career. She also claimed the Blue Riband from her French rival and her 1938 record crossings in both directions of just under four days, at an average speed of around 31 knots, remained unbroken for fourteen years.

QUEEN MARY 1936-1967 Quadruple screw

O.N 164282 80,773g 34,118n;
1937: 81,235g 34,293n
975.2 x 118.6 x 68.5 feet.
Four sets of steam turbines by John Brown & Co. Ltd., Clydebank; 160,000 SHP, 28.5 knots.
Passengers: 776 cabin, 784 tourist, 579 third;
1947: 704 first, 751 cabin, 583 tourist
27.12.1930: Keel laid.
12.12.1931: Work suspended.
3.4.1934: Work resumed.
26.9.1934: Launched by John Brown & Co. Ltd., Clydebank (Yard No. 534) as QUEEN MARY.
21.3.1936: Registered at Liverpool under the ownership of Cunard White Star Ltd., Liverpool.
27.5.1936: Left on maiden voyage from Southampton to New York.
8.1936: Record crossings in both directions: 4 days 27 minutes from Bishops Rock, Scilly Isles to Ambrose Light Vessel and 3 days 23 hours 57 minutes from Ambrose Light Vessel to Bishops Rock, Scilly Isles.
3-8.8.1938: Record crossing Southampton-Cherbourg-New York: 3 days 21 hours 48

minutes from Bishops Rock, Scilly Isles to Ambrose Light Vessel.
10-15.8.1938: Record crossing New York-Cherbourg-Southampton: 3 days 20 hours 42 minutes from Ambrose Light Vessel to Bishops Rock, Scilly Isles. This record stood until the arrival of UNITED STATES (53,329/1952) in July 1952.
9.1939: Laid up in New York.
1.3.1940: Requisitioned by the Ministry of Shipping, London as a troopship.
21.3.1940: Sailed for Sydney for conversion into a troopship. The company code name for the ship was MIDAS.
2.10.1942: The anti-aircraft cruiser HMS CURACOA was sliced in two by QUEEN MARY about 20 miles north west of the Bloody Foreland, Ireland with the loss of 338 lives. QUEEN MARY was on a voyage from New York to the Clyde with troops. A new stem was fitted at Boston.
9.1946-7.1947. Refit at Southampton by

John Brown & Co., Ltd. as main contractors and John I. Thornycroft and Co. Ltd. as sub-contractors.
31.7.1947: Resumed Southampton to New York service.
31.12.1949: Transferred to the Cunard Steam Ship Co. Ltd., Liverpool.
1.1.1950: Owners restyled as the Cunard Steam-Ship Co. Ltd., Liverpool.
1-3.1958: Refit included fitting of Denny-Brown stabilisers.
18.8.1967: Sold to the City of Long Beach, California.
16.9.1967: Final voyage from Southampton to New York.
31.10.1967: Sailed from Southampton to Long Beach via Cape Horn, her last voyage with fare-paying passengers.
9.12.1967: Arrived Long Beach.
12.12.1967: Register closed.
10.5.1971: Open to public as museum and convention centre.

At anchor as a troopship. Note the anti-magnetic mine degaussing strip.

Above: *Queen Mary* entering the King George V Graving Dock at Southampton on 27th March 1936 for her final pre-maiden voyage overhaul. Below: Arriving at New York.

Above; *Queen Mary* at speed, photographed from the deck of the *Nieuw Amsterdam* whilst crossing the Indian Ocean as a troop carrier. *[V.H.Young and L.A.Sawyer]*

Below: Dressed overall for her final sailing from Southampton on 31st October 1967.

Queen Mary commences her last transatlantic crossing to New York (top) on 16th September 1967. On 31st October 1967 she sailed from Southampton for Long Beach, California (middle and bottom) Due to her size she had to go around Cape Horn rather than through the Panama Canal. *[V.H.Young and L.A.Sawyer]*

At Long Beach *Queen Mary* became a museum and convention centre. On the 23rd February 2006 *Queen Mary 2* met her namesake at Long Beach and the two Queens greeted each other with a whistle salute (below). One of *Queen Mary's* whistles is used on *Queen Mary 2*. [Above: V.H.Young and L.A.Sawyer, below: Ian Shiffman]

Although not as fast as *Queen Mary*, *Queen Elizabeth* was the largest ship in the world. Her record size as a passenger ship remained unchallenged for 56 years.

Her elegant public rooms were designed in an understated British modern style and made great use of soft colour schemes and restrained hidden lighting. With two funnels instead of three, her passengers also had considerably more deck space than her running mate.

QUEEN ELIZABETH 1940-1969
Quadruple screw

O.N 166290 83,673g 42,239n;
1966: 82,998g 41,261n
987.4 x 118.6 x 68.4 feet.
Four sets of steam turbines by John Brown & Co. Ltd., Clydebank; 160,000 SHP, 28.5 knots.
Passengers: 822 first, 668 cabin, 798 tourist; *1966*: 724 first, 694 cabin, 844 tourist.
27.9.1938: Launched by John Brown & Co. Ltd., Clydebank (Yard No. 552) as QUEEN ELIZABETH.
19.2.1940: Registered at Liverpool under the ownership of Cunard White Star Ltd., Liverpool.

2.3.1940: Departed the Clyde for New York.
12.11.1940: Left New York for Singapore via Trinidad and Cape Town.
11.2.1941: Troopship conversion at Singapore completed. The company code name for the ship was EROS.
31.3.1946: Arrived at Gourock for first stage of post-war refit by John Brown & Co. Ltd.
16.6-6.10.1946: Refit completion at Southampton.
16.10.1946: Left on maiden commercial voyage from Southampton to New York.
31.12.1949: Transferred to the Cunard Steam Ship Co. Ltd., Liverpool.
1.1.1950: Owners restyled as the Cunard Steam-Ship Co. Ltd., Liverpool.
20.1-27.3.1955: Refit included fitting of Denny-Brown stabilisers.
11.12.1965-12.3.1966: Major refit on the Clyde by John Brown & Co. Ltd. so that she could also be used as a cruise ship. This included fitting air-conditioning throughout the ship and a new lido area aft with a new heated outdoor pool, the largest in the fleet.
28.3.1968: Transferred to the Cunard Line Ltd., London.
23.10.1968: Final voyage from Southampton to New York.

10.1968: Leased as a visitor attraction at Port Everglades, Florida to The Elizabeth Corporation, in which Cunard had an 85% shareholding and who continued to own the ship.
29.11.1968: Left Southampton for Port Everglades.
14.2.1969: Opened to public as THE ELIZABETH. Because of poor revenues, was offered for sale by Cunard.
18.7.1969: Transferred to the Cunard Steam-Ship Co. Ltd., London. Sold to Rolepont Ltd., London (The Queen Ltd.). Cunard had no stake in this company.
29.7.1969: Register closed.
6.1970: The Queen Ltd. filed for bankrupcy.
9.1970: Sold at auction to the Island Navigation Corporation Ltd. (C.Y. Tung), Hong Kong.
10.2.1971: Sailed from Port Everglades for Hong Kong under the name SEAWISE UNIVERSITY (a play on C.Y. Tung's name).
14.7.1971: Arrived Hong Kong after a 10-week stop at Aruba for boiler repairs.
9.1.1972: Caught fire in Hong Kong, capsized and sank in shoal water.
1974-79: Broken up in situ.

Opposite page, top: *Queen Elizabeth* departing New York and being pushed back by the Moran tug *Moira Moran* (238/1949).

Above: *Queen Elizabeth* had a more streamlined and better-balanced profile than the rather old-fashioned-looking *Queen Mary*.

Right: *Queen Elizabeth* arriving at New York for the first time, 7th March 1940. Berthed on her starboard side were *Queen Mary*, *Normandie* and *Mauretania*.

Below: *Queen Elizabeth* photographed by the Royal New Zealand Air Force crossing the Hauraki Gulf, north of Auckland, New Zealand. *[Ian J. Farquhar collection]*

Top: *Queen Mary* arriving at Southampton for her post-war refit on 27th September 1946 as *Queen Elizabeth* prepares for her maiden commercial voyage to New York on 16th October.

Right: *Queen Elizabeth*'s 1966 refit included a lido area aft with a new heated outdoor pool, the largest in the fleet.

Below: Also given full-air-conditioning, she was used as a cruise ship during the winter months.

Top: A fine view of *Queen Elizabeth* by Lindsay Rex. [*Russell Priest collection*]
Right: *Queen Elizabeth* at sea. [*R.M. Parsons/ Malcolm Cranfield collection*]
Bottom right: Towards the end of her career and showing signs of wear.
Below: In the King George V drydock at Southampton in 1967 - her anchors and chains are laid out for inspection and the starboard propellers are undergoing repairs and cleaning. [*V.H. Young and L.A. Sawyer*]

With no fanfare, *Queen Elizabeth* sailed from Southampton for the final time in the early hours of 29th November 1968. Just over three years later she was destroyed by fire in Hong Kong harbour.

The delivery voyage of *Seawise University* took her round the Cape of Good Hope and she called in to Cape Town to take on bunkers (middle left). She is also seen sailing from Cape Town (middle right and bottom left). The final photograph was taken after her arrival in Hong Kong (bottom right). [*Middle left and right, lower left: V.H. Young and L.A. Sawyer*]

The former *Queen Elizabeth* as *Seawise University* at Hong Kong. [*Stephen Berry*]

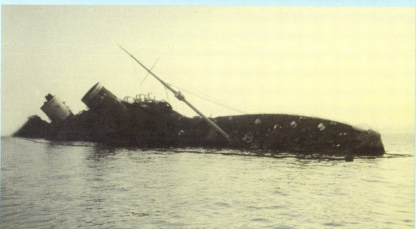

Seawise University burns fiercely. Note that C.Y. Tung's Orient Overseas Line's plum blossom logo has been attached to her funnels (middle left). Despite efforts to fight the blaze she listed to starboard and settled on the bottom of Hong Kong Harbour. She was surrounded by booms in an attempt to minimise the risk of pollution from the oil remaining on board (middle right and bottom left). In due course the scrap merchants took over and all that could be salvaged was brought ashore for the steel furnaces (bottom right). [*Middle left: Ian Shiffman; others: V.H. Young and L.A. Sawyer*]

Queen Elizabeth 2 was Cunard Line's final transatlantic liner. She was designed as a dual purpose liner and cruise ship, with a two-class configuration for transatlantic crossings and as a single-class ship when cruising. She was originally conceived as a liner-only replacement for *Queen Mary*.

After a spectacular launch by Her Majesty Queen Elizabeth in September 1967, the completion of *Queen Elizabeth* 2 in late 1968 was an embarrassment, not just for Britain but British shipbuilding in particular. During her final acceptance trials and shake-down cruise, she developed a major technical problem with her starboard turbine and Cunard refused to accept the ship until these issues were resolved. Despite these initial problems, *Queen Elizabeth 2* went on to become one of the best loved passenger ships of the 20th century.

QUEEN ELIZABETH 2 1969-2008
Twin screw

O.N 336703 67,139g 37,218n;
1987: 69,053g 36,038n
917.0 x 105.2 x 41.7 feet.
Two sets of steam turbines by John Brown Engineering (Clydebank) Ltd., Clydebank; 110,000 SHP, 28.5 knots; *1987*: Nine 9-cyl. oil engines by MAN-B&W Diesel G.m.b.H., Augsburg; 130,000 BHP.
Passengers: 564 first, 1,441 tourist (cruising: 1,400 single class); *1972*: 604 first, 1,223 tourist (cruising: 1,740 single class); *1987*: 1,900 single class; *1996*: 1,500 single class; *1997*: 1,756 single class.
20.9.1967: Launched by John Brown & Co. (Clydebank) Ltd. (Upper Clyde Shipbuilders Ltd. in 1968), Clydebank (Yard No. 736) as QUEEN ELIZABETH 2.
11.12.1968: Registered at Southampton under the ownership of Cunard Line Ltd., Southampton.
23.12.1968: Left Greenock for Las Palmas, Canary Islands on final acceptance trials and shake-down cruise with Cunard staff and their families.
2.1.1969: Arrived at Southampton but engine problems meant that Cunard refused to accept delivery of the ship.
30.3.1969: Left Southampton on a shake-down cruise to West Africa and final trials.
20.4.1969: Delivery accepted.
2.5.1969: Left on maiden voyage Southampton-Havre-New York.
13.10-6.11.1972: Refit at Southampton by Vosper Thornycroft, which included the addition of ten penthouse suites on the Sports Deck and replacement of stabilisers.
4.1.1975: Left Southampton on first world cruise.
10.1977: Two split-level suites added to Signal Deck at Bayonne, New Jersey by Bethlehem Steel Corporation.
3.5.1982: Requisitioned by the British Government as a troopship during the Falkland Islands Campaign and helicopter pads were added.
12.5.1982: Sailed from Southampton for the Falkland Islands, returning on *11.6.1982*.
12.6-7.8.1982: Refit at Southampton by Vosper Thornycroft. Funnel repainted in traditional Cunard colours whilst her hull was a light pebble grey.
6.1983: Hull reverted to original Federal grey.

Queen Elizabeth 2's name was only revealed when she was launched by Her Majesty Queen Elizabeth.

28.11-12.1983: Magradome fitted on the Lido Deck and two large tenders added aft by Lloyd Werft at Bremerhaven.
27.10.1986-25.4.1987: Re-engined at Bremerhaven by Lloyd Werft. Funnel replaced with a wider and more substantial one.
1.1.1994: Transferred to the Cunard Steam-Ship Co. Ltd., London
20.1.1994: Arrived at Hamburg for major refit at Blohm & Voss and removal of magradome.
17.12.1994: Sailed for New York but incomplete work generated much negative publicity.
22.11-11.12.1996: SOLAS upgrade and refit at

Southampton by A&P.
28.5.1998: Following the majority acquisition of Cunard by the Carnival Corporation, ownership was transferred to Cunard White Star Ltd., Hamilton, Bermuda although she remained registered at Southampton.
1.1.2008: Transferred to Carnival plc, London.
26.11.2008: Arrived Dubai having been acquired by QE2 Enterprises, Dubai for use as a floating hotel.
27.11.2008: British register closed.
18.8.2009: Registered at Vanuatu.

Queen Elizabeth 2 on trials (above) and at New York (below). *Queen Elizabeth 2* originally had a white and black funnel, which enhanced her distinctive profile.

Over the years *Queen Elizabeth 2* visited many ports - far more than were ever envisaged when she was completed in 1969. These two pages depict her in some of these ports of call. We start off with her sailing from Southampton in May 1969 at the start of her maiden voyage. We then see her at Wellington, New Zealand in February 1983. The middle right photo shows her sailing from Bremerhaven early in 1987 after her conversion from steam to diesel during the course of which her new funnel was fitted. Our final picture on this page is of her sailing into Auckland, New Zealand on 7th March 1989 escorted by a variety of local craft. *[All: V.H.Young and L.A.Sawyer]*

Top: *Queen Elizabeth 2* in Lisbon 21st April 2006, passing the 'Monument to the Discoveries' with its statue of Henry the Navigator (top left) and passing under the Ponte 25 de Abril in December 2005 (top right). *[Both: Luis Miguel Correia]*
Middle: *Queen Elizabeth 2* at Rejkjavik on 3rd August 2005. *[Ian Boyle]*
Bottom: *Queen Elizabeth 2* at Dubai where she awaits conversion to a floating hotel. *[Shaun Jones]*

Queen Elizabeth 2 as seen through the lenses of FotoFlite cameras; above in her early days with her original black and white funnel and Federal grey hull. The second view shows her with her original funnel, now in the traditional Cunard funnel colours, and grey, post-Falklands hull. When the last picture was taken she had reverted to her Federal grey hull but her funnel had been replaced with a more substantial structure, again in Cunard colours. *[FotoFlite incorporating Skyfotos, 200726, 9579 and 178671]*

INTERMEDIATE TRANSATLANTIC LINERS

The first intermediate liners

In the 1880s the newly-formed Cunard Steamship Co. Ltd. divided its fleet into two distinct categories: the Saturday express passenger-mail service between Liverpool and New York and the intermediate liners, which operated primarily on the weekly Thursday sailing to Boston. These secondary line ships were not only slower but also catered for the growing emigrant trade. In the period from 1880 to 1889, over 4.5 million migrants crossed the Atlantic from Europe to the United States, compared with half that number in the previous decade.

The first purpose-built intermediate ships were delivered between 1881 and 1882. The first to enter service was the 4,841g *Catalonia*. This 13-knot ship, and her slightly larger running mate *Pavonia*, were built on the Clyde by J. and G. Thomson. They were also the last Cunarders with an iron hull. The third ship, *Cephalonia*, had a steel hull, and was constructed at Birkenhead by Laird Brothers. Each of these three vessels had accommodation for around 1,500 steerage passengers and ample cargo space. By the mid-1880s *Bothnia*, *Scythia* and *Gallia* had been outclassed by the new express liners on the New York run and were transferred to the Boston intermediate route. In 1888 the company introduced a fortnightly Tuesday sailing to New York from Liverpool. This new intermediate service was initially operated by *Gallia* and *Scythia* and in the late 1890s by *Servia* and *Aurania*.

In 1894 immigration numbers to the United States fell sharply and did not pick up again until the late 1890s. By then the Cunard Boston ships were too small and outdated for the service. They also faced increasing competition from Leyland Line and Dominion Line. As a result, its new cargo ship *Ultonia* was converted into a steerage-only emigrant ship and replacements for the earlier vessels were ordered. These were the 14,000g passenger-cargo ships *Saxonia* and *Ivernia*, which were delivered in 1900. At the time, they were the third largest ships in the world. They also had the tallest funnels and, with considerable space for cargo, were fitted with stalls for 800 head of cattle. Passengers were carried in three classes, including 1,600 in third. In 1903, *Carpathia*, a slightly smaller version of this pair but with only second and third class passengers, entered service. In the spring of 1903, she and *Aurania* recommenced the fortnightly Liverpool-New York sailings, which had been suspended in 1901 following the withdrawal from service of *Servia*.

Cunard Hungarian-American Line

Also in 1903, the number of immigrants from southern and eastern Europe to the United States rose to over 600,000. Although most came from Italy, a large number were from Hungary. At the time Cunard faced a fierce rates war on the North Atlantic with its German rivals, Hamburg-Amerika Linie and Norddeutscher Lloyd and J. P. Morgan's IMM group. In order to expand its business, Cunard turned to the Mediterranean, a region it knew well, having operated there since 1853. In August 1903 it announced a new service, commencing in October, from Boston to Gibraltar, Naples, Palermo, Trieste and Fiume (present day Rijeka). The terminus for the new fortnightly service was subsequently changed to New York and the veteran Cunarder *Aurania* took the first sailing from there on the 20th October 1903. She

carried first class and steerage passengers and those travelling to see Europe were able to purchase, for each of the ports of call, circular tours across Italy, Switzerland, France and Germany to London and Liverpool for the return sailing to New York. Organised by Thomas Cook and Son, this was Cunard's first venture into the Mediterranean cruise market. In November the brand-new *Carpathia* was placed on the new service, which later became known as the Cunard Hungarian-American Line. Two more ships were added during 1904, *Slavonia*, a two-year-old former British India liner, and *Pannonia*, which had been purchased on the stocks. In June 1904, unable to obtain an agreement with German or local operators, the Hungarian government awarded Cunard the exclusive rights to carry emigrants from Fiume to New York. In response, Hamburg-Amerika Linie and Norddeutscher Lloyd took a controlling interest in the Trieste-based Società Anonima Unione Austriaca di Navigazione, which had been founded in 1903 by the Cosulich brothers. In the years leading up to the First World War, this company grew into one of the major shipping lines in the Mediterranean.

Migration from the Mediterranean area continued to rise and in 1907 almost a million arrived in the United States. In 1909 *Pannonia* was wrecked on the Azores. *Ivernia* was transferred to the route as a replacement. The following year, Messina was added to the schedule whilst occasional calls were also made at Almeira, Spain. In 1913 Patras, Greece was included in the timetable.

A new quartet of intermediates

Meanwhile, on the Liverpool-New York run, White Star Line had taken delivery of its four immense *Celtic*-class liners. These 20,000-ton ships were not only at one time the largest in the world, they also introduced a new type of intermediate vessel which was to become the norm on the North Atlantic. These ships, which were not record breakers, offered considerable comfort for first and second class passengers and also had a large capacity for cargo and steerage passengers. Cunard's answer to the 'Big Four' were two of the most attractive liners ever built for the company, the 19,500g *Caronia* and *Carmania* of 1905. Whilst the latter was famous for being the first Cunard ship to be fitted with turbines, both ships introduced new standards of comfort for Cunard passengers, especially those in first class. They also set the standard for a new generation of Cunard liners, epitomised two years later by the arrival of *Lusitania* and *Mauretania*. Placed on the fortnightly Liverpool-New York service, from 1907 they were also used during the winter months on Mediterranean cruises from New York. The arrival of the two new express liners and the success of *Caronia* and *Carmania* led to the order for two new Boston liners. Delivered in 1911, the 18,100g *Franconia* and *Laconia* were the first Cunard ships designed for winter cruising and the first to feature a gymnasium. Included in the first class accommodation was an open-air veranda café and in the dining saloon four-legged chairs replaced the usual fixed revolving chairs. Externally they were similar to the 1905 *C*-ships and, like the earlier pair, had a large steerage capacity. *Laconia* was also the first British liner to be fitted with a Frahm anti-rolling tank, a German system designed to suppress the rolling motion in heavy Atlantic weather.

The return to Canada

In the early 1900s immigration to Canada also increased significantly and by 1910 over a quarter of a million immigrants had arrived in the country. Cunard, which had not operated to Canada since December 1867, could not ignore the obvious opportunities offered by this lucrative trade. In March 1911 it bought the ships and the London berth of Thomson Line. William Thomson and Sons had been operating cargo services to Canada since the 1880s and in 1908 the company was purchased by the Newcastle-based Cairns, Noble and Company, owners of the Cairn Line of Steamships Ltd. Essentially a cargo line, Cairn decided to expand its business into the passenger market. Under the Thomson Line banner it entered the Canadian immigrant trade and obtained a licence from the Italian government to carry emigrants from Italy to Canada. Two new ships were ordered from Swan, Hunter and Wigham Richardson Ltd. for delivery in 1909 and 1911. It also bought a former Wilson Line freighter which was fitted with steerage accommodation, renamed *Cairnrona* and placed on a Newcastle-Quebec-Montreal service. *Tortona*, the first of the new ships, was delivered in October 1909 and, after carrying poor loads between Italy and Canada, she was transferred in August 1910 to a new service from London to Quebec and Montreal via Southampton. It was this service which attracted Cunard. With its purchase of Thomson Line, not only would it be re-entering the Canadian trade, it would also be obtaining a foothold in London and more importantly, Southampton, the new home port of its arch rival, White Star Line. *Cairnrona* and *Tortona* were renamed *Albania* and *Ausonia* respectively whilst the second Swan Hunter ship, which had been launched as the twin-funnelled *Gerona*, was completed as *Ascania*. This was the start of the *A*-names for Cunard Canadian service ships.

Albania inaugurated the new service on the 2nd May 1911 when she sailed from London for Quebec and Montreal via Southampton. Not only was this the return of Cunard to Canada after an absence of 44 years, it was also Cunard's first commercial transatlantic sailing to the St. Lawrence River. However, *Albania* was deemed unsuitable for the new route and a year later she was sold. In the meantime, the company ordered its first pair of purpose-built Canadian ships from Scotts' shipyard at Greenock. Despite their relatively small size, the 13,400g *Andania* and *Alaunia* had two funnels and carried over 2,000 passengers. Both ships were delivered in 1913 whilst a third sister, *Aurania*, was completed in 1917, only to be sunk a year later by a German submarine. In fact, all the *A*-ships were lost during the First World War.

In 1916 Cunard's presence on the transatlantic Canadian route was further enhanced when it bought from Canadian Northern Railway the four ships and goodwill of the Toronto-based Canadian Northern Steamships Ltd. This

Caronia in the Mersey. *[J. and M. Clarkson collection]*

company formed Royal Line in 1910, offering fortnightly passenger-mail sailings between Avonmouth (Bristol) and Quebec and Montreal in direct competition with Canadian Pacific's Liverpool service. With links to London via the Great Western Railway, its two main liners were the handsome *Royal Edward* and *Royal George*. Canadian Northern Steamships also operated an immigrant line from Rotterdam under the banner of the Uranium Steamship Co. Ltd. In 1913 the Royal Line name was dropped in favour of Canadian Northern Steamships. With the outbreak of war, both *Royal Edward* and *Royal George* were requisitioned as troopships. Despite this, the Avonmouth route continued to operate with the three remaining Uranium Line ships. *Royal Edward* was sunk by a German U-boat in 1915, and with its parent company, Canadian Northern Railway, in a precarious financial situation, its four ships were sold to Cunard. The main reason for this purchase was the Avonmouth and Rotterdam berths. *Royal George* remained in service as a troop transport, whilst the other three ships were given *F*-names and continued the Avonmouth service. However, all the *F*-ships were later sunk by German U-boats.

Joint operations with Anchor Line

Following Cunard's acquisition of Anchor Line's ordinary shares in 1912, the two companies established a close working relationship. In 1915 a joint Cunard-Anchor Line service from Glasgow to New York via Liverpool was established. One of the ships used on this route, *Transylvania*, had been built for Cunard as its contribution to a joint Cunard-Anchor Mediterranean service to New York, and was the first large transatlantic liner fitted with geared turbines. With the outbreak of war, the Italian route was abandoned and her ownership was transferred to Anchor Line. She and her sister *Tuscania* were both sunk in the war and during 1919 the keels for two replacement liners were laid. This pair, *Tyrrhenia* (Cunard) and *Tuscania* (Anchor), were also destined not to operate on their planned Mediterranean-New York route. Delayed by strikes, by the time they were completed in 1922 the United States Government had passed a series of acts which restricted immigrant numbers, especially those from southern and eastern Europe. This, combined with Italian government requirements for Italian emigrants to travel in Italian ships, brought about the end to Cunard's Mediterranean emigrant service. *Pannonia*, the sole survivor on this run, took the final sailing from Trieste on 17th September 1921. In the meantime Anchor-Donaldson Line, which had been formed in 1916 to operate joint liner services between Glasgow and Canada, also had two new 13,600g liners under construction *Athenia* and *Letitia*. Completed in 1923 and 1925 respectively, both ships were used on a joint Cunard-Anchor-Donaldson service between Glasgow and Canada via Liverpool.

Letitia at anchor in the Mersey. Note the funnel colours - she may be in Anchor Line or Cunard colours as pre-war film did not reproduce reds very well. [B. and A. Feilden/J. and M. Clarkson]

Post-war reconstruction and the 1920s

The attrition rate for Cunard's intermediate ships during the 1914-1918 war was very high, with only *Pannonia*, *Saxonia*, *Carmania*, *Caronia* and *Royal George* surviving the conflict. Thirteen ships were lost whilst 265 people lost their lives. To replace war losses, in 1919 Cunard embarked on an ambitious replacement programme for the intermediate service. This included five 20,000g liners for the New York and Boston service, and six 14,000g liners for the Canadian route. However, the construction of these new ships soon became embroiled in major problems with the shipyards, which faced spiralling cost increases through labour disputes and shortages of steel. Many ship owners were unable to sustain these huge rises in construction costs, and orders were either cancelled or put on hold. Cunard also saw its third class traffic fall by a quarter in 1922, the first year after the new United States' emigrant quota scheme was introduced. The company renegotiated contracts with the shipyards, and the delivery programme was spread over four years from 1921 to 1925. Meanwhile, Anchor Line suspended work on its new builds in 1922, whilst the construction of Donaldson Line's *Letitia* was also put on hold.

The first new intermediate ship to be delivered was the 12,768g *Albania*. Ordered in 1916 as the fourth of the pre-war A-class, work had been delayed because of the war. She was completed in 1921 as a cargo-passenger ship. However, she did not fit into the new intermediate fleet. In 1925 she was laid up and eventually sold in 1930. The first of a new class of large intermediates was the oil-fired, 19,730g *Scythia* of 1921. She and her sisters were single funnel, enlarged but slower versions of the pre-war

Franconia and *Laconia*. They became very popular ships, especially among U.S. tourists and students bound for Europe, and were used extensively for cruising. In the winter of 1922-1923 the new *Laconia* made the first ever world cruise by a passenger liner whilst the last in the *Scythia*-class, *Carinthia* and *Franconia*, were the first in the fleet designed for world-wide cruising. They were also fitted with a 'sports arena', consisting of swimming pool, gymnasium and racket court.

The six A-class liners were smaller versions of the *Scythia*-class and only carried cabin and third class passengers. With relatively plain accommodation, they were designed primarily to carry emigrants to Canada. The first to be delivered was the 13,950g *Andania* in 1922 and she revived the London-Southampton-Quebec-Montreal (Halifax in winter) service on 1st June 1922. The new joint Cunard-Anchor-Donaldson Liverpool to Quebec and Montreal (Halifax in winter) service commenced on 20th April 1922. Cunard worked closely with the Canadian government to encourage emigration to Canada. In 1926 it established a joint venture with the Hudson's Bay Company. The Hudson's Bay Company Overseas Settlement Ltd. was set up to assist emigrants wishing to start a new life in the Hudson's Bay territory. By the late 1920s Cunard

Antonia, one of the six 1920s 'A' class, anchored in the Mersey on 27th May 1939. [John McRoberts/J. and M. Clarkson]

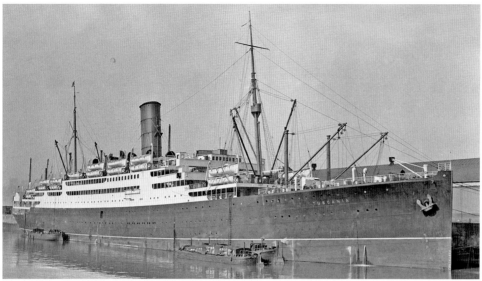

Tuscania on Cunard charter. *[B. and A. Feilden/J. and M. Clarkson]*

offered weekly sailings to Canada from Liverpool, London and Southampton with calls at Havre and Plymouth on the London-Southampton route.

Meanwhile, in April 1922 Cunard started a new route from Hamburg to New York via Southampton and Cherbourg and established Cunard See Transport G.m.b.H. in Hamburg to oversee its German operation. With the revival of German shipping this was a short-lived service and was withdrawn in October 1926. By then the post-war reconstruction programme was complete and Cunard was able to focus on its prime routes. On 3rd June 1926 the Anchor Line charter *Tuscania* inaugurated a weekly London-Havre-Southampton-New York service. This route became of major importance to the company. After the formation of Cunard White Star Ltd. in 1934, White Star Line's large new motor ships *Britannic* and *Georgic* were transferred to the service in 1935. At the time, they were the largest ships to operate on the Thames.

Tuscania remained on charter to Cunard until 1930, whilst her sister *Tyrrhenia*, Cunard's first liner with a cruiser stern, was renamed *Lancastria* in 1924, and spent most of her career on the New York run. By the late 1920s services no longer terminated in Boston and calls were made fortnightly by the Liverpool-New York intermediate liners. The failure of Anchor Line (Henderson Brothers Ltd.) in 1935 also brought an end to the Anchor-Donaldson Line agreement. However, Donaldson continued its Cunard association with the formation of Donaldson Atlantic Line, which operated the joint weekly Liverpool service to Canada with Cunard. Calls were also made at Greenock and Belfast with sailings taken by Donaldson's *Athenia* and *Letitia* and Cunard's *Antonia* and *Andania*.

The great depression and the 1930s

Unlike the express service which operated older tonnage in the early 1930s, the Cunard intermediate fleet was in a relatively strong position to weather the impact of the Great Depression. Whilst the larger new ships were used for cruising, *Andania* was laid up for two years. The veterans *Caronia* and *Carmania* were also sold for demolition in 1932, having given the company excellent service for over a quarter of a century. After the completion of *Queen Mary* in 1936, tenders were sought for the building of a pair of large intermediate liners for the London-Southampton-New York

service, which would be similar to *Georgic* in terms of size, passenger layout and comfort. The new ships would also need to be able to use the entrance lock for London's King George V Dock. The contract for the first ship was awarded at the end of December 1936 to Cammell Laird and Co. Ltd., Birkenhead. With a profile similar to *Queen Elizabeth*, the 35,739g *Mauretania* was completed in May 1939. She had a service speed of 22 knots and was also designed as a replacement liner when either of the *Queens* was taken out of service for the annual refit. Unfortunately, the intervention of war once again put paid to Cunard's ambitions and, after only three voyages, *Mauretania* was sent to New York for lay-up and subsequent transformation into a troopship. Plans for a second ship were put on hold.

Another war and post-war reconstruction programme

At the start of the Second World War, Cunard had sixteen intermediate liners. By the end of the war the fleet had been reduced to only six: *Mauretania, Britannic, Franconia, Scythia, Samaria* and *Ascania*. As was the case at the end of the First World War, the company built up a fleet of freighters with *V*-names to make up for the lost intermediate liner cargo capacity (see page 196). It also ordered two large 13,300g intermediate cargo-passenger liners, *Parthia* and *Media*, which were similar in size to the 1920s A-class liners but with considerably more cargo space. They were originally designed for the London-New York service, but used instead on the Liverpool-New York run alongside *Britannic*. However, unlike the pre-war liners, these ships only carried 250 first class passengers.

On her return from war duty in 1947, *Mauretania* was placed on the Southampton-Cherbourg-New York route. In 1949, she was joined by a new running mate, the 34,183g *Caronia*, which had originally been conceived as her sister. However, because post-war conditions were radically different from the 1930s, the new ship was designed as a dual purpose transatlantic liner and cruise ship. Her passenger capacity was less than a thousand in two classes and she carried no cargo. With a huge single funnel, the largest at that time, she was painted in four shades of green. Known as the 'Green Goddess', she became one of the most exclusive cruise ships of her day. During the summer months she operated on the North Atlantic and in winter she usually cruised out of New York. On 6th January 1951 she sailed from New York on the first of her many world cruises.

Meanwhile, the four remaining intermediate liners from the 1920s were used extensively on the Canada service. In 1948 *Scythia* and *Samaria* were chartered by the International Refugee Organisation and the Canadian Government to carry emigrants on a Cuxhaven-Havre-Quebec (summer) and Halifax (winter) austerity service. Three years later Cunard decided that services from London would be cargo-only and *Scythia* and *Samaria* were transferred to a new Southampton-Havre-Quebec route.

Ascania and *Franconia* were placed on the Liverpool-Quebec-Montreal service. As these four liners were nearing the end of their careers, plans were drawn up for replacement ships.

The final intermediates
Between 1954 and 1957 four 22,000g intermediate liners were built on the Clyde by John Brown for the Canadian service. Built in pairs, *Saxonia*, *Ivernia*, *Carinthia* and *Sylvania* were handsome, fully air-conditioned ships with distinctive domed-top funnels. They were the first Cunard liners designed with stabilisers and had a large cargo capacity of 300,000 cubic feet. They were also the first Cunarders wth a balconied cinema. Whilst the first pair had bright and colourful interiors, the second pair were given more traditional interior designs.

Initially used on the Liverpool service, *Saxonia* and *Ivernia* were transferred to the Southampton-Havre-Quebec-Montreal route in 1957. The second pair remained at Liverpool, and in 1960 *Sylvania* replaced *Britannic* on the Liverpool-New York service. A 28,000g replacement for *Britannic* had been announced in 1957, but the order was later postponed, then cancelled.

In 1961 *Parthia* and *Media* were sold. On 30th November 1967 *Sylvania* sailed for Halifax and New York on the last transatlantic voyage for Cunard from Liverpool. This was also the last Cunard intermediate sailing. In 1968, she and *Carinthia* were sold to Sitmar Line. Meanwhile, their elder sisters which had been converted in 1963 into dual-purpose cruise and transatlantic liners had been renamed *Franconia* (ex *Ivernia*) and *Carmania* (ex *Saxonia*). They were placed on a new Rotterdam-Southampton-Havre-Quebec-Montreal route and, in 1966 and 1967 respectively, became full time cruise ships.

Mauretania was also used as a cruise ship in the early 1960s and in March 1963 she inaugurated a new passenger-cargo service between New York and Cannes, Genoa and Naples. Because of poor passenger numbers this service only lasted seven months. In 1965 she was withdrawn and sold to breakers. Also in 1965 *Caronia* was extensively modernised and had a new lido deck fitted aft. However, her operating costs remained high, and in 1967 she was laid up and sold the following year. *Carmania* and *Franconia* were laid up in 1971 and sold to the Russian Government in 1973.

A helicopter hovers overhead as *Ivernia* arrives in New York for the first time in December 1955. *[J. and M. Clarkson collection]*

Catalonia was the first purpose-built intermediate ship and, like her two running mates, was designed to carry large numbers of steerage passengers. She also had ample cargo space. Note the men on the yards.

CATALONIA 1881-1901 Iron barque rigged screw

O.N. 84126 4,841g 3,093n
429.6 x 43.0 x 18.7 feet.
C.2-cyl. by J. and G. Thomson, Clydebank; 600 HP, 13 knots.
Passengers: 100 first, 1,500 third.
14.5.1881: Launched by J. and G. Thomson, Clydebank (Yard No. 180) as CATALONIA.
3.8.1881: Registered at Liverpool under the ownership of the Cunard Steamship Co. Ltd., Liverpool.
6.8.1881: Left on maiden voyage from Liverpool to New York.
18.4.1883: Left on first voyage from Liverpool to Boston.
24.7-19.9.1882: Chartered by the British Government as a transport during the Egyptian Campaign.
19.9.1899: Final transatlantic crossing.
1.10.1899-15.4.1901: Chartered by the British Government as the Boer War Transport No. 21.
1901: Sold to Italian breakers.
3.5.1901: Register closed.
24.5.1901: Arrived Genoa for demolition.

CEPHALONIA 1882-1900 Barque rigged screw

O.N. 86205 5,517g 3,490n
430.6 x 46.5 x 18.4 feet.
C.2-cyl. by Laird Brothers, Birkenhead; 700 HP, 14 knots.
Passengers: 200 first, 1,500 steerage.
20.5.1882: Launched by Laird Brothers, Birkenhead (Yard No. 498) as CEPHALONIA.
4.8.1882: Registered at Liverpool under the ownership of the Cunard Steamship Co. Ltd., Liverpool.
23.8.1882: Left on maiden voyage from Liverpool to Boston.

4.7.1897: Disabled because of damage to propeller shaft 365 miles west of Fastnet Rock, Ireland. Towed by FLORIDAN (3,257/1884) to Queenstown and then by tugs to Liverpool for repairs.
12.9.1899: Final transatlantic crossing.
1.10.1899-5.5.1900: Chartered by the British Government as the Boer War Transport No. 23.
10.7.1900: Registered under the ownership of Thos. W. Ward Ltd., Sheffield, presumably for demolition, but later resold to the Chinese Eastern Railway Co. Ltd., St. Petersburg, Russia and renamed HAYLAR.
30.8.1900: Register closed.
16.3.1904: Scuttled in the approaches to Port Arthur as a defensive blockship during the Russo-Japanese War.

PAVONIA 1882-1900 Iron barque rigged screw

O.N. 86215 5,588g 3,490n
430.5 x 46.4 x 27 feet.
C.2-cyl. by J. and G. Thomson, Clydebank; 700 HP, 14 knots.
Passengers: 200 first, 1,500 steerage; *1890s*: 200 first, 100 second.
3.6.1882: Launched by J. and G. Thomson, Clydebank (Yard No. 186) as PAVONIA. She was the last Cunarder with an iron hull.
23.8.1882: Registered at Liverpool under the ownership of the Cunard Steamship Co. Ltd., Liverpool.
13.9.1882: Maiden voyage from Liverpool to New York.
18.10.1882: First voyage from Liverpool to Boston.

Cephalonia was the first intermediate with a steel hull. She and *Pavonia* were the first in the fleet to have individually operated electric lights in first class staterooms.

Pavonia's completion was delayed by a fire at the yard. Ordered as a sister to *Catalonia*, she was slightly larger and was the last Cunarder with an iron hull.

19.1.1892: Arrived Boston in tow of HAPAG steamer RHAETIA (3,353/1883) after her propeller shaft broke.

18.2.1899: Arrived at St. Michael's, Azores under tow of WOLVESTON (2,565/1895) after her boilers were unseated during a storm.

29.8.1899: Final transatlantic crossing.

1.10.1899-9.6.1900: Chartered by the British Government as the Boer War Transport No. 6 (also 19).

13.7.1900: Registered under the ownership of Thos. W. Ward Ltd., Sheffield and later resold to Italian breakers.

14.8.1900: Register closed.

23.9.1900: Arrived Genoa for demolition.

ULTONIA 1898-1917 Twin screw
O.N. 109478 8,056g 5,212n;
1904: 10,402g 6,593n
500.0 x 57.1 x 33.9 feet.
Two T.3-cyl. by C. Furness, Westgarth and Co. Ltd., Middlesbrough; 1,100 HP, 14.5 knots.
Passengers: Cargo only; *1899*: 675 steerage; *1904*: 120 second, 2,100 steerage.

4.6.1898: Launched by C.S. Swan and Hunter Ltd., Wallsend (Yard No. 228) as ULTONIA. Bought on the stocks.

26.10.1898: Registered at Liverpool under the ownership of the Cunard Steamship Co. Ltd., Liverpool.

28.10.1898: Left on maiden voyage from Liverpool to Boston.

1899: Fitted as steerage-only passenger ship.

28.2.1899: Left on first voyage as a passenger ship, Liverpool-Queenstown-New York.

1904: Refit included accommodation for second class and expansion of steerage space. Placed on Mediterranean to New York emigrant service.

29.4.1904: First voyage Fiume-Palermo-New York for the Cunard Hungarian-American Line service.

1915-1916: Made several voyages from New York to St. Nazaire.

11.4.1917: Requisitioned by the British Government as a transport.

27.6.1917: Torpedoed and sunk by the German submarine U 53 190 miles south west of Fastnet Rock, Ireland, in position 48°22′N, 11°28′W. whilst on a voyage New York to London with general cargo. One life was lost.

4.7.1917: Register closed.

To meet the demand for increased numbers of emigrants to the United States, the cargo ship *Ultonia* was converted into a steerage-only emigrant ship.

THE CUNARD HUNGARIAN-AMERICAN LINE

In October 1903 Cunard started a New York-Gibraltar-Naples-Palermo-Trieste-Fiume service. The following year, Cunard was awarded exclusive rights to carry emigrants from Fiume (present day Rijeka) to New York and the Cunard Hungarian-American Line was formed.

This service, which lasted until 1921, was initially operated by *Slavonia*, *Ultonia*, *Pannonia* and *Carpathia*. *Saxonia* and *Ivernia* were transferred to the route in 1909 and 1911 respectively.

SLAVONIA 1904-1909 Twin screw

O.N. 115761 8,831g 5,635n;
1904: 10,606g 6,725n
510.0 x 59.5 x 30.25 feet.
T.3-cyl. by Wallsend Slipway and Engineering Co. Ltd., Wallsend; 930 HP, 13.6 knots.
Passengers: 100 first, 48 second, 800 deck;
1904: 71 first, 74 second, 1,954 third.
15.11.1902: Launched by Sir J. Laing and Sons Ltd., Sunderland (Yard No. 600) for the British India Steam Navigation Co. Ltd., London as YAMUNA. She had been ordered as QUETTA and was intended to be the largest ship on the London to Calcutta service.
9.5.1903: Registered at Glasgow under the ownership of the British India Steam Navigation Co. Ltd., London.
1903: Her owners claimed that changes in the Suez Canal tonnage rules made her uneconomic and, after a single voyage to Savona with a cargo of coal and no passengers, she was laid up in London.
30.1.1904: Acquired by Cunard Steamship Co. Ltd., Liverpool.
24.2.1904: Registered at Liverpool under the ownership of the Cunard Steamship Co. Ltd., Liverpool as SLAVONIA.
29.3.1904: First voyage Trieste-Fiume-Palermo-New York for the Cunard Hungarian-American Line service.
10.6.1909: Wrecked two miles south west of Flores Island, Azores whilst on a voyage New York-Naples-Trieste-Fiume, with passengers and general cargo. 100 cabin passengers were transferred to Norddeutscher Lloyd's PRINZESS IRENE (10,881/1900), whilst the 273 steerage passengers, mainly Italian, were carried to Naples aboard HAPAG's BATAVIA (10,178/1899). Her crew, two thirds of whom were Hungarian, was all saved.
16.7.1909: Register closed.

PANNONIA 1904-1922 Twin screw

O.N. 118080 7,839g 5,046n
486.5 x 59.3 x 37.2 feet.
T.3-cyl. by John Brown & Co. Ltd., Clydebank; 811 HP, 12 knots.
Passengers: 40 first, 800 third.
5.9.1902: Launched by John Brown & Co. Ltd., Clydebank (Yard No. 348) as PANNONIA. She had been purchased on the stocks.

Slavonia was a former British India liner.

13.2.1904: Completed.
8.3.1904: Registered at Liverpool under the ownership of the Cunard Steamship Co. Ltd., Liverpool.
28.5.1904: Maiden voyage Trieste-Fiume-Palermo-New York for the Cunard Hungarian-American Line service.
14.11.1913: Whilst bound for New York, rescued 103 passengers and crew from the Spanish steamer BALMES (3,806/1893) which had caught fire in mid-Atlantic.
21.4.1917-24.1.1919: Requisitioned by the British Government as a transport.
18.5.1919: First voyage Piraeus-Marseilles-New York.
17.9.1921: Final voyage from Trieste to New York. Arrived New York *17.10*.
18.4.1922: Last voyage New York-Plymouth-Cherbourg-Hamburg. Laid up at Hamburg.
9.10.1922: Sold for demolition to buyers in Danzig and broken up at Hamburg.
16.12.1922: Register closed.

Pannonia was bought on the stocks for the Mediterranean to New York emigrant service.

Saxonia and Ivernia were built because
of increased competition from Leyland
Line and Dominion Line on the Boston
service. At the time, they were the third
largest ships in the world and had the
tallest funnels.

    Unlike the earlier intermediates,
passengers were carried in three classes.
They also had considerable space for
cargo, and were fitted with stalls for 800
head of cattle.

IVERNIA (1) 1900-1917 Twin screw
O.N. 110643 13,800g 8,913n;
1901: 14,058g 9,052n
582.0 x 64.9 x 21.8 feet.
Q.4-cyl. by Wallsend Slipway and
Engineering Co. Ltd., Wallsend; 1,200 HP,
16 knots.
Passengers: 164 first, 200 second, 1,600
third.
21.9.1899: Launched by C.S. Swan and
Hunter Ltd., Wallsend (Yard No. 247) as
IVERNIA.
24.3.1900: Registered at Liverpool under
the ownership of the Cunard Steamship Co.
Ltd., Liverpool.
14.4.1900: Left on maiden voyage from
Liverpool to New York.
12.6.1900: First voyage from Liverpool to
Boston.
24.5.1911: Struck Gaunts Rock near
Queenstown on a homeward voyage from
Boston. Beached near Queenstown.
24.6.1911: Refloated and returned to
Liverpool for permanent repairs.
17.10.1911: Returned to service.
21.12.1911: First voyage Trieste-Fiume-
Messina-Naples-New York for the Cunard
Hungarian-American Line service.
9.1914: Requisitioned by the British
Government as a troopship.
11.1914-spring of 1915: Moored off

Southend with SAXONIA and ROYAL
EDWARD (1908/11,117), sister of ROYAL
GEORGE, as an accommodation ship
housing prisoners-of-war and internees.
1.1.1917: Torpedoed and sunk by the
German submarine UB 47 fifty-eight miles
east of Cape Matapan in position 35°30′N,
22°53′E whilst on a voyage to Alexandria
with 2,400 Scottish troops. 36 crew and 85
troops were lost.
29.5.1917: Register closed.

Top: *Ivernia* and her sister had
exceptionally tall funnels.
Middle: *Ivernia* as a troopship in dry
dock at Marseilles.
Bottom: Scottish troops wearing life-
jackets waiting to be rescued, not long
after *Ivernia* had been torpedoed.

SAXONIA (1) 1900-1925 Twin screw

O.N. 110648 13,963g 8,921n;
1901: 14,281g 9,100n
580.0 x 64.2 x 30.4 feet.
Q.4-cyl. by John Brown & Co. Ltd.,
Clydebank; 1,200 HP, 16 knots.
Passengers: 164 first, 200 second,
1,600 third; *1920*: 485 cabin, 978 third.
16.12.1899: Launched by John Brown
& Co. Ltd., Clydebank (Yard No. 339)
as SAXONIA.
24.4.1900: Registered at Liverpool
under the ownership of the Cunard
Steamship Co. Ltd., Liverpool.
22.5.1900: Left on maiden voyage
from Liverpool to Boston.
23.12.1909: First voyage Fiume-
Palermo-Naples-New York for the
Cunard Hungarian-American Line
service.
8.1914: Requisitioned by the British
Government as a troopship.
11.1914-spring of 1915: Moored
off Southend with IVERNIA and
ROYAL EDWARD (11,117/1908)
sister of ROYAL GEORGE) as
an accommodation ship housing
prisoners-of-war and internees.
1.3.1917: Resumed Liverpool to New
York service.
18.7.1917: Requisitioned by the
British Government as a troopship
until *14.3.1919*.
1920: Refit included reduction of
funnel height by 15 feet.
19.10.1924: Laid up at Tilbury after
final London-Hamburg-Southampton-
Cherbourg-New York voyage.
13.3.1925: Register closed.
27.3.1925: Arrived in the New
Waterway under tow. Broken up at
Hendrik-Ido-Ambacht, Holland by
N.V. Frank Rijsdijk's Industrieele
Ondernemingen.

Top: *Saxonia* at anchor in the
River Mersey.
Middle: *Saxonia* in dazzle-paint as
a troopship.
Bottom: *Saxonia*'s final guise in the
1920s with her funnel shortened.

The well-known *Carpathia* was a slightly smaller version of *Ivernia* and *Saxonia* but with only second and third class passenger accommodation. *[Stephen Card collection]*

CARPATHIA 1902-1918 Twin screw
O.N.118014 13,555g 8,764n
540.0 x 64.5 x 37.4 feet.
Two Q.4-cyl. by Wallsend Slipway and
Engineering Co. Ltd., Wallsend; 1,340 HP,
16 knots.
Passengers: 204 second, 1,500 third; *1905*:
100 first, 200 second, 2,250 third.
6.8.1902: Launched by C.S. Swan and
Hunter Ltd., Wallsend (Yard No. 274) as
CARPATHIA.
20.4.1903: Registered at Liverpool under
the ownership of the Cunard Steamship Co.
Ltd., Liverpool.
5.5.1903: Left on maiden voyage from
Liverpool to Boston.
28.5.1903: First voyage from Liverpool to
New York.
24.11.1903: First voyage from New York to
Trieste for the Cunard Hungarian-American
Line service.
15.4.1912: Rescued 703 survivors from
White Star Line's TITANIC (46,329/1912).
13.4.1915: Last voyage Piraeus-Messina-
Palermo-Naples-Genoa-Lisbon-New York.
7.1915: Resumed Liverpool to New York
service.
5.5.1917: Requisitioned by the British
Government as a transport.
17.7.1918: Torpedoed and sunk by the
German submarine U 55 170 miles west
by north from Bishop Rock in position
50°25′N, 10°49′W whilst on voyage
Liverpool to Boston. Five lives were lost.
3.9.1918: Register closed.

The 19,500g *Caronia* (above) and *Carmania*
were Cunard's answer to White Star Line's
'Big Four' 20,000-ton intermediate ships on
the Liverpool-New York route.
      These intermediate liners offered
not only considerable comfort for first
and second class passengers, they also
had large capacity for cargo and steerage
passengers. Until the arrival of *Lusitania*
and *Mauretania* in 1907, they were
Cunard's largest ships.

CARONIA (1) 1905-1932 Twin screw
O.N. 120826 19,594g 10,213n
650.0 x 72.2 x 40.2 feet.
Two Q.4-cyl. by John Brown & Co. Ltd.,
Clydebank; 20,000 IHP, 18 knots.
Passengers: 300 first, 350 second, 900
third, 1,100 steerage; *post war*: 352 first,
370 second, 1,204 third; *1926*: 425 cabin,
365 tourist, 650 third; *1928*: 536 cabin, 222
tourist, 404 third.
13.7.1904: Launched by John Brown & Co.
Ltd., Clydebank (Yard No. 362) as CARONIA.

27.1.1905: Registered at Liverpool under the ownership of the Cunard Steam Ship Co. Ltd., Liverpool.

25.2.1905: Maiden voyage from Liverpool to New York.

2.8.1914-22.9.1916: Requisitioned by the British Government as the armed merchant cruiser HMS CARONIA and fitted at Liverpool with eight 4.7-inch guns.

5.1915: Rearmed with eight 6-inch guns.

10.1916-1918: Used as a troopship.

1917: Dazzle painted.

3.7.1918: Resumed Liverpool to New York service.

1-4.1924: Converted to oil firing by Vickers Ltd., Barrow-in-Furness.

1.5.1924: First voyage from Liverpool to Quebec with cabin and third-class accommodation only.

21.11.1924: Resumed Liverpool-New York and Boston service.

21.8.1925: First voyage London-Southampton-Cherbourg-New York.

11.1927 to 2.1928: Refit included two new funnels.

12.9.1931: Last voyage London-Havre-Southampton-New York.

10.1931: Laid up in the Thames Estuary.

19.5.1932: Arrived at Blyth for demolition by Hughes Bolckow Shipbreaking Co. Ltd.

12.1932: Resold to Japanese breakers Kobe Kaiun K.K. and sailed for Japan as TAISEIYO MARU.

10.12.1932: Register closed.

28.3.1933: Arrived at Osaka.

CARMANIA (1) 1905-1932 Triple screw

O.N. 120901 19,524g 9,982n
650.4 x 72.2 x 40.0 feet.
Three steam turbines by John Brown & Co. Ltd., Clydebank; 21,000 SHP, 18 knots.
Passengers: 300 first, 350 second, 900 third, 1,100 steerage; *post war*: 355 first, 372 second, 1,262 third; *1926*: 425 cabin, 365 tourist, 650 third.

21.2.1905: Launched by John Brown & Co. Ltd., Clydebank (Yard No. 366) as CARMANIA.

28.11.1905: Registered at Liverpool under the ownership of the Cunard Steam Ship Co. Ltd., Liverpool.

2.12.1905: Maiden voyage from Liverpool to New York.

2.6.1912: Whilst lying in the Canada Dock, Liverpool, fire destroyed much of her first class accommodation. After repairs, she returned to service 27.8.1912.

9.10.1913: Assisted in the rescue of passengers and crew from the British emigrant ship VOLTURNO (3,586/1906) which caught fire mid-Atlantic in position 48°49´N, 34°39´W with the loss of 136 lives.

8.8.1914-6.7.1916: Requisitioned by the British Government as the armed

Carmania was Cunard's first turbine-driven ship. *[J. and M. Clarkson collection]*

merchant cruiser HMS CARMANIA. Fitted at Liverpool with eight 4.7-inch guns.

14.9.1914: Engaged the German auxilliary cruiser CAP TRAFALGAR (18,805/1914) which had been coaling off the Brazilian island of Trinidada. In the subsequent two-hour battle (see below) the Hamburg-Süd liner was sunk with sixteen men killed whilst HMS CARMANIA suffered serious damage and the loss of nine lives. Repaired at Gibraltar and rearmed with eight 6-inch guns.

11.11.1916: Resumed Liverpool to New York service.

28.3.1917-8.3.1919: Requisitioned by the British Government as a troopship.

22.10.1921: First voyage Southampton-Cherbourg-New York.

3.5.1922: Reverted to Liverpool to New York service.

3.1924: Converted to oil-firing by John Brown & Co. Ltd., Clydebank.

15.5.1924: First voyage Liverpool to Quebec with cabin and third-class accommodation only.

29.11.1924: First voyage Liverpool-Boston-New York.

27.5.1926: First voyage London-Havre-Southampton-New York.

11.1927 to 2.1928: Refit included two new funnels.

25.7.1931: Last voyage London-Havre-Southampton-New York.

25.8.1931: Laid up in the Thames Estuary.

1932: Sold to Hughes Bolckow Shipbreaking Co. Ltd., Blyth.

22.4.1932: Arrived at Blyth for demolition.

27.11.1933: Register closed.

HMS *Carmania* was also dazzle-painted. *[J. and M. Clarkson collection]*

Franconia (above) and *Laconia* were smaller versions of *Caronia* and *Carmania*. They were also the first Cunard ships designed for winter cruising and the first to feature a gymnasium.

FRANCONIA (1) 1911-1916 Twin screw
O.N. 131315 18,150g 11,247n
600.3 x 71.4 x 40.4 feet.
Two Q.4-cyl. by Wallsend Slipway and
Engineering Co. Ltd., Wallsend; 2,175 HP,
18 knots.
Passengers: 250 first, 450 second, 2,200 third.
23.7.1910: Launched by Swan, Hunter and
Wigham Richardson Ltd., Wallsend (Yard
No. 857) as FRANCONIA.
4.2.1911: Registered at Liverpool under the
ownership of the Cunard Steam Ship Co.
Ltd., Liverpool.
25.2.1911: Left on maiden voyage from
Liverpool to New York. Later used on the
Liverpool to Boston route.
11.3.1911: Sailed from New York on first
Mediterranean cruise to French Riviera,
Italy and Egypt.
1.3.1912: Arrived at New York at the end
of a voyage from Alexandria to Trieste,
Palermo and Naples.
1915: Requisitioned by the British
Government as a troopship.
4.10.1916: Torpedoed and sunk by the
German submarine UB 47 195 miles east
of Malta in position 35°56′N, 18°30′E
whilst on a voyage from Alexandria to
Marseille. Twelve lives were lost.
3.11.1916: Register closed.

LACONIA (1) 1912-1917 Twin screw
O.N. 131412 18,099g 11,226n
600.6 x 71.4 x 40.4 feet.
Two Q.4-cyl. by Wallsend Slipway and
Engineering Co. Ltd., Wallsend; 2,175
HP, 18 knots.
Passengers: 250 first, 450 second, 2,000 third.

27.7.1911: Launched by Swan, Hunter and
Wigham Richardson Ltd., Wallsend (Yard
No. 877) as LACONIA.
12.1.1912: Registered at Liverpool under
the ownership of the Cunard Steam Ship Co.
Ltd., Liverpool.
20.1.1912: Left on maiden voyage from
Liverpool to New York. Later used on the
Liverpool to Boston route.
15.2.1913: Sailed from New York on first
Mediterranean cruise to French Riviera, Italy
and Egypt.
27.10.1914: Requisitioned by the British
Government as an armed merchant cruiser
and fitted with eight 6-inch guns.
24.11.1914: Commissioned at Liverpool as
HMS LACONIA.

16.12.1914: Left Portsmouth for South Africa
with stores, ammunition and three of the
Royal Navy's Short Folder aircraft. Joined the
Cape Squadron based at Simonstown.
4.1915-6.1915: Operated as troopship,
headquarters ship and patrol vessel during
the East African Campaign.
2.8.1916: Decommissioned.
9.9.1916: Resumed Liverpool to New York
service
25.2.1917: Torpedoed and sunk by the
German submarine U 50, 160 miles
from Fastnet Rock, Ireland, in position
52°0′N,13°40′W whilst on a voyage from
New York to Liverpool. Six crew and six
passengers lost their lives.
16.3.1917: Register closed.

Laconia and her sister were both sunk by German submarines during the First World War.

Albania inaugurated a new London-Southampton-Quebec-Montreal service.

In 1911, Cunard bought the three ships and the London-Southampton-Quebec-Montreal service of Thomson Line. These ships marked the start of Cunard sailings from London and Southampton and also the first use of A-names for Cunard Canadian service ships.

ALBANIA (1) 1911-1912 Twin screw
O.N. 110797 6,025g 3,960n;
1908: 7,682g 5,012n
461.5 x 52.1 x 31.1 feet.
T.3-cyl. by Thomas Richardson and Sons, Hartlepool; 800 HP, 11 knots.
Passengers:13; *1908*: 50 first, 800 third; *1911*: 50 second, 800 third; *1912*: cargo only.
3.2.1900: Launched by C.S. Swan and

Hunter Ltd., Wallsend (Yard No. 251) as CONSUELO. Designed as a North Atlantic freighter.
15.6.1900: Registered at Hull under the ownership of Thos. Wilson, Sons and Co. Ltd., Hull.
5.8.1900: Maiden voyage from Hull to New York.
21.5.1908: Registered at Newcastle under the ownership of the Cairn Line of Steamships Ltd. (Cairns, Noble and Co. Ltd., managers), Newcastle-upon-Tyne, renamed CAIRNRONA and operated under the Thomson Line banner.
1.1909: First voyage Newcastle-London-Portland, Maine (the winter terminus. In summer it was Montreal and Quebec).

31.3.1911: Acquired by the Cunard Steam Ship Co. Ltd., Liverpool.
28.4.1911: Registered at Liverpool under the ownership of the Cunard Steam Ship Co. Ltd., Liverpool as ALBANIA.
2.5.1911: Left on inaugural voyage London-Southampton-Quebec-Montreal. This was Cunard's first commercial sailing to the St. Lawrence River and the first to any Canadian port since December 1867.
24.6.1912: Registered at Glasgow under the ownership of Bank Line Ltd. (Andrew Weir and Co.), Glasgow as POLERIC. Converted into a cargo ship.
4.3.1929: Arrived at Osaka for demolition.
6.3.1929: Register closed.

Albania was sold after a year to Bank Line and became the cargo ship *Poleric*, shown here at Fowey, Cornwall.

All the Canadian *A*-ships, including *Ausonia*, were lost during the First World War.

AUSONIA (1) 1911-1918 Twin screw

O.N. 129735 7,907g 4,952n
450.6 x 54.2 x 37.3 feet.
T.3-cyl. by Palmers Shipbuilding and Iron Co. Ltd., Jarrow-on-Tyne; 750 HP, 12 knots.
Passengers: 37 first, 1,200 third; *1910*: 90 second, 1,200 third.

18.8.1909: Launched by Swan, Hunter and Wigham Richardson Ltd., Wallsend (Yard No. 837) as TORTONA.

14.10.1909: Registered at Newcastle under the ownership of the Cairn Line of Steamships Ltd. (Cairns, Noble and Co. Ltd., managers), Newcastle-upon-Tyne. Built for the emigrant trade between Italy and Canada and operated under the Thomson Line banner.

22.10.1909: Maiden voyage Middlesborough-Quebec-Montreal.

20.11.1909: First voyage Montreal-Quebec-Naples-Genoa-Leghorn.

28.5.1910: First voyage Montreal-Quebec-London.

18.8.1910: First voyage London-Southampton-Quebec-Montreal.

31.3.1911: Acquired by the Cunard Steam Ship Co. Ltd., Liverpool and subsequently renamed AUSONIA.

7.4.1911: Registered at Liverpool under the ownership of the Cunard Steam Ship Co. Ltd., Liverpool.

23.3.1917: Requisitioned by the British Government as a transport.

11.6.1917: Damaged in a torpedo attack by the German submarine U 55 in position 51°17′N,17°17′W whilst on voyage from Montreal to Avonmouth with general cargo. One life was lost.

30.5.1918: Torpedoed and sunk by the German submarine U 62 620 miles west of Fastnet Rock, Ireland, in position 47°59′N, 23°42′W whilst on voyage from Liverpool to New York. Forty four lives were lost.

14.6.1918: Register closed.

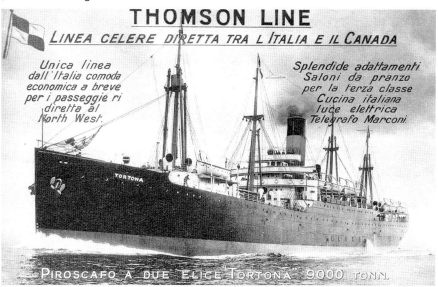

Ausonia was designed for the emigrant trade between Italy and Canada.

With emigrants on the foredeck, *Ausonia* is preparing to sail to Montreal from Southampton on 19th September 1911.

ASCANIA (1) 1911-1918 Twin screw

O.N. 131342 9,111g 5,699n
466.6 x 56.1 x 37.4 feet.
Two T.3-cyl. by Palmers
Shipbuilding and Iron Co. Ltd.,
Jarrow-on-Tyne; 978 HP, 16 knots.
Passengers: 140 second, 1,500 third.
4.3.1911: Launched by Swan,
Hunter and Wigham Richardson
Ltd., Wallsend (Yard No. 869)
for the Cairn Line of Steamships
Ltd. (Cairns, Noble and Co. Ltd.,
managers), Newcastle-upon-Tyne
as GERONA.
31.3.1911: Acquired by the Cunard
Steam Ship Co. Ltd., Liverpool
and renamed ASCANIA.
18.5.1911: Registered at Liverpool
under the ownership of the Cunard
Steam Ship Co. Ltd., Liverpool.
23.5.1911: Left on maiden voyage
from Southampton to Quebec and
Montreal.
Late 1914 to early 1915: Used at
Portsmouth with ANDANIA as
an accommodation ship housing
prisoners-of-war and internees.
13.6.1918: Wrecked 20 miles east
of Cape Ray, Newfoundland whilst
on a voyage from Liverpool to
Montreal in ballast.
16.1.1919: Register closed
'certificate lost on FLAVIA'.

ANDANIA (1) 1913-1918 Twin screw

O.N. 135481 13,405g 8,275n
520.3 x 64.0 x 43.1 feet.
Two Q.4-cyl. by Scotts'
Shipbuilding and Engineering
Co. Ltd., Greenock; 1,097 HP, 15
knots.
Passengers: 520 second, 1,620
third.
22.3.1913: Launched by Scotts'
Shipbuilding and Engineering Co.
Ltd., Greenock (Yard No. 446) as
ANDANIA.
14.7.1913: Registered at Liverpool
under the ownership of the Cunard
Steam Ship Co. Ltd., Liverpool.
14.7.1913: Left on maiden voyage
London-Southampton-Quebec-
Montreal.
Late 1914 to early 1915: Used at
Portsmouth with ASCANIA as
an accommodation ship housing
prisoners-of-war and internees.
27.4.1917: Requisitioned by the
British Government as a transport.
27.1.1918: Torpedoed and sunk by
the German submarine U 46 two
miles north north east of Rathlin
Island Lighthouse, Northern
Ireland in position 55°20′N,
06°12′W whilst on a voyage from
Liverpool to New York. Seven
lives were lost.
8.2.1918: Register closed.

Gerona was under construction when Thomson Line was bought by Cunard. Completed as *Ascania*, she was the first of the Canadian A-ships with two funnels.

Ascania underway. As she was originally intended for the Italy-Canada route, her promenade decks were not enclosed.

Andania was the first of a quartet ordered by Cunard for the Canadian service. Despite their relatively small size, they had two funnels and carried over 2,000 passengers. Here *Andania* is nearing completion at Scotts' yard. The battleship is *HMS Ajax*.

Andania (1) had a career of less than five years. [J. and M. Clarkson collection]

The second of the pre-First World War A-series, Alaunia (1) was in Cunard service for less than a year (middle). In the first photograph of her as a troopship she has her boats slung out (bottom) and in the second looking forward from aft of the mainmast (below).

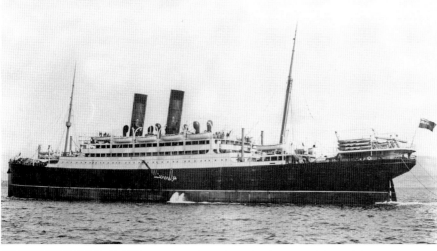

ALAUNIA (1) 1913-1916 Twin screw
O.N. 135513 13,405g 8,260n
520.3 x 64.0 x 43.1 feet.
Two Q.4-cyl. by Scotts' Shipbuilding and Engineering Co. Ltd., Greenock; 1,097 HP, 15 knots.
Passengers: 520 second, 1,620 third.
9.6.1913: Launched by Scotts' Shipbuilding and Engineering Co. Ltd., Greenock (Yard No.

447) as ALAUNIA.
5.11.1913: Registered at Liverpool under the ownership of the Cunard Steam Ship Co. Ltd., Liverpool.
27.11.1913: Left on maiden voyage Liverpool-Queenstown-Portland (Maine)-Boston.
9.1914: Requisitioned by the British Government as a troopship.
19.10.1916: Struck a mine and sank two miles

south of Royal Sovereign Light Vessel (near Eastbourne, Sussex) in position 50°41′N, 00°27′W whilst on a voyage from New York to London with general cargo. The mine had been laid earlier that day by the German submarine U 16. Two lives were lost. The wreck is the largest in Sussex waters and is a popular diving location.
4.11.1916: Register closed.

TRANSYLVANIA 1914-1915 Twin screw
O.N. 136331 14,315g 8,620n
548.8 x 66.6 x 41.7 feet.
Two sets of geared steam turbines by Scotts'
Shipbuilding and Engineering Co. Ltd.,
Greenock; 8,000 IHP, 14.5 knots. She was
the first large transatlantic liner fitted with
geared turbines.
Passengers: 263 first, 260 second, 1,858 third.
23.5.1914: Launched by Scotts' Shipbuilding
and Engineering Co. Ltd., Greenock (Yard
No. 451) as TRANSYLVANIA. She was
designed for an intended joint Cunard-Anchor
Line service between Mediterranean ports

and the United States, which never began
because of the outbreak of the First World
War. Her Anchor Line sister TUSCANIA
(14,348/1915) was sunk in 1918.
19.10.1914: Registered at Glasgow under
the ownership of the Cunard Steam Ship Co.
Ltd., Liverpool.
17.11.1914: Left on maiden voyage from
Liverpool to New York.
4.2.1915: Acquired by Anchor Line Ltd.
(Henderson Brothers), Glasgow.
26.3.1915: First voyage Glasgow-Liverpool-
New York for Anchor-Cunard joint service.
19.5.1915: Requisitioned by the British

Government as a troopship.
4.5.1917: Torpedoed and sunk by the German
submarine U 63, 2.5 miles south of Cape
Vado, Gulf of Genoa in position 44°15′N,
8°30′E whilst on voyage from Marseilles
to Alexandria with troops and government
stores. 402 troops and 12 crew, including her
master, were lost.
22.5.1917: Register closed.
7.10.2011: Her wreck was found by the
remotely operated vehicle PLUTO, close
to the island of Bergeggi at a depth of over
2,000 feet.

Transylvania was built for a joint Cunard-Anchor Mediterranean service to New York. She was the first large transatlantic liner fitted with geared turbines.

Folia is seen as *Principello* (above) and *Flavia* as *Campanello* (opposite top). Both started life as emigrant ships. *[Martin Lindenborn]*

AVONMOUTH ATLANTIC SERVICE
In 1916, Cunard bought Canadian Northern Steamships' four ships and its Avonmouth (Bristol) service to Quebec and Montreal. *Royal George* remained in service as a troopship, whilst the other three ships were given F-names and operated from Avonmouth to Canada and the United States until they were sunk by German submarines.

FOLIA 1916-1917 Twin screw
O.N. 136640 6,365g 4,040n;
1914: 6,705g 4,211n
430.0 x 52.7 x 25.0 feet.
Two T.3-cyl. by George Clark Ltd., Sunderland; 869 HP,14.5 knots.
Passengers: 120 first and 1,700 third;*1914:* 60 second, 1,900 third.
28.2.1907: Launched by Sir James Laing and Sons Ltd., Sunderland (Yard No. 623) for Lloyd Sabaudo S.A. di Nav., Genoa as PRINCIPE DI PIEMONTE. She was the final ship of a trio ordered for Lloyd Sabaudo's Genoa to New York immigrant service.
6.1907: Completed.
1.1914: Acquired by Canadian Northern Steamships Ltd., Toronto as a replacement for VOLTURNO (3,586/1906) which had been destroyed by fire mid-Atlantic with a large loss of life.
12.2.1914: Registered under the ownership of the Principello Steamships Ltd., Toronto (H.W. Harding, London, manager) as PRINCIPELLO. Harding was Company Secretary of Canadian Northern Steamships Ltd. Chartered to the Uranium Steam Ship Co. Ltd. for a Rotterdam-Halifax-New York passenger service.
10.1914: Transferred with CAMPANELLO to Royal Line's Avonmouth to Montreal service as replacements for ROYAL GEORGE and ROYAL EDWARD, which had been requisitioned as troopships. Royal Line was owned by Canadian Northern Steamships.
17.5.1916: Registered under the ownership of the Cunard Steam Ship Co. Ltd., Liverpool

and later renamed FOLIA, she remained on the London register.
11.3.1917: Torpedoed and sunk by the German submarine U 53 four miles east south east of Rame Head, County Waterford in position 51°51′N, 07°41′W whilst on a voyage New York to Avonmouth with general cargo. Seven lives were lost.
1917: Register closed.

FLAVIA 1916-1918 Twin screw
O.N. 115224 7,347g 4,693n
470.0 x 56.8 x 32.1 feet.
Two T.3-cyl. by Palmers Shipbuilding and Iron Co. Ltd., Jarrow; 800 HP, 12.5 knots.
Passengers: *1907:* 90 cabin, 2,200 third.
29.8.1901: Launched by Palmers Shipbuilding and Iron Co. Ltd., Jarrow (Yard No. 755) as BRITISH EMPIRE. She was one of a trio of cargo ships with 'tween deck space for emigrants or troops.
31.10.1901: Registered at Liverpool under the ownership of the British Shipowners' Co. Ltd., Liverpool. Operated on Phoenix Line's Antwerp to New York service.
5.1906: On the liquidation of British Shipowners' Co. Ltd., sold to Navigazione Generale Italiana, Genoa, Italy and renamed CAMPANIA. Refitted as an emigrant carrier by Cantieri Navali Riuniti, Genoa.
20.5.1906: British register closed.
30.10.1906: First voyage Genoa-Naples-River Plate.
3.1907: Placed on Genoa-Naples-Palermo-New York service.
1910: Sold to Canadian Northern Steamships Ltd., Toronto.
4.1910: Began operating under the British flag for the Rotterdam-Halifax-New York passenger service of Uranium Steam Ship Co. Ltd.
16.9.1910: Registered at London under the ownership of H.W. Harding (Company Secretary of Canadian Northern Steamships Ltd.), London as CAMPANELLO.
10.1914: Transferred to Royal Line's Avonmouth to Montreal service. Royal Line

was owned by Canadian Northern Steamships Ltd.
28.4.1915: Transfererred to Campanello Steamships Ltd. (Canadian Northern Steamships Ltd.), Toronto.
20.5.1916: Registered under the ownership of the Cunard Steam Ship Co. Ltd., Liverpool and later renamed FLAVIA, she remained on the London register.
3.6.1917: Requisitioned by the British Government as a transport.
24.8.1918: Torpedoed and sunk by the German submarine U 107, 30 miles north west by west of Tory Island, north west Ireland, in position 55°23′N, 09°40′W whilst on a voyage from Montreal to Avonmouth with general cargo and horses. One life was lost.
28.10.1918: Register closed.

FELTRIA 1916-1917
O.N. 98663 5,324g 3,410n
420.0 x 48.2 x 30.6 feet.
Q.4-cyl by William Denny and Co., Dumbarton; 627 HP, 13 knots.
Passengers: 80 first, 42 second, 400 third; *1908:* 80 first, 1,000 third.
9.6.1891: Launched by William Denny and Brothers, Dumbarton (Yard No. 448) as AVOCA.
20.8.1891: Registered at Glasgow under the ownership of the British India Associated Steamers Ltd., Glasgow.
8.1895: Bareboat chartered to Compañía Trasatlántica, Barcelona as a troopship to Cuba. She was placed under the Spanish flag as SAN FERNANDO.
8.8.1895: British register closed.
21.6.1897: Re-registered at Glasgow as AVOCA.
11.7.1899-2.10.1902: Chartered by the British Government during Boer War as Hospital Ship and Transport No. 6.
3.12.1903: Transferred to the British India Steam Navigation Co. Ltd., London.
29.5.1907: Sold to A/S Det Østasiatiske Kompagni (East Asiatic Co.), Copenhagen

Feltria, seen here as *Uranium*, was the oldest of the Canadian Northern ships. *[Martin Lindenborn collection]*

and later renamed ATLANTA.

17.6.1907: British register closed.

16.3.1908: Registered at London under the ownership of Robertson, Shankland and Co. Ltd., London as AVOCA for the New York and Continental Line's Rotterdam-Halifax-New York emigrant service.

17.5.1908: Collided in fog in the New Waterway with the German steamer NORDSEE (4,439/1907) which sank about three miles off the Hook of Holland with the loss of two lives including the pilot. AVOCA, which was on a voyage from the Hook of Holland to Hamburg, was badly damaged and L. Smit and Sons was engaged to salvage her.

8.1908: Arrested at Rotterdam.

11.1908: Sold at auction to C.G. Ashdown and Co., London.

8.2.1909: Registered under the ownership of the Uranium Steam Ship Co. Ltd., London and later renamed URANIUM. Her manager was William Petersen whilst mortgagee was William Mackenzie of the Canadian Northern Railway. Operated a Rotterdam-Halifax-New York service for North-West Transport Line.

4.1910: Rotterdam-Halifax-New York service now operated under the title of Uranium Steam Ship Co. Ltd.

6.1910: Manager became H.W. Harding, (Company Secretary of Canadian Northern Steamships Ltd.).

2.9.1914: Transferred to Canadian Northern Steamships Ltd., Toronto.

20.5.1916: Registered under the ownership of the Cunard Steam Ship Co. Ltd., Liverpool, and remained on the London register

3.6.1916. Renamed FELTRIA.

5.5.1917: Torpedoed and sunk by the German submarine UC 48 eight miles south east of Mine Head, southern Ireland in position 51°56´N, 07°24´W whilst on a voyage from New York to Avonmouth with general cargo. Forty five lives were lost.

1.6.1917: Register closed.

ROYAL GEORGE 1916-1922 Triple screw

O.N. 125643 10,897g 5,239n; *1910:* 11,145g 5,685n

525.8 x 60.2 x 27.0 feet.

Three steam turbines by the Fairfield Shipbuilding and Engineering Co. Ltd., Govan 18,000 SHP, 20.5 knots.

Passengers: 710 first, 290 second; *1910:* 344 first, 210 second, 560 third.

28.5.1907: Launched by the Fairfield Shipbuilding and Engineering Co. Ltd., Glasgow (Yard No. 449) as HELIOPOLIS. With her sister CAIRO, she was designed for a luxury express service between Marseilles and Alexandria.

10.10.1907: Registered at London under the ownership of the Egyptian Mail Steam Ship Co. Ltd., London.

2.1909: Egyptian Mail liquidated and ownership passed to the mortgagees, Fairfield Shipbuilding and Engineering Co. Ltd. Laid up at Marseilles.

1910: Sold with her sister to Canadian Northern Steamships Ltd., Toronto for use on Royal Line's fortnightly Avonmouth-Quebec-Montreal service. Converted by Fairfield for Atlantic service. To reduce top weight, most of the boat deck was removed and the funnels were shortened. Parts of the stern were

plated over to avoid the ship being pooped by following seas, whilst the forepeak was strengthened for navigation in ice.

14.3.1910: Renamed ROYAL GEORGE.

26.4.1910: Registered at Toronto under the ownership of Canadian Northern Steamships Ltd., Toronto.

1914: Requisitioned by the British Government as a troopship.

1916: Registered at London.

22.5.1916: Acquired by the Cunard Steam Ship Co. Ltd., Liverpool.

10.2.1919: Left on first voyage Liverpool-Halifax-New York.

30.2.1919: Registered at Liverpool.

5.8.1919: Left on first voyage Southampton-Halifax-New York.

1920: Used as a floating emigrant hotel at Cherbourg. Later laid up in the River Fal.

25.7.1922: Register closed.

14.8.1922: Towed to Wilhelmshaven for demolition.

AURANIA (2) 1917-1918 Twin screw

O.N. 137542 13,936g 8,499n

520.5 x 65.3 x 42.6 feet.

Two sets of geared steam turbines by Wallsend Slipway and Engineering Co. Ltd., Wallsend; 7,500 SHP, 14.5 knots.

Passengers: 506 second, 1,538 third.

16.7.1916: Launched by Swan, Hunter and Wigham Richardson Ltd., Wallsend (Yard No. 965) as AURANIA. She was a near sister to ANDANIA and ALAUNIA.

19.3.1917: Registered at Liverpool under the ownership of the Cunard Steam Ship Co. Ltd., Liverpool.

28.3.1917: Left on maiden voyage from the Tyne to New York.

Royal George in Cunard colours (below) and as *Heliopolis* (above). Note the changes to her stern. She did not fit into the post-war fleet and was laid up.

4.2.1918: Torpedoed and badly damaged by the German submarine UB 67, 15 miles north west of Inishtrahull, north of Ireland whilst on a voyage from Liverpool to New York. Eight lives were lost. Taken in tow by a trawler but stranded near Tobermory, Isle of Mull and became a constructive total loss. *23.5.1918*: Register closed.

Right: *Aurania*, the third of the A-class, was completed during the war. She was less than a year old when she sank following an attack by a German submarine. She differed from the earlier pair by having a raised forecastle.

ALBANIA (2) 1920-1930 Twin screw
O.N. 143704 12,768g 7,822n
523.1 x 64.0 x 43.9 feet.
Two sets of geared steam turbines by Scotts Shipbuilding and Engineering Co. Ltd., Greenock; 6,800 SHP, 13 knots.
Passengers: 480 cabin; *1930*: 130 first, 30 second.
6.1916: Ordered as the fourth A-class ship, work suspended for the duration of the war.
1919: When work recommenced, she was redesigned as a cargo-passenger ship.
17.4.1920: Launched by Scotts' Shipbuilding and Engineering Co. Ltd., Greenock (Yard No. 479) as ALBANIA.
21.12.1920: Registered at Liverpool under the ownership of the Cunard Steam Ship Co.

Ltd., Liverpool.
19.1.1921: Left on maiden voyage from Liverpool to New York.
27.8.1925: Left on last voyage London-Southampton-Cherbourg-New York. Laid up.
3.1930: Sold to Navigazione Libera Triestina S.A., Trieste, Italy and refitted at the Arsenale Triestino shipyard. Renamed CALIFORNIA, she was placed on the Italy to west coast U.S.A. service.
5.3.1930: Register closed.
11.12.1930: Left on first voyage from Genoa to Seattle.
10.6.1934: Laid up at Genoa.
3-10.1935: Used as a troopship during the Italian invasion of Ethiopia.
1937: Following the Italian Government's

reorganisation of shipping companies, Navigazione Libera Triestina was dissolved and the fleet was divided between Lloyd Triestino S.A. di Navigazione, Trieste and 'Italia', depending on the routes on which the vessels were employed. CALIFORNIA was allocated to Lloyd Triestino.
13.6.1940: Requisitioned by the Royal Italian Navy at Naples and became a hospital ship.
10-11.8.1941: Beached to prevent sinking in Syracuse harbour after being hit by an aerial torpedo from a RAF aircraft, she subsequently caught fire and suffered structural damage from the swell.
13.10.1941: Salvage attempts were abandoned. Later refloated and broken up.

Albania, the last of the pre-war A-class, was completed as a cargo-passenger ship, hence the four masts and cargo handling gear.

Sold to Navigazione Libera Triestina, *Albania* was renamed *California* and operated between Italy and the U.S. west coast. *[J. and M. Clarkson collection]*

Scythia, the first of the large post-war intermediate liners, was also the longest lasting, and remained in the fleet for 36 years.

SCYTHIA CLASS

Between 1921 and 1925 a new class of five large, oil-fired, intermediate liners were built to replace war losses. These ships were single funnel, enlarged but slower versions of the pre-war *Franconia* and *Laconia*.

SCYTHIA (2) 1921-1957 Twin screw

O.N. 143730 19,730g 11,938n
600.7 x 73.8 x 40.7 feet.
Two sets of geared steam turbines by Vickers Ltd., Barrow-in-Furness; 12,500 SHP, 16 knots.
Passengers: 337 first, 331 second, 1,538 third; *1924*: third reduced; *1928*: cabin, tourist, third; *1940*: 4,800 troops; *1950*: 248 first, 630 tourist.
23.3.1920: Launched by Vickers Ltd., Barrow-in-Furness (Yard No. 493) as SCYTHIA. Completion was delayed by shipyard strikes.
17.3.1921: Registered at Liverpool under the ownership of the Cunard Steam Ship Co. Ltd., Liverpool.
3-7.1921: Because of more shipyard strikes, fitted out at Lorient by Société des Ateliers Lorientais
20.8.1921: Left on maiden voyage from Liverpool to New York.
5.7.1934: Transferred to Cunard White Star Ltd., Liverpool.
29.10.1940-30.8.1948: Requisitioned by the Ministry of Shipping (Ministry of War Transport from *5.1941*) as a troopship.
23.11.1942: Seriously damaged by an aerial torpedo off Algiers during Operation Torch. Subsequently repaired at Gibraltar and New York.
10.1948-10.1949: Used with SAMARIA by the International Refugee Organisation and Canadian Government to carry emigrants on Cuxhaven-Havre-Quebec (summer) and Halifax (winter) austerity service.
11.1949-8.1950: Refit by John Brown & Co. Ltd., Clydebank.

Scythia was almost lost off North Africa during Operation Torch when she was hit by an aerial torpedo. This photograph was taken shortly after the attack.

Scythia leaving Malta in March 1948 as a troopship. *[Ships in Focus]*

22.12.1949: Transferred to the Cunard Steam Ship Co. Ltd., Liverpool.
1.1.1950: Owners restyled as the Cunard Steam-Ship Co. Ltd., Liverpool.
17.8.1950: First voyage after refit Liverpool-Quebec-London.
10.4.1951: Inaugurated Southampton-Havre-Quebec service.

22.12.1957: Arrived Southampton at the end of last voyage Halifax-Havre-Rotterdam-Southampton.
20.1.1958: After sale to British Iron and Steel Corporation (BISCO), arrived Inverkeithing for demolition by Thos. W. Ward Ltd., Sheffield,
23.5.1958: Register closed.

Samaria, seen approaching Liverpool Landing Stage, was the second in the new series and, like her sisters, made at least one cruise during the winter months. *[B. and A. Feilden/J. and M. Clarkson]*

SAMARIA (2) 1922-1956 Twin screw
O.N. 145923 19,602g 11,866n
601.5 x 73.7 x 40.7 feet.
Two sets of geared steam turbines by Cammell
Laird and Co. Ltd., Birkenhead; 12,500 SHP,
16 knots.
Passengers: 350 first, 340 second, 1,422 third;
1924: third reduced; *1929*: cabin, tourist, third;
1940: 4,450 troops; *1951*: 245 first, 641 tourist.
27.11.1920: Launched by Cammell Laird
and Co. Ltd., Birkenhead (Yard No. 836) as
SAMARIA. Completion was delayed by
shipyard strikes.
1.4.1922: Registered at Liverpool under the
ownership of the Cunard Steam Ship Co. Ltd.,
Liverpool.
19.4.1922: Left on maiden voyage from
Liverpool to Boston.
24.1-31.5.1923: First world cruise from New
York. Passenger capacity limited to 400.
5.7.1934: Transferred to Cunard White Star
Ltd., Liverpool.
13.12.1940-18.8.1948: Requisitioned by
the Ministry of Shipping (Ministry of War
Transport from *5.1941*) as a troopship.
9.1948-1950: Used with SCYTHIA by the
International Refugee Organisation and
Canadian Government to carry emigrants
on Cuxhaven-Havre-Quebec (summer) and
Halifax (winter) austerity service.
22.12.1949: Transferred to the Cunard Steam
Ship Co. Ltd., Liverpool.
1.1.1950: Owners restyled as the Cunard
Steam-Ship Co. Ltd., Liverpool.
3.1.1951-6.1951: Refit by John Brown & Co.
Ltd., Clydebank.
14.6.1951: First voyage after refit, Liverpool-
Quebec-Southampton.
12.7.1951: Placed on Southampton-Havre-
Quebec service.

Leaving Cape Town with troops in January 1946. *[Ships in Focus]*

Partially demolished at Inverkeithing.

15.6.1953: Took part in the Coronation Fleet Review at Spithead.
23.11.1955: Last voyage Quebec-Havre-Southampton.
27.1.1956: After sale to British Iron and Steel Corporation (BISCO), arrived at Inverkeithing for demolition by Thos. W. Ward Ltd.
23.8.1957: Register closed.

LACONIA (2) 1922-1942 Twin screw
O.N. 145925 19,679g 11,829n
601.3 x 73.7 x 40.6 feet.
Two sets of geared steam turbines by Wallsend Slipway and Engineering Co. Ltd., Wallsend; 12,500 SHP, 16 knots.
Passengers: 350 first, 350 second, 1,500 third; *1924*: third reduced; *1928*: cabin, tourist, third.
9.4.1921: Launched by Swan, Hunter and Wigham Richardson Ltd., Wallsend (Yard No. 1125) as LACONIA. Launch was delayed for five months because berth was blocked by the capsized wreck of MEDUANA (10,123/1923) which caught fire whilst fitting out in November 1920.
10.4.1922: Registered at Liverpool under the ownership of the Cunard Steam Ship Co. Ltd., Liverpool.
25.5.1922: Left on maiden voyage from Southampton to New York.
21.11.1922-30.3.1923: Departed New York, on charter to American Express for the first world cruise by a passenger ship. She was not only the first vessel to circumnavigate the globe using a gyro-compass but also the first British ship to steer across the Atlantic using an automatic Sperry gyro-pilot.
5.7.1934: Transferred to Cunard White Star Ltd., Liverpool.
25.8.1939: Last voyage from New York to Liverpool.
5.9.1939: Requisitioned by the British Government as an armed merchant cruiser. Converted at Portsmouth and fitted with eight 6-inch guns.
1.1940: Commissioned as HMS LACONIA.
25.9.1941: Paid off at Birkenhead and converted to a troopship.
12.9.1942: Torpedoed and sunk by the German submarine U 156 in position 5°05′S, 11°38′W whilst on a voyage from Cape Town to Freetown with approximately 2,741* persons aboard including crew, passengers, military personnel and about 1,800 Italian prisoners-of-war. U-boats attempted a rescue and were attacked by U.S. anti-submarine aircraft. As a result, Admiral Dönitz, Commander-in-Chief of the U-boat arm, issued an order, known as the 'Laconia order', that U-boats were not to run risks by rescuing survivors. Approximately 1,658* lives were lost.
30.12.1942: Register closed.

*With no official British Government report on the sinking, the published numbers vary considerably.

Probably in the 1920s, *Laconia*'s black hull colour scheme was extended upwards by almost one deck. *[B. and A. Feilden/J. and M. Clarkson]*

Laconia alongside the landing stage at Liverpool. In 1923 *she* made the first world cruise by a passenger ship

In the 1930s *Laconia*'s hull colour scheme was again changed. *[B. and A. Feilden/J. and M. Clarkson]*

FRANCONIA (2) 1923-1956 Twin screw
O.N. 147216 20,158g 12,185n
601.3 x 73.8 x 40.7 feet.
Two sets of geared steam turbines by John
Brown & Co. Ltd., Clydebank; 13,500 SHP,
16 knots.
Passengers: 330 first, 420 second, 950
third (804 single class cruising);*1930*: first,
tourist, third; *1931*: cabin, tourist, third;
1939: 3,950 troops;*1949*: 253 first, 600
tourist.
8.1919: Laid down but work was suspended
in 1920 because of high building costs.
21.10.1922: Launched by John Brown &
Co. Ltd., Clydebank (Yard No. 492) as
FRANCONIA. Accommodation modified
during construction to make her the world's
first purpose-built transatlantic and world-
wide cruise liner.
22.5.1923: Registered at Liverpool under
the ownership of the Cunard Steam Ship Co.
Ltd., Liverpool.
23.6.1923: Left on maiden voyage from
Liverpool to New York.
15.11.1923-27.3.1924: First world cruise
from New York. Passenger capacity limited
to 400.
1923-1933: Winter cruising from New York.
At the end of this period, she was given a
white livery.
11.7.-23.10.1931: After the fire aboard
its flagship BERMUDA (19,086/1927),
chartered by Furness Bermuda Line for 15
round voyages New York-Bermuda-New
York. Funnel painted in Furness Withy and
Co. Ltd. colours. At the end of the charter,
replaced by CARINTHIA
27.8.-10.1932: Chartered by Furness
Bermuda Line for ten round voyages New
York-Bermuda-New York.
20.6.1934: First voyage London-
Southampton-New York.
5.7.1934: Transferred to Cunard White Star
Ltd., Liverpool.
6.1935: Resumed Liverpool to New York
service.
21.9.1939-2.9.1948: Requisitioned by the
Ministry of Shipping (Ministry of War
Transport from *5.1941*) as a troopship.
4-11.2.1945: Headquarters and
communications ship for Winston Churchill
and the British delegation to the Yalta
Conference in the Crimea.
9.1948-22.5.1949: Post-war refit by John
Brown & Co. Ltd., Clydebank.
2.6.1949: First post-refit voyage from
Liverpool to Quebec.
22.12.1949: Transferred to the Cunard Steam
Ship Co. Ltd., Liverpool.
1.1.1950: Owners restyled as the Cunard
Steam-Ship Co. Ltd., Liverpool.
22.7.1955: First voyage Southampton-
Havre-Quebec.
16.11.1956: Final voyage from Liverpool to
New York.
18.12.1956: After sale to British Iron
and Steel Corporation (BISCO), arrived
Inverkeithing for demolition by Thos.W.
Ward Ltd., Sheffield.
22.8.1957: Register closed.

Franconia, seen approaching Port Melbourne, Australia, was the world's first
purpose-built transatlantic and world-wide cruise liner. *[Allen Green/Russell Priest]*

With a white hull, *Franconia* operated from London in 1934 and 1935.

Leaving Cape Town as a troopship in January 1946.

Carinthia berthed on Prince's Pier, Port Melbourne with a P.&O. liner on the opposite side. Because *Franconia*'s design was modified during construction, *Carinthia* became Cunard's first specially-designed dual-purpose transatlantic liner and world-wide cruise ship. *[Allen Green/Russell Priest collection]*

CARINTHIA (2) 1925-1940 Twin screw
O.N. 147318 20,277g 12,088n
600.7 x 73.8 x 40.8 feet.
Two sets of geared steam turbines by Vickers Ltd., Barrow-in-Furness; 13,500 SHP, 16 knots.
Passengers: 331 first, 473 second, 806 third (804 single class cruising); *1930*: first, tourist, third; *1931*: cabin, tourist, third.
3.1921: Laid down as SERVIA but work was suspended because of high building costs.
24.2.1925: Launched by Vickers Ltd., Barrow-in-Furness (Yard No. 586) as CARINTHIA. She was Cunard's first specially designed dual-purpose transatlantic liner and world-wide cruise ship.

21.7.1925: Registered at Liverpool under the ownership of the Cunard Steam Ship Co. Ltd., Liverpool.
22.8.1925: Left on maiden voyage from Liverpool to New York.
Winter 1925-1926: Based in New York for cruises to the Caribbean and a world cruise. This was the pattern for much of her pre-war career. In 1932 she was given a white livery.
24.10.1931-3.1.1932: Chartered by Furness Bermuda Line for nine round voyages New York-Bermuda-New York.
25.5.1934: First voyage London-Southampton-New York.
5.7.1934: Transferred to Cunard White Star Ltd., Liverpool.

5.1935: Resumed Liverpool to New York service.
3.9.1939: Last voyage from New York to Liverpool.
17.9.1939: Requisitioned by the British Government as an armed merchant cruiser and converted at Liverpool. Fitted with eight 6-inch guns.
12.1939: Commissioned as HMS CARINTHIA.
6.6.1940: Torpedoed by the German submarine U 46 in position 53°13′N, 10°40′W whilst on patrol off the coast of Ireland, with the loss of four lives. Taken in tow but sank the following day.
14.7.1941: Register closed.

Photographed on the Mersey on 10th August 1935 *Carinthia* had been painted white with green boot-topping in 1932. *[B. and A. Feilden/J. and M. Clarkson]*

Lancastria was designed for a joint Cunard-Anchor Line Mediterranean to New York service. She was also Cunard's first ship with a cruiser stern. She is shown here at Boston in February 1929. *[Richard Hildebrand/W.A.Schell collection]*

TYRRHENIA/LANCASTRIA 1922-1940 Twin screw
O.N. 145943 16,243g 9,645n
552.8 x 70.4 x 38.8 feet.
Two sets of steam turbines by William Beardmore and Co. Ltd., Glasgow; 12,500 SHP, 16.2 knots.
Passengers: 280 first, 364 second, 1,200 third; *1924*: 580 cabin, 1,200 third.
31.5.1920: Launched by William Beardmore and Co. Ltd., Glasgow (Yard No. 495) as TYRRHENIA. Designed for a joint Cunard-Anchor Line Mediterranean-New York service, she was Cunard's first ship with a cruiser stern. A replacement for TRANSYLVANIA, her completion was delayed because of a shipyard strike.
9.6.1922: Registered at Liverpool under the ownership of the Cunard Steam Ship Co. Ltd., Liverpool.
13.6.1922: Left on maiden voyage Glasgow-Quebec-Montreal.
7.1922: First voyage from Liverpool to Boston.
19.10.1922: Left on first voyage Liverpool to New York.
15.2.1924: Renamed LANCASTRIA.
5.7.1934: Transferred to Cunard White Star Ltd., Liverpool.
4.1940: Requisitioned as a troopship.
17.6.1940: Bombed and sunk in Charpentier Roads, St. Nazaire during the evacuation of British troops and civilian refugees from France. It is estimated that there were over 6,000 men, women and children aboard, of whom 2,477 were saved.
15.7.1941: Register closed.

Lancastria took part in the Jubilee Naval Review at Spithead on 16th July 1935. Note that her black hull colour scheme has been reduced by one deck.

The sinking of *Lancastria* was one of the world's worst maritime disasters. About ten minutes after she was hit, she heeled over onto her port side and sank.

Andania originally had her black hull colour scheme carried one deck higher.

NEW A-CLASS

The six A-class liners of the 1920s were smaller versions of the *Scythia*-class and carried only cabin and third class passengers. With relatively plain accommodation, they were designed primarily to carry emigrants to Canada.

ANDANIA (2) 1922-1940 Twin screw

O.N. 145934 13,950g 8,391n
520.2 x 65.4 x 39.3 feet.
Two sets of geared steam turbines by Hawthorn Leslie and Co. Ltd., Newcastle-upon-Tyne; 8,500 SHP, 15 knots.
Passengers: 484 cabin, 1,222 third; *1928*: cabin, tourist, third.
1.11.1921: Launched by Hawthorn Leslie and Co. Ltd., Newcastle-upon-Tyne (Yard No. 500) as ANDANIA.
22.5.1922: Registered at Liverpool under the ownership of the Cunard Steam Ship Co. Ltd., Liverpool.
1.6.1922: Left on maiden voyage London-Southampton-Quebec-Montreal.
18.11.1924: First voyage Hamburg-Southampton-Halifax-New York.
29.4.1927: First voyage Liverpool-Greenock-Belfast-Quebec-Montreal on a joint Anchor-Donaldson Line service.
1932-1934: Laid up.
5.7.1934: Transferred to Cunard White Star Ltd., Liverpool.
11.8.1939: Last voyage Liverpool-Greenock-Belfast-Quebec-Montreal.
5.9.1939: Requisitioned by the British Government as an armed merchant cruiser.
13.9. to 28.10.1939: Converted by Cammell Laird and Co. Ltd., at Birkenhead. Fitted with eight 6-inch guns.
9.11.1939: Commissioned as HMS ANDANIA.
16.6.1940: Torpedoed and sunk by the German submarine UA whilst on patrol 230 miles west north west of the Faroe Islands in position 62°36′N, 15°09′W. Her entire crew was rescued by the Icelandic trawler SKALLAGRIMUR (403/1920).
12.7.1941: Register closed.

Andania was the first of a new *A*-class of Canadian liners.

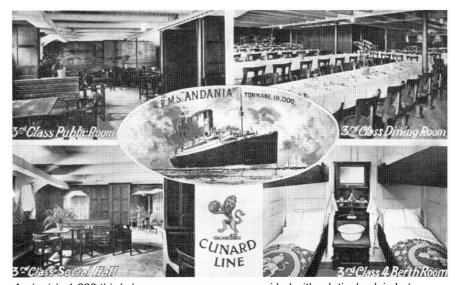

Andania's 1,222 third class passengers were provided with relatively plain but comfortable accommodation.

ANTONIA 1922-1942 Twin screw

O.N. 145937 13,867g 8,445n
519.9 x 65.3 x 39.1 feet.
Two sets of geared steam turbines by Vickers Ltd., Barrow-in-Furness; 8,500 SHP, 15 knots.

Passengers: 510 cabin, 1,178 third; *1927*: cabin, tourist, third.
11.3.1921: Launched by Vickers Ltd., Barrow-in-Furness (Yard No. 498) as ANTONIA.

Andania and *Antonia*, the latter seen here at Torbay during a cruise in the 1930s, operated mainly on the joint Anchor-Donaldson Line Liverpool-Greenock-Belfast-Quebec-Montreal service.

26.5.1922: Registered at Liverpool under the ownership of the Cunard Steam Ship Co. Ltd., Liverpool.

15.6.1922: Left on maiden voyage London-Southampton-Quebec-Montreal.

14.4.1927: First voyage Liverpool-Greenock-Belfast-Quebec-Montreal on joint Anchor-Donaldson Line service.

5.7.1934: Transferred to Cunard White Star Ltd., Liverpool.

30.5.1940: Last voyage Liverpool-Quebec-Montreal.

11.10.1940: Requisitioned by the Ministry of Shipping as a troopship.

23.3.1942: Acquired by the British Government and converted at Portsmouth into a fleet repair ship.

26.3.1942: Register closed.

19.8.1942: Commissioned as HMS WAYLAND (pendant number F137).

31.5.1946: Paid off at Chatham.

21.11.1946: Laid up in the River Dart.

22.1.1948: Sold to the British Iron and Steel Corporation (BISCO) for demoliton.

25.5.1948: Sailed from Dartmouth for Cairnryan, Scotland for destoring and removal of fittings.

2.1949: Arrived at Troon for demolition by the West of Scotland Shipbreaking Co. Ltd.

Four of the A-class became fleet repair ships for the Royal Navy. Here is HMS *Wayland,* ex *Antonia.*

The remaining four A-class ships were used regularly on the London-Southampton-Quebec-Montreal route, which also went via Havre. Here is *Ausonia* on the River Thames.

AUSONIA (2) 1922-1942 Twin screw
O.N. 145970 13,912g 8,527n
520.0 x 65.3 x 39.1 feet.
Two sets of geared steam turbines by Armstrong, Whitworth and Co. Ltd., Walker-on-Tyne; 8,500 SHP, 15 knots.
Passengers: 484 cabin, 1,222 third; *1927*: cabin, tourist, third; *1939*: cabin, third.
22.3.1921: Launched by Armstrong, Whitworth and Co. Ltd., Walker-on-Tyne (Yard No. 970) as AUSONIA.
19.8.1922: Registered at Liverpool under the ownership of the Cunard Steam Ship Co. Ltd., Liverpool.
31.8.1922: Left on maiden voyage Liverpool-

Quebec-Montreal.
21.4.1923: First voyage London-Southampton-Quebec-Montreal.
5.7.1934: Transferred to Cunard White Star Ltd., Liverpool.
18.8.1939: Last voyage London-Havre-Southampton-Quebec-Montreal.
6.9.1939: Requisitioned by the British Government as an armed merchant cruiser and converted on the Tyne by Vickers-Armstrongs Ltd. Fitted with eight 6-inch guns.
8.11.1939: Commissioned as HMS AUSONIA.
3.6.1942: Acquired by the British Government for use as a fleet repair ship.
9.6.1942: Register closed.

2.5.1944: Recommissioned as HMS AUSONIA (pendant number F53, later F153). Conversion work at Portsmouth took two years to complete.
1945: Laid up in the Gareloch.
1947-1948: In Reserve Fleet at Chatham.
1951-1954: Refit at Chatham included new boilers.
16.9.1958: Recommissioned as a fleet repair ship (pendant number A153) for Mediterranean fleet, based at Malta. She replaced the former P&O liner HMS RANPURA (16,601/1925).
9.1964: Laid up at Portsmouth.
13.9.1965: Left Portsmouth for demolition at Castellon, Spain.

Ausonia became the fleet repair ship HMS *Ausonia* in 1942. This is a post-war view of her carrying pendant number A153.

Aurania loading in the Greenland Dock, London in the 1930s.

AURANIA (3) 1924-1942 Twin screw
O.N. 147277 13,984g 8,473n
519.9 x 65.4 x 39.3 feet.
Two sets of geared steam turbines by
Wallsend Slipway and Engineering Co. Ltd.,
Wallsend; 8,500 SHP, 15 knots.
Passengers: 520 cabin, 1,042 third; *1927*:
cabin, tourist, third; *1939*: cabin, third.
6.2.1924: Launched by Swan, Hunter and
Wigham Richardson Ltd., Wallsend (Yard
No. 1127) as AURANIA.
27.8.1924: Registered at Liverpool under
the ownership of the Cunard Steam Ship Co.
Ltd., Liverpool.

13.9.1924: Left on maiden voyage from
Liverpool to New York.
13.3.1928: First voyage London-
Southampton-Quebec-Montreal.
5.7.1934: Transferred to Cunard White Star
Ltd., Liverpool.
4.8.1939: Last voyage London-Havre-
Southampton-Quebec-Montreal.
29.8.1939: Requisitioned by the British
Government as an armed merchant cruiser
and converted at Wallsend by her builders.
Fitted with eight 6-inch guns.
15.10.1939: Commissioned as HMS
AURANIA.

21.10.1941: Damaged by a torpedo whilst on
a voyage from Halifax to the Clyde in convoy.
11.1941-2.1942: Repaired on the Clyde.
9.3.1942: Acquired by the British
Government for use as a heavy repair ship
and converted at Devonport.
26.3.1942: Register closed
10.5.1944: Commissioned as HMS
ARTIFEX (pendant number F128).
Conversion work took two years to
complete.
1946: Laid up in the Gareloch.
8.12.1960: Sold to Italian shipbreakers.
7.1.1961: Left Rosyth under tow for La Spezia.

Aurania was commissioned as HMS *Artifex* in 1944.

ASCANIA (2) 1925-1956 Twin screw

O.N. 147307 14,013g 8,437n
520.0 x 65.4 x 39.2 feet.
Two sets of geared steam turbines by Armstrong, Whitworth and Co. Ltd., Walker-on-Tyne; 8,500 SHP, 15 knots.
Passengers: 520 cabin, 928 third; *1927*: cabin, tourist, third; *1939*: cabin, third; *1950*: 198 first, 498 tourist.
20.12.1923: Launched by Armstrong, Whitworth and Co. Ltd., Newcastle (Yard No. 971) as ASCANIA.
Early1924: Work ceased for a number of months because of industrial problems.
17.4.1925: Registered at Liverpool under the ownership of the Cunard Steam Ship Co. Ltd., Liverpool.
22.5.1925: Left on maiden voyage London-Southampton-Quebec-Montreal.
5.7.1934: Transferred to Cunard White Star Ltd., Liverpool.
24.8.1939: Requisitioned by the British Government as an armed merchant cruiser and converted at Birkenhead. Fitted with eight 6-inch guns.
16.10.1939: Commissioned as HMS ASCANIA (pendant number F68).
5.10.1942: Arrived at Southampton for conversion into a troopship.
1943: Converted into an infantry landing ship and subsequently took part in the invasion of Italy and the Normandy landings.
6.1945: Reverted to a troopship.
25.11.1947: Released from war service.
20.12.1947: Resumed Cunard's Liverpool to Halifax service with austerity accommodation.
22.12.1949: Transferred to the Cunard Steam Ship Co. Ltd., Liverpool.
1.1.1950: Owners restyled as the Cunard Steam-Ship Co. Ltd., Liverpool.
21.4.1950: After refit resumed Liverpool-Quebec-Montreal service.
30.9.1955: Reverted to Southampton-Havre-Quebec-Montreal.
26.10.1956: Final voyage Southampton-Havre-Quebec-Montreal.
23.11.1956: Left Southampton for Cyprus as a troopship.
1956: Sold to the British Iron and Steel Corporation (BISCO).
1.1.1957: Arrived at Newport, Monmouthshire from Southampton for demolition by John Cashmore Ltd.
19.6.1957: Register closed.

A snowy scene in December 1923, not long before *Ascania*'s launch. Because of strikes she was completed only in 1925.

As with other members of the A class *Ascania* was painted white for cruising.
[B. and A. Feilden/J. and M. Clarkson]

Ascania, photographed sailing from Montreal, was the only A class ship which returned to the fleet after the war.

Alaunia, the last A class ship, was delivered in July 1925, more than five years after she had been laid down.

ALAUNIA (2) 1925-1944 Twin screw
O.N. 147315 14,147g 8,528n
519.6 x 65.2 x 39.2 feet.
Two sets of geared geared steam turbines by
John Brown & Co. Ltd., Clydebank; 8,500 SHP,
15 knots.
Passengers: 414 cabin, 1,152 third; *1927*: cabin,
tourist, third; *1939*: cabin, third.
4.1920: Laid down but work was suspended
because of of high building costs.
7.2.1925: Launched by John Brown & Co. Ltd.,
Clydebank (Yard No. 495) as ALAUNIA.
2.7.1925: Registered at Liverpool under the
ownership of the Cunard Steam Ship Co. Ltd.,
Liverpool.
24.7.1925: Left Liverpool on maiden voyage to
Quebec and Montreal.
28.5.1926: First voyage London-Southampton-
Quebec-Montreal.
5.7.1934: Transferred to Cunard White Star Ltd.,
Liverpool.
24.8.1939: Requisitioned by the British
Government as an armed merchant cruiser and
converted at Gibraltar. Fitted with eight 6-inch guns.
27.9.1939: Commissioned as HMS ALAUNIA.
17.5.1944: Paid off.
8.12.1944: Acquired by the British Government
for use as a heavy repair ship and converted at
Devonport.
6.1.1945: Register closed.
21.8.1945: Recommissioned as HMS ALAUNIA
(pendant number F15). Used mainly as a static
training ship for engineering personnel.
10.9.1957: After sale to the British Iron and
Steel Corporation (BISCO), arrived at Blyth for
demolition by Hughes, Bolckow Shipbreaking
Co. Ltd.

LAURENTIC 1934-1940 - see page 137
BRITANNIC 1934-1960 - see page 139
GEORGIC 1934-1942 - see page 140

Like the rest of the A class ships, *Alaunia*'s black hull colour scheme was later reduced by one deck.

After a period as an armed merchant cruiser, *Alaunia* became the heavy repair ship HMS *Alaunia*.

114

A series of pictures from *Mauretania's* early days. *Mauretania* was launched by Lady Bates, wife of Cunard's chairman, Sir Percy Bates. We see the ship on the slipway and after she took to the water. Several tugs then towed her into Cammell Laird's basin to be fitted out. The fifth shows her on the landing stage at Liverpool, not dated, but judging by the bunting it was taken prior to her maiden voyage which commenced on 17th June 1939. The last picture is of her first visit to the Thames, dated 12th August 1939 – the day she sailed on her first voyage from London to New York.

MAURETANIA (2) 1939-1965 Twin screw
O.N 166267 35,739g 20,170n
739.4 x 89.4 x 51.7 feet.
Two sets of steam turbines by Cammell
Laird and Co. Ltd., Birkenhead; 42,000 SHP,
22 knots.
Passengers: 486 cabin, 390 tourist, 502 third;
1947: 475 first, 368 cabin, 304 tourist.
28.7.1938: Launched by Cammell Laird
and Co. Ltd., Birkenhead (Yard No. 1029)
as MAURETANIA. The largest ship yet
built in England. Designed for London-
Southampton-New York service.
31.5.1939: Registered at Liverpool under
the ownership of Cunard White Star Ltd.,
Liverpool.
17.6.1939: Left on maiden voyage from
Liverpool to New York.

12.8.1939: First voyage London-
Southampton-New York. The largest ship yet
to enter the Thames.
12.1939: Laid up in New York.
6.3.1940: Requisitioned by the Ministry of
Shipping, London as a troopship.
20.3.1940: Sailed for Sydney for conversion
into a troopship. The company code name
for the ship was MEDEA.
9.9.1946-15.4.1947: Post-war refit at
Liverpool by Cammell Laird and Co. Ltd.
26.4.1947: First post-war voyage from
Liverpool to New York.
10.6.1947: Southampton-Cherbourg-New
York service.
22.12.1949: Transferred to the Cunard Steam
Ship Co. Ltd., Liverpool.
1.1.1950: Owners restyled as the Cunard

Steam-Ship Co. Ltd., Liverpool.
10-12.1957: Refit including air-conditioning
throughout the ship.
10.1962: Painted in 'cruising green' and
used extensively as a cruise ship.
28.3.1963: First voyage on new passenger-
cargo service New York-Cannes-Genoa-
Naples.
10.1963: Poor passenger numbers led to the
cancellation of the service.
4.8.1965: Final voyage from Southampton to
New York.
10.11.1965: Arrived Southampton at the end
of her final cruise to the Mediteranean.
23.11.1965: Arrived Inverkeithing for
demolition by Thos. W. Ward Ltd., Sheffield.
3.10.1967: Register closed.

Opposite page, top: the second
Mauretania was the largest Cunard
intermediate ship. She was ordered as the
first of a pair of large liners for the London-
Southampton-New York service. Her
profile was similar to *Queen Elizabeth* and
she was also designed as a replacement
liner when either of the *Queens* was taken
out of service for annual refit.

Opposite page, bottom: *Mauretania*
played a major role as a troopship during
the Second World War and carried over
300,000 troops during the war years. As
a troopship, she was heavily armed with
guns on her fore, aft and upper decks. She
was also fitted with a radar tower above
her bridge.

Above: Looking very much the worse
for wear *Mauretania* docks at Fremantle,
Western Australia. *[V.H.Young and
L.A.Sawyer]*

Right: *Mauretania*'s post-war refit took
over seven months and cost over £1.6
million. Her aft funnel was removed
to enable work to be carried out on the
air pre-heaters. The 76-ton funnel was
lifted back in place by the Mersey Dock
and Harbour Board's giant floating crane
Mammoth on 12th December 1946.

Above: By March 1947 *Mauretania*'s refit was nearing completion.
Below: In 1962 she was painted in 'cruising green' and used extensively as a cruise ship

Mauretania in original livery (top) and in 'cruising green' (middle and bottom).
[*Russell Priest collection; Ian Shiffman; R.M. Parsons/Malcolm Cranfield*]

The intermediate cargo-passenger liners, *Media* (above) and *Parthia* were similar in size to the 1920s A-class liners but with considerably more cargo space. They were designed for the London-New York service, but used instead on the Liverpool-New York route.

MEDIA (1) 1947-1961 Twin screw
O.N. 181093 13,342g 7,482n;
1962: 15,465g 8,876n
518.5 x 70.4 x 33.1 feet.
Two sets of geared steam turbines by John Brown & Co. Ltd., Clydebank; 13,600 SHP, 18 knots.
Passengers: 250 first; *1961*: 1,226 tourist; *1968*: 850 single class.
12.12.1946: Launched by John Brown & Co. Ltd., Clydebank (Yard No. 629) as MEDIA. Designed for the London to New York service but used on the Liverpool to New York route.
18.7.1947: Registered at Liverpool under the ownership of Cunard White Star Ltd., Liverpool.
20.8.1947: Left on maiden voyage from Liverpool to New York.

22.12.1949: Transferred to the Cunard Steam Ship Co. Ltd., Liverpool.
1.1.1950: Owners restyled as the Cunard Steam-Ship Co. Ltd., Liverpool.
2.1952: Denny-Brown stabilisers fitted by John Brown & Co. Ltd., Clydebank. She became the first merchant ship to cross the Atlantic with stabilisers. Glazed windows of promenade deck extended aft.
1961: Sold to Cia. Genovese di Armamento S.p.A. (Cogedar Line), Genoa.
9.9.1961: Final voyage from Liverpool to New York.
12.10.1961: Handed over to new owners at Liverpool and later rebuilt by Officine A. & R. Navi, Genoa, Italy as FLAVIA.
14.10.1961: Register closed.
2.10.1962: Left on first voyage Genoa-Fremantle-Melbourne-Sydney.

20.12.1968: After refit at Genoa, sailed on first chartered Caribbean cruise out of Miami for Costa Armatori S.p.A., Genoa.
1.5.1969: Sold to Costa Armatori S.p.A., Genoa.
1.1982: Laid up with engine problems.
24.2.1982: Sold to Flavian Shipping S.A. , Panama (Virtue Shipping Enterprises (Hong Kong) Ltd.) and renamed FLAVIAN.
25.10.1982: Laid up at Hong Kong.
1986: Transferred to Lavia Shipping S.A., Panama (Virtue Shipping Enterprises (Hong Kong) Ltd.) and renamed LAVIA.
7.1.1989: Caught fire whilst undergoing refit at Hong Kong. Beached north of Kau Yi Chau the following day and subsequently capsized, she was later refloated.
19.6.1989: Arrived at Kaohsiung under tow for demolition by Chi Shun Hua Steel Co. Ltd.

In 1962 *Media* was transformed into the Italian liner *Flavia*. [*V.H.Young and L.A.Sawyer*]

PARTHIA (2) 1948-1961 Twin screw

O.N. 182417 13,362g 7,393n
518.5 x 70.4 x 33.1 feet.
Two sets of geared steam turbines
by Harland and Wolff Ltd., Belfast;
13,600 SHP, 18 knots.
Passengers: 250 first; *1962*: 350 first.
25.2.1947: Launched by Harland and
Wolff Ltd., Belfast (Yard No. 1331) as
PARTHIA.
24.3.1948: Registered at Liverpool
under the ownership of Cunard White
Star Ltd., Liverpool. Designed for the
London to New York service but used
on the Liverpool to New York route
1.4.1948: Left on maiden voyage from
Liverpool to New York.
22.12.1949: Transferred to the Cunard
Steam Ship Co. Ltd., Liverpool.
1.1.1950: Owners restyled as the
Cunard Steam-Ship Co. Ltd.,
Liverpool.
1953: Denny-Brown stabilisers fitted
by John Brown & Co. Ltd., Clydebank.
Glazed windows of promenade deck
extended aft.
23.9.1961: Final voyage from
Liverpool to New York.
18.10.1961: Sold to the New Zealand
Shipping Co. Ltd., London. Six-
month refit by Alexander Stephen
and Sons Ltd., Glasgow included full
air-conditioning, promenade deck
extended aft, new smoking room,
sports deck and swimming pool.
24.10.1961: Renamed REMUERA.
1.6.1962: Left on first voyage from
London to Wellington.
12.1.1965: Chartered to Eastern and
Australian Steam Ship Co. Ltd.,
London and renamed ARAMAC.
28.12.1966: Transferred to Federal
Steam Navigation Co. Ltd., London.
9.8.1968: Sold to Eastern and
Australian Steam Ship Co. Ltd.,
London.
22.11.1969: Arrived at Kaohsiung for
demolition by Chin Ho Fa Steel and
Iron Co. Ltd.

Parthia (at New York in August
1960 top and upper middle) and
Media carried only 250 first class
passengers. As *Remuera* (lower
middle) her promenade deck was
extended aft by 60 feet whilst the
aft king posts were replaced with
a mainmast. From 1965 to 1969,
when she went for scrap, *Parthia*
traded in Australian waters as
Aramac. The only obvious
alteration to her was the fitting
of a domed funnel top (bottom).
*[Top, upper and lower middle:
V.H.Young and L.A.Sawyer,
bottom: Russell Priest]*

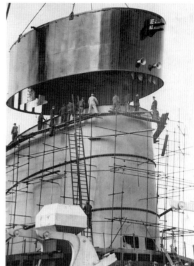

Launched by Princess Elizabeth (later H.M. The Queen), *Caronia* had the largest funnel in the world shown being installed (right).

CARONIA (2) 1948-1968 Twin screw
O.N 182453 34,183g 18,767n
688.0 x 91.4 x 46.7 feet.
Two sets of steam turbines by John Brown & Co. Ltd., Clydebank; 35,000 SHP, 22 knots. Passengers: 582 first, 353 cabin (one class when cruising).
30.10.1947: Launched by John Brown & Co. Ltd., Clydebank (Yard No. 635) as CARONIA. Designed as a dual-purpose cruise ship and transatlantic liner, she was the largest British liner to be launched since the end of the war and had the largest funnel in the world.
23.11.1948: Registered at Liverpool under the ownership of Cunard White Star Ltd., Liverpool.
4.1.1949: Left on maiden voyage from Southampton to New York.
1.1.1950: Owners restyled as the Cunard

Steam-Ship Co. Ltd., Liverpool.
6.1-19.4.1951: First round-the-world cruise from New York to Southampton via the Panama and Suez Canals.
10-12.1956: Refit at Liverpool including air-conditioning throughout the ship.
10-12.1965: Harland and Wolff Ltd., Belfast modified her passenger accommodation and fitted a new lido deck aft, which involved the removal of her docking bridge.
17.11.1967: Final voyage from New York to Southampton.
24.11.1967: Final arrival at Southampton. Laid up.
24.5.1968: Sold to Star Line, Panama.
25.7.1968: Handed over to her new owners and renamed COLUMBIA.
29.7.1968: British register closed and sailed from Southampton to Piraeus.
1968: After refit at Piraeus, renamed

CARIBIA. Ownership changed to Universal Line S.A., Panama (Universal Cruise Line Inc., New York).
11.3.1969: Explosion in engine room during West Indies cruise from New York killed one man. After drifting for almost a day, she returned to St. Thomas.
25.3.1969: Arrived in New York and laid up.
1.1974: Sold to Taiwanese breakers.
27.4.1974: Left New York under tow of the German tug HAMBURG (902/1971).
12.8.1974: Struck the breakwater at the entrance to Apra harbour, Guam during stormy weather. The following day she broke into three sections. The wreck was close to the spot where SCOTIA was wrecked on *11.3.1904*.
6.1975-1977: Wreck removed by the Nippon Salvage Company.

Caronia was originally conceived as *Mauretania*'s sister. However, she was designed as a dual purpose, two-class transatlantic liner and single-class cruise ship. She carried no cargo.

Known as the 'Green Goddess', *Caronia* was painted in four shades of green. During the summer months she operated on the North Atlantic and, in winter, she usually cruised out of New York and became one of the most exclusive cruise ships of her day.

Two pictures of *Caronia* from a scrap book. The Moran tugs confirm the left hand photograph was taken at New York, but why so many tugs and why the bunting, or were both usual? In the right hand photograph she has less bunting flying, and is working passengers probably with her own tender. Note how her landing stage is rigged using the topped-off derrick, and the presence of sightseers in rowing boats. The only clue to the whereabouts is the word 'Belfast' on the photographic negative. *[V.H. Young and L.A. Sawyer]*

Caronia at sea (top), laid up at
Southampton in May 1968 (middle)
and illuminated (bottom). *[Russell
Priest collection; Stephen Berry;
V.H. Young and L.A. Sawyer]*

Caronia was laid up at Southampton when photographed probably in December 1967 with *Carinthia* alongside (top left). As *Caribia*, she is seen in a sorry state at New York (top right), and looking even worse at anchor (middle). The last photograph shows her aground at Apra Harbour. *[V.H. Young and L.A. Sawyer; Stephen Berry; V.H. Young and L.A. Sawyer; Ray Woodmore]*

Saxonia, seen here on her trials and flying the John Brown & Co. house flag, was the first of the final intermediate class.

THE FINAL INTERMEDIATES

Between 1954 and 1957 four intermediate liners were built on the Clyde by John Brown for the Canadian service. Built in pairs, these handsome, fully air-conditioned ships had distinctive domed-top funnels. They were also the first Cunard liners designed with stabilisers and had a large cargo capacity of 300,000 cubic feet.

SAXONIA (2)/CARMANIA (2) 1954-1973
Twin screw

O.N. 185494 21,637g 11,303n
586.4 x 80.3 x 42.5 feet.
Two sets of geared steam turbines by John Brown & Co. (Clydebank) Ltd., Clydebank; 24,500 SHP, 20 knots.
Passengers: 125 first, 800 tourist; *1963*: 117 first, 764 tourist (750 cruising); *1973*: 750 in single class.

17.2.1954: Launched by John Brown & Co. (Clydebank) Ltd., Clydebank (Yard No. 692) as SAXONIA.
20.8.1954: Registered at Liverpool under the ownership of the Cunard Steam-Ship Co. Ltd., Liverpool.
2.9.1954: Left on maiden voyage from Liverpool to Montreal.
19.6.1957: Left on first voyage Southampton-Havre-Quebec-Montreal.
27.9.1962-1.4.1963: Converted at Clydebank by John Brown & Co. (Clydebank) Ltd. into a dual-purpose cruise ship and transatlantic liner.
1.1.1963: Renamed CARMANIA.
8.4.1963: Left on first voyage Rotterdam-Southampton-Havre-Quebec-Montreal.
14.11.1967: Left on final voyage Rotterdam-Southampton-Havre-Quebec-Montreal. Subsequently became full-time cruise ship.

28.3.1968: Transferred to Cunard Line Ltd., Southampton.
12.1.1969: Ran aground on San Salvador Island, Bahamas whilst on a cruise from Port Everglades.
17.1.1969: Refloated and subsequently repaired at Newport News.
5.5.1969: Registered at Southampton.
31.10.1971: Final arrival at Southampton. Laid up with FRANCONIA.
14.5.1972: Following the collapse of the deal to sell both ships to the Japanese company Toyo Yusen K.K., sailed for lay up in the River Fal, Cornwall.
30.8.1973: Sailed from the Fal, having been sold with FRANCONIA to Nikreis Maritime Corporation, Panama acting as representative for the Soviet state-owned shipping company Morflot. Renamed LEONID SOBINOV, transferred to the USSR flag and registered under the ownership of the Far-Eastern Shipping Co. (FESCO), Vladivostok, USSR.
20.11.1973: British register closed.
26.2.1974: After a refit on the Tyne by Swan Hunter Shipbuilders Ltd., sailed on first voyage from Southampton to Australia via Mauritius, Colombo and Singapore. She operated under charter to CTC Lines and spent until *12.1979* mainly on the UK to Australia route.
1980s-early 1990s: Used as a troopship, for cruising in the Black Sea with Soviet passengers and, latterly, cruises from Malta.
1.1990: Registered ownership transferred to Transblasco Four Shipping Co. Ltd., Ta'Xbiex, Malta (Transorient Overseas S.A., Piraeus, managers).
1.1992: Transferred to Black Sea Shipping Co., Odessa, Ukraine (Transorient Overseas S.A., Piraeus, managers).
10.1995: Laid up at Illichivsk, Ukraine.
1.4.1999: Arrived at Alang, India for demolition.

Although used on the Canadian routes, *Saxonia* made her first call at New York on 5th December 1954.

Saxonia (top) is seen again as *Carmania* with a green hull passing beneath the Forth Railway Bridge (middle). The final photograph shows her as *Leonid Sobinov* at Cape Town (bottom). [Russell Priest (2); V.H. Young and L.A. Sawyer]

Ivernia in John Brown's fitting out basin. The tanker is probably the *Stanvac Australia* (17,297/1955).

IVERNIA (2)/FRANCONIA (3) 1955-1973
Twin screw

O.N. 185519 21,717g 11,307n
586.4 x 80.3 x 42.5 feet.
Two sets of geared steam turbines by John
Brown & Co. (Clydebank) Ltd., Clydebank;
24,500 SHP, 20 knots.
Passengers: 110 first, 833 tourist; *1963*: 119
first, 750 tourist (750 cruising); *1973*: 750 in
single class.
14.12.1954: Launched by John Brown & Co.
(Clydebank) Ltd., Clydebank (Yard No. 693)
as IVERNIA.
16.6.1955: Registered at Liverpool under the
ownership of the Cunard Steam-Ship Co.
Ltd., Liverpool.
27.7.1955: Left on maiden voyage from
Liverpool to Montreal.
17.4.1957: Left on first voyage
Southampton-Havre-Quebec-Montreal.
10.10.1962-6.1963: Converted at Clydebank
by John Brown & Co. (Clydebank) Ltd. into
a dual-purpose cruise ship and transatlantic
liner.
1.1.1963: Renamed FRANCONIA.
4.6.1963: Left on first voyage Rotterdam-
Southampton-Havre-Quebec-Montreal.
2.11.1966: Left on final voyage
Southampton-Quebec-Montreal.
Subsequently became a full-time cruise ship.
28.3.1968: Transferred to Cunard Line Ltd.,
Southampton.
19.12.1969: Registered at Southampton.
17.10.1971: Final arrival at Southampton.
Laid up with CARMANIA.
14.5.1972: Following the collapse of the
deal to sell both ships to the Japanese
company Toyo Yusen K.K., sailed for lay up
in the River Fal, Cornwall.

14.8.1973: Sailed from the Fal, having
been sold with CARMANIA to Nikreis
Maritime Corporation, Panama acting as
representative for the Soviet state-owned
shipping company Morflot. Later renamed
FEDOR SHALYAPIN, transferred to
the USSR flag and registered under the
ownership of the Far-Eastern Shipping Co.
(FESCO), Vladivostok.
19.10.1973: British register closed.
20.11.1973: After a refit on the Tyne by
Swan Hunter Shipbuilders Ltd., sailed on
first voyage from Southampton to Australia
via the Panama Canal. She operated under
charter to CTC Lines and spent until *2.1980*
mainly cruising out of Sydney.
1980s-early 1990s: Used as a troopship,

for cruising in the Black Sea with Soviet
passengers and for cruises for the German
market.
5.1992: Transferred to the Odessa Cruise
M.V. 'Fedor Shalyapin' Co. Ltd., Valetta,
Malta (Transorient Overseas S.A., Piraeus,
managers).
1.1995: Transferred to Black Sea Shipping
Co., Odessa, Ukraine.
2.1996: Laid up at Illichivsk, Ukraine.
21.1.2004: After sale to Indian breakers,
ownership changed for final voyage to
Blackpool Investments S.A., Monrovia,
Liberia. Renamed SALONA under the St.
Vincent and Grenadines flag.
5.2.2004: Arrived at Alang, India for
demolition.

After *Ivernia*'s trials, she was anchored in a Scottish loch because of congestion at
Liverpool caused by strikes. Her maiden voyage on 30th June was also delayed.

Ivernia is seen first in liner service (top), and then after conversion for a dual role as cruise ship and transatlantic liner, painted white and renamed *Franconia* (middle). After sale and renaming *Feodor Shalypin* her forward kingposts were removed (bottom). She had a blue band on her funnel whilst *Leonid Sobinov* had a red band. [All: Russell Priest collection]

Carinthia sailing under the Jacques Cartier Bridge on her maiden arrival at Montreal in July 1956.

CARINTHIA (3) 1956-1968 Twin screw
O.N. 187137 21,947g 11,630n
586.4 x 80.3 x 42.5 feet.
Two sets of geared steam turbines by John
Brown & Co. (Clydebank) Ltd., Clydebank;
24,500 SHP, 20 knots.
Passengers: 154 first, 714 tourist; *1971*: 884
in single class.
14.12.1955: Launched by John Brown & Co.
(Clydebank) Ltd., Clydebank (Yard No. 699)
as CARINTHIA.
16.6.1956: Registered at Liverpool under the
ownership of the Cunard Steam-Ship Co.
Ltd., Liverpool.
1.7.1956: Left on maiden voyage from
Greenock to Quebec and Montreal.
27.7.1956: Left on first voyage from
Liverpool to Quebec and Montreal.
13.10.1967: Left on final sailing of
Liverpool-Quebec-Montreal express service.
23.11.1967: Left on final voyage
Southampton-Quebec-Montreal.
9.12.1967: Arrived Southampton and
subsequently laid up.
2.2.1968: Sold with SYLVANIA to Fairsea
Shipping Corporation, Monrovia, Liberia
(Sitmar Line, Milan, Italy) and renamed
FAIRLAND. Intended to be used as
emigrant ships to Australia, but both were
laid up at Southampton.
22.4.1968: British register closed.
21.2.1970: Following Sitmar's loss of the
Australian migrant contract to Chandris
Line, arrived at Trieste for conversion into
an upmarket cruise ship by the Arsenale
Triestino San Marco. Renamed FAIRSEA.
3.11.1971: Delivered to Sitmar subsidiary,

Fairline Shipping Corporation, Monrovia,
Liberia.
14.12.1971: First cruise with commercial
passengers from San Francisco to Mexico.
1980: Transferred to Sitmar Cruises Inc.,
Monrovia.
28.7.1988: Sitmar Line acquired by Princess
Cruises. Subsequently renamed FAIR
PRINCESS.
10.1991: Transferred to Princess Cruises
Liberia Inc., Monrovia,.
3.1997: Transferred to P&O Holidays Ltd.,
London.
2000: Sold to China Sea Cruises Inc., Taipei,
Taiwan (V. Ships Leisure S.A.M., Monaco,
managers) for use as a casino ship based in
Hong Kong.

29.11.2000: Arrived Hong Kong and later
renamed CHINA SEA DISCOVERY.
4.5.2001: Arived Kaohsiung, Taiwan after
being released from arrest in Hong Kong.
9-12.2002: Used on short-stay gambling
cruises based at Keelung, Taiwan.
12.2002: Laid up at Kaohsiung.
2.2003: Management changed to Sophlex Ship
Management Inc., Port Aransas, Texas, U.S.A.
8.2005: Following arrest, sold at auction
to Indian breakers, Mahavir Indecto Melt
Private Ltd.
18.11.2005: Arrived for demolition at Alang,
India under the name DISCOVERY.
17.2.2006: At least nine people suffered
minor injuries following a fire in the engine-
room during demolition.

Fairsea on 9th June 1988. *[Chris Howell]*

Carinthia (top) is also seen as
Fair Princess on 23rd September
1989 (middle) and as *China Sea
Discovery* (bottom). She was the
last Cunard intermediate ship to
survive. *[Top and bottom: Russell
Priest; middle: Chris Howell]*

Sylvania arriving at Montreal at the end of her maiden voyage to Canada in 1957. *[J. and M. Clarkson collection]*

SYLVANIA (2) 1957-1968 Twin screw
O.N. 187164 21,989g 11,665n
586.4 x 80.3 x 42.5 feet.
Two sets of geared steam turbines by John Brown & Co. (Clydebank) Ltd., Clydebank; 24,500 SHP, 20 knots.
Passengers: 154 first, 724 tourist; *1971*: 884 in single class; *1993*: 906 in single class.
22.11.1956: Launched by John Brown & Co. (Clydebank) Ltd., Clydebank (Yard No. 700) as SYLVANIA.
3.6.1957: Registered at Liverpool under the ownership of the Cunard Steam-Ship Co. Ltd., Liverpool.
5.6.1957: Left on maiden voyage Greenock-Quebec-Montreal.
28.11.1958: Left on first voyage Liverpool-Halifax-New York.
5.4.1960: Replaced BRITANNIC on Liverpool to New York service. Operated with MEDIA and PARTHIA.
29.5.1961: First call at Boston.
24.11.1966: Sailed from Liverpool on final express service sailing to New York.
1.1967: Inaugurated a season of fly-cruises with British European Airlines (BEA). Her hull was painted white and she was based at Gibraltar. From 22nd February until 10th May a chartered 38-passenger SR-N6 Hovercraft was carried on the foredeck for use as an excursion craft.
30.11.1967: Left Liverpool on final transatlantic voyage to Halifax-New York-Cobh-Havre-Southampton. During remainder of her Cunard service was used as a cruise ship.
2.2.1968: Sold with CARINTHIA to Fairwinds Shipping Corporation, Monrovia, Liberia (Sitmar Line, Milan, Italy). Intended to be used as emigrant ships to Australia.
7.5.1968: Final arrival for Cunard at Southampton. Renamed FAIRWIND (name announced as FAIRWINDS) and laid up in Southampton with FAIRLAND ex CARINTHIA.
24.6.1968: British register closed.

18.1.1971: Following the loss of the Australian migrant contract to Chandris Line, arrived under tow at Trieste for transformation into an upmarket cruise ship by the Arsenale Triestino San Marco.
14.6.1972: Delivered.
14.8.1972: First cruise with commercial passengers from Los Angeles to Mexico.
1980: Transferred to Sitmar Cruises Inc., Monrovia.
6.1987: Renamed SITMAR FAIRWIND.
28.7.1988: Sitmar Line acquired by Princess Cruises. Subsequently renamed DAWN PRINCESS.

1991: Transferred to Princess Cruises Liberia Inc., Monrovia.
27.4.1992: Sold to the Vlasov Group and registered under the ownership of the Happy Days Shipping Ltd., Nassau, Bahamas.
18.6.1993: Delivered and renamed ALBATROS.
16.5.1997: Ran aground near St. Mary, Scilly Isles. Refloated and repaired at Southampton.
26.12.2003: After sale to Indian breakers, renamed GENOA and placed under Georgian flag.
5.1.2004: Arrived at Alang, India for demolition.

In her final year with Cunard *Sylvania* had her hull painted white (above). She also carried a chartered 38-seater Hovercraft (below), seen here at Gibraltar, on her foredeck which was used as an excursion craft. *[J. and M. Clarkson collection]*

Sylvania (top) had a successful further career as a cruise ship, and is seen again as *Dawn Princess* on 6th July 1991 (middle), and as the German *Albatros* (bottom). *[Russell Priest; Chris Howell; Russell Priest]*

Adriatic was the last of White Star's 'big four' liners.

Cunard White Star Ltd. came into being on 1st January 1934, with the two fleets merging in July.

Nine White Star ships were transferred to the new company and by 1936 the former White Star fleet had been reduced to only three ships. These ships were painted in White Star colours, whilst the White Star flag was always hoisted above the Cunard flag.

ADRIATIC 1934 Twin screw
O.N 124061 24,540g 15,637n
709.2 x 75.5 x 52.6 feet.
Two Q.4-cyl. by Harland and Wolff Ltd., Belfast; 16,000 IHP, 17 knots.
Passengers: 425 first, 500 second, 2,000 third; *1919*: 400 first, 468 second, 1,320 third; *1928*: 506 cabin, 560 tourist, 404 third
20.9.1906: Launched by Harland and Wolff Ltd., Belfast (Yard No. 358) as ADRIATIC.
23.4.1907: Registered at Liverpool under the ownership of the Oceanic Steam Navigation Co Ltd. (White Star Line), Liverpool. The last of White Star's 'big four' and briefly the largest ship in the world.
8.5.1907: Left on maiden voyage from Liverpool to New York.
5.6.1907: First voyage Southampton-Cherbourg-New York.
26.8.1911: Resumed Liverpool to New York service.
13.5.1919: Resumed Southampton to New York service.
1922: Returned to Liverpool route after the introduction of HOMERIC.
9.3.1934: Left New York on final Atlantic crossing. Subsequently used for cruising.
2.7.1934: Acquired by Cunard White Star Ltd., Liverpool.
9.1934: Laid up.
13.12.1934: Sold to Japanese breakers.

19.12.1934: Final sailing from Liverpool.
5.3.1935: Arrived at Osaka.
15.5.1935: Register closed.

CALGARIC 1934 Triple screw
O.N 140579 15,119g 9,449n;
1922: 16,063g 9,614n
550.3 x 67.3 x 43.0 feet.
Two T.3-cyl. with one low pressure turbine by Harland and Wolff Ltd., Belfast; 8,450 IHP, 15 knots.
Passengers: cargo only; *1922*:190 first, 221 second, 473 third; *1927*: 290 cabin, 550 tourist, 330 third.
5.4.1917: Launched by Harland and Wolff Ltd., Belfast (Yard No. 442) as ORCA. Designed as a passenger ship but completed as a cargo ship.
23.5.1918: Registered at Liverpool under the ownership of the Pacific Steam Navigation Company, Liverpool.

18.2.1921: Returned to builders for completion as a passenger ship.
27.12.1922: Ownership transferred to the Royal Mail Steam Packet Company, London. First voyage Hamburg-Southampton-Cherbourg-New York.
8.3.1927: Acquired by White Star Line Ltd., London, following the Royal Mail Steam Packet Company takeover of White Star Line.
7.4.1927: Renamed CALGARIC.
4.5.1927: First voyage Liverpool-Quebec-Montreal.
15.12.1927: Transferred to Oceanic Steam Navigation Co. Ltd., Liverpool.
9.1933: Laid up at Milford Haven.
2.7.1934: Acquired by Cunard White Star Ltd., Liverpool.
25.12.1934: Arrived at Rosyth for demolition by Metal Industries Ltd.
6.8.1935: Register closed.

Calgaric was not a successful ship and had been laid up in 1933.

Olympic was laid up at Southampton six months after her great rival *Mauretania*.

OLYMPIC 1934-1935 Triple screw
O.N 131346 45,323g 20,894n;
1913: 46,358g 22,350n
852.5 x 92.5 x 59.5 feet.
Two T.3-cyl with one low pressure turbine by
Harland and Wolff Ltd., Belfast; 50,000 IHP,
21 knots.
Passengers: 1,054 first, 510 second, 1,020 third;
1920: 750 first, 496 second, 1,100 third; *1933*:
618 first, 447 tourist, 382 third.

20.10.1910: Launched by Harland and Wolff
Ltd., Belfast (Yard No. 400) as OLYMPIC.
25.5.1911: Registered at Liverpool under the
ownership of the Oceanic Steam Navigation
Co Ltd. (White Star Line), Liverpool.
14.6.1911: Left on maiden voyage from
Southampton to New York.
20.9.1911: Rammed by cruiser HMS
HAWKE in the Solent whilst outbound for
New York.
9.10.1912-22.3.1913: Following the sinking
of TITANIC, returned to her builders at
Belfast for extensive modifications.
8.1914: Requisitioned by the British
Government as an armed merchant cruiser but
released as being unsuitable.
2.11.1914: Laid up in Belfast Lough.
9.1915 to 12.1916: Requisitioned by the
British Government as a troopship.
31.3.1917 to 2.1919: Requisitioned by the

British government as an armed merchant
cruiser and fitted with six 6-inch guns. Used
mainly as a troopship.
16.8.1919 to 17.6.1920: Underwent refit and
conversion to oil-firing.
2.7.1934: Acquired by Cunard White Star
Ltd., Liverpool.
27.3.1935: Final voyage from Southampton
to New York. Laid up in Southampton.
9.1935: Bought for breaking up by Sir John
Jarvis to provide work for people in Jarrow.
Resold to Thos. W. Ward Ltd., Sheffield on
condition she was broken up at the former
yard of Palmers' Shipbuilding and Iron Co.
Ltd., Jarrow.
13.10.1935: Arrived Jarrow for demolition.
5.11.1935: Start of ten-day sale of furniture
and fittings by Knight, Frank and Rutley.
19.9.1937: Remains towed to Inverkeithing.
1.2.1939: Register closed.

Above and right: *Olympic* at
Southampton.

Until the arrival of *Queen Mary* in March 1936, *Majestic* was Cunard White Star's largest ship.

MAJESTIC 1934-1936 Quadruple screw

O.N 146555 56,621g 26,249n
915.5 x 100.1 x 58.2 feet.
Four sets of steam turbines by Blohm u. Voss, Hamburg, Germany; 62,000 SHP, 23 knots.
Passengers: 800 first, 708 second, 2,185 third.
20.6.1914: Launched by Blohm u. Voss, Hamburg (Yard No. 214) for Hamburg-Amerikanische-Packetfahrt-Actien-Gesellschaft (HAPAG), Hamburg as BISMARCK. She was the third of HAPAG's IMPERATOR-class.
8.1914: Work was suspended following the outbreak of war.
28.6.1919: Allocated to Britain as war reparations. Building continued under the supervision of Harland and Wolff Ltd.
28.3.1922: Completed. She was the largest ship in the world until 1935.
27.4.1922: Registered at London under the ownership of The Shipping Controller.
2.5.1922: Registered at Liverpool under the ownership of the Oceanic Steam Navigation Co. Ltd. (White Star Line), Liverpool as MAJESTIC.
10.5.1922: Left on maiden voyage from Southampton to New York.
2.7.1934: Acquired by Cunard White Star Ltd., Liverpool.
13.2.1936: Final voyage from Southampton to New York.
3.6.1936: Sold for demolition to Thos. W. Ward Ltd., Sheffield.
1.9.1936: Resold to the British Government and converted into a boy seamen's training ship by John I. Thornycroft and Co. Ltd. at Southampton.
10.4.1937: Arrived at Rosyth with her funnels and masts reduced to pass under the Firth of Forth bridge.
23.4.1937: Commissioned as HMS CALEDONIA.
21.7.1937: Register closed.

29.9.1939: Not long after she ceased to be a training ship, caught fire, burnt out, and sank on an even keel at her moorings in the Firth of Forth.
3.1940: Sold for demolition to Thos. W. Ward Ltd., Sheffield.
17.7.1943: Remains raised and towed to Inverkeithing.

DORIC 1934-1935 Twin screw

O.N 147215 16,484g 9,869n
575.5 x 67.9 x 41.2 feet.
Two sets of steam turbines by Harland and Wolff Ltd., Belfast 15,000 IHP, 16 knots.
Passengers: 594 cabin, 406 tourist, 500 third.
8.8.1922: Launched by Harland and Wolff Ltd., Belfast (Yard No. 573) as DORIC.
16.5.1923: Registered at Liverpool under the ownership of the Oceanic Steam Navigation Co Ltd. (White Star Line), Liverpool.

8.6.1923: Left on maiden voyage Liverpool-Quebec-Montreal.
10.1932: Laid up and subsequently used for cruising, mainly in the Mediterranean.
2.7.1934: Acquired by Cunard White Star Ltd., Liverpool.
5.9.1935: Badly damaged in collision with the French freighter FORMIGNY (2,957/1917) in thick fog near Oporto, Portugal in position 41°19′N, 9°34′W whilst homeward bound from a Mediterranean cruise. After temporary repairs at Vigo, sailed for Tilbury. Damage was too severe and she was sold for demolition.
9.10.1935: Arrived at Newport, Monmouthshire for demolition by John Cashmore Ltd.
26-29.11.1935: Sale of furnishings.
27.10.1936: Register closed.

Unlike most passenger ships of the time, *Doric* was completed as a coal burner.

Although she had become a full-time cruise ship, *Homeric* was also sold for demolition in 1936.

HOMERIC 1934-1936 Twin screw

O.N 146513 34,692g 19,609n
751.0 x 83.3 x 48.6 feet.
Two T.4-cyl. by F. Schichau, Danzig; 28,000 IHP, 18 knots; *1924*: 19.5 knots.
Passengers: 470 first, 538 second, 1,640 third; *1926*: first, second, tourist and third; *1930*: 523 first, 814 tourist, 314 third; *1932*: 472 first, 832 tourist, 659 third.
17.12.1913: Launched by F. Schichau, Danzig (Yard No. 891) for Norddeutscher Lloyd, Bremen, Germany as COLUMBUS. Her sister was to be called HINDENBURG but was completed in 1923 as COLUMBUS.
8.1914: Work was suspended following the outbreak of war, with the ship 80% completed.
28.6.1919: Allocated to Britain as a war reparation. Since she was building in Danzig, which became a Free State under Versailles treaties, she was beyond the reach of the German Government to deliver her on reparations account. Norddeutscher Lloyd was therefore able to barter her to obtain the release of a number of pre-war intermediate

liners which they badly needed to restart services.
6.1920: Building recommenced under the supervision of Harland and Wolff Ltd.
21.1.1922: Arrived Southampton.
25.1.1922: Registered in London under the ownership of The Shipping Controller.
10.2.1922: Registered at Liverpool under the ownership of the Oceanic Steam Navigation Co Ltd. (White Star Line), Liverpool as HOMERIC.
15.2.1922: Left on maiden voyage Southampton-Cherbourg-New York.
11.1923-4.1924: Machinery improvements by Harland and Wolff Ltd. which included conversion to oil-firing.
6.1932: Became full time cruise ship.
2.7.1934: Acquired by Cunard White Star Ltd., Liverpool.
10.1935: Laid up off Ryde, Isle of Wight.
27.2.1936: Sold for demolition to Thos. W. Ward Ltd., Sheffield.
23.3.1936: Arrived at Inverkeithing for demolition.
28.2.1938: Register closed.

LAURENTIC 1934-1940 Triple screw

O.N 149642 18,724g 11,103n
578.2 x 75.4 x 40.6 feet.
Two T.3-cyl. and one low pressure turbine by Harland and Wolff Ltd., Belfast (coal burner); 13,000 IHP, 16 knots.
Passengers: 594 cabin, 406 tourist, 406 third.
16.6.1927: Launched by Harland and Wolff Ltd., Belfast (Yard No. 470) as LAURENTIC.
18.10.1927: Registered at Liverpool under the ownership of the Oceanic Steam Navigation Co Ltd. (White Star Line), Liverpool.
12.11.1927: Left on maiden voyage, Liverpool to New York.
24.4.1928: First voyage Liverpool-Quebec-Montreal.
2.7.1934: Acquired by Cunard White Star Ltd., Liverpool.
1934: Used mainly for cruising.
18.8.1935: Rammed by Blue Star Line's NAPIER STAR (10,583/1927) in fog in the Irish Sea when setting out on a 14-day northern Europe cruise from Liverpool. Six members of LAURENTIC's crew were killed. After repairs, she undertook a single voyage in September from Dublin with Catholic pilgrims bound for Lourdes and was laid up intially at Birkenhead and from December at Southampton.
9.1936: Trooping voyage to Palestine.
3.1938: Laid up in the River Fal, Cornwall.
26.8.1939: Requisitioned by the British government as the armed merchant cruiser HMS LAURENTIC. Converted at Devonport. Fitted with seven 6-inch guns.
3.11.1940: Torpedoed and sunk by the German submarine U 99 off the Bloody Foreland, Ireland in position 54°09′N, 13°44′W with the loss of 49 lives.
15.7.1941: Register closed.

Despite being built as late as 1927, *Laurentic* was another coal burner.

Top and middle: *Britannic*, one of the world's largest motor ships when built, was in the fleet until 1960.

Right: *Britannic* off Cowes, Isle of Wight on 12th December 1944, carrying troops from Italy on Christmas leave.

BRITANNIC 1934-1960 Twin screw
O.N 162316 26,943g 16,445n
683.6 x 82.4 x 48.6 feet.
Two Burmeister & Wain-type 10-cyl 4SCDA
oil engines by Harland and Wolff Ltd.,
Belfast; 18,500 BHP, 18 knots.
Passengers: 504 cabin, 551 second, 498
third; *1949*: 429 first, 564 tourist.
6.8.1929: Launched by Harland and
Wolff Ltd., Belfast (Yard No. 807) as
BRITANNIC.
6.6.1930: Registered at Liverpool under the
ownership of the Oceanic Steam Navigation

Co Ltd. (White Star Line), Liverpool.
28.6.1930: Left on maiden voyage from
Liverpool to New York.
2.7.1934: Acquired by Cunard White Star
Ltd., Liverpool.
19.4.1935: First voyage London-
Southampton-New York.
29.8.1939-1.1947: Requisitioned as a
troopship.
3.1947-1948: Refit in the Gladstone Dock,
Liverpool.
22.5.1948: Resumed Liverpool to New York
service.

22.12.1949: Transferred to the Cunard Steam
Ship Co. Ltd., Liverpool. She remained in
White Star colours.
1.1.1950: Owners restyled as the Cunard
Steam-Ship Co. Ltd., Liverpool.
11.11.1960: Final voyage from Southampton
to New York.
12.1960: Sold to the British Iron and Steel
Corporation (BISCO).
19.12.1960: Arrived Inverkeithing for
demolition by Thos. W. Ward Ltd., Sheffield.
21.11.1961: Register closed.

Unlike *Britannic* (above)
Georgic (right) had a curved
front to her superstructure
whilst her interiors had a more
contemporary look than her
sister. *[Top: B. and A. Feilden/J.
and M. Clarkson collection]*

GEORGIC 1934-1942 Twin screw

O.N 162365 27,759g 16,839n;
1944: 27,268g 15,953n
683.6 x 82.4 x 48.6 feet.
Two Burmeister & Wain-type 10-cyl
4SCDA oil engines by Harland and
Wolff Ltd., Belfast; 18,500 BHP, 18
knots.
Passengers: 479 cabin, 557 second, 506
third; *1944*: 3,000 troops; *1949*: 1,962
single class.
12.11.1931: Launched by Harland and
Wolff Ltd., Belfast (Yard No. 896) as
GEORGIC.
8.6.1932: Registered at Liverpool under
the ownership of the Oceanic Steam
Navigation Co Ltd. (White Star Line),
Liverpool.
25.6.1932: Left on maiden voyage from
Liverpool to New York.
2.7.1934: Acquired by Cunard White
Star Ltd., Liverpool.
3.5.1935: First voyage London-
Southampton-New York.
12.3.1940: Requisitioned as a troopship
and converted on the Clyde.
14.7.1941: Attacked by German aircraft
and set ablaze at Port Tewfik, Suez.
Beached two days later.
27.10.1941: Refloated.
28.12.1941: Left Suez under tow bound
for Karachi where she spent eight
months being repaired.
19.9.1942: Register closed following
acquisition by the Ministry of War
Transport.
14.10.1942: Registered at Liverpool
under the ownership of the Ministry of
War Transport, London.
2.3.1943: Arrived Liverpool.
16.3.1943: Cunard White Star Ltd.
appointed managers.
19.3.1943-21.12.1944: Reconstructed
at Belfast by her builders as a single-
funnel, 3,000-capacity troopship.
1946: Owners became the Ministry of
Transport, London.
7.1948: Arrived on the Tyne for
conversion by Palmer's Hebburn Co.
Ltd. into an Australian and New Zealand
immigrant ship.
11.1.1949: Left Liverpool on first voyage
to Fremantle, Melbourne and Sydney.
4.5.1950: First chartered voyage from
Liverpool to New York for Cunard
Steam-Ship Co. Ltd.
19.10.1954: Left New York on final
voyage for Cunard to Halifax-Cobh-
Havre-Southampton.
19.11.1955: Arrived Liverpool at the end
of final voyage from Australia.
1.1956: Sold to the British Iron and Steel
Corporation (BISCO).
1.2.1956: Arrived Faslane for demolition
by Shipbreaking Industries Ltd.
13.5.1957: Register closed.

Top: With a single funnel and single mast, *Georgic* as a wartime troopship.
Middle: During the summer months of 1950 to 1954, *Georgic* was chartered by Cunard from the Ministry of Transport for voyages to New York from Liverpool and Southampton.
Bottom: Docking at Liverpool on 4th May 1950. *[J. and M. Clarkson]*

Cunard Princess.

CUNARD'S FIRST MASS MARKET CRUISE SHIPS

In 1969, the U.S. airline Overseas National Airways ordered a 15,000g cruise ship from the Rotterdamsche Droogdok Mij. This ship was designed to carry around 800 passengers on short cruises, connecting with air charter flights. In May 1970, ONA and Cunard formed the joint venture Cunard-ONA Ltd., with Cunard taking a 50% share in the new company. A second ship was also ordered. The vessels would be manned and operated by Cunard under the British flag, whilst ONA would be responsible for the marketing of the fly cruises. However, the U.S. Civil Aeronautics Board refused ONA a licence for the air charter operation under anti-trust

legislation, which forbids air and sea transport under the same company management. As ONA was unwilling to set up another airline, it withdrew from the deal before the first ship was delivered in 1971.

Cunard bought ONA's share and the two ships, *Cunard Adventurer* and *Cunard Ambassador,* became Cunard's first purpose-built cruise ships. (Earlier ships were dual purpose transatlantic liners and cruise ships.) They also broke with tradition by having names beginning with *Cunard.* In 1973 Cunard-ONA Ltd. was renamed Cunard Cruise Ships Ltd.

CUNARD ADVENTURER 1971-1977
Twin screw

O.N. 342376 14,150g 8,135n;
1977: 14,110g 7,056n
450.5 x 70.6 x 28.2 feet.
Four 12-cyl. vee oil engines by Stork-
Werkspoor, Amsterdam, Netherlands;
26,800 BHP, 21.5 knots.
Passengers: 806; *1984*: 857; *1990s*: 756.
2.2.1971: Launched by Rotterdamsche
Droogdok Maatschappij N.V., Rotterdam,
Netherlands (Yard No. 329) as CUNARD
ADVENTURER. She had been ordered in
1969 by Overseas National Airways Inc.
15.7.1971: Cunard acquired ONA's 50%
share.
29.10.1971: Registered at Southampton
under the ownership of Cunard-ONA
Ltd., London.
19.11.1971: Left on maiden voyage from
Southampton to San Juan.
16.2.1973: Cunard-ONA Ltd. renamed
Cunard Cruise Ships Ltd.
28.3.1973: Transferred to Cunard Cruise
Ships Ltd. (Cunard Line Ltd.), London.
2.3.1976: Transferred to Cunard Line
Ltd., London.
3.1977: Sold to Kloster Rederi A/S, Oslo,
Norway and renamed SUNWARD II.
1.3.1977: British register closed.
8.3-24.4.1977: Refit at Bremerhaven by
Hapag-Lloyd Werft A.G. Single funnel
replaced by Norwegian Caribbean Line's
trademark split funnel.
1.1982: Transferred to K/S A/S Sunward II.
1.10.1984: Transferred to Norwegian
Caribbean Lines A/S.
1.1.1987: Registered in Bahamas.
11.1991: Sold to Euro Club Cruises
Maritime Co. (Epirotiki Cruise Line),
Piraeus, Greece and renamed TRITON.
1.2001: Transferred to Valentine Oceanic
Inc., Monrovia, Liberia (Royal Olympic
Cruise Line, Piraeus).
6.2003: Transferred to Royal Olympia
Cruise Line, Piraeus.
6.4.2005: Sold to New Wave Nav. S.A.,
Majuro, Marshall Islands (Louis Cruises
Ltd., Nicosia, Cyprus) and renamed
CORAL.
3.2006: Under the Cyprus flag.
2.2010: Under the Malta flag.
2012: Still in existence.

Cunard Adventurer's funnel was white and black (above), with the Cunard name in red on the side of the hull. The same colour scheme was used for *Queen Elizabeth 2*. She was later given traditional Cunard funnel colours. *[Above: Andy Hernandez collection, below: Chris Howell]*

Sunward II at Miami in June 1985 (above) with her single funnel replaced by a pair of uptakes. *Coral* at Civitavecchia in September 2009 (below right) and at Palma (left) in the same year. *[Above: V.H. Young and L.A. Sawyer, below left: W. Mayes]*

Cunard Ambassador on trials flying the Dutch flag.

CUNARD AMBASSADOR 1972-1975
Twin screw
O.N. 359367 14,160g 8,105n;
1976: 5,633g 1,938n
450.5 x 70.6 x 28.2 feet.
Four 12-cyl. vee oil engines by Stork-Werkspoor, Amsterdam, Netherlands; 26,800 BHP, 21.5 knots.
Passengers: 806.
16.3.1972: Launched by N.V. Machinefabriek en Scheepswerf van P. Smit, Jr., Rotterdam, Netherlands (Yard No. 666) as CUNARD AMBASSADOR.
16.10.1972: Registered at Southampton under the ownership of Cunard-ONA Ltd., London.
23.10.1972: Left on maiden voyage from Rotterdam to San Juan.
16.2.1973: Cunard-ONA Ltd. renamed Cunard Cruise Ships Ltd.
21.9.1973: Transferred to Cunard Cruise Ships Ltd. (Cunard Line Ltd.), London.
12.9.1974: Serious engine room fire gutted much of the passenger accommodation. She was about 39 miles south west of Key West in position 24°15′N, 82°27′W on a voyage from Port Everglades to New Orleans without passengers. Towed to Key West and declared a constructive total loss.
1975: Sold to C. Clausen Dampskibsrederi A/S, Graasten, Denmark and towed to Landskrona where she arrived *30.4.1975* for conversion into a livestock carrier by Öresundsvarvet A/B, later renamed LINDA CLAUSEN.
13.3.1975: British register closed.
6.1976: Work complete. Carried sheep between Australia and the Persian Gulf.
1980: Sold to Lembu Shipping Corporation, Panama (Stolt-Nielsen Pte. Ltd., Singapore, managers) and renamed PROCYON.
1983: Sold to Qatar Transport and Marine Services Co. Ltd., Doha (Stolt-Nielsen Pte. Ltd., Singapore, managers) and renamed RASLAN.
16.7.1983: Arrived Singapore from Jeddah after fire in engine control room. Laid up and subsequently arrested.
7.9.1984: Arrived for demolition at Kaohsiung.

Linda Clausen ex *Cunard Ambassador* carried sheep from Australia to the Persian Gulf. *[Russell Priest collection]*

CUNARD COUNTESS 1976-1996
Twin screw

O.N. 365129 17,586g 12,387n
462.6 x 74.9 x 19.8 feet.
Four 7-cyl. 4SCSA Burmeister &
Wain-type geared-oil engine by
Hitachi Zosen, Maizuru, Japan; 21,000
BHP, 21.5 knots.
Passengers: 950; *1990s*: 846.
20.9.1974: Launched by A/S
Burmeister & Wain's Skibsbyggeri,
Copenhagen, Denmark (Yard No. 858)
as CUNARD COUNTESS.
21.5.1975: Registered at Southampton
under the ownership of Cunard
Cruise Ships Ltd. (Cunard Line Ltd.),
London.
28.5.1975: Arrived at La Spezia, Italy
for final fitting out by Industrie Navali
Mechaniche Affini.
7.1976: Completed.
14.8.1976: Left on maiden cruise from
San Juan, Puerto Rico.
10.1982-4.1983: Chartered by the
British Government as a troopship
running between Ascension Island and
Port Stanley, Falkland Islands.
5.4-16.6.1983: Post-charter refit at
Malta by Malta Drydocks.
16.12.1990: Transferred to the
Bahamas register.
20.12.1990: British register closed.
30.9.1992: Transferred to the Cunard
Steam-Ship Co. Ltd., London
12.11.1996: Sold to Awani Cruise Line
(P.T. Pelayaran Awani Modern Hotels),
Jakarta, Indonesia and renamed
AWANI DREAM 2.
1.12.1996: Registered in Panama.
14.2.1998: Sold to Royal Olympia
Cruise Line Inc., Piraeus, Greece and
renamed OLYMPIC COUNTESS.
1.4.1998: Transferred to Ocean Quest
Sea Carriers Inc., Monrovia, Liberia.
2.9.2002: Transferred to Solar
Navigation Corporation, Monrovia and
renamed OLYMPIA COUNTESS.
29.1.2004: Sold to Majestic
International Cruises Inc. (Trading
and Commercial Corporation),
Athens, Greece and renamed OCEAN
COUNTESS.
5.6.2005: Registered at Madeira.
7.12.2005: Chartered to Holiday
Kreuzfahrten G.m.b.H. and renamed
LILI MARLEEN.
2005: Sold to Maximus Navigation
Ltd., Madeira, Portugal (European
Classical Cruises, Piraeus).
11.10.2006: Renamed OCEAN
COUNTESS.
21.5.2007: Renamed RUBY.
1.1.2008: Reverted to OCEAN
COUNTESS.
2012: Still in existence.

Cunard Countess (above) and Cunard Princess were built as replacements for Carmania and Franconia. They were the first mass market cruise ships designed to Cunard's specifications and were larger than the Dutch-built cruise ships, which had been designed for Overseas National Airways. *[David Whiteside collection]*

Cunard Countess, seen as Olympia Countess (above) and Cunard Princess were fitted out in Italy and, although they were intended to have white funnels, their funnels were repainted in traditional Cunard colours. *[Russell Priest]*
Ocean Countess at Lisbon in September 2011 in the colours of Cruise and Maritime Voyages (below). *[Lisa Royall]*

CUNARD CONQUEST/CUNARD PRINCESS 1977-1995 Twin screw
O.N. 365261 17,586g 12,387n
462.6 x 74.9 x 19.8 feet.
Four 7-cyl. 4SCSA Burmeister & Wain-type geared-oil engines by Hitachi Zosen, Maizuru, Japan; 21,000 BHP, 21.5 knots.
Passengers: 950; *1990s*: 788.
12.12.1974: Launched by A/S Burmeister & Wain's Skibsbyggeri, Copenhagen, Denmark (Yard No. 859) as CUNARD CONQUEST.
30.10.1975: Registered at Southampton under the ownership of Cunard Cruise Ships Ltd. (Cunard Line Ltd.), London.
6.11.1975: Arrived at La Spezia, Italy for final fitting out by Industrie Navali Mechaniche Affini.
3.8.1976: Renamed CUNARD PRINCESS.
30.3.1977: Officially named at New York by Princess Grace of Monaco.
2.4.1977: Left on maiden cruise to Bermuda.
10.1980: Transferred to the Bahamas register.
20.10.1980: British register closed.
12.1990-9.1991: Chartered to U.S. Defence Department as rest and recuperation centre for U.S. troops serving in the Gulf War and based in Bahrein.
30.9.1992: Transferred to the Cunard Steam-Ship Co. Ltd., London.
15.4.1995: Sold to Gramerco International Corporation, Panama (Mediterranean Shipping Company S.A., Geneva, Switzerland) and renamed RHAPSODY.
2.6.1995: Transferred to Worldwide Capital Investments Inc., Nassau, Bahamas (Mediterranean Shipping Company S.A., Panama).
1.4.1996: Transferred to Gramerco International Corporation (Mediterranean Shipping Company S.A.), Panama.
25.9.2000: Transferred to Mediterranean Shipping Cruises S.p.A., Naples, Italy.
13.4.2009: Sold to Present Mint Marine Ltd., Panama (Mano Maritime Ltd., Haifa, Israel) and renamed GOLDEN IRIS.
2012: Still in existence.

Top: *Cunard Conquest* en route from Copenhagen to La Spezia for her final fitting out.
Upper middle: Although registered as *Cunard Conquest,* the second ship was completed as *Cunard Princess.* Seen at Vancouver on 12th May 1984 she also became the first passenger ship to be named in the City of New York, when she was officially named by Princess Grace of Monaco. *[V.H.Young and L.A.Sawyer]*
Lower middle: *Cunard Princess* at Madeira, astern of *Enrico Costa* (13,607/1950). *[Luis Miguel Correia]*
Bottom: *Rhapsody* was owned by MSC Cruises for 14 years. *[Luis Miguel Correia]*

CUNARD NAC

In 1983 Cunard bought Norwegian American Cruises' *Sagafjord* and *Vistafjord*, which were at that time among the top cruise ships in the world. They became part of a new company Cunard NAC registered in the Bahamas. Although the funnels were painted in Cunard colours, Cunard wisely retained the Norwegian officers and many of the Norwegian American Cruises' staff.

Sagafjord, post 1980 (above) and *Vistafjord* (below). *Vistafjord* was altered little throughout her career. However, in 1980 *Sagafjord* had a new deck fitted above the bridge with fifteen penthouse suites, many with balconies. For the purists, this addition spoilt *Sagafjord*'s sleek profile. *Vistafjord* was one of the last liners constructed on the Tyne and was Norwegian America Line's final liner. [*Above: V.H.Young and L.A.Sawyer, below: Russell Priest collection*]

SAGAFJORD 1983-1997 Twin screw
24,002g 13,340n;
1980: 24,108g 13,820n
551.4 x 80.3 x 27.1 feet.
  Two 9-cyl. 2SCSA Sulzer-type
oil engines by Société des Forges et
Chantiers de la Méditerranée, Havre,
France; 27,000 BHP, 20 knots.
Passengers: 85 first, 704 tourist; *1972*:
509 single class; *1980s*: 650.
13.6.1964: Launched by Société des
Forges et Chantiers de la Méditerranée,
La Seyne, France (Yard No. 1366) as
SAGAFJORD.
9.1965: Delivered to P/R Sagafjord
(Den Norske Amerikalinje A/S), Oslo,
Norway.
2.10.1965: Maiden voyage from Oslo
to New York.
5.1980: Transferred to K/S Norwegian
American Cruises A/S (Leif Høegh
and Co. A/S, managers), Oslo. Leif
Høegh had 50% of the ownership.
10-12.1980: Refit at Blohm & Voss
A.G., Hamburg, Germany which
included fitting an additional upper
deck with 15 penthouse suites.
1.1981: Leif Høegh and Co. A/S,
Oslo acquired control of Norwegian
American Cruises (later changed to
Norwegian American Line Cruises
A/S).
11.5.1983: Acquired by Cunard Line
Ltd., London for delivery in October
and registered in the Bahamas.
Marketed under the Cunard NAC
banner. The NAC name was dropped
in 1990.
8.4.1991: Ownership transferred to the
Cunard Steam-Ship Co. Ltd., London.
26.2.1996: Disabled by an engine
room fire in the South China Sea and
towed to Subic, near Manila. She was
sailing from Kota Kinabalu, Malaysia
to Hong Kong during a world cruise.
7.1996-4.1997: Chartered to German
tour operator Transocean Tours and
renamed GRIPSHOLM.
30.9.1997: Sold to Saga Shipping Co.
Ltd., Folkestone and renamed SAGA
ROSE.
6.12.2009: Sailed from Southampton
via the Cape of Good Hope bound for
China.
29.5.2010: Arrived Jiangyin for
demolition.

Sagafjord as built (top), at Cape
Town in Cunard colours (upper
middle), as *Gripsholm*, a name
held for less than a year, seen on
the Tilbury Landing Stage on 28th
August 1996 (lower middle) and
finally as *Saga Rose* (bottom).
[*Lower middle: Allan Ryszka-
Onions; bottom: Russell Priest*]

Vistafjord was in the Cunard fleet for 20 years. In 2003 she was reunited in the Saga Cruises' fleet with her near sister. *[Top: V.H. Young and L.A. Sawyer; middle: Luis Miguel Correia; bottom: Ian Shiffman]*

VISTAFJORD/CARONIA (3) 1983-2003 Twin screw

O.N. 902732 24,292g 12,771n
549.9 x 84.1 x 26.9 feet.
Two 9-cyl. 2SCSA Sulzer-type oil
engines by G. Clark and N.E.M. Ltd.,
Wallsend; 24,000 BHP, 20 knots.
Passengers: 635 (later 677).
15.5.1972: Launched by Swan Hunter
Shipbuilders Ltd., Wallsend (Yard No.
39) as VISTAFJORD.
15.5.1973: Delivered to Sameiet Vistafjord
(Den Norske Amerikalinje A/S), Oslo,
Norway.
22.5.1973: Maiden voyage from Oslo to
New York.
5.1980: Transferred to K/S Norwegian
American Cruises A/S (Leif Høegh and
Co. A/S, managers), Oslo.
1.1981: Leif Høegh and Co. A/S,
Oslo acquired control of Norwegian
American Cruises.
11.5.1983: Acquired by Cunard Line
Ltd., London for delivery in October
and registered in the Bahamas. Marketed
under the Cunard NAC banner. The
NAC name was dropped in 1990.
27.5.1991: Transferred to the Cunard
Steam-Ship Co. Ltd., London.
28.5.1998: Reverted to Cunard Line
Ltd., London.
7.12.1999: Registered at Southampton
under the ownership of Cunard Line
Ltd., Hamilton, Bermuda as CARONIA.
2.5.2003: Sold to Saga Shipping Co.
Ltd., Folkestone and renamed SAGA
RUBY.
25.1.2005: Registered at London.
23.11.2009: Transferred to Saga Cruises
Ltd.
2012: Still in existence.

Top: *Caronia*, outbound in the Solent in July 2004. *[Michael Green collection]*
Middle: *Caronia* arriving at Cape Town. *[Andrew Ingpen]*
Bottom: *Saga Ruby*. *[Russell Priest]*

SEA GODDESS CRUISES was the brainchild of the Norwegian former head of Norwegian Caribbean Line, Helge Naarstad, who recognised a niche for smaller ships offering the facilities and style of a modern cruise ship combined with the intimacy and luxury of a private yacht. *Sea Goddess I* and *Sea Goddess II*, seen here at Mykonos, carried only 116 passengers and were able to call at ports and resorts inaccessible to large cruise ships. Sea Goddess Cruises was not a financial success and the ships were chartered to Cunard in 1986 and acquired by the company in 1998. *[Luis Miguel Correia]*

SEA GODDESS I 1986-2000 Twin screw

O.N. 726415 4,253g 1,277n
297.1 x 47.9 x 15.7 feet.
Two 12-cyl. 4SCSA oil engines by O/Y Wärtsilä A/B, Helsinki, Finland; 4.800 BHP, 17.5 knots.
Passengers: 116.
11.7.1983: Launched by O/Y Wärtsilä A/B, Helsinki (Yard No. 466) as SEA GODDESS I.
3.1984: Delivered to A/S Norske Cruise, Oslo, Norway. Marketed as Sea Goddess Cruises.
7.4.1984: Maiden cruise from Malaga to Monte Carlo.
1986: Chartered to Cunard Line Ltd., Southampton.
1.4.1987: Transferred to P/R Norske Cruise A/S (A/S Norske Cruise, managers), Oslo.
4.11.1987: Transferred to the Norwegian International Register.
26.10.1995: Transferred to Norwegian Cruises Ltd., Douglas, Isle of Man.
1998: Acquired by Cunard Line, following the majority acquisition of Cunard by the Carnival Corporation.
1.9.1998: Transferred to Cunard White Star Ltd. (Cunard Line Ltd.), Hamilton, Bermuda and registered in Bahamas.
19.1.2000: Transferred to Seabourn Cruise Line Ltd. (Carnival Corporation), Miami, U.S.A. and renamed SEABOURN GODDESS I.
27.8.2001: Sold to SeaDream Yacht Club A/S, Oslo and renamed SEADREAM I.
2012: Still in existence.

SEA GODDESS II 1986-2000 Twin screw

O.N. 726416 4,260g 1,277n
297.1 x 47.9 x 15.7 feet.
Two 12-cyl. 4SCSA oil engines by O/Y Wärtsilä A/B, Vaasa, Finland; 4.800 BHP, 17.5 knots.
Passengers: 116.
29.9.1984: Launched by Hollming O/Y, Rauma, Finland as SEA GODDESS II. Her hull had been subcontracted by O/Y Wärtsilä A/B, Helsinki, Finland as Yard No. 467.
17.4.1985: Delivered to A/S Norske Cruise, Oslo. Marketed as Sea Goddess Cruises.
11.5.1985: Maiden cruise from Malaga.
1986: Chartered to Cunard Line Ltd., Southampton.
1.4.1987: Transferred to P/R Norske Cruise A/S (A/S Norske Cruise, managers), Oslo, Norway.
4.11.1987: Transferred to the Norwegian International Register.
6.11.1995: Transferred to Norwegian Cruises Ltd., Isle of Man.
1998: Acquired by Cunard, following the majority acquisition of Cunard by the Carnival Corporation.
1.9.1998: Transferred to Cunard White Star Ltd. (Cunard Line Ltd.), Hamilton, Bermuda and registered in Bahamas.
19.1.2000: Transferred to Seabourn Cruise Line Ltd. (Carnival Corporation), Miami, U.S.A. and renamed SEABOURN GODDESS II.
3.9.2001: Sold to SeaDream Yacht Club A/S, Oslo and renamed SEADREAM II.
2012: Still in existence.

Sea Goddess I. [Russell Priest]

Above: *Crown Monarch* at Montreal on 5th September 1992. *[Marc Piché]*
Bottom left: *Crown Monarch's* funnel in Cunard colours. *[Stephen Moore]*
Bottom right: *Crown Monarch* as *Alexander von Humboldt* . *[Fotoflite incorporating Skyfotos, 337248]*

CUNARD CROWN CRUISES

This was a short-lived (1993-1995) venture between Cunard and Crown Cruise Line, a subsidiary of the Effjohn Group, whereby Cunard would take over the sales and marketing of the three Crown ships and market them under the Cunard Crown name. The ships operated in Cunard funnel colours.

CROWN MONARCH 1993-1994 Twin screw

15,271g 5,574n
411.7 x 67.6 x 18.7 feet.
Two sets of 9-cyl. 4SCSA Normo-type oil engines by BMV Bergen Diesel A/S; Bergen, Norway; 17,989 BHP, 18.8 knots.
Passengers: 530.
30.10.1989: Launched by Union Navale de Levante S.A., Valencia, Spain (Yard No. 185) for Cruceros de Valencia S.A.,

Panama (Grundstad Maritime Overseas Inc., Boca Raton, Florida, U.S.A.) as CROWN MONARCH.
1.11.1990: Delivered.
1.12.1990: Maiden cruise for Crown Cruise Line from Palm Beach, Florida to the Caribbean.
1992: Ownership transferred to Crown Cruise Line S.A., Panama (Commodore Cruise Line Ltd., Hollywood, Florida). Ultimate owner was the Effjohn group.
27.1.1993: Formation of Cunard Crown Cruises with Cunard Line responsible for sales and marketing. Marketed as CUNARD CROWN MONARCH but not renamed.
5.11.1993: Arrived at Sydney, Australia for cruises to the South Pacific for Cunard Crown Cruises.
15.10.1994: Final arrival at Sydney where she was renamed NAUTICAN and chartered by Havens Pte. Ltd., Singapore as a gambling ship based at Singapore.
1995: Commodore Cruise Line sold to

a consortium headed by JEMJ Financial Services Inc., Miami, Florida.
1996: Transferred to Hong Kong for overnight gambling cruises for Wide Asia Ltd., Hong Kong and renamed WALRUS.
1997: Managed by SeaHawk Asia Ltd., Hong Kong.
2005: Laid up at Singapore.
5.2006: Sold to Club Cruise. Chartered to Vision Cruceros and renamed JULES VERNES.
5.2008: Chartered to Phoenix Reisen and renamed ALEXANDER VON HUMBOLDT.
11.2008: Club Cruise ceased operations and ship laid up.
11.2009: Bought at auction by All Leisure Group plc.
2010: Resumed Phoenix Reisen charter.
2011: Chartered by Turkish tour operator Bamtur.
4.12.2012: Naming ceremony at Portsmouth for All Leisure subsidiary Voyages of Discovery as VOYAGER.

CROWN JEWEL 1993-1995 Twin screw

19,089g 8,103n
458.8 x 73.8 x 17.7 feet.
Two sets of 8-cyl. 4SCSA oil engines by Echevarria Wärtsilä Diesel S.A., Bermeo, Finland; 17,826 BHP, 18.4 knots.
Passengers: 820.
30.5.1991: Launched by Union Navale de Levante S.A., Valencia, Spain (Yard No. 197) for Crown Jewel Inc., Panama (Commodore Cruise Line Ltd., Hollywood, Florida, U.S.A.) as CROWN JEWEL. Ultimate owner was the Effjohn group.
22.7.1992: Arrived at Barcelona for use as a hotel ship during the 1992 Olympics.
11.8.1992: Maiden voyage from Barcelona to New York.
27.1.1993: Formation of Cunard Crown Cruises with Cunard responsible for sales and marketing. Marketed as CUNARD CROWN JEWEL but not renamed.
5.1995: Sold to Superstar Gemini Ltd., Panama (Star Cruises Private Ltd., Singapore) and renamed SUPERSTAR GEMINI.
5.2007: Sold to Jewel Owner Ltd., Nassau, Bahamas (Star Cruises, managers) and chartered by Star Cruises.
1.2009: Management changed to International Shipping Partners, Miami, Florida.
2010: Chartered by the Spanish company Happy Cruises (Quail Travel Group) and renamed GEMINI.
9.2011: Quail Travel Group ceased trading. Laid up at Tilbury
2012: Transferred to Marshall Islands flag. Still in existence.

CROWN DYNASTY 1993-1997 Twin screw

19,089g 8,103n;
2008: 24,344g 10,164n
458.8 x 73.8 x 17.7 feet;
2008: 639.8 x 73.8 x 17.5 feet.
Two sets of 8-cyl. 4SCSA oil engines by Echevarria Wärtsilä Diesel S.A., Bermeo, Finland; 17,826 BHP, 18.4 knots.
Passengers: 916; *2001*: 727; *2008*: 977.
31.1.1992: Launched by Union Navale de Levante S.A., Valencia Spain (Yard No. 198) for Crown Dynasty Inc., Panama (Commodore Cruise Line Ltd., Hollywood, Florida, U.S.A.) as CROWN DYNASTY. Ultimate owner was the Effjohn group.
1.6.1993: Delivered.
17.7.1993: Maiden cruise under the Cunard Crown Cruises banner. Cunard was responsible for the sales and marketing. Marketed as CUNARD CROWN DYNASTY but not renamed.
1995: Commodore Cruise Line sold to a consortium headed by JEMJ Financial Services Inc., Miami, Florida, U.S.A.

Crown Jewel in Cunard colours. *[Andy Hernandez]*

Super Star Gemini. [Russell Priest]

Crown Dynasty at Vancouver on 18th July 1994. *[Marc Piché]*

5.1995: Cunard chartered the ship and took full operational control. She was based on the United States west coast and marketed as CUNARD DYNASTY although she retained her original name.
1.3.1997: Chartered to Majesty Cruise Line under Cunard management and renamed CROWN MAJESTY.
29.9.1997: Chartered to Norwegian Cruise Line, under their management, and renamed NORWEGIAN DYNASTY.

10.1999: Reverted to CROWN DYNASTY.
11.5.2001: Following the bankruptcy of Commodore Cruise Line, sold to Capital Bank Leasing 6 Ltd., Manchester and leased to Fred. Olsen Cruises Ltd., Ipswich. Managed by Red Band A/S, Oslo, Norway (a Fred. Olsen affiliate) and renamed BRAEMAR
5-6.2008: Lengthened by Blohm & Voss, Hamburg, Germany.
2012: Still in existence.

Braemar, formerly the Crown Dynasty, seen at Oslo in June 2006 (left) and after lengthening (right). *[Lennart Rydberg and Willem van der Moolen]*

CUNARD ROYAL VIKING

In 1994, Cunard purchased the world's highest rated cruise ship, *Royal Viking Sun*, and the Royal Viking Line name from Norwegian Caribbean Line.

The ship was marketed initially as a separate brand, with the Royal Viking colours unchanged. Within two years the distinctive Royal Viking sea eagle motif was incorporated into the traditional Cunard funnel colour scheme.

ROYAL VIKING SUN 1994-2002
Twin screw
37,845g 14,054n
562.5 x 94.8 x 23.8 feet.
Two sets of 8-cyl. 4SCSA Sulzer-type oil engines by Wärtsilä Diesel O/Y, Vaasa, Finland; 28,713 BHP, 21.5 knots.
Passengers: 766.
5.1988: Floated out of building dock by Wärtsilä Marine Industries Inc., Åbo, Finland (Yard No. 1296) as ROYAL VIKING SUN.
26.11.1988: Delivered to Kloster Cruise Ltd., Hamilton, Bermuda and registered at Nassau, Bahamas. Marketed as Royal Viking Line.
30.11.1988. Maiden voyage from Greenwich, London to Miami.
1993: Transferred to subsidiary Royal Viking Line, Nassau, Bahamas.
2.7.1994: Acquired by Cunard Line Ltd., Southampton, remaining on the Bahamian register.
28.5.1998: Following the majority acquisition of Cunard by the Carnival Corporation, transferred to Cunard White Star Ltd. (Cunard Line Ltd.), Hamilton, Bermuda. Registration remained in Bahamas.
26.11.1999: Arrived at Southampton as SEABOURN SUN after a one month refit by Lloyd Werft G.m.b.H., Bremerhaven, Germany. Marketing was transferred to Seabourn Cruise Line.

Upper: *Royal Viking Sun*. *[Ian Shiffman]*
Lower: *Prinsendam*. *[Russell Priest]*

1.6.2002: Transferred within the Carnival Group to HAL Antillen N.V., Willemstad, Curaçao (Holland America Line Westours, Inc., Seattle, U.S.A., managers) and renamed PRINSENDAM under the Dutch flag.
2012: Still in existence.

Seabourn Pride at Lisbon. [Luis Miguel Correia]

SEABOURN CRUISE LINE

The luxury brand Seabourn Cruise Line became a subsidiary of Cunard in 1998, following the majority acquisition of Cunard by the Carnival Corporation. This arrangement lasted until 2005.

SEABOURN PRIDE 1998-2005 Twin screw

9,975g 3,023n
368.7 x 62.3 x 16.4 feet.
Two sets of 4SCSA Normo-type oil engines by BMV Bergen Diesel A/S, Bergen, Norway each set comprised of a 12-cyl. engine of 5,927 BHP (inner) and an 8-cyl. engine of 3,970 BHP (outer); 16 knots.
Passengers: 204.
22.7.1988 Launched by Schichau Seebeckwerft A.G., Bremerhaven, Germany (Yard No. 1065) as SEABOURN PRIDE.
11.1988: Delivered to Seabourn Cruise Line A/S, Lysaker, Norway. Registered at Oslo in Norwegian International Register.
1.1.1992: Transferred to Seabourn Cruise Line Ltd., Monrovia, Liberia but remained under the Norwegian flag.
19.2.1992: Carnival Cruise Lines Inc. purchased a 25% share in the company. This was increased to 50% in 1996 and 100% in 1999.
28.5.1998: Following the majority acquisition of Cunard by the Carnival Corporation, Cunard Line Ltd. and Seabourn Cruise Line A/S were merged and Seabourn Cruise Line became a subsidiary of Cunard Line Ltd.
7.1998: Transferred to Cunard Line Ltd., Bermuda.

24.5.2002: Registered in the Bahamas.
1.2005: Following merger of Cunard operations with Princess Cruises, Seabourn Cruises demerged from Cunard. Ownership changed to Seabourn Cruise Line Ltd., Liberia. Seabourn head office remained in Miami.
2011: Seabourn head office moved to Seattle, headquarters of Holland America Line.
2012: Still in existence.

SEABOURN SPIRIT 1998-2005 Twin screw

9,975g 3,023n
368.7 x 62.3 x 16.4 feet.
Two sets of 4SCSA Normo-type oil engines by BMV Bergen Diesel A/S, Bergen, Norway each set comprising a 12-cyl. engine of 5,927 BHP (inner) and an 8-cyl. engine of 3,970 BHP (outer), 16 knots.
Passengers: 204.
17.3.1989: Launched by Schichau Seebeckwerft A.G., Bremerhaven, Germany (Yard No. 1070) as SEABOURN SPIRIT.
11.1989: Delivered to Seabourn Cruise Line A/S., Lysaker, Norway. Registered at Oslo in Norwegian International Register.
1.1.1992: Transferred to Seabourn Cruise Line Ltd., Monrovia, Liberia but remained under the Norwegian flag.
19.2.1992: Carnival Cruise Lines Inc. purchased a 25% share in the company.

Seabourn Pride. [Russell Priest]

This was increased to 50% in 1996 and 100% in 1999.

28.5.1998: Following the majority acquisition of Cunard by the Carnival Corporation, Cunard Line Ltd. and Seabourn Cruise Line A/S were merged and Seabourn Cruise Line became a subsidiary of Cunard Line Ltd.

7.1998: Transferred to Cunard Line Ltd., Bermuda.

1.11.2001: Registered in the Bahamas.

1.2005: Following merger of Cunard operations with Princess Cruises, Seabourn Cruises demerged from Cunard. Transferred to Seabourn Cruise Line Ltd., Monrovia. Seabourn head office remained in Miami.

2011: Seabourn head office moved to Seattle, headquarters of Holland America Line.

2012: Still in existence.

SEABOURN LEGEND 1998-2005 Twin screw

9,975g 3,023n

368.7 x 62.3 x 16.4 feet.

Two sets of 4SCSA Normo-type oil engines by BMV Bergen Diesel A/S, Bergen, Norway each set comprising a 12-cyl. engine of 5,927 BHP (inner) and an 8-cyl. engine of 3,970 BHP (outer), 16 knots.

Passengers: 204.

24.5.1991: Launched by Schichau Seebeckwerft A.G., Bremerhaven, Germany (Yard No. 1071) as ROYAL VIKING QUEEN. A sister to the earlier Seabourn ships and an option never taken up by Seabourn Cruise Line.

2.1992: Delivered to Kloster Cruise Ltd., Hamilton, Bermuda and registered at Nassau, Bahamas. Marketed as Royal Viking Line.

1993: Transferred to Royal Viking Line, Bahamas.

2.1995: After sale of Royal Viking Line to Cunard, ownership was transferred to a Kloster subsidiary, Royal Cruise Line Ltd., Bermuda and she was renamed QUEEN ODYSSEY.

8.1995: Transferred to Norwegian Cruise Lines Ltd.

18.1.1996: Sold to Seabourn Cruise Line Ltd., Monrovia, Liberia. Registered at Oslo in Norwegian International Register.

22.7.1996: Renamed SEABOURN LEGEND.

28.5.1998: Following the majority acquisition of Cunard by the Carnival Corporation, Cunard Line Ltd. and Seabourn Cruise Line A/S were merged and Seabourn Cruise Line became a subsidiary of Cunard Line Ltd.

7.1998: Transferred to Cunard Line Ltd., Bermuda.

21.1.2002: Registered in the Bahamas.

1.2005: Following merger of Cunard operations with Princess Cruises, Seabourn Cruises demerged from Cunard. Ownership changed to Seabourn Cruise Line Ltd., Monrovia. Seabourn head office remained in Miami.

2012: Seabourn head office moved to Seattle, headquarters of Holland America Line.

2012: Still in existence.

Seabourn Spirit. [Russell Priest]

Seabourn Legend. [Russell Priest]

Seabourn Legend. [Russell Priest]

NEW QUEENS

The French-built *Queen Mary 2* was the first ship to be delivered to the new Cunard fleet. She entered service in January 2004 and at the time was the largest passenger ship in the world. A fast ship, she was designed not only for transatlantic crossings but also world-wide cruising. She was joined respectively in 2007 and 2010 by the 90,000-ton *Queen Victoria* and *Queen Elizabeth*, a pair of ships built in Italy to a standard Carnival company design known as the Vista-class.

QUEEN MARY 2 2003- Quadruple pods
O.N 901558 148,528g 98,720n
988.3 x 134.5 x 33.8 feet.
Four 16-cyl. oil engines by Wärtsilä O/Y, Turku, Finland and two General Electric

gas turbines driving four generators supplying current to electric motors in four azimuthing propulsion pods; 117,200 kW, 29 knots.
Passengers: 3,056.
21.3.2003: Floated out by Chantiers de L'Atlantique, St Nazaire, France (Yard No. G32) as QUEEN MARY 2.
2.12.2003: Registered at Southampton under the ownership of the Cunard Line Ltd., Hamilton, Bermuda (Carnival Corporation, Miami, U.S.A.).
22.12.2003: Delivered.
12.1.2004: Left on maiden voyage from Southampton to Fort Lauderdale, Florida.
2005: Transferred to Carnival plc, London (Carnival Corporation, Miami).
1.12.2011: Registered at Hamilton, Bermuda.
2012: Still in service.

Top and middle: *Queen Mary 2* sailing from Southampton on 13th July 2012. *[Stefan and Sara Venter (upixphotography.com)]*
Below: At Wellington, New Zealand on 26th February 2011. *[Stephen Berry]*

Queen Mary 2 at Melbourne, Australia on 5th March 2012 (upper) and arriving at Cape Town, South Africa (lower).
[Upper: Alf Batchelder; lower: Ian Shiffman]

QUEEN VICTORIA 2007-
Twin pods

O.N 913508 90,049g 50,125n
870.5 x 105.6 x 32.9 feet.
Four 16-cyl. Sulzer-type oil engines by
Wärtsilä Italia S.p.A., Trieste, Italy driving
two generators supplying current to electric
motors in two azimuthing propulsion pods,
64,200kW, 21.7 knots.
Passengers: 2,014.
15.1.2007: Floated out by Fincantieri-

Cantieri Navali Italiani S.p.A., Venice, Italy
(Yard No. 6127) as QUEEN VICTORIA.
A Vista-class Carnival standard ship, she
replaced another Vista-class QUEEN
VICTORIA (Yard No. 6078), which had
been ordered by Holland America Line
but allocated to Cunard and laid down as
QUEEN VICTORIA on *12.7.2003*. Nearing
completion she was transferred to P&O
Cruises and delivered in April 2005 as
ARCADIA.

22.11.2007: Delivered.
30.11.2007: Registered at Southampton
under the ownership of Carnival plc, London
(Carnival Corporation, Miami, U.S.A.)
11.12.2007: Left on maiden cruise from
Southampton to Northern Europe.
27.10.2011: Registered at Hamilton,
Bermuda.
2012: Still in service.

Opposite: Five photographs of *Queen Victoria* under construction, showing the Grand Lobby (top right).
This page: On trials (upper) and in the Solent (lower). *[Fincantieri; Stefan and Sara Venter (upixphotography.com)]*

Queen Victoria sailing from Southampton (top left), at Madeira (top right), a stern view (middle right) and at Lisbon (bottom). *[Stefan and Sara Venter (upixphotography.com); Luis Miguel Correia; M. Green; Luis Miguel Correia]*

QUEEN ELIZABETH (2) 2010- Twin pods
O.N 916716 90,901g 50,125n
870.2 x 106.6 x 32.3 feet.
Four 12-cyl MaK Motoren-type oil
engines by Caterpillar G.m.b.H. and Co.
K.G., Hamburg, Germany driving two
generators supplying current to electric
motors in two azimuthing propulsion pods;

64,000kW, 23.7 knots.
Passengers: 2,092.
6.1.2010: Floated out at Fincantieri-Cantieri
Navali Italiani S.p.A., Monfalcone, Italy
(Yard No. 6187) as QUEEN ELIZABETH.
She is a Vista-class Carnival standard ship.
30.9.2010: Delivered. Registered at
Southampton under the ownership of

Carnival plc, London (Carnival Corporation,
Miami, U.S.A.).
12.10.2010: Left on maiden cruise from
Southampton to Atlantic Isles.
24.10.2011: Registered at Hamilton, Bermuda.
2012: Still in service.

Queen Elizabeth's stern is more vertical than *Queen Victoria* with a larger Lido Deck area. She also has a large enclosed space below her signal mast. She was photographed sailing from Southampton on 13th July 2012. *[Stefan and Sara Venter (upixphotography.com)]*

Queen Elizabeth

Above: To commemorate H.M. The Queen's Diamond Jubilee, Cunard held a spectacular evening celebration at Southampton on 5th June 2012 when all three Cunard Queens were in dock at the same time.

Below: On 13th July 2012 another unique event took place when the three ships sailed in convoy from Southampton for the first time during daylight hours. *[Stefan and Sara Venter (upixphotography.com)]*

AN ODDITY

In 1983, Cunard won a two-year British Government contract to carry construction workers and supplies for a new Falkland Islands airport. The Danish passenger-car ferry *England* was acquired for the service which ran between Cape Town and Port Stanley, Falkland Islands.

ENGLAND 1983-1986 Twin screw
O.N. 703651 8,221g 4,277n
410.0 x 63.3 x 18.2 feet.
Two 10-cyl. 2SCSA Burmeister & Wain-type oil engines by Helsingør Skibsværft og Maskinbyggeri A/S, Elsinore, Denmark; 14,000 BHP, 21 knots.
Passengers: 155 first, 244 second; *1974*: 120.
10.12.1963: Launched by Helsingør Skibsværft og Maskinbyggeri A/S, Elsinore (Yard No. 369) as ENGLAND.
25.5.1964: Delivered to Det Forenede Dampskibs-Selskab A/S (DFDS), Esbjerg, Denmark. Used initially as a passenger-car ferry on the Esbjerg to Harwich route and for cruises during the winter months.
1974: Rebuilt with increased passenger and car capacity.
16.9.1983: Acquired by Cunard Steam-Ship Co. Ltd., London for use between Cape Town and Port Stanley, Falkland Islands carrying construction workers and supplies for a new Falkland Islands airport as part of a two-year British Government contract.
2.7.1985: Arrived at Birkenhead for lay up.

England underway (above) and arriving at Liverpool at the end of her contract in July 1985 (below). *[Above: Russell Priest, below: Malcolm Cranfield]*

1986: Sold to Start Point Investments S.A., Panama (Bilinder Marine Corporation S.A.) (John S. Latsis, Piraeus, Greece) and renamed AMERICA XIII.
23.12.1986: Sailed from Birkenhead for Jeddah for use as an accommodation vessel for oil refinery construction workers.
1987: Laid up at Piraeus and renamed initially EMMA and then EUROPA under the Greek flag. Later partially converted into a luxury private yacht at the Eleusis Shipyards S.A. This plan was abandoned

and she was laid up in Eleusis Bay.
3.2001: Sold for demolition in Alang, India. Renamed EUROPE and registered at Kingstown, St. Vincent and Grenadines for the delivery voyage.
24.3.2001: Sailed for Alang from Laurium, Greece under tow of Russian salvage tug UTYOS (1,160/1983).
3.4.2001: Sailed from Suez and was later reported to have foundered in bad weather near Aden in the Red Sea.

MEDITERRANEAN, HAVRE, CHANNEL ISLANDS AND MIDDLE EAST SERVICES

SERVICES TO THE MEDITERRANEAN

Two of the most significant events for 19th century British shipping occurred in 1849: the repeal of the Navigation Acts and the repeal of the Corn Laws. Both had favoured trade between Britain and its colonial territories. This not only paved the way for a free trade economy in Britain, it also significantly reduced the cost of food, by allowing cheaper foreign imports such as grain from Egypt and the Russian Steppes. This was followed in 1853 by a reduction in duties on fruit, tea, cocoa and other foodstuffs.

To Charles MacIver the opportunities of this laissez-faire approach to trade were obvious. In 1849 he sent Donald Currie, his head of cargo, to France to open agencies in Havre and Paris in order to secure French passengers and freight bound for the United States, which could connect with the Liverpool transatlantic service. Currie, founder of Castle Line, later Union-Castle Line, worked for Charles MacIver from 1844 to 1862. In 1850 Charles MacIver and Company commenced a feeder service between Havre and Liverpool with George Burn's wooden paddle steamer *Commodore* (760/1838). In April the following year, Brownlow, Pearson and Company's screw steamer *British Queen* (773/1849) was chartered to operate a new service between Liverpool and Constantinople (modern day Istanbul). Prior to the completion of the Suez Canal in 1869, much of the cargo from India and the Far East was carried overland from Suez to Alexandria whilst Constantinople remained the crossroads for trade between the East and Europe, as it had done for centuries. In the early part of the 18th century, a number of well-known Liverpool shipping companies started routes to Italy and the eastern Mediterranean. These included Bibby

Line and James Moss and Company, which later became Moss-Hutchison Line. Moss and Bibby were among the first to introduce steam ships to this area, a fact which caused considerable angst among shippers of fruit who felt that steam would damage the flavour of the fruit. Up to that point, fruit tended to be carried in small but fast schooners. Currants, raisins and figs were also packed in small consignments aboard these ships as shippers were convinced that this was one way of keeping prices high.

The success of MacIver's new Mediterranean route persuaded his partners in The British and North American Royal Mail Steam Packet Company to join in the venture. They purchased *British Queen* in 1852 and on 17th July 1852 she sailed under her new owners from Liverpool to Constantinople via Gibraltar and Malta. She was also the company's first screw-driven ship. The following year, a new joint stock company was established with Charles MacIver, the Burns family and Samuel Cunard as trustees. The British and Foreign Steam Navigation Company which, like The British and North American Royal Mail Steam Packet Company, was registered at Glasgow. Operating under the banner of Burns and MacIver, five new ships were completed in 1853 by Denny, Dumbarton, including *Teneriffe*, which extended the route network to Alexandria in June 1853. The company was formally constituted on 1st October 1855 with 1,000 shares divided as follows: Charles MacIver 312; Samuel Cunard 187; James Burns 167; John Burns 167 and George Burns 167.

Soon after the start of the new line, the Crimean War (1853-1856) broke out. Thirteen Cunard ships were chartered by the British Government for use as supply

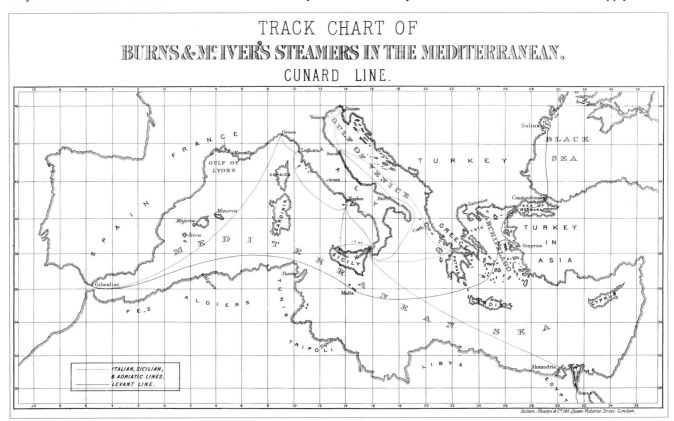

The Mediterranean service was operated under the Burns and MacIver name.

and troopships, including five of the Mediterranean fleet: *Balbec*, *British Queen*, *Karnak*, *Melita* and *Taurus*. For his contribution to the war effort, Samuel Cunard was knighted in 1859.

Between 1853 and 1866 twenty three ships were built for the service. Most were less than 3,000 gross tons, with nine constructed by Denny and nine on the Clyde by J. and G. Thomson. The cargo carried was varied and included tobacco, wool, silk, Indian corn, cotton, barley, wine and all kinds of exotic goods from carpets to boxes of honey. Even opium was carried. Liverpool had a large Chinese community and in the 19th century opium dens were legal and, of course, the drug was used extensively for medicinal purposes. Most of the Mediterranean ships had limited passenger accommodation but in the 1860s a number of the fleet were given expanded steerage space and placed on the Atlantic route carrying immigrants to the United States. In the early 1870s four of the 1860-built ships were also lengthened at Belfast by Harland and Wolff.

In July 1878, The British and Foreign Steam Navigation Company was absorbed into the Cunard Steamship Co. Ltd. By then the Mediterranean fleet consisted of twenty-two ships. The main routes were:

Italian, Sicilian and Adriatic Lines: weekly to Gibraltar, Genoa, Leghorn, Naples, Trieste and Venice and fortnightly to Palermo, Messina, Catania, Patras, Corfu, Bari, Ancona and Alexandria.

Levant Line: every three weeks to Gibraltar, Malta, Smyrna, Constantinople and occasionally, Sulina in Romania.

By 1893 there were seven ships on the Mediterranean service, with an average age of 31 years. In fact, the last ship built for the route, *Palmyra*, had been delivered in 1866. A replacement programme was urgently needed and an order was placed with the Belfast shipbuilder Workman, Clark for three 2,935g cargo-only freighters, which were completed in 1897 and 1898. This trio was followed by a pair of slightly larger ships, which were constructed in north east England and delivered in 1899 and 1903. In 1909, the same year as *Aleppo*, the last of the original fleet was sent to the breakers, three freighters were bought from the Plate Steam Ship Co. Ltd. In 1911 another second-hand vessel was purchased and the fleet size once again stood at nine ships. Unfortunately, five of these were sunk by German submarines during the 1914-1918 conflict.

At the end of the First World War, Cunard acquired a controlling interest in the America-Levant Line Ltd., which had been established in 1912 by Stanley and John Thompson, who went on to found Silver Line in 1925. The America-Levant Line, whose ships had *River* names, was formed to carry goods between the Mediterranean and east coast ports of the United States. The original shareholders in the company were the Thompson brothers (3,300 shares), a Smyrna-based merchant and ship-owner T. Bowen Rees and Co. Ltd. (1,800 shares) and the trading company MacAndrews and Forbes (6,800 shares). Whilst T. Bowen Rees owned the Egypt and Levant Steamship Co. Ltd., MacAndrews and Forbes, which had been founded in the mid-19th century by two Scottish entrepreneurs, was one of the largest producers of liquorice in the world. Much of the liquorice was exported from Turkey to the U.S. for use in the tobacco industry as it not only sweetens the taste, it also helps to keep the tobacco alight. MacAndrews and Forbes sold its controlling shareholding in America-Levant Line to Cunard in 1918 whilst S. and J. Thompson remained the managers of the ships. Cunard bought the shares in the hope of carrying emigrants from south eastern Europe to the U.S., but this was never realised because of changes to emigration quotas and United States government competition in the Mediterranean from the United States Shipping Board. However, in post-war years the America-Levant ships operated between Smyrna, Constantinople, Salonika, Piraeus and New York. Between 1923 and 1926, three of the Cunard V-name freighters were sold to America-Levant Line.

In the latter half of the 1920s, a quartet of Mediterranean traders were ordered from the Thompson family yard in Sunderland, as replacements for Cunard's four elderly Mediterranean ships. The 2,400g B-class ships were delivered in 1928. Initially owned by America-Levant Line and under Thompson management, they were transferred to Cunard Line ownership in 1930 with the sale of Cunard's shareholding in America-Levant Line to S. and J. Thompson. From 1930 to 1946, the B-ships were the sole cargo-only vessels in the Cunard fleet and were not transferred to Cunard White Star Line in 1934.

On Sunday 3rd September 1939 war was declared with Germany and on 5th September *Bosnia* became the second British merchant ship in the Second World War to be sunk by U-boat. The first was the unarmed and unescorted Donaldson liner *Athenia* (13,465/1923) which had been torpedoed without warning by the German submarine *U 30*. *Bosnia* was forced to stop by gunfire from *U 47*, some 120 miles from the north west corner of Spain. One crew member was killed whilst the remaining crew were allowed

LIVERPOOL TO THE MEDITERRANEAN.

FARES

(FROM LIVERPOOL), INCLUDING PROVISIONS, BUT WITHOUT WINES OR LIQUORS, WHICH CAN BE OBTAINED ON BOARD.

To GIBRALTAR	£10 0	To CORFU	£20 0
,, GENOA	13 13	,, ANCONA	21 0
,, LEGHORN	14 14	,, TRIESTE	21 0
,, NAPLES	15 15	,, MALTA	15 0
,, PALERMO and CATANIA		,, SYRA	18 0
(*via Italy*)	16 16	,, SMYRNA	20 0
,, MESSINA (*via*) *Italy*	17 17	,, CONSTANTINOPLE	20 0
,, PATRAS	20 0	,, MALTA and back	25 0

Voyage out and Home, £40.

CHILDREN OVER **2** *AND UNDER* **12** *YEARS OF AGE HALF FARE.*

The Passage-money as above is exclusive of beer, wines, and spirits; and, in the event of quarantine, passengers will be maintained on board at the rate of 5s. per day.

PASSENGERS.—Tickets are granted for the voyage out and home, by any one of the above routes, for £40 each passenger, available for four months, entitling the holder to stop at two ports on the route, and to continue the voyage by succeeding steamers. Malta and Gibraltar are generally the only ports at which the steamers call on the passage home. The voyage out and home usually occupies from seven to eight weeks.

BAGGAGE.—First-class passengers are allowed 20 cubic feet of personal baggage. One shilling per cubic foot will be charged on all above that quantity. Names and destination to be distinctly marked on the packages; and passengers are requested to reduce to the smallest quantity such indispensable articles as they may require to have in the cabins, in which no heavy baggage, trunks, boxes, or portmanteaus are allowed. The Company not to be held liable for any damage to or loss of baggage, nor for unavoidable delays, accidents, fire, steam, or sea risk of any kind whatever.

The length of the passage from Liverpool to Gibraltar is about 5 days; Genoa, 10 days; Leghorn, 12 days; Naples, 14 days; Palermo, 15 days; Messina, 16 days; Patras, 17 days; Corfu, 18 days; Catania, 16 days; Bari, 17 days; Ancona, 18 days; Trieste, 20 days; Venice, 26 days; Malta, 10 days; Syra, 13 days; Smyrna, 14 days; and Constantinople, 16 days.

The stay at Gibraltar, Malta, Syra, Palermo, Messina, Patras, Corfu, Catania, and Bari, is about 12 hours at each; at Leghorn, 1 day; Ancona, 1 day; Naples, 1 day; Genoa, 2 days; Trieste, 6 days; Venice, 6 days; Constantinople, 6 days; Smyrna, outwards 1 day, homewards 6 days; and Alexandria, 8 days.

FOREIGN AGENTS:—M. H. BLAND & Co., Gibraltar; CARLO FIGOLI, Genoa; WILLIAM MILLER, Leghorn; HOLME & Co., Naples; THOMAS BROTHERS, Palermo; EDWARD OATES & NEPHEW, Messina; DENNIS MALTESO, Patras; PANAJOTTI CREMIDI, Corfu; PAOLUCCI PAGANINI & Co., Bari; FRANCIS KANE, Ancona; A. & C. M. SCHRÖDER, Trieste; G. SARFATTI, Venice; ROSE & Co., Malta; ANTONIO E. MAVROGORDATO, Syra; T. & J. MALCOZZI, Smyrna; C. & E. GRACE, Constantinople; WATSON & YOUELL, Sulina & Galatz; R. MUNTZ, Odessa; BARKER & Co., Alexandria; JOSE SERRA Y CALSINA, Barcelona; F. SAGRISTA Y COLL, Valencia and Carthagena; M. SANCHEZ DELGADO, Almeria; ANDREW REYES, Malaga; E. PINTO BASTO & Co., Lisbon; etc., etc.

For further particulars, apply in London to WILLIAM CUNARD, 6, St. Helen's Place, Bishopsgate Street, and 28, Pall Mall, S.W.; in Glasgow to G. & J. BURNS, 267, Argyle Street; in Manchester at 77A, Market Street; or to

BURNS & MAC IVER, 1, RUMFORD STREET, LIVERPOOL.

F   33

List of fares from an 1878 Cunard guide book.

MEDITERRANEAN SAILINGS
Loading Berth: North 2 Huskisson Dock.

GIBRALTAR, MALTA, PATRAS, PIRAEUS, THESSALONIKI, IZMIR, ISTANBUL, HAIDAR-PASHA, BOURGAS, VARNA and CONSTANZA.

STEAMER ... ... Mid. Jan.

CHANNEL ISLANDS and HAVRE
REGULAR SAILINGS MAINTAINED
CUNARD LINE,
Cunard Buildings, Liverpool.
(Tel.: Bank 9200) or Local Agents.

December 1939 Cunard advertisement in 'The Journal of Commerce'.

to get into lifeboats. Just over an hour later, *Bosnia* was sunk by a single torpedo. The commander of *U 47* was Günther Prien, one of the German Navy's most famous submariners. The first U-boat commander to win the Iron Cross, his *U 47* sank 31 ships in only 18 months.

The remaining trio had eventful wartime careers and were joined in 1947 by a replacement for *Bosnia*. The engines-aft U.S.-built C1-M-AV1-type standard ship *Brescia* was not only Cunard's first cargo motor ship, at 3,817g, she was also the largest Cunard Liverpool-Mediterranean trader. Her cargo capacity was 225,000 cubic feet, including 9,830 cubic feet of insulated space.

The B-class ships were replaced between 1953 and 1955 by *Pavia*, *Lycia* and *Phrygia*, the first motor ships built for Cunard. These handsome ships had four holds with over 7,000 cubic feet of upper 'tween deck insulated cargo space. They also had relatively short careers with Cunard. In 1964, *Lycia* and *Phrygia* were transferred to the fortnightly Liverpool-Boston cargo service. They were also used on the summer-only Canadian Great Lakes service before being sold in 1965. In the meantime, the Liverpool-Mediterranean route continued to operate with *Brescia* and chartered vessels. This ceased in 1965 when *Brescia* was sold and the two chartered German ships, *Leabeth* (2,099/1956) and *Johanna* (1,980/1953), were transferred to the Great Lakes run. Although this ended 113 years of Cunard trading between Liverpool and the Mediterranean, the service to North Africa continued to be operated by Cunard's subsidiary Thos. and Jno. Brocklebank.

HAVRE AND CHANNEL ISLAND SERVICE

Opened in 1850, the Liverpool-Havre route was originally operated by Charles MacIver and Company with George Burn's *Commodore* (760/1838) and *Admiral* (929/1840). In 1853 the weekly service came under the banner of Burns and MacIver and ownership of The British and Foreign Steam Navigation Company. *Commodore* was joined by the former Pictou-Quebec feeder paddle steamer *Margaret* and was replaced in 1854 by the screw-driven *Delta*. *Delta* was transferred to the Halifax-Bermuda mail service in 1856 and later in the 1850s *British Queen*, *Stromboli* and *Balbec* were placed on the route. These ships not only carried cargo but also French-speaking immigrants bound for the United States and Canada. In 1856 and 1857 the company briefly operated a direct service to New York from Havre and, during the 1870s, three new ships were built for the Liverpool-Havre service: *Cherbourg*, *Brest* and *Nantes*.

Four of the Havre ships (*Brest*, *Stromboli*, *Nantes* and *Balbec*) were wrecked off the coast of Cornwall between 1878 and 1888, leaving *British Queen* and *Cherbourg* as the sole survivors of the service in the 1890s. The longest-serving deep-sea Cunard ship, with 46 years' service, *British Queen* was sold for scrap in 1898. To replace *British Queen*, the 599g coaster *Liverpool* was chartered from the Barrow-based company J. Mawson and Son. Built in 1864 for the Sligo Steam Navigation Co. Ltd., *Liverpool*'s first voyage to Havre was on the 10th April 1899. She remained on the Havre route until November 1914, when she was sold to breakers. Despite the onset of war, the service continued until June 1916 with short charters of G. Heyn's *Fairhead* (1,093/1879), Leach and Co. Ltd.'s *Sea Gull* (976/1899), *Sea Hound* (1,090/1901) and J. J. Mack and Sons' *Cheshire* (633/1904) and *Fleswick* (674/1900).

In the 1920s and 1930s Cunard continued to charter small coasters for the Havre route whilst the service was also extended to the Channel Islands. Among the charters were Monroe Brothers' *Test* (530/1890) and *Staghound* (468/1894); William Robertson's *Beryl* (568/1924) and J. and A. Gardner's motor

Lycia (2), one of the trio of Mediterranean ships delivered between 1953 and 1955, was only in the fleet for eleven years.

Test passing Anchor Wharf, Chatham. At one time this 1890-built steamer carried Cunard's funnel and flew their flag whilst on charter for the seasonal trade between the Channel Isles and Liverpool. *[Nautical Photo Agency/National Maritime Museum N43935]*

from mid-May to late June each year, and tomatoes from Guernsey in early summer.

After three further sailings on the service, *Alouette* was replaced by John S. Monks's *Clara Monks* (577/1920), which became the main vessel until 1953. Monroe's larger *Kyleglen* (943/1929) took over in 1953, and a call at Avonmouth was included, but was soon discontinued as it was not viable. From October 1954 until March 1961 coasters were chartered for a single voyage only, until the Jersey registered *Fauvic* (485/1951) joined the service in March 1961 and was given a black hull and Cunard funnel colours. She was owned by Channel Shipping Ltd., Jersey, a subsidiary of the Dundee, Perth and London Shipping Co. Ltd. She was replaced by the larger shelter deck coaster *Broughty* (553/1955) in mid-December 1961 when Dublin and Bristol were briefly added to the network. In 1962 the weekly service via Bristol City Docks to Jersey and Guernsey was operated by *Broughty*, *Colette* (480/1956) and *London* (706/1951).

In January 1963 Cunard decided to discontinue Channel Island sailings from Liverpool and the Liverpool-Channel Island service was continued by Channel Shipping Ltd. In 1967 the goodwill of the trade, which had operated from Runcorn since March 1966, was bought by Manchester Shipping Ltd. From 1967 the German shelter decker *Stephan* ran on the route until it was closed down with her final arrival in St. Helier Harbour on the 17th September 1975.

coaster *Saint Angus* (392/1936). For the duration of the charter, the funnel was painted in Cunard colours and, whilst in port, the Cunard flag was flown. The last to sail before the islands were occupied by Germany on 30th June 1940, was *Staghound*, which arrived in St Helier Harbour, Jersey on 19th June 1940 with general cargo from Liverpool. She sailed the following day on British Government orders.

The charters recommenced soon after the war's end and the first arrival at St. Helier was General Steam Navigation's *Alouette* (276/1938) on 13th July 1945. The route was nearly always Liverpool to Jersey first, then Guernsey and Havre, where general cargo was loaded for Liverpool. Limited cargo was carried from the Channel Islands back to Liverpool, with only Jersey Royal potatoes

Broughty in Cunard colours arriving at St. Helier in the early 1960s. *[Dave Hocquard]*

THE FIRST MEDITERRANEAN SERVICES

In 1850 Charles MacIver and Co. started a feeder service between Havre and Liverpool. In the following year the small screw-steamer *British Queen* was chartered to operate a new service between Liverpool and Constantinople (modern day Istanbul).

The success of this venture led to the formation of The British and Foreign Steam Navigation Company by Charles MacIver, the Burns family and Samuel Cunard. *British Queen* was acquired and five new ships were ordered from Denny, Dumbarton. The route network was expanded to Alexandria and the service operated under the Burns and MacIver banner.

BRITISH QUEEN 1852-1898 Iron schooner-rigged

O.N. 1540 773g 566n;
1878: 772g 483n;
1889: 735g 432n
187.1 x 28 x 17.8 feet;
1878: 195.0 x 29.0 x 18.0 feet.
2-cyl. geared engine by Caird and Co., Greenock; 180 HP, 9 knots;
1878: C. 2-cyl. by James Jack and Co., Liverpool; 125 HP.
Passengers: 50 cabin; *1850s/1860s*: 71 cabin, 166 steerage (Board of Trade Passenger Certificate: *28.7.1866*: 71; *15.6.1878*: 221).
8.6.1849: Launched by William Denny and Brothers, Dumbarton (Yard No.18) as BRITISH QUEEN.
19.7.1849: Registered at Hull under the ownership of Brownlow, Pearson and Co., Hull.
10.8.1849: Left on maiden voyage from Hull to Hamburg.
4.4.1850: First sailing from Hamburg to New York with 25 first, 20 second and seven third class passengers. The voyage took 32 days with a stop at St John's, Newfoundland for coal and storm damage repair.
26.4.1851: First voyage from Liverpool to Constantinople on charter to Charles MacIver and Co.
16.7.1852: Registered at Liverpool under the ownership of George Burns, James Burns and Charles MacIver, shareholders in The British and North American Royal Mail Steam Packet Company. She was the company's first screw-driven ship although screw steamers had operated on Samuel Cunard's Halifax to Bermuda mail service since 1848.
17.7.1852: Inaugurated the Liverpool-Gibraltar-Malta-Constantinople service.
8.3.1853: Registered at Glasgow under the ownership of The British and Foreign Steam Navigation Company, Glasgow.
1854: Chartered by the British Government during the Crimean War as a troopship.
1850s: Transferred to the Liverpool-Havre route.
20.4.1862: Sailed from Liverpool to New York as a temporary replacement on the New York-Nassau-Havana service for KARNAK, which had been wrecked in the Bahamas.
1863: Reverted to Liverpool-Havre service.
1878: Rebuilt, lengthened and fitted with a new compound engine
1.7.1878: Transferred to the Cunard Steamship Co. Ltd., Liverpool.
30.9.1892: Registered at Liverpool.
11.1898: Sold to W.R. Pearce, Liverpool.
15.2.1899: Acquired by Thos. W. Ward Ltd., Sheffield.
16.2.1899: Arrived at Preston for demolition.
14.10.1899: Register closed.

British Queen was not only the longest-serving deep-sea Cunard ship (46 years), she was also the first in the fleet to be screw-driven.

British Queen at the end of her career.

Balbec, the first of the new Mediterranean fleet, was wrecked on the Cornish coast. She had been a supply and troopship during the Crimean War.

BALBEC 1853-1884 Iron barque rigged

O.N. 1288 838g 615n;
1873: 774g 484n
206.5 x 29.4 x 17.0 feet.
2-cyl. geared engine by Tulloch and Denny, Dumbarton; 180 HP, 9 knots;

1873: C. 2-cyl. by James Jack, Rollo and Co., Liverpool; 130 HP.
Passengers: 29 cabin, 157 steerage (Board of Trade Passenger Certificate: *23.11.1865*: 109; *8.2.1878*: 186).
9.11.1852: Launched by William Denny

and Brothers, Dumbarton (Yard No. 36) as BALBEC. Bought on the stocks having been ordered by Joseph Gee and Co., Hull.
18.1.1853: Registered at Glasgow under the ownership of The British and Foreign Steam Navigation Company, Glasgow
23.1.1853: Left on maiden voyage Liverpool-Gibraltar-Malta-Constantinople-Smyrna.
5.1854: Chartered by the British Government as Crimean War Transport No. 89 and sailed from Cork with troops.
25.3.1860: First voyage from Liverpool to New York.
1865: Transferred to the Liverpool to Havre service.
1873: New compound engine fitted.
1.7.1878: Transferred to the Cunard Steamship Co. Ltd., Liverpool.
28.3.1884: Struck submerged object off the Longships, Cornwall whilst on a voyage from Liverpool to Havre with a general cargo and chemicals. Beached at Nanjizel Cove, all 29 crew and five passengers were rescued and she was later declared a constructive total loss.
24.4.1884: Register closed.

TAURUS 1853-1859 Iron barque rigged
O.N. 23925 1,127g 812n
210.5 x 29.5 x 24.0 feet.
2-cyl. engine by Tulloch and Denny, Dumbarton; 180 HP, 9 knots.
Passengers: 40 fixed cabin or 140 convertible cabin.
21.2.1853: Launched by William Denny and Brothers, Dumbarton (Yard No. 37) as TAURUS.
8.4.1853: Registered at Glasgow under the ownership of The British and Foreign Steam Navigation Company, Glasgow.
21.4.1853: Left on maiden voyage Liverpool-Gibraltar-Malta-Constantinople.
7.1853: First voyage from Liverpool to New York.
3.1854: Chartered by the British Government as Crimean War Transport No. 23.
18.3.1854: Left Liverpool for Malta with 428 soldiers and officers of the 41st and 47th Regiments.
28.5.1859: Sold with TENERIFFE to the Spanish Government.

Taurus was sold to Spain and became the troopship *Marqués de la Victoria* as shown here. *[Juan Luis Coello collection]*

2.7.1859: Renamed MARQUÉS DE LA VICTORIA following her conversion into a troopship.
28.4.1860: British register closed.
1881: Decommissioned.
1881-11.5.1894: Used as an accommodation hulk in Subic Bay, Luzon, Philippines and was presumably broken up locally.

TENERIFFE 1853-1859 Iron barque rigged
O.N. 24067 1,127g 812n
210.5 x 29.5 x 24.0 feet.
2-cyl. engine by Tulloch and Denny, Dumbarton; 180 HP, 9 knots.
Passengers: 40 fixed cabin or 140 convertible cabin.
14.3.1853: Launched by William Denny and Brothers, Dumbarton (Yard No. 38) as TENERIFFE.
9.5.1853: Registered at Glasgow under the ownership of The British and Foreign Steam Navigation Company, Glasgow.
26.5.1853: Left on maiden voyage on a new route Liverpool-Gibraltar-Malta-Alexandria.
28.5.1859: Sold with TAURUS to the Spanish Government.
2.7.1859: Renamed PATIÑO following her conversion into a troopship.

25.7.1859: British register closed.
11.1860: Engines overhauled on the Clyde.
1885: Sold, possibly for demolition.

MELITA 1853-1861 Iron barque rigged
O.N. 1891 1,060g 749n;
1855: 1,255g 853n
232.6 x 29.0 x 19.0 feet;
1855: 246.0 x 30.3 x 25.6 feet.
2-cyl. oscillating engine by Macnab and Clark, Greenock; 180 HP, 9 knots.
Passengers: probably similar to TENERIFFE and TAURUS.
27.3.1853: Launched by Alexander Denny, Dumbarton (Yard No. 28) as MELITA.
5.5.1853: Registered at Port Glasgow under the ownership of Alexander Denny and William Denny and Brothers, Dumbarton. She had been built on speculation by the yard and initially chartered to The British and Foreign Steam Navigation Company for its Mediterranean service.
20.5.1853: Maiden voyage Liverpool-Gibraltar-Malta-Constantinople.
20.9.1853: Registered at Glasgow under the ownership of The British and Foreign Steam Navigation Company, Glasgow.
3.1854: Chartered by the British Government during the Crimean War as a transport

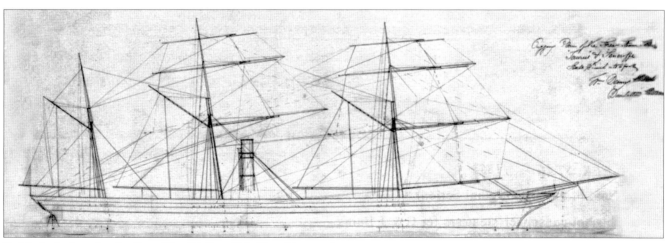

Builder's rigging plan for *Teneriffe*. *[National Maritime Museum]*

18.4.1854: Left Liverpool for Malta and Gallipoli with 300 tons of stores, 40 soldiers and 27 officer's servants of the 19th Regiment.
1855: Rebuilt and lengthened.
13.6.1860: Left Liverpool for Quebec and Montreal on a round voyage charter to Allan Line.
5.9.1860: First voyage Liverpool-Halifax-New York for The British and North American Royal Mail Steam Packet Company.
1861: Sold with DAMASCUS to William Denny and Brothers in part exchange for SIDON and MOROCCO.
13.12.1861: Registered under the ownership of Peter Denny, J. McAusland, Dumbarton and T. S. Begbie, London.
28.3.1862: Registered under the ownership of Samuel and Saul Isaac, London who reportedly used her during the American Civil War as a blockade runner.
30.4.1862: Registered at London.
27.11.1863: Registered at Liverpool under the ownership of C.E. Dixon, Liverpool.
6.1866: Chartered to Warren Line on the Liverpool-Boston-Philadelphia service.
5.9.1868: Caught fire about 800 miles from Queenstown whilst on a voyage from Boston to Liverpool. Her passengers and crew were rescued by the U.S. sailing ship JACOB A. STAMLER (1,000/1856).
12.10.1868: Register closed

KARNAK 1853-1862 Iron barque rigged

O.N. 1791 1,127g 794n
210.5 x 29.5 x 24.0 feet.
2-cyl. direct acting engine by Tulloch and Denny, Dumbarton; 180 HP, 9 knots.
Passengers: probably similar to TENERIFFE and TAURUS.
22.9.1853: Launched by William Denny and Brothers, Dumbarton (Yard No. 42) as KARNAK. She was ordered as a repeat of BALBEC but with the addition of a spar deck was completed as a sister of TENERIFFE and TAURUS.
12.12.1853: Registered at Glasgow under the ownership of The British and Foreign Steam Navigation Company, Glasgow
28.12.1853: Left on maiden voyage Liverpool-Gibraltar-Malta-Constantinople-Smyrna-Alexandria.
5.1854: Chartered by the British Government as a Crimean War transport and sailed from Cork with troops on *27.5.1854*.
1860s: Transferred to the New York-Nassau-Havana service.
14.4.1862: Stranded on Nassau bar, Bahamas whilst on a voyage from Havana to New York with sixty passengers and general cargo. She had a pilot aboard and all passengers and crew were rescued.
7.1862: Sold at auction to Kimball and Arnold for $825, later refloated and sailed to New York.
18.8.1862: British register closed.
1863: Sold to C.C. Duncan and Co., New York, U.S.A.
11.1863: Sold to the U.S. Quartermaster's Department (U.S. Army).

11.1865: Sold to J.H. Sears, Boston, U.S.A. trading as the Merchants Steamship Co., and renamed SAINT LOUIS.
circa 1872: Sold to H.B. Cromwell and Co., New York.
9.12.1872: Abandoned at 02:00, having sprung a leak the previous evening about 170 miles from Southwest Passage whilst on voyage from New Orleans to New York with a cargo of cotton, molasses and general cargo. Her crew was rescued the following day by the British ship RECORD and later landed at Key West.

LEBANON 1855-1859 Iron barque rigged

O.N. 1287 1,383g 818n
252.6 x 30.5 x 24.3 feet.
2-cyl. geared oscillating engine by J. and G. Thomson, Govan; 220 HP, 10 knots.
Passengers: probably similar to TENERIFFE and TAURUS.
22.11.1854: Launched by J. and G. Thomson, Govan (Yard No. 16) as AEROLITH for Robert Miles Sloman, Hamburg, she was bought on the stocks. Another AEROLITH was completed in 1857 for Sloman by Robert Napier (Yard No. 84).
24.1.1855: Registered at Glasgow under the ownership of The British and North American Royal Mail Steam Packet Company, Glasgow as LEBANON.
3.2.1855: Maiden voyage from Liverpool to Constantinople.
31.7.1855: First voyage from Liverpool to New York.
1.10.1855: Ownership transferred to The British and Foreign Steam Navigation Company, Glasgow.
28.6.1856: First voyage from Havre to New York.
8.1857: Chartered by the British Government as an Indian Mutiny troopship.
28.5.1859: Sold to the Spanish Government.
18.8.1859: British register closed.
2.7.1859: Renamed GENERAL ÁLAVA following her conversion into a troopship.
12.11.1863: Sank at Santa Cruz de La Palma,

Teneriffe after a fire in her coal bunker whilst on a voyage from La Coruña to Puerto Rico and Havana with troops, guns and stores.

DAMASCUS 1856-1860 Iron brig rigged

O.N. 16246 1,214g 825n;
1870: 1,517g 960n;
1877: 1,808g 1,158n
253.5 x 32 x 22.2 feet;
1870: 288.3 x 32.0 x 22.2 feet.
2-cyl. engine by Tulloch and Denny, Dumbarton; 200 HP, 11 knots;
1870: C. 2-cyl. by Greenock Foundry Co., Greenock; 165 HP.
Passengers: 40 cabin, steerage; *1885*: 512 steerage (Board of Trade Passenger Certificates: *21.3.1866*: 311; *9.5.1878*: 357).
30.9.1856: Launched by William Denny and Brothers, Dumbarton (Yard No. 59) as DAMASCUS. Bought on the stocks, she had been ordered as ST. ANDREW (her sister was to be ST. GEORGE) by Captain D.R. MacGregor, James Miller and Sons, D. Lindsay and Robert Sinclair. The contract was cancelled because of delays by the yard.
27.10.1856: Registered at Glasgow under the ownership of The British and Foreign Steam Navigation Company, Glasgow.
10.11.1856: Maiden voyage from Liverpool to Constantinople.
30.7.1860: First voyage Liverpool-Halifax-New York.
14.9.1860: Registered under the ownership of P. Denny and J. McAusland (William Denny and Brothers), Dumbarton, having been taken in part exchange with MELITA for SIDON and MOROCCO.
6.2.1862: Registered under the ownership of James and Alexander Allan (Montreal Ocean Steamship Company (Allan Line), Glasgow.
29.4.1862: First voyage from Liverpool to Quebec and Montreal for Allan Line.
9.3.1870: Register closed 'sold to foreigners' and renamed CORINTHIAN. Such a sale was often the only way in which a British ship could be renamed.
1870: Rebuilt, lengthened and fitted with a new compound engine and a single funnel.

Damascus of 1856 was the company's first screw-driven steamer with two funnels.
[J. and M. Clarkson collection]

9.9.1870: Re-registered at Glasgow under the ownership of James and Alexander Allan, Glasgow and Hugh Allan, Montreal, Quebec and others.
1881: Sold to Francesco Zenoglio, Genoa, Italy.
4.7.1881: British register closed.
1883: Sold to Paolo Gaggino, Genoa and renamed GENOVA.
1883: Sold to Stefano Castagnola, Genoa and renamed GIOVANNI LANZA.
1885: Sold to Società di Assicurazioni 'L'Italia' and renamed GIUSEPPE GARIBALDI as an emigrant ship to South America.
1886: Sold to İdare-I Mahsusa, İstanbul, Turkey and renamed FİRAZ-İ OSMANİYE ('Blessed are the Ottomans').
1889: Renamed SAKARYA (name of a river on Black Sea coast).
28.8.1910: Company restyled as Osmanlı Seyr-I Sefain İdaresi (Ottoman Steam Navigation Company), Istanbul.
1912: Sold for demolition at Istanbul.

Palestine was the first of a new series of brig rigged Mediterranean traders.

PALESTINE 1858-1870 Iron brig rigged
O.N. 21385 1,377g 936n;
1872: 2,867g 2,128n
255.2 x 34.2 x 24.3 feet;
1872: 352.1 x 36.1 x 23.8 feet.
2-cyl. engine by McNab and Clark, Greenock; 260 HP, 10 knots;
1872: C. 2-cyl. by J. and J. Thomson, Glasgow; 300 HP, 10.5 knots.
Passengers: Board of Trade Passenger Certificates: *27.3.1866*: 484 including crew; *3.3.1879*: 100 including crew.
17.4.1858: Launched by Robert Steele and Company, Greenock (Yard No. 16) as PALESTINE.
1.7.1858: Registered at Glasgow under the ownership of The British and Foreign Steam Navigation Company, Glasgow.
31.7.1858: Maiden voyage from Liverpool to Constantinople.
5.1860: Chartered by Allan Line for Liverpool-Quebec-Montreal service.
25.12.1860: First voyage from Liverpool to New York.

1.1866: First voyage Liverpool-Boston-New York.
23.11.1870: Registered under the ownership of James Reid Stewart, Glasgow.
14.7.1871: Registered under the ownership of William Henry Jones, Liverpool.
1872: Rebuilt, lengthened, and fitted with a third mast (barque rig) and a new compound engine.
5.10.1872: Registered at Liverpool.
3-9.1873: Chartered to Dominion Line for the Liverpool-Boston-Portland and Liverpool-Quebec-Montreal routes.
1876-1892: Chartered by Warren Line for the Liverpool to Boston service.
10.3.1896: Registered under the ownership of G.O. Wight, Sunderland and later broken up at Sunderland.
5.2.1898: Register closed.

STROMBOLI 1859-1878 Iron probably brig rigged
O.N. 13532 724g 598n
198.8 x 28.5 x 17.7 feet.
2-cyl. engine by J. and G. Thomson, Govan; 100 HP, 10 knots:
1873: C. 2-cyl. by James Jack, Rollo and Co., Liverpool; 118 HP.
Passengers: 9 cabin, 200 steerage.
25.3.1856: Launched by J. and G. Thomson,

Govan (Yard No. 25) as JAMES BROWN.
9.5.1856: Registered at Glasgow under the ownership of J. Brown and W. Marr, London.
15.6.1858: Registered at Liverpool in the name of Charles MacIver, Liverpool.
21.6.1859: Register closed 'sold to foreigners' and renamed STROMBOLI. Such a sale was often the only way in which a British ship could be renamed.
2.7.1859: Re-registered at Liverpool.
4.11.1859: Registered at Glasgow under the ownership of The British and Foreign Steam Navigation Company, Glasgow and used on the Liverpool to Havre service.
5.1873: New compound engine fitted.
20.3.1878: Ran ashore a mile west of Kynance Cove and broke her back having struck one of the Stag Rocks off the Lizard, Cornwall whilst on voyage from Le Havre to Liverpool with 16 passengers, 32 crew and general cargo. All aboard were saved.
12.4.1878: Register closed.

OLYMPUS 1860-1881 Iron brig rigged
O.N. 28216 1,794g 1,220n;
1872: 2,415g 1,585n
276.8 x 36.2 x 26.0 feet:
1872: 340 x 36.6 x 25.8 feet.
2-cyl. engine by J. and G. Thomson, Govan; 250 HP, 10 knots;
1872: C. 2-cyl. by J. and G. Thomson, Glasgow; 270 HP, 10.5 knots.
Passengers: *1870s*: 40 cabin, 900 steerage. (Board of Trade Passenger Certificates: *29.3.1866*: 531; *21.5.1878*: 72)
10.1.1860: Launched by J. and G. Thomson, Govan (Yard No. 45) as OLYMPUS.
20.2.1860: Registered at Glasgow under the ownership of The British and Foreign Steam Navigation Company, Glasgow.
6.3.1860: Maiden voyage from Liverpool to Constantinople.
2.6.1863: First voyage from Liverpool to New York.
1866: Advertised as a 'Cunard emigrant steamer'.
1872: Rebuilt and lengthened by Harland and Wolff, Belfast, she was fitted with a third mast (barque rig) and a new compound engine.
1872-1881: Used mainly on the Liverpool

Olympus was one four Mediterranean vessels which were lengthened at Belfast by Harland and Wolff, and became transatlantic emigrant ships. This image shows her before she was stretched.

to Boston service as an emigrant ship plus some Liverpool to Mediterranean voyages.
1.7.1878: Transferred to the Cunard Steamship Co. Ltd., Liverpool.
1879: Chartered as a Zulu War transport.
22.8.1881: Registered under the ownership of J. and G. Thomson, having been sold in part payment for PAVONIA.
19.8.1887: Registered under the ownership of W. Ker, A.C. Scott and A. Colville, Glasgow.
20.8.1889: Registered under the ownership of W. MacKinnon, Glasgow.
15.9.1891: Register closed, broken up.

MARATHON 1860-1898 Iron brig rigged

O.N. 28220 1,784g 1,213n;
1873: 2,403g 1,553n
274.0 x 36.2 x 25.8 feet;
1873: 336.4 x 36.6 x 25.7 feet.
2-cyl. engine by Robert Napier and Sons, Glasgow, 300 HP, 10 knots;
1873: C. 2-cyl. by J. and G. Thomson, Clydebank; 300 HP, 10.5 knots.
Passengers: *1870s*: 70 cabin, 950 steerage.
(Board of Trade Passenger Certificates: *29.3.1866*: 527; *13.5.1878*: 1,088).
1860: Launched by Robert Napier and Sons, Glasgow (Yard No. 96) as MARATHON.
19.3.1860: Registered at Glasgow under the ownership of The British and Foreign Steam Navigation Company, Glasgow.
4.1860: Maiden voyage from Liverpool to Constantinople.
8.1.1861: First voyage from Liverpool to New York.
1866: Advertised as a 'Cunard emigrant steamer'.
1873: Rebuilt and lengthened by Harland and Wolff, Belfast, she was fitted with a third mast (barque rig) and a new compound engine.
1873-1884: Used mainly on Liverpool-Queenstown-Boston service as an emigrant ship.
1.7.1878: Transferred to the Cunard Steamship Co. Ltd., Liverpool.
28.7-23.10.1882: Chartered by British Government as an Egyptian Campaign transport.
1884 onwards: Mainly Liverpool to Mediterranean service.
5.1898: Sold to Workman, Clark and Co. Ltd., Belfast as part payment for CYPRIA.
3.6.1898: Register closed after sale to Italian buyers.
8.1898: Demolished in Italy by L. Pittaluga fu F., Genoa.

ATLAS 1860-1896 Iron brig rigged

O.N. 28477 1,794 g 1,220n;
1872: 2,393g 1,553n
276.9 x 36.2 x 26.0 feet
1873: 339.0 x 36.5 x 25.7 feet.
2-cyl. engine by J. and G. Thomson, Govan; 250 HP, 10 knots;
1872: C. 2-cyl. by J. and G. Thomson, Glasgow; 300 HP, 10.5 knots.
Passengers: *1870s*: 69 cabin, 943 steerage.

The four lengthened ships were fitted with a third mast (barque rig) and a new compound engine. This is *Marathon* after her rebuild.

(Board of Trade Passenger Certificates: *22.11.1865*: 76; *4.1.1878*: 1,012)
8.3.1860: Launched by J. and G. Thomson, Govan (Yard No. 46) as ATLAS.
30.3.1860: Registered at Glasgow under the ownership of The British and Foreign Steam Navigation Company, Glasgow.
6.1860: Maiden voyage Liverpool to Constantinople.
1873: Rebuilt and lengthened by Harland and Wolff, Belfast, she was fitted with a third mast (barque rig) and a new compound engine and used on the transatlantic service as an emigrant ship.
1.7.1878: Transferred to the Cunard Steamship Co. Ltd., Liverpool.
13.7.1896: Registered under the ownership of J.J. King, Manchester and broken up on the Mersey at Tranmere.
8.9.1896: Register closed.

HECLA 1860-1881 Iron brig-rig

O.N. 28225 1,785 g 1,214 n;
1871: 2,421g 1,578n
274.1 x 36.2 x 25.8 feet;
1871: 338.7 x 36.4 x 25.6 feet.
2-cyl. engine by Robert Napier and Sons, Glasgow; 300 HP, 10 knots;
1871: C. 2-cyl. by J. and G. Thomson, Govan; 270 HP, 10.5 knots;
1919: T.4-cyl; 4,000 HP, 14 knots.
Passengers: *1870s*: 40 cabin, 494 steerage.

(Board of Trade Passenger Certificates: *24.3.1866*: 531; *22.3.1878*: 40)
1860: Launched by Robert Napier and Sons, Glasgow (Yard No. 97) as HECLA.
30.3.1860: Registered at Glasgow under the ownership of The British and Foreign Steam Navigation Company, Glasgow.
21.4.1860: Maiden voyage from Liverpool to Constantinople.
10.6.1863: First voyage from Liverpool to New York, advertised as a 'Cunard emigrant steamer'.
1871: Rebuilt and lengthened by Harland and Wolff, Belfast, she was fitted with a third mast (barque rig) and a new compound engine and used on the transatlantic service as an emigrant ship.
23.5.1872: First voyage from Liverpool to Boston.
1.7.1878: Transferred to the Cunard Steamship Co. Ltd., Liverpool.
5.2.1881: Last voyage from Liverpool to Boston.
3.1881: Sold to Laird Brothers, Birkenhead as part payment for CEPHALONIA.
22.3.1881: Handed over at Huskisson Dock and towed to Birkenhead.
30.4.1881: Registered under the ownership of Jonathan Laird, Birkenhead.
8.1881-2.1882: Chartered to Société Anonyme de Navigation Belge-Américaine (Red Star Line), Antwerp for the Antwerp to

Many of the iron-hulled Mediterranean ships had lengthy careers with the company. *Atlas* was in the fleet for 36 years.

New York and Philadelphia service.
5.1882: Sold to Compañía de Transportes Marítimos, Barcelona and renamed CLARIS for Barcelona to River Plate service.
9.5.1882: British register closed.
29.7.1883: Arrived at Rio de Janeiro under tow of the German steamer NEKO (1882/1,718), having broken down in the south Atlantic whilst on a voyage from Barcelona to Buenos Aires with 200 passengers.
1884: Laid up under arrest at Barcelona following the bankruptcy of Compañía de Trasportes Marítimos.
12.1885: Acquired by Laird Brothers from liquidators, probably because they were the main mortgagee for the ship.
1.3.1886: Arrived at Liverpool from Barcelona as CLARIS.
17.4.1886: Registered at Liverpool under the ownership of W. Laird, Birkenhead as HECLA.
9.5.1886: Register closed 'sold to Spanish owners and renamed CLARIS'.
1888: Sold to Conde de Vilana, Barcelona, Spain and renamed CONDE DE VILANA
8.1889: Arrived at Buenos Aires as a floating Spanish exhibition ship.
1892: Sold to Peter A. Garland, Buenos Aires, Argentina and renamed PEDRO TERCERO.
1895: Renamed TIEMPO
9.4.1897: Acquired by the Argentinean Government for use as training ship and renamed RIO NEGRO.
16.9.1899: Towed to Ushuaia for use as a coal hulk.
1919: Towed to Buenos Aires and fitted with the triple expansion engine from cruiser 25 DE MAYO.
28.2.1920: Conversion work complete, she was subsequently used as an Argentine Navy coastal transport.
1924: Collided with Nelson Line's HIGHLAND LOCH (7,493/1911) at Buenos Aires and subsequently repaired.
10.1930: Returned to Ushuaia as a hulk having had her engines removed.

Hecla was the longest-surviving Cunard ship and lasted ninety-four years.

27.2.1951: Towed to Buenos Aires by the Argentine Navy tugs CHIRIGUANO and SANAVIRON, having been stricken from service.
1954: Broken up Buenos Aires.

KEDAR 1860-1897 Iron brig rigged
O.N. 28890 1,783g 1,212n
275.8 x 36.2 x 25.7 feet.
2-cyl. geared oscillating engine by Tulloch and Denny, Dumbarton; 224 HP, 12 knots:
1873: C. 2-cyl. by James Jack, Rollo and Co., Liverpool; 212 HP.
Passengers: *1870s*: 40 cabin, 800 steerage.
(Board of Trade Passenger Certificate: *5.1.1866*: 534)
17.8.1860: Launched by William Denny and Brothers, Dumbarton (Yard No. 76) as KEDAR.
13.10.1860: Registered at Glasgow under the ownership of The British and Foreign Steam Navigation Company, Glasgow.

27.11.1860: Maiden voyage from Liverpool to New York. From 1864 used mainly on Liverpool to Mediterranean service apart from twelve round voyages from Liverpool to Boston in 1872.
1873: New compound engine fitted.
1.7.1878: Transferred to the Cunard Steamship Co. Ltd., Liverpool.
4.9.1896: Registered at Liverpool.
7.8.1897: Registered under the ownership of Workman, Clark and Co. Ltd., Belfast having been sold presumably as part payment for TYRIA.
12.1897: Broken up at Genoa.
12.8.1898: Register closed.

SIDON 1861-1885 Iron brig rigged
O.N. 43687 1,782g 1,268n
275.6 x 36.2 x 25.8 feet.
2-cyl. geared oscillating engine by Tulloch and Denny, Dumbarton; 224 HP, 12 knots;
1873: C. 2-cyl. by James Jack, Rollo and

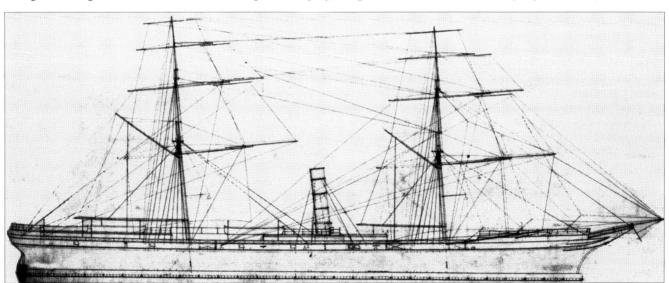

Kedar was typical of the Mediterranean brig rigged ships, which were sometimes known as 'MacIver's yachts'. *[National Maritime Museum]*

Co., Liverpool; 212 HP.
Passengers: *1870s*: 69 cabin, 462 steerage.
(Board of Trade Passenger Certificate:
19.9.1866: 531)
20.8.1861: Launched by William Denny
and Brothers, Dumbarton (Yard No. 79) as
SIDON.
18.9.1861 Registered at Glasgow under the
ownership of The British and Foreign Steam
Navigation Company, Glasgow.
3.10.1861: Maiden voyage from Liverpool
to Genoa.
19.5.1863: First voyage from Liverpool to
New York.
1866: Advertised as a 'Cunard emigrant
steamer'.
1867 onwards: Used mainly on the
Liverpool to Mediterranean service.
1873: New compound engine fitted.
1.7.1878: Transferred to the Cunard
Steamship Co. Ltd., Liverpool.
27.10.1885: Wrecked near Malpica, north
west Spain (roughly 20 miles west of La
Coruña) on a voyage from Liverpool to
Constantinople with general cargo, 43 crew
and 14 passengers. Four passengers were
drowned and she became the first Cunarder
to lose passengers during peace time.
7.11.1885: Register closed.

Sidon was the first Cunarder to lose passengers during peacetime.

MOROCCO 1861-1896 Iron brig rigged
O.N. 43696 1,783g 1,268n
275.5 x 36.2 x 25.8 feet.
2-cyl. geared oscillating engine by Tulloch
and Denny, Dumbarton; 212 HP, 10 knots;
1874: C. 2-cyl. by James Jack, Rollo and
Co., Liverpool; 212 HP.
Passengers: 76 cabin. (Board of Trade
Passenger Certificate: *25.4.1866*: 76)
22.10.1861: Launched by William Denny
and Brothers, Dumbarton (Yard No. 80) as
MOROCCO.
18.11.1861: Registered at Glasgow under the
ownership of The British and Foreign Steam
Navigation Company, Glasgow.
4.12.1861: Maiden voyage from Liverpool
to Genoa.
1874: New compound engine fitted.
1.7.1878: Transferred to the Cunard
Steamship Co. Ltd., Liverpool.
9.7.1896: Registered at Liverpool.
1.9.1896: Registered under the ownership
of Workman, Clark and Co. Ltd., Belfast,
having been sold presumably as part
payment for PAVIA.
7.9.1896: Registered under the ownership of
J.S. Turnbull, Glasgow and broken up on the
Mersey at Hale.
16.9.1896: Register closed 'being broken
up'.

CORSICA 1863-1867 Iron probably brig rigged
O.N. 44819 1,134g 681n;
1878: 1,581g 1,036n
224.2 x 32.2 x 24 feet;
1878: 272.7 x 32.7 x 23.8
2-cyl. geared oscillating engine by J. and G.
Thomson, Govan; 200 HP, 10 knots;
1878: C. 2-cyl. by Wallsend Slipway and

Morocco spent most of her career on the Liverpool to Mediterranean routes.

Engineering Co. Ltd., Wallsend; 160 HP.
Passengers: probably similar to TRIPOLI.
21.1.1863: Launched by J. and G. Thomson,
Govan (Yard No. 62) as CORSICA.
23.2.1863: Registered at Glasgow under the
ownership of The British and Foreign Steam
Navigation Company, Glasgow.
28.3.1863: Maiden voyage Liverpool-
Halifax-New York.
20.11.1867: Registered under the ownership
of the Royal Mail Steam Packet Company,
London, having been sold as a replacement
for WYE (1853/919), which sank in a
hurricane at St. Thomas on *29.10.1867*, with
the loss of 41 lives.
13.1.1868: Registered at London.
1878: Registered under the ownership of
various partners including S.P. Austin, H.
F. Wilcox, Sunderland and C.L. Dodgson,
Oxford (the writer Lewis Carroll).
1878: Rebuilt, probably by S.P. Austin at
Sunderland, lengthened and fitted with a
new compound engine.
12.1879: Sold to the Bristol Steam
Navigation Co. Ltd., Bristol.
6.12.1879: Registered at Bristol.
11.10.1881: Struck a reef off Cape Roca,
Portugal and sank within ten minutes whilst
on a voyage from London to Bombay with
a crew of 26 and general cargo. There were
only five survivors.
26.10.1881: Register closed.

TRIPOLI 1863-1872 Iron brig rigged
O.N. 45997 2,061g 1,458n
292.3 x 38.2 x 26.5 feet.
2-cyl. engine by J. and G. Thomson, Govan;
280 HP, 11 knots.
Passengers: 50 cabin, 650 steerage. (Board of
Trade Passenger Certificate: *11.1.1866*: 50)
15.8.1863: Launched by J. and G. Thomson,
Govan (Yard No. 63) as TRIPOLI.
26.8.1863: Registered at Glasgow under the
ownership of The British and Foreign Steam
Navigation Company, Glasgow.
26.9.1863: Maiden voyage from Liverpool to
Genoa.
19.8.1865: First voyage from Liverpool to
New York, she was advertised as a 'Cunard
emigrant steamer'.
1865-1872: Used mainly on the Liverpool
to New York service with many voyages via
Boston.
17.5.1872: Ran on to rocks near Tuskar Rock
Lighthouse, County Wexford, Ireland in fog
whilst on a voyage from Liverpool to Boston
with 328 passengers and crew and two pilots,.
All on board were saved.
6.7.1872: Register closed.

ALEPPO 1865-1909 Iron brig rigged
O.N. 50370 2,057g 1,459n
292.5 x 38.2 x 26.2 feet.
2-cyl. engine by J. and G. Thomson, Govan;
280 HP, 11 knots;

1878: C. 2-cyl. by James Jack, Rollo and Co., Liverpool; 212 HP;
1890: T. 3-cyl. by J. Howden and Co., Glasgow; 220 HP, 12.5 knots.
Passengers: 46 cabin;. *1870s*: 46 cabin, 500 steerage. (Board of Trade Passenger Certificate: *20.12.1865*: 46; *3.9.1881*: 752)
1.11.1864: Launched by J. and G. Thomson, Govan (Yard No. 78) as ALEPPO.
3.1.865: Registered at Glasgow under the ownership of The British and Foreign Steam Navigation Company, Glasgow
12.1.1865: Maiden voyage from Liverpool to Constantinople.
15.9.1865: First voyage from Liverpool to New York, she was advertised as a 'Cunard emigrant steamer'.
1865-1872: Used mainly on the Liverpool to New York service with many voyages via Boston.
1872 onwards: Transferred to Liverpool to Mediterranean service with seventeen transatlantic crossings between 1877 and 1892.
1.7.1878: Transferred to the Cunard Steamship Co. Ltd., Liverpool.
1880: New compound engine fitted.
1890: New triple expansion engine fitted.
24.3.1892: Last transatlantic sailing from Liverpool.
19.5.1898: Registered at Liverpool.
1909: Sold for demolition to Thos. W. Ward Ltd., Sheffield.
25.11.1909: Arrived for demolition at Preston in tow of STORM COCK (64/1891). ALEPPO's figurehead is now in the Mystic Seaport Museum, Connecticut.
15.4.1910: Register closed.

TARIFA 1865-1899 Iron brig rigged
O.N. 50378 2,058g 1,459n
292.5 x 38.2 x 26.2 feet.
2-cyl. engine by J. and G. Thomson, Govan; 280 HP, 11 knots;

Tripoli was the first of five ships of just over 2,000g which were built between 1863 and 1866. All were used for the transatlantic emigrant trade from the mid-1860s to the early 1870s.

Tripoli was wrecked off the coast of Ireland in 1872.

1879: C. 2-cyl. by James Jack, Rollo and Co., Liverpool; 212 HP.
Passengers: 50 cabin; *1870s*: 50 cabin, 589 steerage. (Board of Trade Passenger Certificates: *28.2.1866*: 50; *19.8.1879*: 639)
12.1.1865: Launched by J. and G. Thomson,

Govan (Yard No. 79) as TARIFA.
3.3.1865: Registered at Glasgow under the ownership of The British and Foreign Steam Navigation Company, Glasgow.
15.3.1865: Maiden voyage from Liverpool to Alexandria.

Aleppo seen at Liverpool (above left) was the longest-serving (44 years) Mediterranean ship. She was also used extensively on the Atlantic routes.. Note the donkey boiler mini-funnel forward of the bridge. On her way into Preston for demolition *Aleppo* ran aground outside the dock entrance (above right). *[Right: J. and M. Clarkson collection]*

22.7.1865: First voyage Liverpool to New York, she was advertised as a 'Cunard emigrant steamer'.

1865-1871: Used mainly on the Liverpool to New York service, with many voyages via Boston.

1873 onwards: Used mainly on the Liverpool to Mediterranean service.

1.7.1878: Transferred to the Cunard Steamship Co. Ltd., Liverpool.

1879: New compound engine fitted.

8.11.1888: Last transatlantic sailing from Liverpool

19.5.1898: Registered at Liverpool.

First quarter1899: Broken up at Naples.

25.2.1899: Register closed.

MALTA 1865-1889 Iron brig rigged

O.N. 53378 2,132g 1,541n

303.1 x 39.3 x 25.0 feet.

2-cyl. engine by J. and G. Thomson, Govan; 280 HP, 11 knots:

1879: C. 2-cyl. by James Jack, Rollo and Co., Liverpool; 212 HP.

Passengers: 62 cabin; *1870s*: 40 cabin, 555 steerage; (Board of Trade Passenger Certificates: *4.12.1865*: 62; *11.11.1879*: 40)

19.10.1865: Launched by J. and G. Thomson, Govan (Yard No. 84) as MALTA.

22.11.1865: Registered at Glasgow under the ownership of The British and Foreign Steam Navigation Company, Glasgow.

12.1865: Maiden voyage from Liverpool to Constantinople.

20.2.1866: First voyage from Liverpool to New York, she was advertised as a 'Cunard emigrant steamer'.

1866-1871: Used mainly on the Liverpool to New York service.

1871-1873: Used mainly on the Liverpool to Boston service.

1873 onwards: Used mainly on the Liverpool to Mediterranean service apart from between *7.1881* and *9.1882* when she was used on the Liverpool to Boston route.

1.7.1878: Transferred to the Cunard Steamship Co. Ltd., Liverpool.

1879: Compound engine fitted.

30.8.1888: Last transatlantic sailing from Liverpool

15.10.1889: Struck rocks half a mile north of Cape Cornwall, near Land's End, Cornwall in fog whilst on a voyage from Liverpool to Adriatic ports via Falmouth with 21 passengers, 40 crew and general cargo. All were rescued and much of the cargo salvaged.

29.10.1889: Register closed.

PALMYRA 1866-1896 Iron brig rigged

O.N. 53391 2,044g 1,390n

290.8 x 38.0 x 26.1 feet.

2-cyl. oscillating engine by Caird and Co., Greenock; 260 HP, 11 knots;

1878: C. 2-cyl. by James Jack, Rollo and Co., Liverpool; 212 HP.

Passengers: 46 cabin, 650 steerage; *1870s*: 46 cabin, 500 steerage. (Board of Trade Passenger Certificates: *19.4.1866*: 692; *21.9.1878*: 546)

Malta was wrecked near Land's End, Cornwall in 1889.

23.12.1865: Launched by Caird and Co., Greenock (Yard No. 125) as PALMYRA.

12.4.1866: Registered at Glasgow under the ownership of The British and Foreign Steam Navigation Company, Glasgow.

25.4.1866: Maiden voyage from Liverpool to New York, she was advertised as a 'Cunard emigrant steamer'.

1866-1870: Used mainly on the Liverpool to New York service.

1870-1873: Used mainly on the Liverpool to Boston service.

1873 onwards: Used mainly on the Liverpool to Mediterranean service apart from 23 transatlantic crossings between 1880 and 1891.

1878: New compound engine fitted.

1.7.1878: Transferred to the Cunard Steamship Co. Ltd., Liverpool.

1879: Chartered as a Zulu War transport.

1881: Chartered as a transport during the First Boer War (1880-1881). Troops were on passage when peace was signed.

23.4.1881: Lost her propeller whilst on a

voyage from Liverpool to New York with general cargo and 770 passengers and crew. Towed to St. John's, Newfoundland by Bristol City Line's BROOKLYN CITY (1,726/1881), which was on her maiden voyage.

24.7-22.11.1882: Chartered as an Egyptian Campaign transport.

9.7.1896: Registered at Liverpool.

7.1896: Sold for demolition to J.S. Turnbull, Glasgow and broken up on the Mersey at Tranmere.

16.9.1896: Register closed.

NANTES 1873-1888 Iron barque rigged

O.N. 68056 1,473g 949n

238.3 x 32.2 x 19.0 feet.

2-cyl. engine by Blackwood and Gordon, Glasgow; 160 HP;

1878: C. 2-cyl. by James Jack, Rollo and Co., Liverpool; 212HP.

Passengers: 8 cabin, 386 steerage. (Board of Trade Passenger Certificate: *18.6.1882*: 44 including crew).

Palmyra was the last of the 1860s iron brigs to be delivered.

Between 1878 and 1889 four of the Mediterranean ships were lost off the coast of Cornwall, including *Brest* in 1879.

Cherbourg was the final ship of a trio built in the 1870s for the Liverpool to Havre service. Here she is in the Langton Graving Dock, Liverpool. *[National Martime Museum G3608]*

28.5.1873: Launched by Blackwood and Gordon, Glasgow (Yard No.122) as NANTES.

27.10.1873: Registered at Glasgow under the ownership of The British and Foreign Steam Navigation Company, Glasgow.

9.12.1873: Maiden voyage from Liverpool to Genoa, she was subsequently used on the Liverpool to Havre route.

1.7.1878: Transferred to the Cunard Steamship Co. Ltd., Liverpool.

1878: New compound engine fitted.

6.11.1888: Collided with the German sailing ship THEODORE RUGER (1,629/1872) 40 miles east south east of the Lizard, Cornwall in a force nine gale whilst on a voyage from Liverpool to Havre with 26 crew and a cargo of coal and general cargo. Both ships sank with the loss of 23 men from NANTES and eight from THEODORE RUGER.

14.11.1888: Register closed.

BREST 1874-1879 Iron barque rigged

O.N. 68088 1,473g 949n
238.3 x 32.2 x 19.0 feet.
2-cyl. engine by Blackwood and Gordon, Glasgow; 160 HP.
Passengers: 8 cabin, 386 steerage. (Board of Trade Passenger Certificate: *28.3.1878*: 44 including crew)

22.8.1873: Launched by Blackwood and Gordon, Glasgow (Yard No.123) as BREST.

10.4.1874: Registered at Glasgow under the ownership of The British and Foreign Steam Navigation Company, Glasgow.

17.4.1874: Maiden voyage from Liverpool to Palermo. She was subsequently used on the Liverpool to Havre route.

1.7.1878: Transferred to the Cunard Steamship Co. Ltd., Liverpool.

6.9.1879: Ran aground at full speed between Polpeor and Church Cove, near the Lizard, Cornwall in thick fog whilst on a voyage from Havre to Liverpool with 132 emigrants, 34 crew and 500 tons of cargo. All aboard were saved and the ship was later declared a constructive total loss. The wreck was a few miles from where STROMBOLI had been lost the previous year.

6.10.1879: Register closed.

CHERBOURG 1875-1909 Iron brig rigged

O.N. 71694 1,614g 1,038n
251.2 x 32.4 x 19.4 feet.
C. 2-cyl. by J. and G. Thomson, Clydebank; 170 HP, 10 knots.
Passengers: 4 cabin. (Board of Trade Passenger Certificate: *13.11.1878*:44 (including crew)

12.11.1874: Launched by J. and G. Thomson, Clydebank (Yard No. 133) as CHERBOURG. Designed for Liverpool to Havre cargo service.

2.2.1875: Registered at Glasgow under the ownership of The British and Foreign Steam Navigation Company, Glasgow.

14.2.1875: Maiden voyage from Liverpool to Genoa. She was subsequently used on the Liverpool to Havre route.

1.7.1878: Transferred to the Cunard

Steamship Co. Ltd., Liverpool.
19.5.1898: Registered at Liverpool.
1909: Sold for demolition to Thos. W. Ward
Ltd., Sheffield.
28.12.1909: Arrived at Preston for
demolition.
6.6.1910: Register closed.

PAVIA (1) 1897-1928
O.N. 106853 2,935g 1,883n
332.1 x 45.7 x 22.5 feet.
T.3-cyl. by Barclay, Curle and Co. Ltd.,
Glasgow; 360 HP, 11 knots.
4.3.1897: Launched by Workman, Clark and

Co. Ltd., Belfast (Yard No. 140) as PAVIA.
5.6.1897: Registered at Liverpool under the
ownership of the Cunard Steamship Co.
Ltd., Liverpool.
12.6.1897: Maiden voyage from Liverpool
to Venice.
8.6.1917: Requisitioned by the British
Government as a transport until *8.3.1919*.
1928: Sold for demolition to Thos. W. Ward
Ltd., Sheffield.
19.1.1928: Demolition commenced at
Barrow-in-Furness.
2.7.1928: Register closed.

TYRIA 1897-1928
O.N. 106870 2,936g 1,884n
332.1 x 45.7 x 22.5 feet.
T.3-cyl. by Barclay, Curle and Co. Ltd.,
Glasgow; 360 HP, 11 knots.
17.4.1897: Launched by Workman, Clark
and Co. Ltd., Belfast (Yard No. 141) as
TYRIA.
16.8.1897: Registered at Liverpool under
the ownership of the Cunard Steamship Co.
Ltd., Liverpool.
21.8.1897: Maiden voyage from Liverpool
to Trieste.
21.4.1917: Requisitioned by the British

In the late 1890s, a programme commenced to replace the iron ships of the 1860s. Three cargo-only freighters built by Workman, Clark were followed by a pair of slightly larger ships, which were constructed in north east England. *Pavia* (top) was the first to be delivered. She was followed two months later by *Tyria* (bottom). *[Both: B. and A. Feilden]*

Remarkably, the Belfast trio, including *Cypria*, all survived the First World War and were sold in 1928.

Government as a transport until *25.3.1919*.
2.6.1928: Registered under the ownership of the Niger Co. Ltd. (Lever Brothers), London for trading to West Africa.
2.7.1928: Renamed ARS.
19.5.1930: Transferred to United Africa Co. Ltd., London, a company which later became Palm Line.
5.9.1930: Registered under the ownership of Sea and Land Securities Ltd., London and resold for demolition to Petersen and Albeck, Copenhagen.
24.11.1930: Register closed.
29.11.1930: Arrived at Cork under tow for demolition at the Haulbowline Dockyard.

CYPRIA 1898-1928
O.N. 109406 2,935g 1,884n
332.1 x 45.7 x 22.5 feet.

T.3-cyl. by Barclay, Curle and Co. Ltd., Glasgow; 360 HP, 11 knots.
20.7.1897: Launched by Workman, Clark and Co. Ltd., Belfast (Yard No. 142) as CYPRIA.
6.4.1898: Registered at Liverpool under the ownership of the Cunard Steamship Co. Ltd., Liverpool.
16.4.1898: Maiden voyage from Liverpool to Genoa.
25.4.1917: Requisitioned by the British Government as a transport until *7.4.1919*.
1928: Sold to Cie. Franco-Africaine de Navigation 'Francafrica', Rouen, France.
31.5.1928: Register closed.
11.10.1937: Arrived at Rosyth for demolition by Metal Industries Ltd.

VERIA 1899-1915
O.N. 110564 3,229g 2,064n

330.6 x 45.2 x 24.7 feet.
T.3-cyl. by Wallsend Slipway and Engineering Co. Ltd., Wallsend; 360 HP, 11 knots.
15.11.1898: Launched by W.G. Armstrong, Whitworth and Co. Ltd., Newcastle-upon-Tyne (Yard No. 686) as VERIA.
30.3.1899: Registered at Liverpool under the ownership of the Cunard Steamship Co. Ltd., Liverpool.
1.4.1899: Maiden voyage from Newcastle to Constantinople.
7.12.1915: Sunk with explosives by the German submarine U 39 twenty four miles north west by west of Alexandria, in position 31°30´N, 29°28´E, having been captured on a voyage from Patras to Alexandria in ballast.
7.1.1916: Register closed.

Veria had almost the same length and beam as the three Belfast ships.

BRESCIA (1) 1903-1930
O.N. 118021 3,235g 2,058n
330.0 x 45.2 x 25.0 feet.
T.3-cyl. by Wallsend Slipway and
Engineering Co. Ltd., Wallsend; 371 HP, 11
knots.
9.4.1903: Launched by Joseph L. Thompson
and Sons Ltd., Sunderland (Yard No. 409) as
BRESCIA.
5.6.1903: Registered at Liverpool under the
ownership of the Cunard Steamship Co.
Ltd., Liverpool.
27.6.1903: Maiden voyage from Liverpool
to Genoa.
27.4.1917: Requisitioned by the British
Government as a transport until *11.3.1919*.
1930: Sold for demolition to Thos. W. Ward
Ltd., Sheffield.
20.6.1930: Arrived at Preston for demolition.
1930: Register closed.

LYCIA (1) 1909-1917
O.N. 106521 2,715g 1,739n
308.0 x 43.3 x 22.7 feet.
T.3-cyl. by North Eastern Marine
Engineering Co. Ltd., Wallsend; 250 HP, 10
knots.
28.7.1896: Launched by Sir Raylton Dixon
and Co. Ltd., Middlesbrough (Yard No. 428)
as OCEANO.
5.10.1896: Registered at Rochester under
the ownership of the Plate Steam Ship Co.
Ltd. (Gellatly, Hankey and Co., managers),
London.
25.10.1909: Registered at Liverpool under
the ownership of the Cunard Steam Ship Co.
Ltd., Liverpool as LYCIA for the Liverpool
to Mediterranean cargo service.
12.2.1910: First sailing for Cunard from
Liverpool to Constantinople.
11.2.1917: Sunk with explosives by the
German submarine UC 65 twenty miles
north east by north of the South Bishop
Lighthouse in position 52°12′N, 05°27′W
having been captured on a voyage from
Genoa and Bougie to Liverpool via Swansea
with general cargo.
27.2.1917: Register closed.

THRACIA 1909-1917
O.N. 109921 2,891g 1,850n
310.0 x 44.1 x 23.7 feet.
T.3-cyl. by Thomas Richardson and Sons,
Hartlepool; 265 HP, 9 knots.
30.8.1898: Launched by Sir Raylton Dixon
and Co. Ltd., Middlesbrough (Yard No. 459)
as OROÑO.
14.11.1898: Registered at Rochester under
the ownership of the Plate Steam Ship Co.
Ltd., (Gellatly, Hankey and Co., managers)
London.
25.10.1909: Registered at Liverpool under
the ownership of the Cunard Steam Ship
Co. Ltd., Liverpool as THRACIA for the
Liverpool to Mediterranean cargo service.
9.3.1910: First sailing for Cunard from
Liverpool to Constantinople.
27.3.1917: Torpedoed and sunk by the
German submarine UC 69 twelve miles
north of Belle Ile, France in position
47°32′N, 03°19′W whilst on a voyage from
Bilbao to Ardrossan with a cargo of iron ore.
Thirty six lives were lost.
17.4.1917: Register closed.

Brescia was the last new ship to be ordered for the Mediterranean service for a quarter of a century. Between 1909 and 1911 four second-hand freighters were bought for the service, including three from the Plate Steam Ship Co. Ltd.

Oroño, seen in the Avon Gorge (above), became *Thracia* (below).

Phrygia was the third of the freighters bought from the Plate Steam Ship Co. Ltd. *[Below: J. and M. Clarkson collection]*

PHRYGIA (1) 1909-1928
O.N. 110973 3,352g 2,147n
340.0 x 47.1 x 23.4 feet
T.3-cyl. by Sir Christopher Furness,
Westgarth and Co. Ltd., Middlesbrough; 350
HP, 9.5 knots.
21.10.1899: Launched by Sir Raylton Dixon
and Co. Ltd. Middlesbrough (Yard No. 465)
as ORO.
15.1.1900: Registered at Rochester under
the ownership of the Plate Steam Ship Co.
Ltd., (Gellatly, Hankey and Co., managers),
London.
25.10.1909: Acquired by the Cunard Steam
Ship Co. Ltd., Liverpool for the Liverpool to
Mediterranean cargo service.
29.10.1909: Registered at Liverpool under
the ownership of the Cunard Steam Ship Co.
Ltd., Liverpool as PHRYGIA.
1.2.1910: First sailing for Cunard from
Liverpool to Venice.

13.6.1917: Requisitioned by the British
Government as a transport until *26.7.1919*.
28.3.1928: Registered under the ownership
of Frederick L. Dawson, Newcastle and
subsequently sold to Commercial Navigation
Co. Ltd. (Raymond Olivier, manager),
Piraeus, Greece and renamed ALKYON.
27.8.1928: British register closed.
11.12.1931: Registered at London under the
ownership of Anglo Maritime Shipping Ltd.,
London and reverted to PHRYGIA.
1933: Sold to Maurice Olivier, Algiers and
registered at Panama.
13.1.1933: British register closed.
1933: Broken up in Italy in third quarter.

CARIA 1911-1915
O.N. 131328 3,032g 1,928n
318.0 x 43.0 x 25.2 feet.
T.3-cyl. by Wallsend Slipway and Engineering
Co. Ltd., Wallsend; 286 HP, 9.5 knots.

13.6.1900: Launched by Tyne Iron
Shipbuilding Co., Willington Quay,
Newcastle-upon-Tyne (Yard No. 129) as
CLEMATIS.
8.1900: Completed for S.A. des Produits
Résineux, Antwerp, Belgium.
1908: Company restyled as S.A.
d'Entreposage et de Transports, Antwerp.
20.3.1911: Registered at Liverpool under
the ownership of the Cunard Steam Ship Co.
Ltd., Liverpool as CARIA for the Liverpool
to Mediterranean cargo service.
11.7.1911: First sailing for Cunard from
Liverpool to Naples.
6.11.1915: Sunk by gunfire from the German
submarine U 35 120 miles south east of
Cape Martello, Crete in position 33°14′N,
25°47′E, having been captured on a voyage
from Liverpool to Alexandria in ballast.
7.12.1915: Register closed.

Bosnia was the first of four 2,400-ton Mediterranean traders ordered as replacements for Cunard's four elderly Mediterranean ships. From 1930 to 1946, they were the sole cargo-only vessels in the Cunard fleet. Bosnia was the second British merchant ship in the Second World War to be sunk by U-boat.

BOSNIA 1928-1939

O.N. 160388 2,396g 1,247n
292.3 x 45.0 x 23.4 feet.
T.3-cyl. by J. Dickinson and Sons Ltd.,
Sunderland; 403 HP, 9 knots.
6.2.1928: Launched by J.L. Thompson and
Sons Ltd., Sunderland (Yard No. 560) as
BOSNIA.
14.3.1928: Registered at London under the
ownership of the America-Levant Line Ltd.,
London (Stanley and John Thompson Ltd.,
managers). Cunard owned a controlling
interest in this company.
28.3.1928: Maiden voyage from Liverpool
to Constantinople.
5.12.1930: Ownership transferred to the
Cunard Steam Ship Co. Ltd., Liverpool.
1.1931: Cunard sold its shares in the
America-Levant Line Ltd. to Stanley and
John Thompson Ltd.
13.1.1938: Registered at Liverpool.
5.9.1939: Torpedoed and sunk by the
German submarine U 47 about 120 miles
north north west of Cape Ortegal, Spain
in position 45°29′N, 09°45′W whilst on a
voyage from Sicily to Manchester with a
cargo of sulphur, having been stopped by
gun fire from the submarine. One life was
lost.
21.10.1939: Register closed.

BACTRIA 1928-1954

O.N. 160411 2,402g 1,209n
292.3 x 45.0 x 20.3 feet.
T.3-cyl. by J. Dickinson and Sons Ltd.,
Sunderland; 403 HP, 9 knots.
6.3.1928: Launched by J.L. Thompson and
Sons Ltd., Sunderland (Yard No. 561) as
BACTRIA.

Bactria in the River Mersey.

Catalina S, the former Bactria, suffered serious damage after grounding near San Juan, Puerto Rico.

Bothnia had an active wartime career and was the last of the B-Class to be sold.

18.4.1928: Registered at London under the ownership of the America-Levant Line Ltd. (Stanley and John Thompson Ltd., managers), London. Cunard owned a controlling interest in this company.
2.5.1928: Maiden voyage from Liverpool to Constantinople.
5.12.1930: Ownership transferred to the Cunard Steam Ship Co. Ltd., Liverpool.
1.1931: Cunard sold its shares in the America-Levant Line Ltd. to Stanley and John Thompson Ltd.
17.1.1938: Registered at Liverpool.
13.4.1940: Requisitioned by the British Government as an ammunition ship.
7 to 8.1940: Used as a personnel ship.
22.8.1940: Transferred to the Liner Division and operated mainly between the UK and West Africa.
4.3.1946: End of requisition.
1.1.1950: Owners restyled as the Cunard Steam-Ship Co. Ltd., Liverpool.
12.5.1954: Final arrival at Liverpool.
1954: Sold to Cia. Isla Bella Ltda., Puerto Limon, Costa Rica (Panaghis G. Anghelatos, London) and renamed THEO.
1954: British register closed.
1958: Sold to Capital S.A. (Antonio Scoufalos), Montevideo, Uruguay and renamed CATALINA S.
1962: Sold to Bahamas Pearl Co. Ltd., Nassau, Bahamas and renamed BAHAMAS PEARL.
1962: Sold to National Shipping Trinidad Co. (J.M. O'Sullivan and Associates), Port of Spain, Trinidad and reverted to CATALINA S.
21.12.1962: Ran aground about two miles west of San Juan, Puerto Rico whilst on a voyage from Belize and San Juan to West Indies ports with a cargo of lumber and was subsequently declared a constructive total loss.

BOTHNIA (2) 1928-1955
O.N. 160475 2,402g 1,209n
292.3 x 45.0 x 20.3 feet.
T.3-cyl. by J. Dickinson and Sons Ltd., Sunderland; 403 HP, 9 knots.
5.4.1928: Launched by J.L. Thompson and Sons Ltd., Sunderland (Yard No. 562) as BOTHNIA.
15.5.1928: Registered at London under the ownership of the America-Levant Line Ltd. (Stanley and John Thompson Ltd., managers), London. Cunard owned a controlling interest in this company.
30.5.1928: Maiden voyage from Liverpool to Genoa.
5.12.1930: Ownership transferred to the Cunard Steam Ship Co. Ltd., Liverpool.
1.1931: Cunard sold its shares in the America-Levant Line Ltd. to Stanley and John Thompson Ltd.
17.1.1938: Registered at Liverpool.
30.10.1939: Requisitioned by the British Government.

6.1940-7.1944: Operated between the UK and West Africa.
12.1944-4.1946: Based in Ceylon and operated to Singapore and India.
2.7.1946: End of requisition.
1.1.1950: Owners restyled as the Cunard Steam-Ship Co. Ltd., Liverpool.
3.9.1955: Final arrival at Liverpool.
1955: Sold to Vivalet Shipping and Trading Co. S.A., Panama (A.I. Romano, Athens, Greece) and renamed EMILY.
1955: British register closed.
1958: Sold to Alex. G. Sigalas (George Sigalas Sons), Athens and renamed CAPETAN MANOLIS under the Lebanese flag.
24.12.1960: Ran aground one mile north of Casablanca whilst on a voyage from Fedala to Nemours in ballast,
16.3.1961: Refloated and subsequently declared a constructive total loss.
18.5.1961: Arrived at Valencia for demolition.

BANTRIA 1928-1953

O.N. 160500 2,402g 1,209n
292.3 x 45.0 x 20.3 feet.
T.3-cyl. by J. Dickinson and Sons Ltd.,
Sunderland; 403 HP, 9 knots.
17.5.1928: Launched by J. L.
Thompson and Sons Ltd., Sunderland
(Yard No. 563) as BANTRIA.
11.6.1928: Registered at London under
the ownership of America-Levant Line
Ltd. (Stanley and John Thompson Ltd.,
managers), London. Cunard owned a
controlling interest in the company.
26.6.1928: Maiden voyage from
Liverpool to Genoa.
5.12.1930: Ownership transferred
to the Cunard Steam Ship Co. Ltd.,
Liverpool.
1.1931: Cunard sold its shares in the
America-Levant Line Ltd. to Stanley
and John Thompson Ltd.
17.1.1938: Registered at Liverpool.
21.2.1940: Requisitioned by the British
Government until *15.3.1946* and used
mainly by the Liner Division based in
the Eastern Mediterranean, sailing to
Cyprus, Alexandria and North African
ports.
1.1.1950: Owners restyled as the
Cunard Steam-Ship Co. Ltd.,
Liverpool.
12.12.1953: Arrived Venice and sold
to Marco Celli, Venice, Italy and later
renamed GIORGINA CELLI.
1953: British register closed.
1955: Sold to Lauro and Montella
(Gennaro Montella), Naples, Italy and
renamed SACRUM COR.
1963: Transferred to Gennaro Montella,
Naples.
11.1968: Broken up at Vado Ligure,
Italy.

Bantria underway (top and middle) and loading steam locomotives at Swansea (below).

BRESCIA (2) 1947-1966
O.N. 180517   3,817g 2,165n
326.9 x 50.0 x 26.4 feet.
6-cyl oil engine by Nordberg Manufacturing Company, Milwaukee, Wisconsin; 1,700 BHP, 11.5 knots.
12.3.1945: Pre-registered at London*.
5.5.1945: Launched by Consolidated Steel Corporation Ltd., Wilmington, California (Yard No. 1,323) for the United States War Shipping Administration as HICKORY ISLE, a C1-M-AV1-type standard ship.
7.1945: Completed and bareboat chartered to the Ministry of War Transport, London (Common Brothers Ltd., Newcastle-upon-Tyne, managers).

17.7.1947: Registered at Liverpool under the ownership of the Cunard Steam Ship Co. Ltd., Liverpool as BRESCIA, a replacement for BOSNIA.
1.1.1950: Owners restyled as the Cunard Steam-Ship Co. Ltd., Liverpool.
6.1.1966: Register closed after sale to Timber Shipping Company, Panama (Letasa S.A., Bilbao, Spain).
8.1.1966: Sailed from Liverpool for Baddock, Nova Scotia, Canada as TIMBER ONE.
1969: Sold to Deepsea Miner Inc., Panama (Tenneco Oil Co., Houston, U.S.A.), refitted as a deepsea mineral mining vessel and renamed DEEPSEA MINER.

9.1973: Sold for demolition to Eckhardt and Co. K.G., Hamburg, Germany.
26.1.1974: Arrived at Santander, Spain under tow for demolition by Recuperaciones Submarinas S.A.

* The C1-M-AV1s (and the later T1 tankers) were pre-registered at London, the C1-M-AV1s in a block of thirty official numbers (180498-180527) in strict alphabetical order of the intended 'Hickory' names. In the event, not all of them were even laid down and only ten were leased to the U.K. and actually used the British registers provided for them.

Brescia was bought as a replacement for *Bosnia*. This United States-built ship was not only Cunard's first cargo motor ship, she was also the largest Cunard Liverpool-Mediterranean trader. The C1-M-AV1 type U.S. standard ships had a very distinctive profile.

PAVIA (2) 1953-1965
O.N. 185468 3,411g 1,828n
330.4 x 49.8 x 25.5 feet.
4-cyl 2SCSA Doxford-type oil engine by
David Rowan and Co. Ltd., Glasgow; 3,600
BHP, 14 knots.
19.3.1953: Launched by William Hamilton
and Co. Ltd., Glasgow (Yard No. 501) as
PAVIA.
22.5.1953: Registered at Liverpool under the
ownership of the Cunard Steam-Ship Co.
Ltd., Liverpool.
2.6.1953: Maiden voyage from Liverpool to
Piraeus.
1963-1964: On a Greek charter between
Piraeus and Southern and East African ports.
2.7.1965: Sailed from Liverpool to New
York.
5.8.1965: Arrived at London and
subsequently sold to Seaswift Maritime Co.
Ltd., Panama (Loucas Nomicos, Piraeus,
Greece) and renamed TOULA N under the
Greek flag.
25.8.1965: British register closed.
12.3.1974: Arrived at Suao, Taiwan for
demolition by Fukao Shipping Enterprise
and Jwi Lin Steel and Iron Works.

The B-class ships were replaced by *Pavia* (above), *Lycia* and *Phrygia*, the first
motor ships built for Cunard. These handsome vessels were the final purpose-built
Mediterranean ships.

LYCIA (2) 1954-1965

O.N. 185499 3,534g 1,731n
330.4 x 49.8 x 25.5 feet.
4-cyl 2SCSA Doxford-type oil engine by David Rowan and Co. Ltd., Glasgow; 3,600 BHP, 14 knots.
17.6.1954: Launched by William Hamilton and Co. Ltd., Glasgow (Yard No. 502) as LYCIA.
16.9.1954: Registered at Liverpool under the ownership of the Cunard Steam-Ship Co. Ltd., Liverpool.
24.9.1954: Maiden voyage from Liverpool to Piraeus.
4.1964: Transferred with PHRYGIA (2) to the Cunard North Atlantic services to the Great Lakes (summer-only), Boston and Canadian east coast ports.
1965: Sold to Diapori S.A., Panama (Loucas Nomicos, Piraeus, Greece) and renamed FLORA N. under the Greek flag.
23.9.1965: British register closed.
1970: Transferred to Cia. Mar. Louninosa, Panama (Loucas Nomicos reformed as Bluebird Maritime Co. Ltd., Piraeus) and renamed NEA TYHI, remaining under the Greek flag.
1974: Sold to Allied Shipping Co. Ltd., Bangkok, Thailand and renamed SOTHON.
1975: Renamed PATANPORN.
4.1977: Broken up at Hong Kong by Loy Kee Shipbreaker and Transportation Co. Ltd.

Like her sisters, *Lycia* had a relatively short career with Cunard. *Lycia* spent her last year with Cunard on the North Atlantic services to the Great Lakes. Here she is at Toronto in June 1965 (middle). The last name *Lycia* held was *Patanporn* (bottom) and was photographed as such at Singapore on 15th February 1976. *[Middle: Fred Sankoff/ W.A.Schell collection, bottom: Malcolm Cranfield]*

PHRYGIA (2) 1955-1965
O.N. 185515 3,534g 1,730n
330.4 x 49.8 x 25.5 feet.
4-cyl 2SCSA Doxford-type oil engine by
David Rowan and Co. Ltd., Glasgow; 3,600
BHP, 14 knots
29.12.1954: Launched by William Hamilton
and Co. Ltd., Glasgow (Yard No. 503) as
PHRYGIA.
25.3.1955: Registered at Liverpool under the
ownership of the Cunard Steam-Ship Co.

Ltd., Liverpool.
3.1964: Transferred with LYCIA (2) to
Cunard's North Atlantic routes to the Great
Lakes (summer-only), Boston and Canadian
east coast ports.
12.8.1965: Arrived at London and
subsequently sold to Firgounes S.A.,
Panama (Loucas Nomicos, Piraeus, Greece)
and renamed DIMITRIS N. under the Greek
flag.
7.9.1965: British register closed.

1970: Loucas Nomicos reformed as Bluebird
Maritime Co. Ltd., Piraeus.
1974: Sold to Kai Fah Maritime, Panama
and renamed ASIA DEVELOPER.
1975: Sold to Shun Fong Maritime S.A.,
Panama and renamed FONG CHI.
9.2.1975: Holds flooded and the ship
capsized following repairs at Kaohsiung.
29.10.1975: Raised and later sold to Long
Jong Industry Co. Ltd. for demolition.
16.7.1976: Demolition commenced.

Phrygia on trials (above) and working cargo (below).

CUNARD ELLERMAN SERVICES TO PORTUGAL AND THE MEDITERRANEAN

At its peak, Ellerman Lines had one of the largest fleets owned in Britain. Badly hit by the container revolution and the fuel price hikes of the 1970s, the number of ships owned by the company fell from 94 ships in 1953 to only six in the early 1980s. Among these were five 300-TEU capacity ships built at the Appledore shipyard. These vessels had been designed for Ellerman's joint P&O (Ellerman Strath) and Furness Withy (Ellerman Prince) services to the Mediterranean and Middle East from Ellesmere Port and Hull. The company also had a 20% share in Ben Line's Europe-Far East container service, a 65% share of Ellerman Harrison Container Lines and a shareholding in ACTA, the Associated Container Transportation (Australia) Ltd. Cunard had been a founding partner in ACTA through its Port Line subsidiary.

Despite heavy investment in the container business, Ellerman City Liners, the shipping division of the Ellerman Group, continued to operate with considerable losses. On the 15th November 1983 the reclusive Barclay brothers bought the entire group. The twins David and Frederick were primarily property developers and were mainly interested in Ellerman's brewery, property and leisure businesses. As a result, in February 1985 the Barclays agreed to a management buyout of the Ellerman shipping interests.

In 1987 the Ellerman company, now a profitable business, attracted the attention of Trafalgar House, which had failed in its bid to take over P&O in 1983. On 1st July 1987 Trafalgar House bought Ellerman Lines plc and formed Cunard Ellerman Shipping Services Ltd. to manage the company's cargo operations. This deal also included the five Appledore-built container ships which continued to serve on the UK-Portugal and Mediterranean routes.

However, this was a short-lived venture as the all-conquering Trafalgar House stumbled and, faced with a serious downturn in its profitability, agreed to sell Cunard Ellerman to P&O on 18th July 1991. This was to be one of the most complicated shipping deals in recent history. On 30th September 1991 P&O Containers took control of ACTA, the Associated Container Transportation (Australia) Ltd. with the transfer of the Cunard Ellerman's shares of the line. It also acquired its share of Ellerman Harrison Container Lines on 11th October 1991. Meanwhile, the Cunard Ellerman share in Ben Line's Europe-Far East container service had already been bought by Ben Line to prevent it coming under P&O control. P&O also sold ACTA's North American trades to Blue Star Line whilst Cunard Ellerman interests in the Mediterranean, Middle East, India and East Africa were sold to Andrew Weir Shipping, which formed a new division called Ellerman Container Line Services. On 31st December 2002 Andrew Weir's short sea activities, comprising Macandrews and the former Cunard Ellerman UK-Portugal service, were sold to CMA-CGM, who marketed them under the Macandrews name and for the first time since 1902 there was no Ellerman connection with the shipping business.

City of Plymouth was the first of five small 300 TEU container ships built between 1978 and 1981 by the Appledore Shipyard for Ellerman Line's UK-Portugal and Mediterranean services. This route continued during the Cunard Ellerman period. *[FotoFlite incorporating Skyfotos, 4265]*

CITY OF PLYMOUTH 1987-1991

O.N. 379751 1,599g 1,084n
316.1 x 54.1 x 26.6 feet.
3-cyl 2SCSA oil engine by Doxford
Engines Ltd., Sunderland; 5,000 BHP, 15
knots.
Containers: 300 TEU (twenty-foot
equivalent container units).
23.6.1978: Floated out by Appledore
Shipbuilders Ltd., Appledore (Yard No. A.S.
121) as CITY OF PLYMOUTH. Designed
for the UK to Mediterranean and Middle
East services.
11.1978: Completed and registered at
London under the ownership of Investors
in Industry plc (Ellerman City Lines Ltd.)
(Denholm Ship Management (Isle of Man
Ltd.), Douglas, managers) London.
1985-1987: Lloyd's Register prototype 'black
box' accident recorder installed and tested.
1.7.1987: Trafalgar House bought Ellerman
Lines plc and Cunard Ellerman Shipping
Services Ltd. was formed to operate the
group's cargo ships.
11.1991: Sold to Andrew Weir Shipping Ltd.
(AWS), London and registered on the Isle
of Man.
5.1993: Renamed CERVANTES.
5.1996: Renamed CITY OF LISBON.
4.1998: Renamed PACHECO.
1.1.2003: Sold to Macandrews & Co. Ltd.,
London (CMA CGM S.A., Marseilles,
managers).
1.7.2004: Management changed to CMA
CGM (UK) Shipping Ltd., Liverpool.
14.9.2007: Sold to Pm/s Kinnoul Ltd.,
Kingstown, St. Vincent and Grenadines
(KNK Ship Management, Mumbai, India,
managers) and renamed PACHECO 1 under
the Tuvalu flag.
3.8.2008: Sold to Perfetto Maritime Ltd.,
Majuro, Marshall Islands and renamed

City of Plymouth in the English Channel (top) and alongside a container terminal.
[Top: FotoFlite incorporating Skyfotos, 4266]

SARAH HANEM under the Moldova flag.
20.8.2009: Capsized in bad weather off
the cost of Yemen whilst on a voyage from
Sharjah to Bosaso with general cargo. One
life was lost

CITY OF LISBON 1987-1988

O.N. 379845 1,599g 1,084n
316.1 x 54.1 x 26.6 feet.
3-cyl 2SCSA oil engine by Doxford
Engines Ltd., Sunderland; 5,000 BHP, 15
knots.
Containers: 300 TEU (twenty-foot
equivalent container units).
14.10.1978: Floated out by Appledore
Shipbuilders Ltd., Appledore (Yard No. A.S.
122) as CITY OF PERTH. Designed for
the UK to Mediterranean and Middle East
services.

2.1979: Completed and registered at London
under the ownership of Investors in Industry
plc (Ellerman City Lines Ltd.), London.
10.1985: Renamed CITY OF LISBON.
1.7.1987: Trafalgar House bought Ellerman
Lines plc and Cunard Ellerman Shipping
Services Ltd. was formed to operate the
group's cargo ships.
8.1988: Sold to Troubadour Shipping Co.
Ltd., Limassol, Cyprus (Erka-Shipping
G.m.b.H., Neu Wulmstorf, Germany) and
renamed ERKA SUN.
11.1998: Renamed SINAR BANDUNG.
7.1999: Reverted to ERKA SUN.
3.2000: Renamed CTE TARRAGONA,
under the British flag.
5.2001: Reverted to ERKA SUN under the
Antigua and Barbuda flag.
23.7.2003: Arrived at Alang for demolition.

City of Lisbon was the only ship in the Appledore quintet which had been sold for demolition by 2012. *[Malcolm Cranfield]*

CITY OF MANCHESTER 1987-1991

O.N. 379965 1,599g 1,084n
316.1 x 54.1 x 26.6 feet.
3-cyl 2SCSA oil engine by Doxford
Engines Ltd., Sunderland; 5,000 BHP, 15
knots.
Containers: 300 TEU (twenty-foot
equivalent container units).
3.2.1979: Floated out by Appledore
Shipbuilders Ltd., Appledore (Yard No. A.S.
123) as CITY OF HARTLEPOOL. Designed
for the UK to Mediterranean and Middle
East services.
5.1979: Completed and registered at London

under the ownership of Container Rentals
Ltd. (Ellerman City Lines Ltd.), London.
5.1984: Chartered to Hf. Eimskipafélag
Íslands (Icelandic Steamship Co.),
Reykjavik, Iceland and renamed LAXFOSS
under the Bahamas flag.
8.1985: Renamed CITY OF
MANCHESTER.
1.7.1987: Trafalgar House bought Ellerman
Lines plc and Cunard Ellerman Shipping
Services Ltd. was formed to operate the
group's cargo ships.
9.1988: Reverted to the British register.
11.1991: Sold to Andrew Weir Shipping Ltd.

(AWS), London and registered on the Isle
of Man.
6.2007: Sold to Netherlands Antilles South
Seas Shipping N.V., Netherlands Antilles
(Derin Denizcilik Gemi Tasimacilik Sanayi
ve Ticaret Limited Sirketi, Istanbul, Turkey)
and renamed CITY.
6.2008: Renamed ZEELAND.
12.2009: Sold to North Bulkers S.A.,
Istanbul (Alfamarine Shipping Com. Ltd.,
Tartous, Syria) and renamed GOLDEN BAY
under the Panama flag.
2012: Still in existence.

City of Manchester in Cunard Ellerman colours. *[Malcolm Cranfield]*

LIVERPOOL STAR 1987-1991

O.N. 386250 1,599g 1,084n
316.1 x 54.1 x 26.6 feet.
3-cyl 2SCSA oil engine by Doxford
Engines Ltd., Sunderland; 5,000 BHP,
15 knots.
Containers: 300 TEU (twenty-foot
equivalent container units).
9.5.1979: Floated out by Appledore
Shipbuilders Ltd., Appledore (Yard
No. A.S. 124) as CITY OF IPSWICH.
Designed for the UK to Mediterranean
and Middle East services.
7.1979: Completed and registered at
London under the ownership of Lloyds
Leasing Ltd. (Ellerman City Lines
Ltd.), London.
10.1981: Chartered to Manchester
Liners Ltd., Manchester and renamed
MANCHESTER FULMAR.
7.1983: Reverted to CITY OF
IPSWICH.
1.1984: Renamed LIVERPOOL STAR.
1.7.1987: Trafalgar House bought
Ellerman Lines plc and Cunard
Ellerman Shipping Services Ltd. was
formed to operate the group's cargo
ships.
11.1991: Sold to Andrew Weir Shipping
Ltd. (AWS), London, registered on the
Isle of Man and reverted to CITY OF
IPSWICH.
3.1992: Sold to Pella Shipping Co.
S.A., Panama City (Sarlis Group,
Piraeus, Geece) and renamed
PELMARINER under the Greek flag.
26.7.1999: Sank after a collision
in thick fog with the container ship
PELRANGER (6,562/1978), also Sarlis
Group-owned, whilst on a voyage from
Iraklion to Gemlik with containerized
cargo, five miles south west of Tenedos
in position 39°48′N, 25°51′E. One life
was lost.

During her time with Cunard Ellerman, the former *City of Ipswich* was named *Liverpool Star*. [*FotoFlite incorporating Skyfotos, 27822*]

OXFORD 1987-1992

O.N. 390997 1,599g 1,084n
316.1 x 54.1 x 26.6 feet.
3-cyl 2SCSA oil engine by Doxford Engines
Ltd., Sunderland; 5,000 BHP, 15 knots.
Containers: 300 TEU (twenty-foot equivalent
container units).
6.3.1981: Floated out by Appledore
Shipbuilders Ltd., Appledore (Yard No. A.S.
125) as CITY OF OXFORD. Designed for the
UK to Mediterranean and Middle East services.
5.1981: Completed and registered at London
under the ownership of Investors in Industry
plc (Ellerman City Lines Ltd.), London.
3.1983: Chartered to Hf. Eimskipafélag Íslands
(Icelandic Steamship Co.), Reykjavik, Iceland and
renamed BAKKAFOSS under the Bahamas flag.
1.7.1987: Trafalgar House bought Ellerman
Lines plc and Cunard Ellerman Shipping
Services Ltd. was formed to operate the group's
cargo ships.

9.1987: Renamed OXFORD at the end of the
charter.
12.1992: Sold to Andrew Weir Shipping Ltd.
(AWS), London.
4.1993: Sold to HSH Aquarius Inc., Nassau,
Bahamas (Norasia Schiffahrts G.m.b.H.,
Fribourg, Switzerland) and renamed NORASIA
MALACCA.
2.1994: Renamed HYUNDAI MALACCA.
1.1995: Transferred to HSH Aquarius
Incorporated, Nassau, Bahamas (Hai Sun Hup
Co. (Private) Ltd., Singapore).
5.1996: Rename HUB MELAKA.
9.1996: Renamed MELAKA.
4.2003: Under Malaysian flag.
10.2005: Sold to Joo Tat Shipping Private Ltd,
Singapore and renamed JTS SENTOSA under
the Tuvalu flag.
8.2006: Renamed SYSTEMINDO PERDANA
under the Indonesian flag.
2012: Still in existence.

Following her sale to Andrew Weir, *Oxford* has had six name changes. [*FotoFlite incorporating Skyfotos, 66373*]

CUNARD ARABIAN MIDDLE EAST LINE (CAMEL)

One of the main beneficiaries of the oil price hikes during the 1973 'fuel crisis' was Saudi Arabia, then the world's main oil exporting country. In the mid-1970s the country underwent a huge transformation from a semi-feudal state to a modern economy. Goods flooded into the country and, in 1976, the Saudi Ports Authority was created to develop and improve the country's ports, which at the time had limited cargo handling facilities. Chaos ensued at the main port Jeddah. Conventional ships often had to wait up to three months before they could unload their cargo. Cunard's subsidiary, Thos. and Jno. Brocklebank, had been operating in the region since the 1950s as it had switched the emphasis of its services away from the Bay of Bengal to Red Sea ports. It was therefore ideally placed to offer shippers the opportunity to beat the congestion with a new containerised roll-on-roll-off (ro-ro) service to Jeddah and other Red Sea ports.

In February 1976 Cunard Brocklebank announced the establishment of the Cunard Arabian Middle East Line (CAMEL) which would operate a monthly express service from Felixstowe to Jeddah via the Jordanian port of Aqaba using chartered ships. One of Sea Containers' 3,391g Strider-class ro-ro ships was chartered for the service and was renamed *Jeddah Crown*. This type of vessel had been specially designed for under-developed ports such as Jeddah. Fitted with an angular stern ramp and a travelling gantry crane mounted on deck, containers could be easily loaded onto lorries driven onto the deck via the stern ramp. In Jeddah this discharge and delivery service was operated by Arabian International Road Transport, a Cunard-Saudi Arabian joint venture. Sporting the familiar Brocklebank funnel colours with the Cunard name (later CAMEL) in red on the aft superstructure, the 330-TEU (twenty-foot equivalent container units) capacity *Jeddah Crown* inaugurated the new service on 5th May 1976.

In April 1977, a second Strider-class vessel *Aqaba Crown* was added and, for the 3rd May sailing from Felixstowe, a call at the North Yemen port of Hodeida was included. By the time the third Strider-class ship *Saudi Crown* joined the fleet that summer, the

The 1976-built Strider-class ro-ro *Jeddah Crown* inaugurated the CAMEL service from Felixstowe to Jeddah in 1976. *[FotoFlite incorporating Skyfotos, 329129]*

Hodeidah Crown of 1977 was on the CAMEL service from 1979 to 1981. *[Fotoflite incorporating Skyfotos, 341702]*

frequency of sailings had increased to one every ten days. Hamburg, Havre and Rotterdam had also been added to the schedule. By the end of the decade, Jeddah was fully operational as a container port and the Strider-class ships were replaced by a trio of larger container ships. The sisters *Jeddah Crown* (6,216/1978) and *Hodeidah Crown* (6,216/1977) and the *Petra Crown* (7,681/1974) had travelling gantry cranes which enabled the ships to load and discharge containers independently of shore based facilities.

In a relatively short time, the number of companies offering regular services to the Red Sea region from Northern Europe had risen from four to over forty. Containerisation also brought to an end Brocklebank's break-bulk cargo operation and in 1983 the

last Brocklebank conventional cargo liners were sold. Meanwhile, despite increased competition, the Cunard Arabian Middle East Line continued to operate with chartered tonnage throughout the 1980s. In 1985 a new service called Red Sea Express was launched by Merzario and Cunard who were joined in 1986 by the Compagnie Maritime d'Affrètement (CMA) and in 1988 by the East German State Line, Deutsche Seereederei VEB (DSR). CAMEL became Cunard's trading name in the new service, each partner chartering ships which were given a 'Red Sea E...' name. The trading name of CAMEL passed to Andrew Weir Shipping Ltd. in October 1991 after the sale of Cunard Ellerman to P&O but was subsequently replaced in the joint service by the Ellerman brand name.

Until 1986 the Crown-names on the CAMEL service were repeated a number of times. There were three *Aqaba Crown*s, four *Hodeidah Crown*s and three *Jeddah Crown*s. Here are *Petra Crown* (7,680/1974) chartered from 1980 to1983, *Hodeidah Crown* (12,758/1978) from 1979 to 1983 and *Jeddah Crown* (11,269/1977) which was used between 1984 and 1986. *[Fotoflite incorporating Skyfotos, 366643; 30553; 40114]*

THE TRANSATLANTIC CARGO FLEET

THE ATLANTIC CARGO FLEET

Although Cunard is known primarily as a passenger ship company, it was also an important cargo operator across the Atlantic. From the start, its passenger ships carried not only mail but also freight. This was the main reason for the sporadic use of freighters from the 1870s until after the Second World War.

In February 1871 the company announced that it had placed an order with J. and G. Thomson for a pair of 1,900g steamers for a new cargo route between Glasgow, the West Indies (Barbados, Trinidad, Demerara and Cuba) and South America. *Trinidad* and *Demerara*, completed in 1872, had a large cargo capacity and limited passenger accommodation. Interestingly, whilst *Jackal* was the first ship built by Thomson at Govan (the company moved the yard in 1871 to Clydebank), *Demerara* was the last. A slightly larger ship, *Saragossa*, was ordered from Thomson in May 1872 for the new service. Although she was laid down in December 1872, she was only completed in June 1874, possibly because of financial difficulties at the yard. By that time, the service had been terminated after only one year, probably because of poor returns. The three ships were transferred to the Liverpool-Mediterranean service. *Trinidad* and *Saragossa* had lengthy careers with the company, whilst *Demerara* vanished in 1888 off the coast of south west England, with the loss of two passengers and thirty-nine crew. Three years earlier, *Sidon* had become the first Cunarder to lose passengers during peace time, when four passengers drowned after the ship was wrecked off north west Spain.

It was not until the early 1890s that Cunard again ordered purpose-built freighters for the North Atlantic. Relatively large ships, the 5,600g *Sylvania* and *Carinthia* carried no passengers and were designed primarily for the Liverpool-Boston cattle and cargo trade. At the time of their completion in 1895, Liverpool had the largest livestock market in Europe. Imports of heads of cattle to the UK across the Atlantic ran into the hundreds of thousands per annum. In 1865 Chicago became the centre for the United States meat industry with the formation by a group of railroad companies of the Union Stock Yards. This led to a more efficient distribution of livestock to the major seaports on the eastern seaboard and a number of Liverpool-based companies such as White Star, Leyland and Warren Line had ships fitted with stalls for the carriage of large numbers of cattle. In 1898 Cunard bought on the stocks an even larger ship, the 8,056g *Ultonia*, for the Boston cargo service. She not only had cattle fittings but also insulated space in the lower 'tween decks for chilled beef. However, within a few months she was fitted as an emigrant ship for the Liverpool-Queenstown-New York route. During the Boer War, *Sylvania* and *Carinthia* were chartered to carry mules from New Orleans

to South Africa, and it was during one of these voyages in 1900 that *Carinthia* was wrecked off Haiti. With the rapid development of refrigerated meat ships and the importation of Argentinean beef, the live cattle trade fell away dramatically in the early 1900s. The Cunard company also concluded that larger passenger ships could also handle sufficient cargo with no need for cargo-only vessels at ports such as New York and Boston. As a result, *Sylvania* was sent to the breakers in 1910, after a career of only fifteen years.

The need for freighters on the North Atlantic became apparent during the first two years of the 1914-1918 war when most of the passenger ships were requisitioned as troopships. In 1916 four second-hand cargo ships were purchased, two from Lawther, Latta and two from the Dundee company C. Barrie and Sons. They were all given V-names, a naming process which continued for transatlantic freighters until 1947 when the company returned to more familiar Cunard names such as *Asia* and *Arabia*.

The losses among the Cunard cargo fleet during the First World War were high, and included all four V-ships. The company also managed eight freighters for the British Government; four ex-German ships belonging to Woermann Line and given *Pol* names and four U.S.-built vessels with *War* names. Only two of these survived the conflict. To replace war losses, which included most of the intermediate liner fleet, ten cargo ships were bought for the North Atlantic trade, including six wartime standard ships. Such was the need for cargo capacity that the 12,768g intermediate *Albania*, which had been laid down in 1914 as the fourth A-class intermediate passenger liner, was completed as a cargo-passenger ship in 1920. By then Cunard operated cargo services from Liverpool, London, Avonmouth (Bristol), Rotterdam and Antwerp to Canada and eastern seaboard U.S. ports such as Philadelphia, Baltimore, Portland, Boston and New York. From 1922 the sailings from Avonmouth were taken up by Cunard's associate, Donaldson Line.

Between 1921 and 1925, a dozen intermediate liners were built for the New York, Boston and Canadian routes, all with considerable cargo space. The cargo-only fleet was gradually phased out throughout the decade and by 1931 the last one, *Valacia*, had been sold, leaving the Mediterranean

Albania was completed as a passenger-cargo ship in 1920. *[Ships in Focus]*

B-class quartet the only company-owned freighters. Interestingly, the amount of cargo carried on Cunard transatlantic ships in 1929 was 500,000 tons eastbound and 337,000 tons westbound.

During the Second World War and in the immediate post-war era, the company managed thirty-one ships, including nineteen cargo ships. Among these were eight U.S. Liberty-type standard ships with *Sam*-names and seven Canadian standard ships with *Park* or *Fort* names. Two of the war-managed Liberties were bought by Cunard in 1947 and given V-names. They joined two British–built *Empire* partially-refrigerated wartime standard ships with V-names, which had been purchased a year earlier. As was the case in the 1920s, these four ships acted as stop-gaps until replacements for war losses had been completed. The last of the V-ships were the two Liberties, which were sold in 1954.

However, unlike in the 1920s, the company decided to build up its fleet of freighters. For the first time in over fifty years, purpose-built transatlantic cargo ships were ordered. These were the A-class, a trio of fast 8,700g ships, designed for the weekly Liverpool-Canada freight service and given traditional Cunard names ending in *ia*. Three-island types, they had six holds and ten 'tween deck compartments. With almost 500,000 cubic feet capacity and 130,000 cubic feet of insulated space, the cargo was handled with electric winches and twenty-one derricks, including a 50-ton heavy lift derrick at Number 2 hatch. These traditional-looking ships were joined in 1951 by a pair of second-hand ships, which were the most distinctive of all the Cunard cargo ships. With a raked bow, extended forecastle, streamlined bridge and twin funnels, *Andria* and *Alsatia* looked more like small passenger ships than cargo liners. Completed for Silver Line's New York service, they were sold to Cunard after the company decided to abandon its liner trade.

By the mid-1950s Cunard's transatlantic freighter routes included: Liverpool-Montreal; Liverpool-St. John, New Brunswick and Halifax, Nova Scotia; London-Havre-New York and London-Havre-St. John, New Brunswick.

Vasconia, seen in April 1949, had been completed as Empire Pendennis in 1944. [Ships in Focus]

In the spring of 1957, Cunard started a new Cunard Lakes Service from London to Chicago and Milwaukee using a small chartered German ship, *Erin Nübel* (827/1954). A Liverpool service commenced the following year with the chartered *Concordia* (1,367/1953) and Toronto, Hamilton, Cleveland and Detroit were later added to the schedule. For most of the 1960s, chartered tonnage was used on the Cunard Lakes Service with many of the ships given well-known Cunard names ending in *ia* (see page 284). This naming process continued until 1968, when the service, still with chartered ships, became the Transatlantic Lakes Line, a joint operation with Oranje Lijn, French Line and Fjell Line.

The St. Lawrence Seaway was officially opened by Queen Elizabeth II and President Dwight D. Eisenhower on the 26th June 1959. This enabled larger ships to use the route and the first Cunarders designed for service in the St. Lawrence Seaway and the Great Lakes were *Andania* and *Alaunia*. Delivered in 1960, these 7,000g ships were also the first designed to negotiate the Manchester Ship Canal and were given telescopic topmasts, hinged radar masts and removable funnel tops. Not long after their introduction, they were placed on a new cargo service from London and Glasgow via Liverpool to the United States Gulf of Mexico ports, mainly Galveston, Houston and New Orleans. The London service also called at Havre.

By 1961, the intermediate passenger-cargo liners *Media* and *Parthia* had become too expensive to operate profitably. The pair were withdrawn and sold. Their places on the Liverpool-New York route were taken in October 1961 by two chartered, newly-completed Swedish ships, *Nordic* (4,560/1961) and *Marion* (4,364/1961) which were renamed *Nordia* and *Maronia* respectively. These charters and the older steam ships *Andria*, *Alsatia* and the A-class would eventually be replaced by a new class of engines aft motor ships. The *Media*-class ships, delivered between 1963 and 1966, were also the last conventional freighters built for Cunard. They were designed primarily for a weekly service between

Nordia (above) and her sister Maronia replaced Media and Parthia on the Liverpool to New York route on 6th October and 20th October 1961 respectively. [Malcolm Cranfield collection]

Liverpool and New York and were also able to transit the Manchester Ship Canal. Their deadweight of 7,000 tons was considered, at that time, to be the optimum size for a cargo liner operating a regular service between Great Britain and New York. The forward section of the ship was ice-strengthened and the four main holds were square in shape so that fork-lift trucks could work freely aboard. The first four ships were completed for Cunard, whilst the final trio were built and owned by their builders, Cammell Laird, and bareboat chartered to Cunard. They were also used on the UK-Canada services and were slightly longer and more powerful versions of the earlier quartet.

With the arrival of container ships in the 1960s, the writing was on the wall for conventional cargo ships. In 1966 Cunard joined the Atlantic Container Line consortium. Three years later, *Atlantic Causeway*, its first container ship, was delivered. In the meantime, on 1st January 1968, the Cunard company was split into two separate businesses. Whilst the passenger ships were transferred into Cunard Line Ltd., all the Cunard-owned and chartered ships, together with those owned by Thos. and Jno.

Brocklebank and Moss Tankers, were managed by a new company, Cunard Brocklebank Ltd.

By 1971, all the conventional Cunard freighters had been sold, with the exception of *Saxonia* and *Ivernia*, which had been lengthened, given Brocklebank names, and operated with the remaining Brocklebank cargo liners, under the Cunard Brocklebank banner.

On the *Media*-class the holds were served by twelve 10-ton derricks, four 5-ton derricks and one 25-ton derrick. They were controlled from weatherproof shelters situated on the masthouse platforms.

Hydraulic steel hatch covers were fitted to all hatchways.

The holds on the *Media*-class were designed to reduce obstructions in the cargo space to a minimum and were square in shape for the carriage of containers and palletised cargo. The decks were also strengthened for the use of fork lift trucks.

GLASGOW-WEST INDIES 1872-1873

In 1872 a new cargo service was started from Glasgow to the West Indies (Barbados, Trinidad, Demerara and Cuba) and South America. Three cargo ships were ordered for the route, each with limited passenger accommodation. The service lasted only a year and the vessels were subsequently used on the Liverpool to Mediterranean services.

TRINIDAD 1872-1898 Iron brig rigged

O.N. 67981 1,899g 1,228n
307.5 x 34.1 x 24.5 feet.
C. 2-cyl. by J. and G. Thomson, Govan; 300 HP, 10.5 knots.
Passengers: 46 cabin, 16 steerage. (Board of Trade Passenger Certificate: *27.8.1878*: 46)
9.4.1872: Launched by J. and G. Thomson, Govan (Yard No. 121) as TRINIDAD.
4.7.1872: Registered at Glasgow under the ownership of The British and North American Steam Packet Company, Glasgow.
5.10.1872: Maiden voyage from Glasgow to Demerara.
1873: Transferred to the Liverpool-Mediterranean routes after the termination of the West Indies service.
1.7.1878: Transferred to the Cunard Steamship Co. Ltd., Liverpool.
16.5.1898: Registered at Liverpool. Register closed the same day following the sale to Heinrich Diederichsen, Kiel, Germany who intended to use her as a coal hulk at Kiao Chou, China.
30.8.1898: Foundered off Turnabout Island, near Foochow, China during her delivery voyage from Hong Kong to Kiao Chou with a cargo of coal.

DEMERARA 1872-1887 Iron brig rigged

O.N. 68003 1,904g 1,231n
307.4 x 34.7 x 24.6 feet.
C. 2-cyl. by J. and G. Thomson, Govan; 300 HP, 10.5 knots.
Passengers: 46 cabin, 22 steerage. (Board of Trade Passenger Certificate: *26.9.1879*: 68)
6.9.1872: Launched by J. and G. Thomson, Govan (Yard No. 122) as DEMERARA. She was the last ship to be built at Thomsons' Govan yard. JACKAL (page 252) was the first in 1862.
18.11.1872: Registered at Glasgow under the ownership of The British and North American Steam Packet Company, Glasgow.
3.2.1873: Maiden voyage from Glasgow to Demerara.
1873: Transferred to the Liverpool-Mediterranean routes after the termination of the West Indies service.
1.7.1878: Transferred to the Cunard Steamship Co. Ltd., Liverpool.

Demerara was lost without a trace in 1887.

Saragossa remained in service for 35 years. *[National Maritime Museum N.21843]*

25.12.1887: Sailed from Liverpool for Trieste with two passengers, 39 crew and general cargo, including 307 tons of bar iron.
27.12.1887: Sighted 200 miles south of the Scilly Islands and never seen again.
7.3.1888: Register closed.

SARAGOSSA 1874-1909 Iron brig rigged

O.N. 68098 2,263g 1,430n
316.3 x 35.3 x 17.7 feet.
2-cyl. compound engine by J. and G. Thomson, Clydebank; 300 HP, 11 knots.
Passengers: 74 first, 548 steerage. (Board of Trade Passenger Certificate: *12.8.1879*: 74)
5.5.1874: Launched by J. and G. Thomson, Clydebank (Yard No. 130) as SARAGOSSA. Designed for the Glasgow to West Indies service but was not used on this route.
20.5.1874: Registered at Glasgow under the ownership of The British and North American Steam Packet Company, Glasgow.
18.6.1874: Completed.
23.7.1874: Maiden voyage from Liverpool to Boston. Subsequently used on the Liverpool-Mediterranean service.
1.7.1878: Transferred to the Cunard Steamship Co. Ltd., Liverpool.
19.5.1898: Registered at Liverpool

1909: Sold for demolition to Thos. W. Ward Ltd., Sheffield.
12.3.1909: Arrived at Preston for demolition.
17.8.1910: Register closed.

SYLVANIA (1) 1895-1910 Twin screw

O.N. 105282 5,598g 3,623n
445.0 x 49.0 x 23.9 feet.
Two T.3-cyl. by London and Glasgow Engineering and Iron Shipbuilding Co. Ltd., Glasgow; 570 HP, 14.5 knots.
24.1.1895: Launched by London and Glasgow Engineering and Iron Shipbuilding Co. Ltd., Glasgow (Yard No. 280) as SYLVANIA. Designed for the transatlantic cattle and cargo trade.
3.4.1895: Registered at Liverpool under the ownership of the Cunard Steamship Co. Ltd., Liverpool.
27.4.1895: Maiden voyage from Liverpool to Boston.
4.1901: Chartered by the British Government during the Boer War to carry mules from New Orleans to South Africa.
20.7.1910: Register closed after sale to Italian buyers.
2.8.1910: Arrived at La Spezia for demolition.

Sylvania was the company's first purpose-built North Atlantic freighter.

CARINTHIA (1) 1895-1900 Twin screw
O.N. 105318 5,598g 3,623n
445.0 x 49.0 x 23.9 feet.
Two T.3-cyl. by London and Glasgow
Engineering and Iron Shipbuilding Co. Ltd.,
Glasgow; 570 HP, 14.5 knots.
24.5.1895: Launched by London and
Glasgow Engineering and Iron Shipbuilding
Co. Ltd., Glasgow (Yard No. 281) as
CARINTHIA. Designed for the transatlantic
cattle and cargo trade.
19.7.1895: Registered at Liverpool under
the ownership of the Cunard Steamship Co.
Ltd., Liverpool.
24.10.1895: Maiden voyage from Liverpool
to Boston.
10.1899: Chartered by the British
Government during the Boer War to carry
mules from New Orleans to South Africa.
15.5.1900: Wrecked on Gravois Point, Haiti
during a voyage from New Orleans to Cape
Town with 1,450 mules, 64 crew and 64
muleteers. 995 mules were saved although
the ship was later declared a constructive
total loss.
20.6.1900: Register closed.

VANDALIA (1) 1916-1918
O.N. 132711 7,333g 4,618n
425.0 x 56.3 x 36.3 feet.
Q.4-cyl by North Eastern Marine
Engineering Co. Ltd., Newcastle; 601 HP,
12 knots.
21.2.1912: Launched by Short Brothers Ltd.,
Sunderland (Yard No. 372) as ANGLO-
CALIFORNIAN.
7.5.1912: Registered at London under the
ownership of Nitrate Producers' Steamship
Co. Ltd., (Lawther, Latta and Co.,
managers), London.
7.1.1916: Acquired by the Cunard Steam
Ship Co. Ltd., Liverpool.
15.1.1916: Registered at Liverpool under

Like her sister, *Carinthia* carried no passengers and was designed primarily for the Liverpool to Boston cattle and cargo trade.

Vandalia, seen here as *Anglo-Californian*, was the first Cunard freighter to be given a V-name. *[David Whiteside collection]*

the ownership of the Cunard Steam Ship Co.
Ltd., Liverpool as VANDALIA.
21.4.1917: Requisitioned by the British
Government as a transport.
9.6.1918: Torpedoed and sunk by the
German submarine U 96 eighteen miles west

north west of the Smalls Lighthouse, Irish
Sea, in position 51°44′N, 06°10′W whilst
on a convoy voyage from Liverpool to
Montreal in ballast. No lives were lost.
15.6.1918: Register closed.

VINOVIA 1916-1917

O.N. 123758 5,503g 3,520n
418.2 x 54.5 x 29.3 feet.
Q.4-cyl by North Eastern Marine
Engineering Co. Ltd., Newcastle; 539 HP,
11 knots.
3.10.1906: Launched by Short Brothers Ltd.,
Sunderland (Yard No. 335) as ANGLO-
BOLIVIAN.
24.11.1906: Registered at London under the
ownership of Southern Steam Shipping Co.
Ltd. (Lawther, Latta and Co., managers),
London.
18.12.1907: Transferred to Nitrate
Producers' Steamship Co. Ltd. (Lawther,
Latta and Co., managers), London.
15.2.1916: Acquired by the Cunard Steam
Ship Co. Ltd., Liverpool.
19.2.1916: Registered at Liverpool under
the ownership of the Cunard Steam Ship Co.
Ltd., Liverpool as VINOVIA.
3.5.1917: Requisitioned by the British
Government as a transport.
19.12.1917: Torpedoed and sunk by the
German submarine U 105 eight miles
south of Wolf Rock Lighthouse, Cornwall
in position 49°56′N, 05°33′W whilst on
a voyage from New York to London with
general cargo. Nine lives were lost.
9.1.1918: Register closed.

VOLODIA 1916-1917

O.N. 123342 5,689g 3,616n
423.5 x 56.0 x 28.7 feet.
T.3-cyl. by Rankin and Blackmore,
Greenock; 585 HP, 12 knots.
22.9.1913: Launched by Russell and Co.,
Port Glasgow (Yard No. 651) as DEN OF
OGIL.
21.10.1913: Registered at Dundee under the
ownership of the Barrie Shipping Co Ltd.
(C. Barrie and Sons, managers), Dundee.
21.1.1916: Acquired by the Cunard Steam
Ship Co. Ltd., Liverpool
24.1.1916: Registered at Liverpool under
the ownership of the Cunard Steam Ship Co.
Ltd., Liverpool as VOLODIA.
5.1917: Requisitioned by the British
Government as a transport.
21.8.1917: Torpedoed and sunk by the
German submarine U 96 285 miles west
of Ushant, in position 46°30′N, 11°30′W,
whilst on a voyage from Montreal to London
with general cargo. Ten lives were lost.
11.9.1917: Register closed.

VALERIA 1916-1918

O.N. 123340 5,865g 3,736n
423.4 x 56.0 x 28.8 feet.
T.3-cyl. by Rankin and Blackmore,
Greenock; 579 HP, 12 knots.
22.1.1913: Launched by Russell and Co.,
Port Glasgow (Yard No. 643) as DEN OF
AIRLIE.
13.2.1913: Registered at Dundee under
the ownership of Steamship Den of Airlie
Co. Ltd. (C. Barrie and Sons, managers),
Dundee.
16.2.1916: Acquired by the Cunard Steam
Ship Co. Ltd., Liverpool.

Volodia was the former *Den of Ogil*, shown here in ballast.

Valeria.

19.2.1916: Registered at Liverpool under
the ownership of the Cunard Steam Ship Co.
Ltd., Liverpool as VALERIA.
9.5.1917: Requisitioned by the British
Government as a transport.
20.6.1917: Rammed a German submarine,
believed to be U 99, off the coast of Ireland
whilst on a voyage from New York to
Liverpool. Although the submarine was
reported to have been sunk by the ship's
guns, she was in fact torpedoed and sunk by
the Royal Navy submarine J2 on *7.7.1917*.
21.3.1918: Grounded on Taylor's Bank,
River Mersey and caught fire at the end of
a voyage from New York with a cargo of
oil and general. She was later declared a
constructive total loss.
15.4.1918: Register closed.

VALACIA (1) 1916-1931

O.N. 129524 6,526g 4,100n
460.0 x 57.0 x 28.9 feet.
T.3-cyl. by Rankin and Blackmore,
Greenock; 690 HP, 12 knots.
6.9.1910: Launched by Russell and Co., Port
Glasgow (Yard No. 606) as LUCERIC.
15.10.1910: Registered at Glasgow under
the ownership of Bank Line Ltd. (Andrew
Weir and Co.), London.

6.10.1916: Acquired by the Cunard Steam
Ship Co. Ltd., Liverpool
13.10.1916: Registered at Liverpool under
the ownership of the Cunard Steam Ship Co.
Ltd., Liverpool.
17.11.1916: Renamed VALACIA.
30.3.1917: Damaged by a torpedo fired
from a German submarine not far from
the Eddystone Lighthouse whilst on a
voyage from London to New York. She was
subsequently towed to Plymouth for repairs.
21.4.1917: Requisitioned by the British
Government as a transport until *27.2.1919*.
1.3.1919: First voyage from London to New
York.
13.7.1930: Arrived in the Truro River,
Cornwall to be laid up.
1931: Sold to Industrie Navale S.A., Genoa,
Italy and renamed ERNANI.
16.12.1931: British register closed.
1938: Transferred to Ditta Giovanni
Gavarone fu G., Genoa.
28.6.1941: Torpedoed and sunk in error
by the German submarine U 103 about
450 miles west of Las Palmas in position
27°52′N, 26°17′W whilst attempting to
reach Bordeaux from Teneriffe, disguised
as the Dutch cargo ship ENGGANO
(5,412/1920).

Valacia was the last of the 1916-1919 V-ships and the only one to survive the First World War, in service above and below laid up in the Truro River, Cornwall in 1930 or 1931. *[Below: Ships in Focus]*

VENNONIA 1919-1924

O.N. 142630 5,225g 3,193n
400.6 x 52.2 x 28.6 feet.
T.3-cyl. by Caledon Ship Building and Engineering Co. Ltd., Dundee; 517 HP, 11.5 knots.

7.1918: Launched by Caledon Ship Building and Engineering Co. Ltd., Dundee (Yard No. 258) as WAR CARP, a B-type wartime standard ship.

30.8.1918: Registered at London under the ownership of The Shipping Controller, London (William Thomson and Co., Leith, managers) .

19.1.1919: Requisitioned by the British Government as a transport until *5.4.1919*.

22.1.1919: Acquired by the Cunard Steam Ship Co. Ltd., Liverpool.

8.2.1919: Registered at Liverpool under the ownership of the Cunard Steam Ship Co. Ltd., Liverpool as VENNONIA.

12.2.1919: First voyage from London to New York.

1924: Sold to the America-Levant Line Ltd. (Stanley and John Thompson Ltd.), London. Cunard owned a controlling interest in the company.

23.1.1924: Registered at London under the ownership of the America-Levant Line Ltd. (Stanley and John Thompson Ltd.), London as RIVER HUDSON.

1.1931: Cunard sold its shares in the American-Levant Line Ltd. to Stanley and John Thompson Ltd.

1931: Sold to 'Corrado' S.A. di Navigazione, Genoa, Italy and renamed ZEFFIRO.

6.5.1931: British register closed.

20.5.1941: Struck an Italian-laid mine and sunk about 5.8 miles from Cap Bon, Tunisia whilst on a voyage from Sfax to Naples

The four B-type standard ships, with their distinctive goalpost masts, were probably the most unattractive ships operated by Cunard. *Vennonia* was the first to join the fleet.

VERENTIA 1919-1926

O.N. 142429 5,185g 3,152n
400.4 x 52.3 x 32.1 feet.
T.3-cyl. by Harland and Wolff Ltd., Belfast;
518 HP, 11.5 knots.
9.5.1918: Launched by Harland and Wolff
Ltd., Belfast (Yard No. 532) as WAR
LEMUR, a B-type wartime standard ship.
25.5.1918: Registered at London under
the ownership of The Shipping Controller,
London (Thomas Dunlop and Sons,
Glasgow, managers).
22.1.1919: Acquired by the Cunard Steam
Ship Co. Ltd., Liverpool.
6.2.1919: Registered at Liverpool under the
ownership of the Cunard Steam Ship Co.
Ltd., Liverpool as VERENTIA.
21.7.1926: Acquired by Cree Investment Co.
Ltd. (Andrew Weir and Co.), Glasgow and
later renamed FORERIC.
1927: Transferred to Bank Line Ltd.,
Glasgow.
26.8.1927: Acquired by the Buenos Ayres
Great Southern Railway Co. Ltd. (A.
Holland and Co. Ltd., managers), London.
29.8.1927: Registered at London under
the ownership of the Buenos Ayres Great
Southern Railway Co. Ltd. (A. Holland and
Co. Ltd., managers), London as GALVAN.
22.3.1935: Sold to Kaye, Son and Co. Ltd.,
London.
1937: Sold to Pedder and Mylchreest Ltd.,
London and subsequently sold to Chang
Shu Chang (Nisshin Kaiun Shokai K.K.),
Tsingtao, China and renamed PEI TAI.
7.10.1937: British register closed.
1938: Sold to Kitagawa Sangyo Kaiun K.K.,
Osaka, Japan and renamed HOKUTAI MARU.
30.3.1944: Beached off Babelthuap, Palau
Atoll following air attack from U.S. aircraft
carriers.

VENUSIA 1919-1923

O.N. 142627 5,225g 3,172n
400.4 x 52.3 x 28.4 feet.
T.3-cyl. by Harland and Wolff Ltd., Belfast;
518 HP, 11.5 knots.
22.8.1918: Launched by Harland and
Wolff Ltd., Belfast (Yard No. 538) as WAR
SNAKE, a B-type wartime standard ship.

Verentia, as built with a signal mast abaft her funnel (above) and later (below).

28.8.1918: Registered at London under
the ownership of The Shipping Controller,
London (G. Heyn and Sons, Belfast,
managers).
22.1.1919: Acquired by the Cunard Steam
Ship Co. Ltd., Liverpool.
27.1.1919: Requisitioned by the British
Government as a transport until *21.3.1919*.
4.2.1919: Registered at Liverpool under the
ownership of the Cunard Steam Ship Co.
Ltd., Liverpool as VENUSIA.
1.6.1923: Final sailing from London to New
York.
11.7.1923: Acquired by the America-Levant
Line Ltd. (Stanley and John Thompson
Ltd.), London. Cunard owned a controlling

interest in the company.
21.7.1923: Registered at London under the
ownership of the America-Levant Line Ltd.
(Stanley and John Thompson Ltd.), London
as RIVER DELAWARE.
1.1931: Cunard sold its shares in America-
Levant Line Ltd. to Stanley and John
Thompson Ltd.
1931: Sold to 'Corrado' S.A. di Navigazione,
Genoa, Italy and renamed RINA CORRADO.
20.4.1931: British register closed.
9.11.1941: Sunk by gunfire from British
warships about 120 miles south east of
Punta Stilo, Calabria in position 37°08′N,
18°09′E whilst on a voyage from Messina
to Tripoli with war supplies,.

Three of the B-type ships, including *Venusia*, were sold to the Cunard associate company, American-Levant Line.

Vellavia in the River Mersey. *[B. and A. Feilden/J. and M. Clarkson]*

VELLAVIA 1919-1926
O.N. 142434 5,273g 3,195n
400.2 x 52.3 x 28.5 feet.
T.3-cyl. by G. Clark Ltd., Sunderland; 517
HP, 11.5 knots.
12.3.1918: Launched by Armstrong,
Whitworth and Co. Ltd., Newcastle-upon-
Tyne (Yard No. 933) as WAR SETTER, a
B-type wartime standard ship.
27.5.1918: Registered at London under
the ownership of The Shipping Controller
(Cairns, Noble and Co. Ltd., managers),
London.
22.1.1919: Acquired by the Cunard Steam
Ship Co. Ltd., Liverpool.
2.6.1919: Registered at Liverpool under the
ownership of the Cunard Steam Ship Co.
Ltd., Liverpool as VELLAVIA.
3.6.1919: First voyage from Liverpool to
New York.
1926: Sold to the American-Levant Line Ltd.
(Stanley and John Thompson Ltd.), London.
Cunard owned a controlling interest in the
company.
26.4.1926: Registered at London under the
ownership of the America-Levant Line Ltd.
(Stanley and John Thompson Ltd.), London
as RIVER TIGRIS.
1.1931: Cunard sold its shares in America-
Levant Line Ltd. to Stanley and John
Thompson Ltd.
1931: Sold to 'Corrado' S.A. di Navigazione,
Genoa, Italy and renamed INES
CORRADO.
27.4.1931: British register closed..
6.1940: Laid up at Bahia Blanca, Argentina
after Italy's entry into the Second World War.
25.8.1941: Taken over by the Argentine
Government-owned Flota Mercante del
Estado, Buenos Aires, Argentina and
renamed RIO DIAMANTE.

1946: Returned to her owners and reverted to
INES CORRADO.
16.4.1959: Arrived at Tokyo for demolition by
Ishikawajima Heavy Industries.

VITELLIA 1919
O.N. 142699 4,449g 2,681n
375.6 x 51.7 x 26.5 feet.
T.3-cyl. by Earle's Shipbuilding and
Engineering Co. Ltd., Hull; 517 HP, 11.5 knots.
10.1918: Launched by Earle's Shipbuilding
and Engineering Co. Ltd., Hull (Yard No.
633) as WAR PINTAIL, an E-type wartime
standard ship.
30.11.1918: Registered at London under
the ownership of The Shipping Controller,
London (Headlam and Rowland, Whitby,
managers).
29.1.1919: Requisitioned by the British
Government as a transport until *4.4.1919*.

6.2.1919: Registered at Liverpool under the
ownership of the Cunard Steam Ship Co.
Ltd., Liverpool as VITELLIA. First Cunard
voyage was from Liverpool to New York.
5.6.1919: Sold to Anchor Line Ltd.
(Henderson Brothers), Glasgow.
13.12.1923: Sold to Scindia Steam
Navigation Co. Ltd., Bombay, India and later
renamed JALARASHMI.
1953: Sold to Jhajharia Trading Co. Ltd.,
Calcutta, India and renamed ASHA.
24.2.1954: Arrived at Singapore on voyage
from Bombay to Osaka with scrap metal
and because of her poor condition the crew
subsequently refused to sail on her and she
was laid up.
4.1955: Sold for demolition to C. Itoh and
Co., Hirohata, Japan and renamed ASHA
MARU for tow to breakers.
8.6.1955: Arrived at Hirohata.

Vitellia at Boston, U.S.A. on 8th August 1920. *[J. and M. Clarkson collection]*

VINDELIA 1919

O.N. 142653 4,430g 2,698n

376.0 x 51.9 x 26.4 feet.

T.3-cyl. by Central Marine Engine Works, Hartlepool; 517 HP, 11.5 knots.

25.7.1918: Launched by William Gray and Co. Ltd., West Hartlepool (Yard No. 906) as WAR WAGTAIL, an E-type wartime standard ship.

20.9.1918: Registered at London under the ownership of The Shipping Controller (Lawther, Latta and Co., managers), London.

13.2.1919: Registered at Liverpool under the ownership of the Cunard Steam Ship Co. Ltd., Liverpool as VINDELIA.

30.6.1919: Sold to Anchor Line Ltd. (Henderson Brothers), Glasgow.

16.1.1924: Sold to Scindia Steam Navigation Co. Ltd., Bombay and later renamed JALAJYOTI.

1949: Sold for demolition to Hindustan Iron Co., Bombay.

3.1950: Demolition commenced.

VARDULIA (1) 1919-1929

O.N. 137835 5,691g 3,613n

423.3 x 56.0 x 28.7 feet.

T.3-cyl. by Rankin and Blackmore Ltd., Greenock; 564 HP, 11 knots.

3.2.1917: Launched by Russell and Co., Port Glasgow (Yard No. 691) as VERDUN.

30.3.1917: Registered at Glasgow under the ownership of Verdun Steamship Co. Ltd. (Gow, Harrison and Co.), Glasgow.

7.6.1919: Acquired by the Cunard Steam Ship Co. Ltd., Liverpool.

10.6.1919: Registered at Liverpool under the ownership of the Cunard Steam Ship Co. Ltd., Liverpool as VARDULIA.

27.2.1929: Sold to Donaldson Line Ltd., Glasgow.

8.4.1929: Registered at Glasgow under the ownership of Donaldson Line Ltd., Glasgow.

19.10.1935: Abandoned in the Atlantic in position 58°N,18°30′W after a distress signal was sent saying that she was listing, whilst on a voyage from West Hartlepool to Botwood, Newfoundland with a cargo of coal and general cargo. Her 37 crew members were lost.

23.12.1935: Register closed.

VIRGILIA 1919-1925

O.N. 141888 5,697g 3,619n

423.3 x 56.0 x 28.7 feet.

T.3-cyl. by J.G. Kincaid and Co. Ltd., Greenock; 550 HP, 10.25 knots.

27.9.1918: Launched by Russell and Co., Port Glasgow (Yard No. 707) as VIRGILIA.

4.11.1918: Registered at Glasgow under the ownership of Virgilia Steamship Co Ltd. (Gow, Harrison and Co.), Glasgow.

7.7.1919: Acquired by the Cunard Steam Ship Co. Ltd., Liverpool.

9.8.1919: Registered at Liverpool under the ownership of the Cunard Steam Ship Co. Ltd., Liverpool.

20.6.1925: Final sailing from London to New York.

10.8.1925: Acquired by the Lancashire Shipping Co. Ltd. (J. Chambers and Co.), Liverpool, and later renamed CORBY CASTLE.

1928: Sold to Tatsuuma Kisen K.K., Nishinomiya, Japan and renamed TATSUHA MARU.

19.1.1928: British register closed.

1937: Transliteration of name modified to TATUHA MARU.

17.2.1944: Sunk by U.S. Navy aircraft 40

miles west of Truk Lagoon in the Caroline Islands whilst on a voyage from Yokohama to Truk with troops,.

VERBANIA 1919-1927

O.N. 141875 5,021g 3,180n

405.3 x 53.0 x 27.5 feet.

T.3-cyl. by J.G. Kincaid and Co. Ltd., Greenock; 538 HP, 11 knots.

26.12.1917: Launched by Robert Duncan and Co., Port Glasgow (Yard No. 329) as TRAFALGAR.

21.2.1918: Registered at Glasgow under the ownership of Laurence Glen (Glen and Co.), Glasgow.

5.8.1919: Acquired by the Cunard Steam Ship Co. Ltd., Liverpool.

11.9.1919: Registered at Liverpool under the ownership of the Cunard Steam Ship Co. Ltd., Liverpool as VERBANIA.

16.2.1927: Sold to Lyle Shipping Co. Ltd., Glasgow and later renamed CAPE CORNWALL.

27.4.1927: Registered at Glasgow under the ownership of Lyle Shipping Co. Ltd., Glasgow.

28.1.1934: Arrived at Shanghai and broken up locally.

20.2.1934: Register closed.

Vardulia (above) was the first of four second-hand freighters acquired in 1919. Sold to Donaldson Line in 1929 (below) she was lost with all hands six years later. *[Below: John McRoberts/J. and M. Clarkson]*

VASCONIA (1) 1919-1927

O.N. 141885 5,680g 3,612n
423.3 x 56.0 x 28.7 feet.
T.3-cyl. by Rankin and Blackmore
Ltd., Greenock; 574 HP, 11 knots.
24.6.1918: Launched by Russell and
Co., Port Glasgow (Yard No. 703) as
VALVERDA.
29.8.1918: Registered at Glasgow
under the ownership of the Valverda
Steamship Co. Ltd. (Gow, Harrison
and Co.), Glasgow.
29.8.1919: Acquired by the Cunard
Steam Ship Co. Ltd., Liverpool.
30.8.1919: Registered at Liverpool
under the ownership of the Cunard
Steam Ship Co. Ltd., Liverpool as
VASCONIA.
1.9.1919: First voyage for Cunard
from Manchester to New York.
1927: Sold to Tatsuuma Kisen K.K.,
Nishinomiya, Japan and renamed
SHIRAHA MARU.
18.1.1927: British register closed.
1938: Transliteration of name modified
to SIRAHA MARU.
14.1.1943: Torpedoed and sunk by
USS SEARAVEN 200 miles east
of Mindanao in position 09°12′N,
130°38′E whilst on a voyage from
Palau to Manila.

Top: *Virgilia* was sold to Chambers and Company of Liverpool in 1925 and renamed
Corby Castle. In 1928 she was sold to Tatsuuma Kisen, Japan.
Middle: *Verbania* was only sixteen years old when she was sold for demolition.
Bottom: *Vasconia* remained with Cunard until 1927 when she too was sold to Tatsuuma
Kisen, the buyers of *Corby Castle*. Both ships were lost during the Pacific War.

After the Second World War, four wartime standard ships were acquired as stop-gaps until replacements for war losses had been delivered. These were two British–built Empire ships, with split superstructures, and two Liberty ships. These freighters were also the last to be given V-names.

VALACIA (2) 1946-1950

O.N. 169124 7,052g 4,760n
431.0 x 56.3 x 35.2 feet.
T.3-cyl. by North East Marine Co. (1938) Ltd., Newcastle-upon-Tyne; 542 HP, 11 knots.
17.6.1943: Launched by Short Brothers Ltd., Sunderland (Yard No. 477) as EMPIRE CAMP, a partially-refrigerated wartime standard ship.
4.10.1943: Registered at Sunderland under the ownership of the Ministry of War Transport (Blue Star Line Ltd., managers), London.
1946: Sold to Cunard White Star Ltd., Liverpool.
29.3.1946: Registered at Liverpool under the ownership of Cunard White Star Ltd., Liverpool.
9.5.1946: Renamed VALACIA.
22.12.1949: Transferred to the Cunard Steam Ship Co. Ltd., Liverpool.
1.1.1950: Owners restyled as the Cunard Steam-Ship Co. Ltd., Liverpool.
29.12.1950: Sold to the Bristol City Line of Steamships Ltd. (Charles Hill and Sons Ltd.), Bristol and later renamed NEW YORK CITY.
12.8.1955: Sold to Steamship 'Induna' Co. Ltd. (Maclay and McIntyre Ltd.), Glasgow and later renamed LOCH MORAR.
1959: sold to Lütfi Yelkenci Evlatları Donatma İştirakı, Istanbul, Turkey and later re-named YELKENCI.

Valacia had a long career and was broken up only in 1971.

9.9.1959: British register closed.
20.2.1971: Arrived at Istanbul for demolition at Istanbul to Hasköy by Imdat Gündoğdu ve Zaven Esseyan.

VASCONIA (2) 1946-1950

O.N. 180136 7,058g 4,757n
431.0 x 56.3 x 35.2 feet.
T.3-cyl. by Harland and Wolff Ltd., Glasgow; 542 HP, 11 knots.
11.4.1944: Launched by Short Brothers Ltd., Sunderland (Yard No. 481) as EMPIRE PENDENNIS, a partially-refrigerated 'Empire' wartime standard ship.
5.6.1944: Registered at Sunderland under the ownership of the Ministry of War Transport (Ellerman and Bucknall Steamship Co. Ltd., managers), London.
5.4.1946: Registered at Liverpool under the ownership of Cunard White Star Ltd., Liverpool.
1.6.1946: Renamed VASCONIA.
22.12.1949: Transferred to the Cunard Steam Ship Co. Ltd., Liverpool.

1.1.1950: Owners restyled as the Cunard Steam-Ship Co. Ltd., Liverpool.
30.12.1950: Sold to Blue Star Line Ltd., London and later renamed FRESNO STAR.
12.1957: Bareboat chartered to Lamport and Holt Line Ltd., Liverpool and renamed MILLAIS.
13.3.1958: Registered at London.
22.2.1960: Sold to Grosvenor Shipping Co. Ltd., London (Mollers' Ltd., Hong Kong) and renamed GROSVENOR NAVIGATOR.
9.9.1966: Arrived at Kaohsiung for demolition by Sing Chien Yung Steel and Ironworks Co. Ltd.
20.9.1966: British register closed.

VARDULIA (2) 1947-1954

O.N. 169864 7,243g 4,375n
422.8 x 57.0 x 34.8 feet.
T.3-cyl. by Filer and Stowell Co., Milwaukee, Wisconsin, U.S.A.; 574 HP, 11 knots.
23.3.1944: Launched by J.A. Jones Construction Co. Inc., Brunswick,

Vasconia, seen at Port Chalmers, New Zealand in July 1948 was sold to Blue Star Line in 1950. The hulk in the background is that of *Broxton* (3,585 tons gross), completed at Seattle, U.S.A. as a steamship in 1919. She was one of the world's largest wooden ships. She was bought in 1922 by the Union Steam Ship Co. of New Zealand for use as a storage hulk. *[Ian Farquhar]*

Prior to their acquisition in 1947, the Liberty ships *Vardulia* (above) and *Vandalia* (bottom) had been managed by Cunard White Star Line.

Georgia, U.S.A. (Yard No. 136) as SAMFOYLE, a Liberty-type wartime standard ship built for the United States War Shipping Administration and bareboat chartered to the Ministry of War Transport, London.
31.3.1944: Completed in 52 days.
31.3.1944-9.7.1947: Managed by Cunard White Star Ltd., Liverpool.
7.5.1944: Left Boston on maiden voyage to U.K.
26.5.1944: Registered at London under the ownership of the Ministry of War Transport, London.*
17.4.1947: Acquired by Cunard White Star Ltd., Liverpool.
29.5.1947: Registered at Liverpool under the ownership of Cunard White Star Ltd., Liverpool as VARDULIA.
22.12.1949: Transferred to the Cunard Steam Ship Co. Ltd., Liverpool.
1.1.1950: Owners restyled as the Cunard Steam-Ship Co. Ltd., Liverpool.
1954: Sold to Nueva Valencia Cia. Nav. S.A., Panama (N.J. Goulandris, London) and renamed VALENCIA.
18.11.1954: British register closed.
1957: Sold to Cia. de Navegacion Almirante S.A., Panama (Salvatores e C., Genoa, Italy) and renamed SEACOB.
2.12.1968: Arrived at Hong Kong for demolition by Mollers Ltd.

VANDALIA (2) 1947-1954
O.N. 169642 7,219g 4,380n
422.8 x 57.0 x 34.8 feet.
T.3-cyl. by Joshua Hendy Iron Works, Sunnyvale, California, U.S.A.; 574 HP, 11 knots.
11.7.1943: Launched by California

Shipbuilding Corporation, Los Angeles, California, U.S.A. (Yard No. 221) as GRANVILLE STUART, a Liberty-type wartime standard ship built for United States War Shipping Administration and bareboat chartered to the Ministry of War Transport, London.
23.7.1943: Completed as SAMARITAN in 38 days.
23.7.1943-5.6.1947: Managed by Cunard White Star Ltd., Liverpool.
19.8.1943: Left Iquique, Chile for Egypt on her first voyage with cargo.
20.11.1943: Registered at London under the ownership of the Ministry of War Transport, London.*
6.6.1947: Registered at Liverpool under the ownership of Cunard White Star Ltd.,

Liverpool as VANDALIA.
22.12.1949: Transferred to the Cunard Steam Ship Co. Ltd., Liverpool.
1.1.1950: Owners restyled as the Cunard Steam-Ship Co. Ltd., Liverpool.
1954: Sold to Marine Transport Co. S.A., Panama (Pandias Margaronis, London) and renamed SIDERIS under the Liberian flag.
10.12.1954: British register closed.
7.5.1971: Arrived at Barcelona for demolition at Villanueva y Geltru by Salvamentos y Demolicion Naval S.A.

* In wartime, official numbers and registration documentation were only allocated once the ship had reached a British port.

Asia (above and below) was the first ship to be delivered in Cunard's post-war rebuilding programme.

Each of these new cars in *Asia*'s 'tween decks had to be individually loaded by derricks. What a contrast to the scene over twenty years later on *Atlantic Conveyor* (see page 224).

The three post-war A-class freighters were the first purpose-built transatlantic, cargo-only ships built for Cunard in over fifty years.

They were three-island types, with two continuous decks and a third one in the forward well. There were two hatches in the forward well, three in the after one and one, served by two kingposts, between the bridge and funnel. These handsome ships were designed for the weekly Liverpool-Canada freight service.

ASIA (2) 1947-1963
O.N. 181080 8,723g 5,001n
488.5 x 64.1 x 32.3 feet.
Geared steam turbines by Richardson, Westgarth and Co. Ltd., Hartlepool; 7,250 SHP, 16 knots.
12.9.1946: Launched by Sir James Laing and Sons Ltd., Sunderland (Yard No. 769) as ASIA.
24.3.1947: Registered at Liverpool under the ownership of Cunard White Star Ltd., Liverpool.
15.4.1947: Maiden voyage Liverpool-Quebec-Montreal.
25.8.1948: In collision with the Italian Liberty-type steamer CICLOPE (7,189/1944) fifteen miles off St. Catherine's Point, Isle of Wight at 04.30 whilst on a voyage from Montreal to London with general cargo. Berthed at Southampton later that day and it was found that many cars and vans in number 3 hold were crushed or water damaged.
31.8.1948: Dry-docked for repair John I. Thornycroft and Co. Ltd.
22.12.1949: Transferred to the Cunard Steam Ship Co. Ltd., Liverpool.
1.1.1950: Owners restyled as the Cunard Steam-Ship Co. Ltd., Liverpool.

19.11.1956: Collided with the German freighter WOLFGANG RUSS (2,963/1955) in the St. Lawrence River whilst on a voyage from Quebec to London. After temporary repairs to her damaged bow at Quebec, she spent three months in the Halifax Navy Dockyard undergoing permanent repairs.

1963: Sold to Waywiser Navigation Corporation Ltd. (W.H. Eddie Hsu), Keelung, Taiwan and renamed SHIRLEY.

17.5.1963: British register closed.

14.1.1969: Prior to this date arrived at Kaohsiung, Taiwan for demolition.

ARABIA (3) 1947-1963

O.N. 182394 8,720g 5,073n

488.5 x 64.1 x 32.4 feet.

Geared steam turbines by Richardson, Westgarth and Co. Ltd., Hartlepool; 7,250 SHP, 16 knots.

18.7.1947: Launched by Sir James Laing and Sons Ltd., Sunderland (Yard No. 774) as ARABIA.

9.12.1947: Registered at Liverpool under the ownership of Cunard White Star Ltd., Liverpool.

8.1.1948: Maiden voyage from Liverpool to Halifax.

22.12.1949: Transferred to the Cunard Steam Ship Co. Ltd., Liverpool.

1.1.1950: Owners restyled as the Cunard Steam-Ship Co. Ltd., Liverpool.

1963: Sold to Neptune Marine Corporation, Monrovia, Liberia (P.S. Li, Hong Kong) and renamed ONSHUN.

22.4.1963: British register closed.

1967: Sold to Cosmos Marine Development Corporation and Showa Kaiun K.K., Monrovia (Y.C. Sa, Hong Kong).

10.5.1972: Arrived at Kaohsiung for demolition by Jui Long Steel and Copper Works.

Arabia was delivered nine months after her virtually-identical sister ship (top and above). After being sold she was renamed *Onshun* and was photographed as such in the Straits of Malacca (below) by Captain Peter Foxley. *[Below: David Whiteside collection]*

The success of the *Asia* and *Arabia*, led to an order for a third ship, *Assyria* (above and below). The first Cunard vessel to be built by Swan Hunter since 1928, she can be distinguished from the earlier pair by the addition of winch houses and lack of forward kingposts. For some reason, possibly storm damage, the square windows on the forward bridge deck of the Asia-class ships were later replaced with portholes. *[Above: Malcolm Cranfield]*

ASSYRIA 1950-1963

O.N. 183787 8,683g 5,014n
488.7 x 64.1 x 31.2 feet.
Geared steam turbines by Richardson, Westgarth and Co. Ltd., Hartlepool; 7,250 SHP, 16 knots.

19.1.1950: Launched by Swan, Hunter and Wigham Richardson Ltd., Wallsend (Yard No. 1801) as ASSYRIA.

18.8.1950: Registered at Liverpool under the ownership of the Cunard Steam-Ship Co. Ltd., Liverpool.

24.8.1950: Maiden voyage London-Havre-Montreal.

1963: Sold to Stala Cia. Naviera S.A. Monrovia, Liberia (N. and J. Vlassopoulos, London) and renamed LAERTIS.

26.7.1963: British register closed.

1970: Sold to Ambelos Development Corporation S.A., Chios, Greece and renamed HOLY TRINITY

1972: Renamed DROMON.

16.3.1974: Delivered to China National Metals and Minerals Import and Export Corporation, Shanghai for possible demolition. There is no information as to when she was demolished or if she continued to trade along the Chinese coast.

Laertis ex-*Assyria*.

Designed for Silver Line's New York service, *Silverbriar* and *Silverplane* were among the most distinctive British-built cargo ships of the 20th century. With a raked bow, streamlined bridge and twin funnels, they looked more like small passenger ships than cargo liners. The forward funnel was a dummy and housed the captain's cabin, chartroom, wheelhouse, and a 'ye-olde' English pub.

The passenger accommodation on the bridge deck was of a very high standard with a dining saloon facing aft and lounge forward. All cabins also had an adjacent bathroom. They never carried passengers during their time with Cunard and had a high fuel consumption of around 70 to 80 tonnes per day.

Silverplane (top) became *Alsatia* for Cunard in 1951 (middle) and was sold to Taiwan in 1963 as *Union Freedom* (bottom). *[Top and middle: Ships in Focus (2); bottom: J. and M. Clarkson collection]*

ALSATIA (2) 1951-1963
O.N. 182833 7,242g 4,098n
483.3 x 64.9 x 28.6 feet.
Geared steam turbines by Parsons Marine Steam Turbines, Wallsend; 8,000 SHP, 16 knots.
Passengers: 12; *1951*: Cargo only.
29.11.1947: Launched by J.L. Thompson and Sons Ltd., Sunderland (Yard No. 652) as SILVERPLANE.
25.8.1948: Registered at London under the ownership of Silver Line Ltd., London.
1951: Acquired by Cunard Steam-Ship Co. Ltd., Liverpool.
21.9.1951: Registered at Liverpool under the ownership of the Cunard Steam-Ship Co. Ltd., Liverpool.
25.9.1951: Renamed ALSATIA.
6.10.1951: First sailing for Cunard:

Liverpool-Boston-New York.
1963: Sold to China Union Lines Ltd., Keelung, Taiwan and renamed UNION FREEDOM.

28.1.1963: British register closed.
1.1977: Demolition commenced at Kaohsiung by Nan Fu Steel and Iron Co. Ltd.

The forward funnel of *Alsatia* and *Andria,* seen above, was a dummy.

ANDRIA (1) 1951-1963

O.N. 181841 7,242g 4,098n
483.3 x 64.9 x 28.6 feet.
Geared steam turbines by Parsons Marine
Steam Turbines, Wallsend; 8,000 SHP, 16
knots.
Passengers: 12; *1951*: Cargo only.
21.5.1947: Launched by J.L. Thompson and
Sons Ltd., Sunderland (Yard No. 651) as
SILVERBRIAR.
9.2.1948: Registered at London under the

ownership of Silver Line Ltd., London.
1951: Acquired by Cunard Steam-Ship Co.
Ltd., Liverpool.
20.12.1951: Registered at Liverpool as
ANDRIA.
1963: Sold to China Union Lines Ltd.,
Keelung, Taiwan and renamed UNION FAITH.
4.2.1963: British register closed.
6.4.1969: Collided off the foot of Canal
Street, New Orleans, U.S.A. with the tank
barge I.O.C. NO. 7, one of three barges

under tow of the tug WARREN J. DOUCET
(116/1967). The barge exploded and UNION
FAITH caught fire and subsequently capsized
and sank in the early hours of the following
morning. Twenty five crew and a river pilot
died. The pilot and the master apparently
perished when they left the bridge and
attempted to drop anchor to stop her drifting
into wharves and other ships. At the time,
UNION FAITH was loaded with a cargo of
cotton cloth, plywood and general cargo.

Andria sailing from the Royal Docks, London in 1955. *[Malcolm Cranfield collection]*

ANDANIA (3) 1960-1971
O.N. 301337 7,004g 3,501n;
1969: 8,717g 4,657n
471.0 x 63.3 x 27.2 feet.
Geared Pametrada-type steam turbines
by David Rowan and Co. Ltd.,
Glasgow; 9,500 SHP, 17 knots.
19.12.1959: Launched by William
Hamilton and Co. Ltd., Port Glasgow
(Yard No. 521) as ANDANIA. She
and ALAUNIA were the first Cunard
ships designed for service in the St.
Lawrence Seaway and to negotiate the
Manchester Ship Canal.
25.4.1960: Registered at Liverpool
under the ownership of the Cunard
Steam-Ship Co. Ltd., Liverpool.
3.5.1960: Maiden voyage from
Glasgow via Liverpool to the Gulf
of Mexico. Presumably because of
problems with soot, her funnel was
fitted around this time with a similar
smoke deflector as ALAUNIA.
8.12.1969: Renamed MACHARDA
following her charter to Cunard-
Brocklebank Ltd., London
1971: Sold to Soja Shipping (Liberia)
Inc., Panama (Ocean Shipping and
Enterprises, Ltd., Hong Kong) and

Andania (above) and *Alaunia* were the first Cunarders built for service in the St. Lawrence Seaway and the Great Lakes. They were also first in the fleet designed to negotiate the Manchester Ship Canal and were given telescopic topmasts, hinged radar masts and removable funnel tops. *Andania* was later fitted with a similar smoke deflector to *Alaunia* (middle). This addition, which carried smuts away from the deck, slightly marred her appearance.

renamed HUMI MAHIS.
19.5.1971: British register closed.
1973: Sold to Ocean Tramping Co. Ltd.,
Mogadiscio and renamed YUNGJIAN. This
company was a front company owned by the
People's Republic of China.

1975: Ownership transferred to People's
Republic of China Bureau of Maritime
Transport Administration, Kwangtung Branch,
Guangzhou, China and renamed HONG QI 107
1986: Reported broken up in China.

Andania's officers' smoke room on the boat deck (left) and her wheelhouse (right).

ALAUNIA (3) 1960-1971

O.N. 301359 7,004g 3,501n;
1970: 8,717g 4,657n
471.0 x 63.3 x 27.2 feet.
Geared Pametrada-type steam turbine by David Rowan and Co. Ltd., Glasgow; 9,500 SHP, 17 knots.
12.5.1960: Launched by William Hamilton and Co. Ltd., Port Glasgow (Yard No. 522) as ALAUNIA.
15.9.1960: Registered at Liverpool under the ownership of the Cunard Steam-Ship Co. Ltd., Liverpool.
26.9.1960: Maiden voyage from London to Montreal cancelled because of strike by London tally clerks.
10.1960: Maiden voyage from Glasgow to New York.
1.1.1970: Renamed MALANCHA following her charter to Cunard-Brocklebank Ltd., London
1971: Sold to Soja Shipping (Liberia) Inc., Panama (Ocean Shipping and Enterprises, Ltd., Hong Kong) and renamed HUMI NASITA.
25.5.1971: British register closed.
1973: Sold to Ocean Tramping Co. Ltd., Mogadiscio and renamed YUNGMING. This was a front company owned by the People's Republic of China.
1975: Ownership transferred to People's Republic of China Bureau of Maritime Transport Administration, Kwangtung Branch, Guangzhou, China and renamed HONG QI 108
1993: Deleted from 'Lloyd's Register'.

Alaunia is seen on trials on the Clyde (top), in the Thames (middle) and as *Malancha* leaving Durban in Brocklebank colours (bottom).

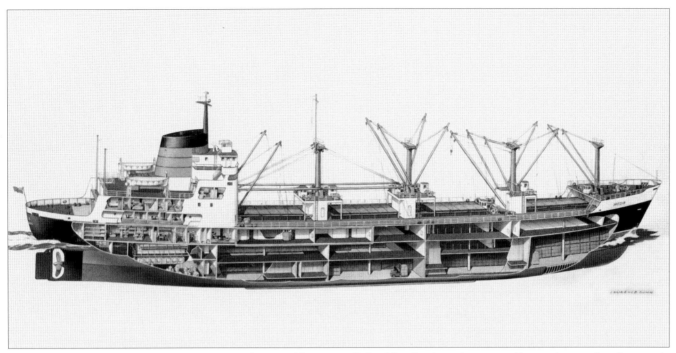

The engines-aft *Media*-class ships were Cunard's last conventional freighters. They were designed primarily for a weekly service between Liverpool and New York and were able to transit the Manchester Ship Canal. The forward section of the ship was ice-strengthened and, as this fine cut-away drawing of *Media* by Laurence Dunn shows, the four main holds were rectangular in shape, except in the forward end of Number 1 hold, so that fork-lift trucks could work freely aboard.

Media was the first of seven similar ships delivered between 1963 and 1966.

MEDIA (2) 1963-1971
O.N. 303887 5,586g 2,658n
419.2 x 60.1 x 24.9 feet.
7-cyl 2SCSA Sulzer-type oil engine
by Hawthorn Leslie (Engineers) Ltd.,
Newcastle-upon-Tyne; 7,700 BHP, 17 knots.
20.6.1963: Launched by John Readhead and Sons Ltd., South Shields (Yard No. 612) as MEDIA.
9.10.1963: Registered at Liverpool under the ownership of the Cunard Steam-Ship Co.

Ltd., Liverpool.
18.10.1963: Maiden voyage from Liverpool to New York.
13.5.1971: Sold to the Western Australian Coastal Shipping Commission, Fremantle for use on the coastal route between Fremantle and Darwin.
19.8.1971: Registered at Fremantle under the ownership of the Western Australian Coastal Shipping Commission, Fremantle, Australia as BEROONA

1978: Sold to Seaforth Investment Trust Inc. (Manta Shipping Co. Ltd. of Liberia), Piraeus, Greece and renamed PALM TRADER.
13.10.1983: Accommodation gutted and engine room seriously damaged during a fire at Bandar Abbas whilst on a voyage to Bombay with a cargo of beans. Later declared a constructive total loss and laid up off Bandar Abbas.
circa 7.1987: Reported capsized at Larakh Island.

Parthia was the second in the new series to be delivered.

PARTHIA (3) 1963-1971

O.N. 303894 5,586g 2,658n
419.2 x 60.1 x 24.9 feet.
7-cyl 2SCSA Sulzer-type oil engine by
John Brown & Co. (Clydebank) Ltd.,
Glasgow; 7,700 BHP, 17 knots.
18.7.1963: Launched by Caledon
Shipbuilding and Engineering Co. Ltd.,
Dundee (Yard No. 539) as PARTHIA.
18.11.1963: Registered at Liverpool under
the ownership of the Cunard Steam-Ship Co.
Ltd., Liverpool.
29.11.1963: Maiden voyage from Liverpool
to New York.
1.1966: First to use the new London Cunard

berth at Number 14-16 Royal Albert Dock.
Cunard had operated from Number 7 Berth,
King George V Dock since the 1930s.
23.2.1966: Steering gear and rudder carried
away in heavy weather about 360 miles
east south east of St. John's, Newfoundland
in position 45°56′N, 44°40′W whilst
on a voyage from New York to London.
She drifted until *27.2.1966* when tug
FOUNDATION VIGILANT (719/1952)
took her under tow and towed her about
2,000 miles to Southampton, where she
arrived on *11.3.1966*.
13.5.1971: Sold to the Western Australian
Coastal Shipping Commission, Fremantle

for use on the coastal route between
Fremantle and Darwin and later renamed
STASHIP 1.
6.9.1971: Renamed WAMBIRI.
18.11.1971: Registered at Fremantle under
the ownership of the Western Australian
Coastal Shipping Commission, Fremantle,
Australia.
1979: Sold to Sport Maritime Co. Ltd.
E.P.E. (Manta Shipping Co. Ltd. of Liberia),
Piraeus, Greece and renamed RICE
TRADER.
4.8.1984: Arrived at Gadani Beach, Pakistan
for demolition by Yaqoob and Sons Ltd.

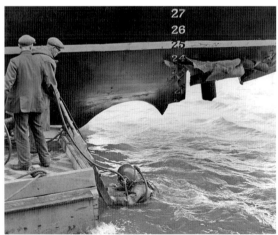

Left: *Parthia* arriving at Southampton in March 1966
after her steering gear and rudder had been torn off
in rough weather.
Above: Divers examine the extensive damage.

SAXONIA (3) 1964-1978

O.N. 306471 5,586g 2,658n;
1970: 8,783g 5,126n
419.2 x 60.1 x 24.9 feet;
1970: 499.2 x 60.1 x 24.9 feet.
7-cyl 2SCSA Sulzer-type oil engine
by Hawthorn Leslie (Engineers) Ltd.,
Newcastle-upon-Tyne; 7,700 BHP, 17
knots.
17.10.1963: Launched by John Readhead
and Sons Ltd., South Shields (Yard No.
613) as SAXONIA.
19.2.1964: Registered at Liverpool under
the ownership of the Cunard Steam-Ship
Co. Ltd., Liverpool.
28.2.1964: Maiden voyage from Liverpool
to New York.
20.9.1970: Arrived in the Tyne for
lengthening by Swan Hunter Shiprepairers
Ltd.
6.10.1970: Chartered to Cunard-
Brocklebank Ltd., London and renamed
MAHRONDA.
3.1972: Chartered to Chr. Haaland,
(Concordia Line), Haugesund.
25.7.1972: Renamed CONCORDIA FOSS.
15.12.1972: Reverted to MAHRONDA.
18.1.1978: Sold to Chung Chiao Shipping
Pte. Ltd. (Sin Chiao Shipping (Private)
Ltd.), Singapore and renamed NEW
DEER.
18.6.1978: Register at Singapore.
21.5.1983: Sailed from Hong Kong for
delivery to breakers at Ningpo, China.

IVERNIA (3) 1964-1977

O.N. 306479 5,586g 2,658n;
1970: 8,783g 5,125n
419.2 x 60.1 x 24.9 feet;
1970: 499.2 x 60.1 x 24.9 feet.
7-cyl 2SCSA Sulzer-type oil engine by
John Brown & Co. (Clydebank) Ltd.,
Glasgow; 7,700 BHP, 17 knots.
28.1.1964: Launched by Caledon
Shipbuilding and Engineering Co. Ltd.,
Dundee (Yard No. 540) as IVERNIA.
17.4.1964: Registered at Liverpool under
the ownership of the Cunard Steam-Ship
Co. Ltd., Liverpool.
1.5.1964: Maiden voyage from Liverpool
to New York
1970: Chartered to Cunard-Brocklebank,
Ltd., London.
14.6.1970: Arrived in the Tyne for
lengthening by Swan Hunter Shiprepairers
Ltd.
23.6.1970: Renamed MANIPUR.
7.1971: Chartered to Chr. Haaland
(Concordia Line), Haugesund, Norway
renamed CONCORDIA MANIPUR, she
later reverted to MANIPUR.
1977: Sold to Cia. Naviera Philippa
S.A., Panama (G. Aponte, Naples, Italy)
(Mediterranean Shipping Company) and
renamed PHILIPPA.
1977: British register closed.
9.2.1985: Arrived at Chittagong for
demolition by Rahman Shipbreakers Ltd.,
work began *19.2.1985* at Sitalpur, near
Chittagong.

Saxonia was the last conventional conventional dry cargo ship in the Cunard fleet.

Following the arrival of *Atlantic Causeway*, the company's first container ship, *Saxonia* (shown here as *Mahronda* in May 1976) and *Ivernia*, were lengthened. With an extra hold amidships, they were transferred to the Cunard Brocklebank fleet.

Ivernia ended her career with the Mediterranean Shipping Company.

The final trio, which included *Scythia*, were 17-feet longer and were fitted with more powerful engines. They were owned by their builders and bareboat chartered to Cunard.

SCYTHIA (3) 1964-1969
O.N. 306495 5,837g 2,829n
436.4 x 60.1 x 24.9 feet.
6-cyl 2SCSA oil engine by Sulzer Brothers Ltd., Winterthur, Switzerland; 9,600 BHP, 17.5 knots.
25.8.1964: Launched by Cammell Laird and Co. (Shipbuilders and Engineers) Ltd., Birkenhead (Yard No. 1314) as SCYTHIA.
14.12.1964: Registered at Liverpool under the ownership of North Western Line (Mersey) Ltd., Birkenhead, a Cammell Laird subsidiary, and bareboat chartered to the Cunard Steam-Ship Co. Ltd., Liverpool.
1.12.1969: Acquired by the Cunard Steam-Ship Co. Ltd., London.
9.12.1969: Sold to the Charente Steam Ship Co. Ltd. (Thos. and Jas. Harrison Ltd., managers), Liverpool.
23.12.1969: Renamed MERCHANT.
1.1979: Laid up at Leith.
6.7.1979: Sold to Totnes Shipping Corporation, Monrovia, Liberia (Manta Shipping Co. Ltd. of Liberia, Piraeus) and later renamed SISAL TRADER under the Greek flag.
1979: British register closed.
13.1.1984: Arrested at Dzaoudzi, Comoro Islands for non-payment of debts and subsequently abandoned by crew.
12.4.1984: Driven ashore in cyclone and later refloated by a French naval tug.
3.5.1984: Arrived at Mombasa under tow of the tug BISON 1 (476/1974).
30.9.1986: Departed Mombasa under tow for demolition at Gadani Beach, Pakistan.

SAMARIA (3) 1965-1969
O.N. 306499 5,837g 2,844n
436.4 x 60.1 x 24.9 feet.
6-cyl 2SCSA oil engine by Sulzer Brothers Ltd., Winterthur, Switzerland; 9,600 BHP, 17.5 knots.
22.10.1964: Launched by Cammell Laird and Co. (Shipbuilders and Engineers) Ltd., Birkenhead (Yard No. 1315) as SAMARIA.
1.2.1965: Registered at Liverpool under the ownership of North Western Line (Mersey) Ltd., Birkenhead, a Cammell Laird subsidiary, and bareboat chartered to the Cunard Steam-Ship Co. Ltd., Liverpool.
1.12.1969: Acquired by the Cunard Steam-Ship Co. Ltd., London.
23.12.1969: Sold to the Charente Steam Ship Co. Ltd. (Thos. and Jas. Harrison Ltd., managers), Liverpool.
15.1.1970: Renamed SCHOLAR.
1.1979: Laid up at Manchester.
18.7.1979: Sold to Brora Shipping Corporation, Monrovia, Liberia (Manta Shipping Co. Ltd. of Liberia, Piraeus, Greece) and later renamed STEEL TRADER under the Greek flag.
1980: British register closed.
23.9.1980: Trapped at Khorramshahr with ninety other vessels in the Shatt-el-Arab waterway at the start of the Iran-Iraq War.
5.10.1980: Seriously damaged by gunfire and abandoned by her crew, she was later declared a constructive total loss. She was reported to have been towed by Iraqi forces to Basra, where she remained in a sunken condition until at least 1993.

SCOTIA (2) 1966-1970
O.N. 308687 5,825g 2,822n
436.4 x 60.1 x 24.9 feet.
6-cyl 2SCSA oil engine by Sulzer Brothers Ltd., Winterthur, Switzerland; 9,600 BHP, 17.5 knots.
17.8.1966: Launched by Cammell Laird and Co. (Shipbuilders and Engineers) Ltd., Birkenhead (Yard No. 1321) as SCOTIA.
13.12.1966: Registered at Liverpool under the ownership of United Dominions Leasing Ltd., London, a Cammell Laird subsidiary, and bareboat chartered to the Cunard Steam-Ship Co. Ltd., Liverpool.
23.1.1970: Sold to Neptune Orient Lines Ltd., Singapore and later renamed NEPTUNE AMBER.
1970: British register closed.
12.1.1971: Registered at Singapore under the ownership of Neptune Orient Lines Ltd., Singapore.
1.1977: Sold to Himalaya Shipping Co. Ltd., Calcutta, India and renamed SRI KAILASH.
5.1982: Laid up at Bombay.
1984: Broken up at Bombay by Akbarally and Sons.

Top: *Samaria* on the Thames.

Right: *Scythia* and *Samaria* were sold to Harrison Line in 1969. *Samaria* was renamed *Scholar*.

Bottom: *Scotia*, the final ship in the *Media* class, was delivered only in 1966, despite being ordered in June 1964. She was the first Cunard vessel to have remote control of the engines from the bridge.

Transatlantic cargo fleet in colour
Top: *Alsatia* at London in August, 1957
[V.H.Young and L.A.Sawyer]
Left: *Andania*. *[V.H.Young and L.A.Sawyer]*
Below: *Alaunia*. *[Russell Priest]*
Opposite page, top: The sisters *Media*
and *Parthia* were sold to Australian buyers
becoming *Beroona* (left) and *Wambiri* (right)
respectively. *[Both Russell Priest]*
Middle: *Saxonia* (right) and her sister *Ivernia*
were chartered to Cunard-Brocklebank,
lengthened and took the names *Mahronda* and
Manipur (bottom) sailing from Avonmouth in
March 1975. *[Middle right: V.H. Young and L.A.
Sawyer, bottom: Ray Perry/Malcolm Cranfield
collection]*

Scythia, Samaria (opposite bottom) and Scotia (above and right) were all sold off by 1970 after only four or five years service. The first two went to T. and J. Harrison, the Scythia becoming Merchant (opposite page, top), seen sailing from Eastham on 27th May 1978, and Scholar. The Scotia (bottom) went to Singapore owners and, renamed Neptune Amber is shown at Cape Town on 1st September 1972. [Opposite page, top: Allan Ryszka-Onions/Malcolm Cranfield collection, bottom: FotoFlite incorporating Skyfotos, 198553, this page, top: V.H.Young and L.A.Sawyer, middle: Russell Priest, bottom V.H.Young and L.A.Sawyer]

CONTAINERISATION AND THE ATLANTIC CONTAINER LINE

On 26th April 1956, *Ideal X* (10,441/1945), a converted T2 U.S. standard tanker, inaugurated the world's first modern container ship operation when she sailed from Port Newark, New Jersey to Houston, Texas with a cargo of 58 standardised containers stowed topside and oil in her tanks. She was owned by Malcom McLean's Pan-Atlantic Steamship Corporation , which later became Sea-Land Service Inc. Although the idea of ships carrying containers was not new, what McLean, often known as the father of containerisation, came up with was an intermodal system using large standardised containers which could be easily transferred between shipper and consignee using ships, trucks and railcars. In 1957 his company converted *Gateway City* (9,006/1942), a C2 U.S. standard cargo ship, into the world's first all-container ship. After a slow start, McLean's invention revolutionised cargo handling around the world. Shippers and ship owners soon came to recognise the cost advantages of this efficient and labour-saving cargo-handling system. However, the cost of re-engineering the business was immense, especially among traditional shipping lines, which had run their business with large fleets of relatively small break-bulk ships manned by large crews. Many companies went out of business during this period of great change. A number of the major shipping lines also formed consortia to run their container operations.

On the North Atlantic, one of the first consortia was Atlantic Container Line (ACL) which had been formed in 1965 as a partnership between Holland America Line and three Swedish lines, Rederi A/B Transatlantic, Swedish America Line and Wallenius Lines. The last mentioned, under the leadership of Olaf Wallenius, was one of the first companies to operate specialist car carriers. It is for this reason that ACL opted for ships which were a combination of container transports and roll-on roll-off (ro-ro) car carriers with stern ramps. At the time, this was a radical concept and the vessels were the first large ships of the type to operate on deep-sea routes. This type of ship could also carry trailers, buses, excavators and large non-standard loads such as generators and machinery.

Four 12,000g ships were ordered for the new line, each owned by one of the partners. Delivered in 1967, the design of these ships evolved from the world's first true ro-ro, the 3,300g *Undine*, which had been completed at

Papenburg by Jos. L. Meyer for Wallenius Lines the previous year. Diesel-driven, they had a service speed of over 21 knots and space for 500 containers, 70 trailers and 1,100 cars. The new ACL service offered weekly sailings from Gothenburg, Bremerhaven, Rotterdam and Antwerp to New York, Baltimore and Portsmouth, Virginia. The first in the series, Rederi A/B Transatlantic's *Atlantic Song*, sailed on her maiden voyage from Gothenburg to New York on 4th September 1967.

Meanwhile, in December 1966, Cunard decided to join the consortium and ordered two 15,000g roll-on-roll-off container ships from Swan Hunter for delivery in 1969. Cie. Générale Transatlantique (French Line) also joined and placed an order for a pair of ships with Chantiers de L'Atlantique, Dunkerque. The ACL's head office was moved from Stockholm to Southampton in 1968 with Philip Bates, Cunard's former Managing Director, appointed ACL's Chairman.

These four Cunard and French Line ships were part of a six-ship second generation ACL series, which included one each from Holland America and Wallenius. This brought the fleet size to ten ships and, as a result, the ownership of ACL was divided into five 20% shares. Holland America Line, Wallenius Lines, Cunard and French Line each held a share whilst Rederi A/B Transatlantic and Swedish America Line divided a share between them.

The new ships were not only larger and faster, they also had twin screws driven by steam turbines. Cunard's *Atlantic Causeway* was the first in the series to be delivered and on 4th December 1969 she departed from Southampton on her maiden voyage to New York. The company's second ship, *Atlantic Conveyor*, followed in March 1970. With a fleet of ten ships, ACL's weekly sailings operated from Greenock, Liverpool and Southampton to New York, Baltimore and Portsmouth, Virginia. Havre also became part of the route network. The company was a pioneer in the use of computers for its operation. In the 1970s, it introduced the first 'real time' computer system in the transportation industry with electronically transmitted documents.

In 1975, Holland America Line withdrew from the consortium following the sale of its main cargo division, including its two ACL ships, to Swedish America Line's parent

The versatile *Atlantic Conveyor* carried not only containers but also cars and trailers.

company, the Broström Group. Also in the mid-1970s the four first generation ships were lengthened and direct services to Halifax and Montreal were added to the route network. From 1978 to 1981 two new Korean-built 5,466g ro-ro/container ships were bareboat chartered from Stena Line for the Canadian service and renamed *Atlantic Project* and *Atlantic Prosper*. They were registered at London and managed by Cunard Brocklebank. The first captain of *Atlantic Prosper* was Captain Ian North who lost his life during the Falklands War whilst in command of *Atlantic Conveyor*.

The Falklands War started on 2nd April 1982 when, without warning, Argentina invaded the Falkland Islands, a British Overseas Territory. Britain rapidly put together a task force of ships and sent an expeditionary force to reclaim the islands. *Atlantic Conveyor*, which had been laid up in Liverpool, and *Atlantic Causeway* were requisitioned by the British Government as transports. They were refitted at the Devonport naval dockyard and given a flight deck for Harrier 'jump jets'. Loaded with supplies, Sea Harriers and helicopters, they sailed for the Falkland Islands on 25th April and 6th May respectively. Unfortunately on 25th May, just north east of the Falkland Islands, *Atlantic Conveyor* was mistaken for an aircraft carrier and was hit by two Exocet missiles fired by two Argentinean Super Étendard fighters. Twelve lives were lost and the ship later sank under tow. She was the only British merchant ship lost in the Falklands War. As an interim replacement, Cunard bought *Atlantic Star* from Broström. This first generation ACL ship started life in 1967 as Holland America Line's first ACL ship.

With rising fuel prices, the second generation steam turbine ships had by now become expensive to operate. After much research and planning, ACL ordered five 25,000g replacement ships in 1982. Not only were these vessels the largest ro ro/container ships in the world, they were more fuel efficient and offered greater cargo handling flexibility than their predecessors. On the weather deck, containers could be stacked four high without the need for lashing whilst below

deck there was sufficient space for more containers plus cars, trailers and cargoes such as steel and forestry products. The two-lane ramp also allowed cars and ro-ro traffic to be loaded and discharged simultaneously. The first in the series, *Atlantic Companion*, left Liverpool on her maiden voyage to Canada and the United States in March 1984.

However, Cunard's contribution to the new fleet became mired in controversy when it was learned in June 1982 that Cunard was the only company in the ACL consortium which would not be ordering its ship from a local shipyard. In fact, Cunard was considering placing the order with Hyundai in South Korea as its quote was considerably cheaper than any British yard. Coming so soon after the loss of *Atlantic Conveyor*, the opposition Labour Party, press and unions had a field day and accused Cunard's chairman Lord Matthews of being unpatriotic. Pressure mounted on Cunard and eventually Prime Minister Margaret Thatcher became involved. A deal was reached on 28th June for the ship to be built on the Tyne by Swan Hunter Shipbuilders. Part of the agreement specified that she should have strengthened decks, extra tanks for helicopter fuel, and to be made available, when needed, for Ministry of Defence exercises. The new ship completed in January 1985, was named *Atlantic Conveyor* in honour of the ship lost in 1982. In 1987 *Atlantic Conveyor* was lengthened by 139 feet at Greenock by Trafalgar House's Scott-Lithgow yard.

In 1990 the ACL consortium was dissolved and the Bilspedition Group acquired 100% ownership of Atlantic Container Line whilst the head office moved from Southampton to South Plainfield, New Jersey. Despite this and the sale of Cunard Ellerman to P&O in 1991, *Atlantic Conveyor* remained in Cunard ownership. She continued to be chartered to Atlantic Container Line until her sale to ACL in 1995. *Atlantic Conveyor* was also Cunard's final cargo ship and, although ACL is now part of the Italian Grimaldi group, *Atlantic Conveyor* remains in service.

Atlantic Prosper. [Marc Piché]

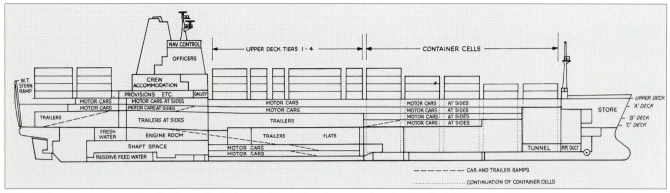

Atlantic Causeway was not only Cunard's first container ship, she was also the first in ACL's second generation series. They were larger and faster than the earlier ACL ships and carried containers aft of the superstructure.

Atlantic Causeway at Rotterdam in August 1979. *[Marc Piché]*

ATLANTIC CAUSEWAY 1969-1986 Twin screw
O.N. 337229 14,946g 7,405n
645.9 x 92.0 x 30.4 feet.
Two sets of geared steam turbines by Associated Electrical Industries Ltd., Manchester; 38,500 SHP, 24 knots.
Containers: 750 TEU (twenty-foot equivalent container units) plus 920 cars and 144 trailers.
2.4.1969: Launched by Swan Hunter Shipbuilders Ltd., Newcastle-upon-Tyne (Yard No. 1) as ATLANTIC CAUSEWAY.
11.1969: Completed and registered at Liverpool under the ownership of the Cunard Steam-Ship Co. Ltd. (Cunard-Brocklebank Ltd., managers), Liverpool. Operated for Atlantic Container Line.
4.12.1969: Maiden voyage from Southampton to New York.
6.5.1982: Arrived at Devonport having been requisitioned by the British Government as a transport during the Falkland Islands War. Fitted with a flight deck for Sea Harriers and an aviation fuel system.
14.5.1982: Sailed from Devonport for the Falkland Islands via Ascension Island,

carrying eight Sea Harriers and twenty Wessex helicopters.
27.7.1982: Returned to Devonport after serving with the Falkland Islands Task Force.
16.8.1986: Under the name ATLANTIC, arrived at Kaohsiung for demolition by Ming Hsieh Steel Mill Inc.

ATLANTIC CONVEYOR (1) 1970-1982 Twin screw
O.N. 337245 14,946g 7,408n
645.9 x 92.0 x 30.4 feet.
Two sets of geared steam turbines by Associated Electrical Industries Ltd., Manchester; 38,500 SHP, 24 knots.
Containers: 750 TEU (twenty-foot equivalent container units), 920 cars, 144 trailers.
25.8.1969: Launched by Swan Hunter Shipbuilders Ltd. , Newcastle-upon-Tyne (Yard No. 2) as ATLANTIC CONVEYOR.
3.1970: Completed and registered at London under the ownership of the Cunard Steam-Ship Co. Ltd. (Cunard-Brocklebank Ltd., managers), Liverpool. Operated for Atlantic Container Line.
31.3.1970: First arrival at Southampton.
8.1981: Laid up at Liverpool.

16.4.1982: Arrived at Devonport having been requisitioned by the British Government as a transport during the Falkland Islands campaign.
25.4.1982: Departed Devonport for the Falkland Islands via Ascension Island. A flight deck for Harriers had been fitted and she was loaded with supplies and helicopters.
5.5.1982: Arrived at Ascension and embarked six Sea Harriers and six G3 Harriers - these took off from the ship on *20* and *21.5.1982*.
25.5.1982: Just north east of the Falkland Islands, hit at 19:42 by two Exocet missiles fired by two Argentinean Super Étendard fighters. These missiles were meant for the aircraft carrier HMS HERMES. Twelve lives were lost, including her master, Captain Ian North, and she was abandoned by her crew at 20:15.
27.5.1982: With her bow section blown away, she was taken in tow by the tug IRISHMAN (686/1978).
28.5.1982: Tow parted at 03:50 and she sank in position 50°40′S, 54°28′W. She was the only British merchant ship lost in the Falklands conflict.

Atlantic Causeway and Atlantic Conveyor (above) were built on the Tyne by Swan Hunter. [Marc Piché]

Atlantic Conveyor during the Falklands conflict. Middle right: Taking bunkers from the Royal Fleet Auxiliary Tidepool (14,130/1963) whilst on her way south. Above: Container stacks either side of the ship disguised the fact that she was carrying helicopters. She was also fitted with a flight deck for Harrier 'jump jets', one of which can be seen in this photograph. Bottom right: Ablaze after she had been struck by two Exocet missiles. [Right middle and bottom: Imperial War Museum, FKD 161 and FKD 217]

ATLANTIC STAR 1983-1987

O.N. 389219 11,839g 5,530n;
1976: 15,055g 7,624n
600.2 x 86.8 x 30.0 feet;
1976: 685.4 x 98.4 x 30.0 feet.
9-cyl 2SCSA oil engine by Maschinenbau Augsburg-Nürnberg (MAN), Augsburg, West Germany; 20,700 BHP, 19.5 knots.
Containers: 500 TEU (twenty-foot equivalent container units), 1,100 cars, 70 trailers;
1976: 1,154 TEU plus cars.
27.6.1967: Launched by Ateliers et Chantiers de Dunkerque et Bordeaux (France-Gironde), Dunkerque, France (Yard No. 255) as ATLANTIC STAR.
11.1967: Completed and registered at Rotterdam under the ownership of N.V. Nederlandsche-Amerikaansche Stoomvaart-Maatschappij, Rotterdam, Netherlands. Operated for Atlantic Container Line.
15.1.1973: Transferred to the N.A.S.M. subsidiary Scheepvaart Maatschappij Trans-Ocean B.V., Rotterdam.
1.1975: Transferred to Intercontinental Transport B.V., Rotterdam (Holland America's freight operation) and sold to the Broström Group, Gothenburg.
7.1976: Arrived at Innoshima, Japan to be lengthened and widened by installation of an additional cargo section by Hitachi Zosen K.K. Sponsons were also added to the side of the hull to improve stability.
1983: Acquired by Cunard Steam-Ship Co. Ltd. (Cunard Brocklebank Ltd., managers), London as an interim replacement for ATLANTIC CONVEYOR and registered at Liverpool.
1.7.1987: Trafalgar House bought Ellerman Lines plc and Cunard Ellerman Shipping Services Ltd. was formed to operate the group's cargo ships.
14.12.1987: Arrived at Kaohsiung for demolition by Kuo Dar Steel Enterprise Co. Ltd.

The first generation ACL ship *Atlantic Star* was acquired as an interim replacement for *Atlantic Conveyor*. The above photo was taken from Staten Island, New Jersey as *Atlantic Star* was passing under the Verrazano Narrows Bridge outbound from New York in May 1975. The lower photograph shows her after 1976 when lengthened, widened and fitted with sponsons. *[Above: Marc Piché; below: FotoFlite incorporating Skyfotos, 264582]*

The order with Swan Hunter for a new *Atlantic Conveyor* (above) came about only after the intervention of the British Government. This ship, one of the largest ro-ro/container ships in the world, was Cunard's contribution to ACL's third generation fleet and their final cargo ship. The five third generation ships were lengthened in 1987. The contract for A*tlantic Conveyor* was given to Trafalgar House's Scott-Lithgow yard where 139 feet were added (below). *[FotoFlite incorporating Skyfotos 50659; Marc Piché]*

ATLANTIC CONVEYOR (2) 1985-1995
Twin screw
O.N. 704464 25,301g 12,993n;
1987: 58,438g 21,660n
766.2 x 105.8 x 35.7 feet;
1987: 905.7 x 105.8 x 35.7 feet.
6-cyl. 2SCSA Burmeister & Wain-type oil engine by J.G. Kincaid Ltd., Greenock, 23,791 BHP, 17.5 knots.
1987: Engines uprated to 27,450 BHP.
Containers: 2,130 TEU (twenty-foot equivalent container units), 600 cars;
1987: 2,908 TEU, 1,756 cars.

12.7.1984: Launched by Swan Hunter Shipbuilders Ltd. , Newcastle-upon-Tyne (Yard No. 121) as ATLANTIC CONVEYOR.
14.1.1985: Delivered and registered at London under the ownership of the Cunard Steam-Ship Co. Ltd. (Cunard Brocklebank Ltd., managers), London. Operated for Atlantic Container Line.
22.1.1985: Maiden transatlantic voyage from Liverpool.
1.7.1987: Trafalgar House bought Ellerman Lines plc and Cunard Ellerman Shipping

Services Ltd. was formed to operate the group's cargo ships.
7 to 9.1987: Lengthened by Scott-Lithgow Ltd., Greenock, a Trafalgar House-owned yard.
1.7.1995: Sold to ACL Shipowners Holding Inc., Nassau, Bahamas.
23.6.2003 Registered in Sweden for bare-boat charter to Atlantic Container Line A/B, Gothenburg, Sweden.
2012: Still in existence.

Following the granting of independence to India and Pakistan in 1947, Cunard's subsidiary Thos. and Jno. Brocklebank struggled to maintain a profitable position on its prime routes to the Indian subcontinent. Pooling arrangements also meant that half of the Gulf of Bengal to United Kingdom traffic was allocated to Indian and Pakistani national carriers. As a result, there was chronic British overcapacity on these services with Clan Line, British India, Ellerman and P&O all seeking a greater share of a much reduced market. In order to stem its losses, Brocklebank decided to diversify its business. In 1964 it bought the Liverpool tanker firm H.E. Moss and Co.'s Tankers Ltd. and its ship broking parent company, H. E. Moss and Co. Ltd. The origins of this Liverpool-based company go back to 1827. In 1854 Henry E. Moss founded the ship broking and coal merchant firm H.E. Moss and Company and in 1860 a London office was opened. The company was among the first in Britain to recognise the opportunities offered to ship owners of transporting oil in bulk instead of in barrels. Moss arranged for one of the first bulk petroleum cargoes to be offloaded in Liverpool and in 1889 took delivery of *Lumen* (2,402g) its first purpose-built tanker. Shell's first tanker *Murex* was completed only in 1892.

After the death of Henry E. Moss, the business was continued by his nephew, Edward Asher Cohan, and in later years by his great nephew, C.M. Cohan. H.E. Moss and Co's Tankers Ltd. was founded in 1913 and, shortly before the start of the First World War, Moss apparently played a major behind the scenes role on behalf of the Norwegian ship owner Wilhelm Wilhelmsen in securing ten tanker orders with north east England shipyards. Six of these ships built between 1916 and 1918 were requisitioned by the British Government and managed by H.E Moss and Co. H.E. Moss and Co. had a modest fleet, usually less than a dozen ships, and in 1957 the privately-owned firm was listed on the London Stock

Exchange. Up to that point, company policy had dictated that every new ship should be financed out of existing capital. With the immense cost of building crude carriers in the early 1960s, this was not an option without either significantly increasing company capital or amalgamation with another company. The latter path was chosen and H.E. Moss with its fleet of three tankers was bought by Brocklebank in 1964. The ships were registered in the ownership of the Cunard Steam-Ship Co. Ltd. with T. and J. Brocklebank Ltd. as managers. They also continued to use the Moss livery.

For Brocklebank this was a wise move and in 1965 it recorded its first profit since 1958. In 1966 the name of the tanker arm of the business was changed to Moss Tankers Ltd. and between 1968 and 1972 five motor-driven product tankers of just under 15,000g were built for the company at Gothenburg by Eriksbergs. *Lumiere*, the last of these, remained in the fleet for almost twenty years. In the meantime, on the 1st January 1968, the Cunard company was split into two separate businesses. Whilst the passenger ships were transferred into Cunard Line Ltd., all the Cunard-owned and chartered ships together with those owned by Thos. and Jno. Brocklebank and Moss Tankers were managed by a new company, Cunard-Brocklebank Ltd. It was also the UK agent for the recently-formed Atlantic Container Line (ACL). In March 1970 it was decided to enter the world-wide bulk dry cargo trade, i.e. coal, grain, fertiliser, lumber and steel products. A number of British and foreign yards were asked to bid for the eight-ship order. The contract was awarded to the Spanish shipbuilder Astilleros Españoles as it was not only able to deliver the ships within the required two year time span, its bid was also 25% lower than the best British quote. The 15,498g single deck vessels were practically identical and were a standard bulk carrier design developed at the company's yard in Bilbao, but with four electrically-

Luxor, one of the three tankers bought by Brocklebank in 1964, photographed at Singapore on 18th March 1974. *[V. H. Young and L. A. Sawyer]*

operated 15-ton cranes and grabs instead of derricks. This allowed the ships greater flexibility as they were able to self-load/discharge directly to and from barges in shallow draught ports. Tank tops were specially strengthened for grab discharges and fork-lift truck operations and the ships were also fitted to navigate the St. Lawrence Seaway. The eight bulkers were delivered at regular intervals between 1972 and 1973 and, like the recently-built cruise ships, *Cunard Adventurer* and *Cunard Ambassador,* were given names beginning with *Cunard*. Interestingly, the six ships built at Seville were given second names starting with *Ca* whilst the two from Bilbao had second names starting with *Ch*. Despite the *Cunard* names, the bulkers had Brocklebank funnel colours and were each manned by eleven British officers and twenty-nine Indian seamen. In 1972 a new management company, Cunard-Brocklebank Bulkers Ltd., was formed to manage the bulk carriers and the product tankers. Three of the new bulkers secured time charters, whilst the remainder traded on the spot market. They also joined the pool of the Norwegian A/S Bulkhandling fleet and, during their first year of operation, carried a variety of cargoes, including pig iron, wheat, timber, tapioca, logs, and scrap iron.

In 1975 two Canadian-built 23,736g tankers were added to the tanker fleet, which now stood at seven ships. These were the largest ships ever owned by Moss and replaced the last of the original pre-1964 fleet. The brand new *Lucerna* and *Lucellum* also spent time in South America,

working for the burgeoning Venezuelan, Colombian and Peruvian oil companies. The last mentioned ship was in fact sold to Flota Mercante Grancolombiana. However, after the massive increases in the price of oil during the 1973 'fuel crisis', and the subsequent stock market crash, the demand for oil fell sharply. This led to an over supply of bulk carriers and tankers. As Cunard bulkers and tankers relied heavily on charters, the decision was taken to sell the bulker fleet and a number of the tankers. By the end of 1978 only three tankers remained and these were placed under the management of Cunard Shipping Services Ltd., which was formed as the charter and ship management arm of the Cunard company.

Trafalgar House bought Ellerman Lines plc in July 1987 and Cunard Ellerman Shipping Services Ltd. was formed to operate the company's cargo ships, which included the product tankers. At the time of the sale of Cunard Ellerman in 1991 to P&O, *Lumiere* was the sole tanker and after a brief spell in the ownership of P&O Containers, she was transferred to a P&O Hong Kong company, Moss Tankers Ltd. After a year she was sold, thus bringing an end 103 years of tankers under the Moss name. The ship-broking firm H.E. Moss and Co Ltd, which came with the sale to Brocklebank in 1964, also played an important role within the Cunard organisation as the in-house shipbroker and brokered the sale of *Queen Mary* in August 1967 to the City of Long Beach. Sold to P&O Containers in 1991, it traded until 2005.

Cunard Campaigner was the first of eight Spanish-built bulkers delivered between 1972 and 1973.

Lucellum was a typical British-built general purpose tanker of the 1950s.

LUCELLUM (1) 1964-1969
O.N. 187187 12,202g 6,800n
530.0 x 69.5 x 30 feet.
Geared steam turbines by Cammell Laird and Co. (Shipbuilding and Engineering) Ltd., Birkenhead; 6,800 SHP, 14.5 knots.
10.12.1957: Launched by Cammell Laird and Co. (Shipbuilding and Engineering) Ltd., Birkenhead (Yard No. 1252) as LUCELLUM.
4.1958: Completed and registered under the ownership of H.E. Moss and Co.'s Tankers Ltd., Liverpool.
10.1964: Acquired by the Cunard Steam-Ship Co. Ltd. (T. and J. Brocklebank Ltd., managers), Liverpool.
1968: Management changed to Cunard-Brocklebank Ltd., Liverpool.
1969: Sold to True Mariners S.A., Monrovia,

Liberia and renamed JULIANA. (V.K. Eddie Hsu, Hong Kong).
1969: British register closed.
30.11.1971: Broke in two having dragged her anchor in rough weather and struck the breakwater at Niigata, Japan whilst carrying a cargo of Kuwaiti crude oil.
6.1972: Both sections refloated and taken to Kure for demolition by Taisei Kaihatsu K.K.

LUXOR 1964-1975
O.N. 301336 12,700g 7,298n.
530 x 72.0 x 31.3 feet.
6-cyl 2SCSA oil engine by William Doxford and Sons (England) Ltd., Sunderland; 6,800 BHP, 14.5 knots.
15.12.1959: Launched by J.L Thompson and Sons Ltd., Sunderland (Yard No. 697) for A/S Dovrefjell and A/S Haukefjell, (Olsen

and Ugelstad) Oslo as HAUKEFJELL.
5.1960: Completed as LUXOR and registered under the ownership of H.E. Moss and Co.'s Tankers Ltd., Liverpool.
10.1964: Acquired by the Cunard Steam-Ship Co. Ltd., Liverpool (T. and J. Brocklebank Ltd., managers).
1968: Management changed to Cunard-Brocklebank Ltd., Liverpool.
1972: Management changed to Cunard-Brocklebank Bulkers Ltd, London.
1975: Sold to Vinstra Shipping Co. (Pte.) Ltd. (Norse Management Co. (Pte.) Ltd.), Singapore and renamed CHERRY PRINCE.
1975: British register closed.
21.7.1980: Demolition commenced at Kaohsiung by Nan Ya Metal Industrial Co.

Luxor sailing from Avonmouth in March 1965. *[Malcolm Cranfield]*

Lucigen was H.E. Moss's first tanker with her superstructure aft. Seen in the Malacca Strait in 1971. *[W.A.Schell collection]*

LUCIGEN 1964-1975

O.N. 303864 12,800g 7,446n
533.9 x 71.5 x 31.0 feet.
6-cyl 2SCSA Doxford-type oil engine
by Hawthorn Leslie (Engineers) Ltd.,
Newcastle-upon-Tyne; 10,000 BHP, 15
knots.
1.6.1962: Launched by Smith's Dock Co.
Ltd., Middlesborough (Yard No. 1271) as
LUCIGEN.
9.1962: Completed and registered under the
ownership of H.E. Moss and Co's Tankers
Ltd., Liverpool.
10.1964: Acquired by the Cunard Steam-
Ship Co. Ltd. (T. and J. Brocklebank Ltd.,
managers), Liverpool.
1968: Management changed to Cunard-
Brocklebank Ltd., Liverpool.
1972: Management changed to Cunard-
Brocklebank Bulkers Ltd., London.
1975: Sold to Probity Shipping Corporation,
Piraeus, Greece (Southern Shipping
and Finance Co., London) and renamed
ANATOLI.
1975: British register closed.
1981: Sold to Maralma Cia. Nav. S.A.,
Panama (Aegis Shipping Co. Ltd., Athens,
Greece) and renamed NYALA.
1987: Sold to Ontario Shipping Ltd.,
Limassol, Cyprus (L. Hajiioannou, Piraeus)
and renamed ONTARIO.
23.2.1988: Arrived at Kaohsiung for
demolition by Progress Steel and Iron Co. Ltd.

LUSTROUS 1968-1977

O.N. 334253 14,923g 9,629n
525.6 x 81.4 x 31.3 feet.
Two 12-cyl 4SCSA Pielstick-type geared-
oil engines by Eriksbergs M/V A/B,

Gothenburg; 10,080 BHP, 14.7 knots.
8.8.1968: Launched by Eriksbergs M/V A/B,
Gothenburg (Yard No. 624) as LUSTROUS.
10.1968: Completed and registered under
the ownership of the Cunard Steam-Ship Co.
Ltd. (Cunard-Brocklebank Ltd., managers),
Liverpool.
1972: Management changed to Cunard-
Brocklebank Bulkers Ltd., London.
1977: Sold to Al Hofuf Navigation Co. Ltd.,
Jeddah, Saudi Arabia (Varnima Corporation
International S.A., Piraeus, Greece) and

renamed AL HOFUF.
1977: British register closed.
1984: Transferred to Cyclades Maritime
Co. S.A., Panama (Varnima Corporation
International S.A., Piraeus) and renamed
KRITI GERANI under the Greek flag.
1995: Ownership transferred to Kriti Gerani
Shipping Co., Panama (Varnima Corporation
International S.A., Piraeus).
22.4.1999: Arrived at Alang for demolition
by Gohilwal Shipbreakers.

Lustrous was the first of five motor tankers ordered by the Cunard group from the Swedish Eriksbergs yard.

233

LUMINOUS 1968-1977

O.N. 334260 14,923g 9,629n
526.6 x 81.4 x 31.3 feet.
Two 12-cyl 4SCSA Pielstick-type
geared-oil engines by Eriksbergs M/V
A/B, Gothenburg; 10,080 BHP, 14.7
knots.
3.10.1968: Launched by Eriksbergs
M/V A/B, Gothenburg (Yard No. 625)
as LUMINOUS.
16.12.1968: Delivered and later
registered under the ownership of
the Cunard Steam-Ship Co. Ltd.
(Cunard-Brocklebank Ltd., managers),
Liverpool.
1972: Management changed to
Cunard-Brocklebank Bulkers Ltd,
London.
19.3.1977: Sold to Al Khafji
Navigation Co. Ltd., Jeddah, Saudi
Arabia (Varnima Corporation
International S.A., Piraeus, Greece)
and renamed AL KHAFJI.
1977: British register closed.
1984: Transferred to Melea Maritime
Co. S.A., Panama (Varnima
Corporation International S.A.,
Piraeus) and renamed KRITI
EPISKOPI under the Greek flag.
1995: Transferred to Kriti Episkopi
Shipping Co., Panama (Varnima
Corporation International S.A.,
Piraeus).
17.4.1999: Arrived at Alang for
demolition by Raj Metal Works (Pvt.)
Ltd.

LUMEN 1971-1977

O.N. 341740 14,923g 9,629n
525.6 x 81.4 x 31.3 feet.

Luminous at Singapore on 9th March 1975. *[Russell Priest]*

Two 12-cyl 4SCSA Pielstick-type geared-
oil engines by Lindholmen Motor A/B,
Gothenburg, Sweden; 10,080 BHP, 14.8 knots.
18.5.1971: Launched by Eriksbergs M/V A/B,
Gothenburg (Yard No. 652) as LUMEN.
4.11.1971: Completed and registered under
the ownership of the Cunard Steam-Ship Co.
Ltd. (Cunard-Brocklebank Ltd., managers),
Liverpool.
1972: Management changed to Cunard-
Brocklebank Bulkers Ltd, London.
1.1977: Sold to Al Dammam Navigation
Co. Ltd., Jeddah, Saudi Arabia (Varnima
Corporation International S.A., Piraeus,
Greece) and renamed AL DAMMAM 1.

1977: British register closed.
2.1984: Transferred to Cyclades Maritime
Co. S.A., Panama (Varnima Corporation
International S.A., Piraeus) and renamed KRITI
SAMARIA under the Greek flag.
6.1986: Sold to Morfini S.p.A., Bari, Italy and
renamed EGNAZIA.
11.1996: Transferred to Minosse Shipping Co.
Ltd., Valletta, Malta (Gemarfin S.A., Lugano,
Switzerland, operators).
1998: Transferred to Midday Shipping Co. Ltd.,
Valletta (Medcare Shipping, Athens, operators
for Morfini).
19.2.1999: Arrived at Alang for demolition.

The first three Eriksbergs tankers, including *Lumen*, were sold to Greek owners for operations out of Saudi Arabia.

Lumiere, seen here arriving at Cape Town, was the last tanker in the Cunard fleet.

LUMIERE 1972-1991
O.N. 357413 14,925g 9,631n
525.6 x 81.4 x 31.3 feet.
Two 12-cyl 4SCSA Pielstick-type geared-oil engines by Lindholmen Motor A/B, Gothenburg, Sweden 10,080 BHP, 14.8 knots.
22.12.1971: Launched by Eriksbergs M/V A/B (Lindholmen yard), Gothenburg (Yard No. 651) as LUMIERE.
23.3.1972: Delivered and later registered

under the ownership of the Cunard Steam-Ship Co. Ltd. (Cunard-Brocklebank Ltd., managers), London. Management subsequently changed to Cunard-Brocklebank Bulkers Ltd, London.
1978: Management changed to Cunard Shipping Services Ltd.
1.7.1987: Trafalgar House bought Ellerman Lines plc and Cunard Ellerman Shipping Services Ltd. was formed to operate the group's cargo ships.

11.1991: Sold to P&O Containers Ltd. (Peninsular and Oriental Steam Navigation Co., London), London.
7.1992: Transferred to Moss Tankers (Hong Kong) Ltd., Hong Kong (Peninsular and Oriental Steam Navigation Co., London).
7.1993: Sold to Broome Navigation Corporation, Monrovia, Liberia (Alfa Marine Services Ltd., Apapa, Nigeria) and renamed LEONA III.
20.6.1995: Arrived at Alang for demolition.

Despite being owned by Cunard, *Luminetta* and the rest of the tanker fleet wore Moss funnel colours. *[FotoFlite incorporating Skyfotos 325656]*

LUMINETTA 1972-1990
O.N. 357414 14,925g 9,631n
525.6 x 81.4 x 31.3 feet.
Two 12-cyl 4SCSA Pielstick-type geared-oil engines by Eriksbergs M/V A/B, Gothenburg, Sweden; 10,080 BHP, 14.8 knots.
1.11.1971: Launched by Eriksbergs M/V A/B, Gothenburg (Yard No. 653) as LUMINETTA.

9.3.1972: Delivered and later registered under the ownership of the Cunard Steam-Ship Co. Ltd. (Cunard-Brocklebank managers), London. Management subsequently changed to Cunard-Brocklebank Bulkers Ltd, London.
1978: Management changed to Cunard Shipping Services Ltd.
1.7.1987: Trafalgar House bought Ellerman Lines plc and Cunard Ellerman Shipping

Services Ltd. was formed to operate the group's cargo ships.
3.1990: Sold to Tankersud S.p.A., Genoa, Italy (Morfini S.p.A., Bari, Italy) and renamed ENOTRIA.
1990: British register closed.
8.1993: Management transferred to Petrolifera Tankers S.r.l., Genoa.
28.7.1996: Arrived at Alang for demolition.

Lucellum was the first of a new design of product tankers built on the St. Lawrence River by Davie Shipbuilding.

LUCELLUM (2) 1975-1978
O.N. 365847 23,736g 17,030n
569.9 x 106.0 x 37.5 feet.
7-cyl 2SCSA Sulzer-type oil engine by
Hitachi Zosen, Maizuru, Japan; 14,000 BHP,
15 knots.
17.12.1974: Launched by Davie
Shipbuilding Ltd., Lauzon, Canada (Yard
No. 685) as LUCELLUM.
7.1975: Completed and registered under the
ownership of the Cunard Steam-Ship Co.
Ltd. (Cunard-Brocklebank Bulkers Ltd.,
managers), London.
2.1978: Sold to Flota Mercante
Grancolombiana S.A., Bogota,
Colombia, and renamed CIUDAD DE
BARRANCABERMEJA and registered at
Cartagena de Indias, Colombia.
1978: British register closed.
5.1987: Sold to Tankersud S.p.A. (Morfini
S.p.A.), Bari, Italy and renamed MARVEA.
10.1989: Sold to Misano di Navigazione
S.p.A., Ravenna, Italy and renamed
RAVENNA TRADER
7.1991: Sold to Seaserpent Navigation
Co. Ltd., Malta (Compagnie Monegasque
Maritime S.A.M., Monte Carlo) and
renamed ATLANTIC SEA under the Cypriot
flag.
12.1997: Sold to Mostyn Navigation Ltd.
Malta (Trader Navigation Agencies Ltd.,
Windsor, U.K.) and renamed TN TOPAZ
under the Maltese flag.
6.2000: Sold to Ecologiki Naftiki Eteria,
Piraeus, Greece and renamed SLOPS X.
22.4.2007: Arrived at Aliaga, Turkey for
demolition.

LUCERNA 1975-1989
O.N. 365989 23,736g 17,030n
569.9 x 106.0 x 37.5 feet.
7-cyl 2SCSA Sulzer-type oil engine by G.
Clarke and N.E.M. Ltd., Wallsend; 14,000
BHP, 15.5 knots.
3.5.1975: Launched by Davie Shipbuilding

Ltd., Lauzon, Canada (Yard No. 686) as
LUCERNA.
11.1975: Completed and registered under
the ownership of the Cunard Steam-Ship
Co. Ltd. (Cunard-Brocklebank Bulkers Ltd.,
managers), London.
1978: Management changed to Cunard
Shipping Services Ltd.
1.7.1987: Trafalgar House bought Ellerman
Lines plc and Cunard Ellerman Shipping
Services Ltd. was formed to operate the
group's cargo ships.
3.1988: Renamed AL AROUS.
18.9.1989: Placed on the Norwegian
International Register following sale to K/S
Herlofson Tank II (Sigurd Herlofson and
Co. A/S), Oslo, Norway, renamed TANK
QUEEN.
1989: British register closed.
1991: Following Herlofson's withdrawal

from shipping, management assumed by
Tschudi & Eitzen A/S, Oslo.
12.1991: Transferred to Tschudi & Eitzen
Tankers A/S, Oslo and renamed SITAXA.
28.2.1996: Stranded on rocks off Magnisi,
while entering Santa Panagia Bay on a
voyage from Amsterdam to Santa Panagia,
Italy.
7.3.1996: Refloated and later dry docked at
Messina and declared a constructive total
loss.
3.1996: After repairs sold to Galea
Maritime Ltd., Valletta, Malta (Sougerka
Maritime Co. Ltd., Piraeus, Greece) and
renamed GALEA II.
5.2000: Sold to Castle Bay Shipping Ltd.,
Valletta (Univan Ship Management Ltd.,
Hong Kong), renamed IONA and registered
at Hong Kong.
11.2003: Sold to Chinese breakers.

Lucerna had an eventful career and was broken up only in 2003. She was the last of the Moss tankers. *[Fotoflite incorporating Skyfotos, 277143]*

236

CUNARD-BROCKLEBANK BULKERS LTD.

Cunard Campaigner. [Russell Priest]

CUNARD CAMPAIGNER 1972-1974
O.N. 358490 15,498g 11,227n
576.4 x 73.7 x 41.9 feet.
6-cyl 2SCSA Sulzer-type oil engine by
Astilleros Españoles S.A., Manises, Spain;
9,900 BHP, 15.5 knots.
23.10.1971: Launched by Astilleros
Españoles S.A., Seville, Spain (Yard No.
149) as CUNARD CAMPAIGNER.
19.7.1972: Registered at London under the
ownership of the Cunard Steam-Ship Co.
Ltd. (Cunard-Brocklebank Bulkers Ltd.,
managers), London.
1974: Sold to the Great Eastern Shipping
Co. Ltd., Bombay, India.
5.9.1974: British register closed.
21.5.1975: Renamed JAG SHANTI.

1994: Transferred to Infrastructure Leasing
and Finance Services Ltd., India.
28.5.1994: Abandoned by 30 of her 45 man
crew in the Arabian Sea about 125 miles
from New Mangalore after her engine
room flooded from leaking pipes whilst
on a voyage from New Mangalore, India
to Eregli, Turkey with a cargo of iron ore
pellets
5.6.1994: Foundered during a storm whilst
at anchorage 25 miles off New Mangalore,
having been towed there by the tug/salvage
vessel SALVANGUARD (2,938/1978).

CUNARD CARAVEL 1972-1974
O.N. 358582 15,498g 11,227n
576.4 x 73.7 x 41.9 feet.

6-cyl 2SCSA Sulzer-type oil engine by
Astilleros Españoles S.A., Manises, Spain;
9,900 BHP, 15.5 knots.
4.12.1971: Launched by Astilleros
Españoles S.A., Seville, Spain (Yard No.
150) as CUNARD CARAVEL.
19.9.1972: Registered at London under the
ownership of the Cunard Steam-Ship Co.
Ltd. (Cunard-Brocklebank Bulkers Ltd.,
managers), London.
1974: Sold to the Great Eastern Shipping
Co. Ltd., Bombay, India.
5.9.1974: British register closed.
16.2.1975: Renamed JAG SHAKTI.
8.4.1997: Arrived at Alang, India for
demolition.

Cunard Caravel.

Cunard Carronade at Vancouver, Canada on 14th January 1974. *[J. and M. Clarkson collection]*

CUNARD CARRONADE 1972-1978

O.N. 358696 15,498g 11,227n
576.4 x 73.7 x 41.9 feet.
6-cyl 2SCSA Sulzer-type oil engine by
Astilleros Españoles S.A., Bilbao, Spain;
9,900 BHP, 15.5 knots.
17.3.1972: Launched by Astilleros
Españoles S.A., Seville, Spain (Yard No.
151) as CUNARD CARRONADE.
11.1972: Completed.
1972: Registered at London under the
ownership of the Cunard Steam-Ship Co.
Ltd. (Cunard-Brocklebank Bulkers Ltd.,
managers), London.
3.10.1978: Sold to Rossway Transportation
Co., Monrovia, Liberia (Olympic Maritime
S.A., Panama) and later renamed OLYMPIC
HISTORY under the Greek flag.
1978: British register closed.
8.8.1985: Laid up at Eleusis Bay near Piraeus.
10.1987: Sold to Panagia Odigitria Shipping
Co. Ltd., Nicosia, Cyprus (Constantinos and
Charalambos Ventouris Co. Ltd., Piraeus,
Greece) and renamed CHARALAMBOS B.
12.1989: Transferred to Kyklades
Navigation Co. Ltd., Valletta, Malta and
renamed CHARALAMBOS.
5.1991: Transferred to Aghios Charalambos
Shipping Co. Ltd., Nicosia, Cyprus and
reverted to CHARALAMBOS B.
1.1995: Sold to Türkol Deniz T.A.Ş. (Turan
Companies Group), Istanbul, Turkey and
renamed MERYEM ANA.
5.1998: Transferred within the Turan Group
to Avrasya Ekspres Denizcilik ve T.L.Ş.
19.3.2002: Arrived at Alang, India for
demolition.

CUNARD CALAMANDA 1973-1978

O.N. 358820 15,498g 11,237n
576.4 x 73.7 x 41.9 feet.
6-cyl 2SCSA Sulzer-type oil engine by
Astilleros Españoles S.A., Bilbao, Spain;
9,900 BHP, 15.5 knots.
4.5.1972: Launched by Astilleros Españoles
S.A., Seville, Spain (Yard No. 152) as
CUNARD CALAMANDA.
5.2.1973: Registered at London under the
ownership of the Cunard Steam-Ship Co.
Ltd. (Cunard-Brocklebank Bulkers Ltd.,
managers), London.
9.7.1978: Sold to Neville Corporation,
Monrovia, Liberia (Arktias Shipping
Enterprises Co. Ltd., Piraeus, Greece) and
later renamed IONIAN CARRIER under
the Greek flag. She was also fitted for the
carriage and self-discharge of cement.
21.7.1978: British register closed.

1981: Management transferred to Naftitan
Maritime and Transportation Enterprises,
S.A., Piraeus.
1.1987: Sold to Poliaigos Nav. Co. Ltd.,
Nicosia, Cyprus (Constantinos and
Charalambos Ventouris Co. Ltd., Piraeus)
and renamed MASTROGIORGIS B. There
is no record of the removal of the cement-
handling equipment although the vessel's
voyage record indicates she was now
carrying other bulk cargoes.
7.1995: Sold to Türkol Deniz T.A.Ş.,
Istanbul, Turkey and renamed BÜYÜK
ANA.
7.1998: Transferred within the Turan Group
to Avrasya Ekspres Denizcilik ve T.L.Ş.
11.2001: Sold to Indian breakers and
renamed YU for the delivery voyage under
the Tonga flag.
8.12.2001: Arrived at Alang, India.

Cunard Calamanda.

CUNARD CHAMPION 1973-1978
O.N. 360662 15,448g 11,221n
576.4 x 73.7 x 41.9 feet.
6-cyl 2SCSA Sulzer-type oil engine
by Astilleros Españoles S.A., Manises,
Spain; 9,900 BHP, 15.5 knots.
7.4.1973: Launched by Astilleros
Españoles S.A., Bilbao, Spain (Yard
No. 258) as CUNARD CHAMPION.
20.8.1973: Registered at London
under the ownership of the Cunard
Steam-Ship Co. Ltd. (Cunard-
Brocklebank Bulkers Ltd., managers),
London.
26.6.1978: Acquired by Litonjua
Shipping Co. Inc., Manila, Philippines
and later renamed EL CHAMPION.
She was subsequently registered
in Panama and operated with dual
Philippine/Panamanian registration.
21.7.1978: British register closed.
12.1984: Sold to Seadove Shipping
Inc., Monrovia, Liberia (Zodiac
Maritime Agencies Ltd./Ofer
Brothers, London) and renamed
OCEAN PINE. Vessel management
functions within the Ofer Brothers
group were carried out by S.A.
Monegasque d'Administration
Maritime et Aerienne, Monte Carlo.
12.1985: Renamed FRIENDLY
ISLANDS.
9.1994: Sold to Orient Shipping
and Trading (Private) Ltd., Valletta,
Malta (Unipak Shipping and Trading
(Private) Ltd., Karachi, Pakistan)
and renamed FRIENDLY. Reported
as acquired for resale to Pakistani
shipbreakers but continued trading.
9.6.1997: Arrived at Alang, India for
demolition.

Cunard Champion. [Matterson Marine collection]

CUNARD CAVALIER 1973-1978
O.N. 360826 15,498g 11,227n
576.4 x 73.7 x 41.9 feet.
6-cyl 2SCSA Sulzer-type oil engine by
Astilleros Españoles S.A., Bilbao, Spain; 9,900
BHP, 15.5 knots.
10.2.1973: Launched by Astilleros Españoles
S.A., Seville, Spain (Yard No. 153) as
CUNARD CAVALIER.
20.9.1973: Registered at London under the
ownership of the Cunard Steam-Ship Co. Ltd.
(Cunard-Brocklebank Bulkers Ltd., managers),
London.
4.9.1978: Sold to Eastside Transportation Co.
(Olympic Maritime S.A.), Panama and later
renamed OLYMPIC HARMONY under the
Liberian flag.
11.9.1978: British register closed.
27.10.1985: Laid up in Eleusis Bay near
Piraeus.

1987: Sold to Starlight Shipping Ltd., Nicosia,
Cyprus (Overlink Maritime Inc., Piraeus,
Greece) and renamed SAGA under the Cypriot
flag. Management was subsequently transferred
to Drytank S.A., Piraeus.
1989: Sold to Villar's Shipping Ltd., Cyprus
(Fiesta Investment Trust Inc., Athens, Greece)
and renamed VILLAR.
2.7.1990: Suffered steering gear failure and ran
aground in Port Muhammad Bin Qasim channel
whilst on a voyage from Port Muhammad Bin
Qasim, Pakistan to Douala, Cameroon with a
cargo of rice. She was later abandoned and her
cargo discharged into lighters.
30.11.1990: Refloated and anchored.
16.1.1991: Towed to Colombo.
16.5.1991: Towed to Singapore and later
declared a constructive total loss.
6.2.1992: Arrived at Alang, India for demolition.

Cunard Cavalier.

CUNARD CHIEFTAIN 1973-1978

O.N. 360920 15,448g 11,221n
576.4 x 73.7 x 41.9 feet.
6-cyl 2SCSA Sulzer-type oil engine by
Astilleros Españoles S.A., Sestao, Spain;
9,900 BHP, 15.5 knots.

28.6.1973: Launched by Astilleros
Españoles S.A., Bilbao, Spain (Yard No.
258) as CUNARD CHIEFTAIN.

3.12.1973: Registered at London under the
ownership of the Cunard Steam-Ship Co.
Ltd. (Cunard-Brocklebank Bulkers Ltd.,
managers), London.

25.8.1978: Acquired by Superblue Trading
Inc., Panama (Orconsult S.A., Zurich,
Switzerland) and later renamed CHIEFTAIN.

8.9.1978: British register closed.

3.1981: Sold to Great City Nav. S.A., Panama
(Far East Enterprising Co. (H.K.) Ltd., Hong
Kong) and renamed GREAT CITY.

1983: Management transferred to Wah Tung
Shipping Agency Co. Ltd., Hong Kong (at
the same premises).

7.1987: Sold to Wolf Marine S.A., Panama
(Byzantine Maritime Corporation, Piraeus,
Greece) and renamed FANNIE ANNA under
the Greek flag.

11.1995: Sold to Pamaev St. Ltd., Valletta,
Malta (Astin Financiera Ltd., Athens,
Greece) and renamed AG. APOSTOLOS.

17.10.1996: Fire broke out in galley whilst
off the coast of South Korea in position
36°10′N, 125°45′E on a voyage in ballast
from Kunsan, Republic of Korea to People's
Republic of China.

24.10.1996: Towed to Kunsan outer
anchorage and later declared a constructive
total loss.

4.1.1997: Arrived at Zhenjiang, People's
Republic of China for demolition under
tow of tug PACIFIC CHALLENGE
(1,383/1983).

Cunard Chieftain in dry-dock at Malta (top) and in Australian waters (bottom). *[Top: World Ship Society Ltd.; bottom: Russell Priest]*

CUNARD CARRIER 1973-1978
O.N. 360951 15,498g 11,227n
576.4 x 73.7 x 41.9 feet.
6-cyl 2SCSA Sulzer-type oil engine by
Astilleros Españoles S.A., Sestao, Spain;
9,900 BHP, 15.5 knots.
31.3.1973: Launched by Astilleros
Españoles S.A., Seville, Spain (Yard No.
154) as CUNARD CARRIER.
21.12.1973: Registered at London under the
ownership of the Cunard Steam-Ship Co.
Ltd. (Cunard-Brocklebank Bulkers Ltd.,
managers), London.
18.8.1978: Sold to Silverdale Co. Ltd.,
Hamilton, Bermuda (Ocean Transport
and Trading Ltd., Liverpool, managers).
(Ocean Transport and Trading were vessel
managers only whilst Silverdale was owned
by Continental European interests, which
from 1979 operated as Agence Maritime
Transoceanique, Antwerp, Belgium and
Transocean Maritime Agencies, Monte Carlo).
4.9.1978. Renamed AENEAS.
4.1983: Transferred to Caroline Maritime
Pte. Ltd., Singapore. All management
functions assumed by the owner's offices in
Antwerp and Monte Carlo.
21.4.1983: British register closed.
4.1987: Sold to Saltlake Shipping Co. Ltd.,
Limassol, Cyprus (Dayak Corporation,
Piraeus, Greece) and renamed LEROS
ENDEAVOUR.
8.4.1989: Placed on the Norwegian
International Register following sale to
Gaard Shipping A/S (K/S Gaard Partners
II), Grimstad, Norway and renamed ELI
MARIE.

1.4.1995: Put into Valletta, Malta with a
hull crack sustained whilst on a voyage
from Ventspils to Taiwan. Detained under
port state control regulations for multiple
deficiencies and required replacement of
about 350 tons of steel work.
7.1995: Sold to Shoreham Sailor S.A.,
Monrovia, Liberia (Norbel Shipping Inc.
Ninove, Belgium) and renamed NORBEL
BULK.
29.8.1995: Sailed from Malta, having
completed sufficient provisional repairs
to permit her release to proceed to Piraeus
for permanent repairs. She was later re-
registered at Kingstown, St. Vincent and

placed under the Grenadines flag.
3.1996: Reported to have been registered in
Panama to a company named 'Hebron' and
renamed SUNNY BULK.
11.1996: Sold to Fujian Shipping Co.
(FUSCO), Fuzhou, China (Hainan Tongli
Shipping Co. Ltd., Beijing, China)
and renamed HUA HAI.
1.2008: Transferred to Fuzhou Taihai
Shipping Co. Ltd., Fuzhou (Hao Xing
Marine Ltd., Hong Kong) and renamed
HAOXING 1 under the Panama flag.
24.5.2009: Arrived at Alang, India for
demolition.

Cunard Carrier survived until 2009. *[Top: Russell Priest; bottom: Ships in Focus]*

REFRIGERATED SHIPS

In 1973, the Haifa-based Maritime Fruit Carriers Co. Ltd. placed an order for twenty six British-built ships, including ten 260,000 to 330,000-dwt tankers and ore-oil carriers. Spread across three yards, Harland and Wolff, Swan Hunter and Scott Lithgow, this was the largest single-customer shipbuilding transaction ever undertaken in Britain. Founded in 1964, Maritime Fruit Carriers, with the backing of the Israeli-government, had built up a large fleet of reefers which were all leased to the Swedish Salen Reefer Services. However, in 1975, following the collapse in the tanker market, Maritime Fruit Carriers found itself saddled with enormous debt. Unable to repay the banks, in 1976 many of its 37 ships were seized by creditors, including the British Government which had provided loans for the building of the new ships. Swan Hunter was particularly badly hit by the failure of the company and had to be rescued by the British Government.

For Trafalgar House this was a unique opportunity to purchase a reasonably-priced fleet of modern reefers, especially as the Cunard subsidiary, Port Line, had considerable expertise in what was then a growing market. In mid-1976 it offered to buy sixteen of the Maritime Fruit Carriers reefers, but this offer was rejected. In September, after a bid by Sea Containers had been abandoned, Trafalgar House tried again, this time bidding for thirteen British-flagged reefers. Because of on-going problems with creditors, it was agreed that the offer would be for twelve ships, two of which would be sold on to the Hamburg firm, W. Bruns and Co. These were *Maranga* (9,742/1972) and *London Clipper* (6,676/1972), which were renamed *Brunsland* and *Salinas* respectively.

The ten fruit ships were delivered to Cunard during the latter part of 1976 and were given classic Cunard names ending in *ia*. The names given also denoted the three distinct types of ships:

A-class: four British-built 23-knot 4,938g ships, originally had names ending in *Clipper*.
C-class: two Norwegian-built 7,323g ships, were originally named after fruits.
S-class: four Danish-built 12,059g ships, originally had flower names.

After renaming the ships continued to be chartered to Salen and in due course they all came under Cunard-Brocklebank management. For most of their time with Cunard they featured Salen funnel colours and only latterly had funnels painted in the familiar Cunard red and black. Their hulls were also initially white but, after a short time, were painted grey with red boot-topping. In November 1979, the reefer fleet was chartered to United Brands, the giant U.S. fruit company. In July 1981 the four A-class ships were sold to the Greek reefer company, Restis and four years later, at the end of their time charter to United Brands, the remaining ships were laid up in Vittoria Dock, Birkenhead. With a depressed reefer market and limited prospects for future long-term charters, they were offered for sale. Purchased by another Greek company, Kappa Maritime, they sailed from Birkenhead under new names between December 1985 and February 1986. The former *Saxonia* was the last to leave.

The A-class, including *Alsatia* (above), were the smallest reefers and were in the fleet for only five years.   *[David Salisbury]*

ALSATIA (3) 1976-1981
O.N. 357471 4,938g 2,636n
426.4 x 60.3 x 38.1 feet.
9-cyl. 2SCSA Sulzer-type oil engine by
George Clark and North Eastern Marine
Engineering Co. Ltd., Wallsend; 14,850
BHP, 23 knots.
19.1.1972: Launched by Smith's Dock Co.
Ltd., South Bank, Middlesbrough (Yard No.
1318) as EDINBURGH CLIPPER
5.1972: Completed for Chichester Shipping
Lines Ltd., North West Shipping Co. Ltd.
and Island Fruit Shipping Co. Ltd., London
(Maritime Fruit Carriers Co. Ltd., Haifa,
Israel), and registered at Glasgow.
1976: Acquird by the Cunard Steam-
Ship Co. Ltd. (Cunard-Brocklebank Ltd.,
managers), London and renamed ALSATIA.
1981: Sold to Alaska Maritime Co. S.A.,
Panama (Enterprises Shipping and Trading
S.A. (S. Restis), Piraeus, Greece) and
renamed AMERICA FREEZER under the
Greek flag.
1985: Transferred to Daiko Shipping Ltd.,
Monrovia, Liberia (Enterprises Shipping
and Trading S.A. (S. Restis), Piraeus) and
renamed ANGELMAR under the Greek flag.
1990: Sold to Nema Compania Naviera
S.A., Panama (Transcontinental Maritime
and Trading S.A., Piraeus) and renamed
ATLANTICO under the Bahamas flag.
1990: Transferred to Lucida Navigation
S.A., Panama (Transcontinental Maritime

and Trading S.A., Piraeus) and renamed
NETWORK SWAN under the Bahamas flag.
1991: Sold to Del-Monte Fresh Fruit
(International) Ltd., Monrovia, Liberia
(Irgens Larsen A/S, Oslo, Norway, managers).
1992: Transferred to Del-Monte Fresh Fruit
(International) Ltd., Panama City (Network
Shipping Ltd., Coral Gables, Florida, U.S.A.,
managers) (Irgens Larsen A/S, Oslo).
1992: Transferred to Del-Monte Fresh Fruit
International Ltd., Hamilton, Bermuda and
renamed BANANA REEFER.
2.9.1994: Arrived in Chittagong Roads for
demolition by Diamond Steel Products Co.
(Private) Ltd. at Bhatiary, Bangladesh.

ANDANIA (4) 1976-1981
O.N. 357490 4,938g 2,636n
426.4 x 60.3 x 38.1 feet.
9-cyl. 2SCSA Sulzer-type oil engine by
George Clark and North Eastern Marine
Engineering Co. Ltd., Wallsend; 14,850
BHP, 23 knots.
11.6.1972: Launched by Smith's Dock Co.
Ltd., South Bank, Middlesbrough (Yard No.
1320) as GLASGOW CLIPPER.
12.1972: Completed for Sovertur Shipping
Co. Ltd., North West Shipping Co. Ltd.
and Island Fruit Shipping Co. Ltd., London
(Maritime Fruit Carriers Co. Ltd., Haifa,
Israel) and registered at Glasgow.
1976: Acquird by the Cunard Steam-
Ship Co. Ltd. (Cunard-Brocklebank Ltd.,

managers), London and renamed ANDANIA
1981: Sold to Acadimos Maritime Co.
S.A., Panama (Enterprises Shipping and
Trading S.A. (S. Restis), Piraeus, Greece)
and renamed EUROPE FREEZER under the
Greek flag.
1986: Transferred to Ribarosa Shipping Ltd.,
Monrovia, Liberia (Enterprises Shipping
and Trading S.A. (S. Restis), Piraeus) and
renamed BALMAR under the Greek flag.
1990: Sold to Ultima Compania Naviera
S.A., Panama (Transcontinental Maritime
and Trading S.A., Piraeus) and renamed
PACIFICO under the Bahamas flag.
1990: Sold to Oriental Galaxy S.A., Panama
(Transcontinental Maritime and Trading
S.A., Piraeus) and renamed NETWORK
STORK under the Bahamas flag.
1991: Sold to Del-Monte Fresh Fruit
(International) Ltd., Monrovia (Irgens
Larsen A/S, Oslo, Norway, managers) .
1992: Owners became Del-Monte Fresh
Fruit (International) Ltd., Panama (Network
Shipping Ltd., Coral Gables, Florida,
U.S.A.,managers) (Irgens Larsen A/S, Oslo).
1992: Transferred to Del-Monte Fresh Fruit
International Ltd., Hamilton, Bermuda and
renamed BANANA PLANTER under the
Panama flag.
14.1.1995: Laid up at Malalag Bay,
Philippines.
29.4.1995: Beached at Alang for demolition
by Virat Shipbreaking Corporation.

Andania. [FotoFlite incorporating Skyfotos, 244794]

Andria. [Russell Priest]

ANDRIA (2) 1976-1981

O.N. 357505 4,938g 2,636n
426.4 x 60.3 x 38.1 feet.
9-cyl. 2SCSA Sulzer-type oil engine by
George Clark and North Eastern Marine
Engineering Co. Ltd., Wallsend; 14,850
BHP, 23 knots
20.11.1972: Launched by Smith's Dock Co.
Ltd., South Bank, Middlesbrough (Yard No.
1321) as TEESSIDE CLIPPER.
3.1973: Completed for Curtis Shipping
Co. Ltd. and others, London (Maritime
Fruit Carriers Co. Ltd., Haifa, Israel) and
registered at Glasgow.
1976: Acquired by the Cunard Steam-
Ship Co. Ltd. (Cunard-Brocklebank Ltd.,
managers), London renamed ANDRIA
1981: Sold to Akropol Navigation Co. S.A.,
Panama (Enterprises Shipping and Trading
S.A. (S. Restis), Piraeus, Greece) and
renamed AUSTRALIA FREEZER under the
Greek flag.
1986: Transferred to Rubisun Marine S.A.,
Monrovia, Liberia (Liberia Enterprises
Shipping and Trading S.A. (S. Restis),
Piraeus) and renamed ACECHILLY under
the Greek flag.
1988: Sold to Durango Shipping Co. Ltd.,
Limassol, Cyprus (Laskaridis Shipping
Co. Ltd., Piraeus) and renamed FRIO
HAMBURG.
1993: Transferred to Marine Shield S.A.,
Panama (Laskaridis Shipping Co. Ltd.,
Piraeus).
1994: Sold to UB Shipping Ltd. (Ugland
Interocean Management Ltd.), London and
renamed BANANOR under the Panama flag.
1996: Transferred to Ugland Reefers Ltd.

(Ugland International Holdings plc), Grand
Cayman, Cayman Islands.
1998: Renamed UB PRUDENT.
12.1998: Sold to Green Navigation Ltd.
(Star Entech Ltd.), St. Vincent and renamed
PRIDE III.
17.1.1999: Arrived at Mumbai for
demolition.

ALAUNIA (4) 1976-1981

O.N. 361584 4,938g 2,636n
426.4 x 60.3 x 38.1 feet.
9-cyl. 2SCSA Sulzer-type oil engine by
George Clark and North Eastern Marine
Engineering Co. Ltd., Wallsend; 14,850
BHP, 23 knots.
6.3.1973: Launched by Smith's Dock Co.
Ltd., South Bank, Middlesbrough (Yard
No.1323) as CARDIFF CLIPPER.
6.1973: Completed for Cardigan Bay
Shipping Co. Ltd., London (Maritime
Fruit Carriers Co. Ltd., Haifa, Israel) and
registered at Glasgow.
1974: Transferred to Abeyreuth Shipping
Co. Ltd. and Adelaide Shipping Lines Ltd.,
London (Maritime Fruit Carriers Co. Ltd.,
Haifa).
1976: Acquired by the Cunard Steam-
Ship Co. Ltd. (Cunard-Brocklebank
Ltd., managers), London and renamed
ALAUNIA.
1981: Sold to Amorgos Maritime Co. S.A.,
(Enterprises Shipping and Trading S.A.,
Panama (S. Restis), Piraeus, Greece) and
renamed OCEANIA FREEZER under the
Greek flag.
1986: Transferred to Laval Maritime Ltd.,
Monrovia, Liberia (Enterprises Shipping

and Trading S.A. (S. Restis), Piraeus) and
renamed FROSTY under the Greek flag.
1987: Sold to Acefrosty Navigation Co.
Ltd., Valletta, Malta (Government of Cuba,
Havana, Cuba) and renamed ACE FROSTY.
1988: Sold to Mazatlan Shipping Co. Ltd.,
Limassol, Cyprus (Laskaridis Shipping Co.
Ltd., Piraeus) and renamed FRIO BREMEN.
1993: Transferred to Lilium Maritime S.A.,
Panama (Laskaridis Shipping Co. Ltd.,
Piraeus).
1994: Sold to UB Shipping Ltd. (Ugland
Interocean Management Ltd.), London and
renamed GOLDEN B. under the Panama
flag.
1996: Transferred to Ugland Reefers Ltd.
(Ugland International Holdings plc), Grand
Cayman, Cayman Islands.
1997: Renamed UB PEARL.
2.11.1998: Arrived Alang for demolition.

CARINTHIA (4) 1976-1985

O.N.361582 7,330g 3,542n
471.3 x 70.1 x 41.7 feet.
9-cyl. 2SCSA Sulzer-type oil engine by
Nylands M/V, Oslo, Norway; 17,400 BHP,
20 knots
19.1.1973: Launched by Nylands Verksted,
Oslo (Yard No. 655) for Sagar Shipping Co.
Ltd., London as CANTALOUP.
7.1973: Completed for Druidstan Ltd.,
London (I.F.R. Services Ltd., managers)
(Maritime Fruit Carriers Co. Ltd., Haifa) and
registered at Glasgow.
1976: Acquired by the Cunard Steam-
Ship Co. Ltd. (Cunard-Brocklebank
Ltd., managers), London and renamed
CARINTHIA

20.9.1985: Arrived in the Mersey for lay up in Vittoria Dock, Birkenhead.
1985: Sold to Arlen Shipping Corporation, Monrovia, Liberia (Kappa Maritime Ltd. (G. and P.E. Kollakis), London).
15.1.1986: Sailed from Liverpool renamed PEGASUS under the Greek flag.
1994: Owners became Emperor Investment Corporation, Monrovia (Chartworld Shipping Corporation, Piraeus, Greece) (Kappa Maritime Ltd. (G. and P.E. Kollakis), London), managers) and renamed STAR LIGHT.
1995: Transferred to Caparison Shipping Corporation, Monrovia (Chartworld Shipping Corporation, Piraeus) (Kappa Maritime Ltd. (G. and P.E. Kollakis), London, managers) and renamed PELAGOS under the Bahamas flag.
1997: Managers became Kosmos Maritime Ltd. (D. Kastellis, Nikolaos Haberis, Nikolaos Markou), London.
2.7.2000: Arrived at Alang for demolition.

Alaunia in United Brands colours. *[David Whiteside collection]*

Carinthia. [FotoFlite incorporating Skyfotos, 7351]

Carmania. [FotoFlite incorporating Skyfotos, 244739]

CARMANIA (3) 1976-1986

O.N.357467 7,323g 3,546n
471.3 x 70.1 x 41.7 feet.
9-cyl. 2SCSA Sulzer-type oil engine by
Nylands M/V, Oslo; 17,400 BHP, 22 knots.
19.11.1971: Launched by Nylands Verksted,
Oslo (Yard No. 652) as ORANGE.
3.1972: Completed for Chichester Shipping
Lines Ltd., London (I.F.R. Services Ltd.,
managers) (Maritime Fruit Carriers Co. Ltd.,
Haifa, Israel) and registered in Glasgow.
1976: Acquired by the Cunard Steam-Ship
Co. Ltd., London (Cunard-Brocklebank Ltd.,
managers) renamed CARMANIA
14.6.1985: Arrived in the Mersey for lay up
in the Vittoria Dock, Birkenhead.
1986: Sold to Garton Shipping Corporation,
Monrovia, Liberia (Kappa Maritime Ltd. (G.
and P.E. Kollakis), London).
7.2.1986: Sailed from Liverpool renamed
PERSEUS under the Greek flag.
1995: Managers became Chartworld
Shipping Corporation, Piraeus, Greece
(Kappa Maritime Ltd. (G. and P.E. Kollakis),
London), managers) under the Bahamas flag.
1997: Managers became Kosmos Maritime
Ltd. (D. Kastellis, Nikolaos Haberis,
Nikolaos Markou), London.
13.6.1999: Arrived at Alang for demolition.

SAMARIA (4) 1976-1986

O.N. 357499 12,059g 6,915n
533.4 x 75.0 x 44.3 feet.
9-cyl. 2SCSA Sulzer-type oil engine by
Burmeister & Wain, Copenhagen, Denmark;
23,200 BHP, 23.5 knots.
31.8.1972: Launched by Aalborg Vaerft
A/S, Aalborg, Denmark (Yard No. 198) as
CHRYSANTEMA.
2.1973: Completed for Paravon Shipping Co.
Ltd., London (Maritime Fruit Carriers Co.
Ltd., Haifa, Israel) and registered at Glasgow.
1976: Acquired by the Cunard Steam-

Ship Co. Ltd. (Cunard-Brocklebank Ltd.,
managers), London and renamed SAMARIA
26.5.1985: Arrived in the Mersey for lay up
in the Vittoria Dock, Birkenhead.
1986: Sold to Cepheus Shipping Corporation,
Monrovia, Liberia (Kappa Maritime Ltd. (G.
and P.E. Kollakis), London).
19.2.1986: Sailed from Liverpool renamed
CAPRICORN under the Greek flag.
1986: Transferred to Diamond Seal Shipping
Co. Ltd., Limassol, Cyprus (Kappa Maritime

Ltd. (G. and P.E. Kollakis), London).
1992: Transferred to Daphnis Shipping
Corporation, Monrovia (Chartworld
Shipping Corporation, Piraeus, Greece
(Kappa Maritime Ltd. (G. and P.E. Kollakis),
London), managers) under the Bahamas flag.
1997: Managers became Kosmos Maritime
Ltd. (D. Kastellis, Nikolaos Haberis,
Nikolaos Markou) London.
30.7.1997: Arrived at Alang for demolition
by Gupta Steel.

Perseus ex-Carmania in the New Waterway in August 1969 (middle) and arriving at
Cape Town (bottom). *[Middle: David Salisbury]*

246

Samaria. [David Whiteside collection]

Saxonia, photographed on the New Waterway in June 1977 was the last Cunard reefer. *[David Salisbury]*

SAXONIA (4) 1976-1986
O.N. 357465 12,029g 6,900n
533.4 x 75.0 x 44.3 feet.
9-cyl. 2SCSA Sulzer-type oil engine by
Burmeister & Wain, Copenhagen, Denmark;
23,200 BHP, 23.5 knots.
2.6.1971: Launched by Aalborg Vaerft

A/S, Aalborg, Denmark (Yard No. 195) as
GLADIOLA.
2.1972: Completed for Adelaide Shipping
Lines Ltd., London (Maritime Fruit Carriers
Co. Ltd., Haifa, Israel) and registered at
Glasgow.
1976: Acquired by the Cunard Steam-

Ship Co. Ltd. (Cunard-Brocklebank Ltd.,
managers), London and renamed SAXONIA
4 to 6.1982: Requisitioned by the British
Government as a transport during the
Falklands campaign.
7.6.1985: Arrived in the Mersey for lay up in
the Vittoria Dock, Birkenhead.

247

1986: Sold to Cepheus Tondo Shipping Corporation, Monrovia, Liberia (Kappa Maritime Ltd. (G. and P.E. Kollakis), London).
21.2.1986: Sailed from Liverpool renamed CARINA under the Greek flag.
1986: Transferred to Skyrocket Shipping Co. Ltd., Limassol, Cyprus (Kappa Maritime Ltd. (G. and P.E. Kollakis), London).

1992: Transferred to Chloe Shipping Corporation, Monrovia (Chartworld Shipping Corporation) (Kappa Maritime Ltd., London, managers) under the Bahamas flag.
7.7.1995: Damaged in collision with the container ship MSC SAMIA (40,944/1973) in position 51°22´N, 02°46´E whilst on a voyage from Bellingham, Washington State, U.S.A. to

Vlissingen with a cargo of frozen potato chips. The vessels were separated by tugs and after temporary repairs and partial discharge of her cargo, CARINA was taken to Zeebrugge and later declared a constructive total loss.
12.3.1996: Arrived at Aliaga, Turkey for demolition by Dortel Gemi Sokum Demir Celik.

The damaged *Carina*. *[FotoFlite incorporating Skyfotos, 186317, 186319 and 186320]*

SCYTHIA (4) 1976-1986

O.N. 357489 12,059g 6,915n
533.4 x 75.0 x 44.3 feet.
9-cyl. 2SCSA Sulzer-type oil engine
by Burmeister & Wain, Copenhagen,
Denmark; 23,200 BHP, 23.5 knots.
23.5.1972: Launched by Aalborg
Vaerft A/S, Aalborg, Denmark (Yard
No. 197) as IRIS QUEEN.
11.1972: Completed for Adelaide
Shipping Lines Ltd., London (Maritime
Fruit Carriers Co. Ltd., Haifa, Israel)
and registered at Glasgow.
1976: Acquired by the Cunard Steam-
Ship Co. Ltd. (Cunard-Brocklebank
Ltd., managers), London and renamed
SCYTHIA.
17.6.1985: Arrived in the Mersey
for lay up in the Vittoria Dock,
Birkenhead.
1986: Sold to Toulon Shipping
Corporation, Monrovia, Liberia
(Kappa Maritime Ltd. (G. and P.E.
Kollakis), London).
6.2.1986: Sailed from Liverpool
renamed CENTAURUS under the
Greek flag.
1989: Transferred to Shipping Co.
Ltd., Limassol, Cyprus (Kappa
Maritime Ltd. (G. and P.E. Kollakis),
London).
8.2.1989: Abandoned after a fire
broke out in her engine room whilst
alongside at Wilmington, Delaware
with a cargo of bananas from La
Ceiba, Honduras. She was towed to
an anchorage in the Delaware River
where the fire was extinguished.
18.2.1989: Towed into Philadelphia
and subsequently declared a
constructive total loss.
16.7.1989: Arrived Chittagong for
demolition by Abdul Motaleb.

SERVIA (2) 1976-1985

O.N. 357481 12,059g 6,920n
533.4 x 75.0 x 44.3 feet.
9-cyl. 2SCSA Sulzer-type oil engine
by Burmeister & Wain, Copenhagen,
Denmark; 23,200 BHP, 24 knots.
20.10.1971: Launched by Aalborg
Vaerft A/S, Aalborg, Denmark (Yard
No. 196) as ORCHIDEA.
7.1972: Completed for Austral
Shipping Lines Ltd., London (Maritime
Fruit Carriers Co. Ltd., Haifa, Israel)
and registered at Glasgow.
1976: Acquired by the Cunard Steam-
Ship Co. Ltd. (Cunard-Brocklebank
Ltd., managers), London and renamed
SERVIA
21.9.1985: Arrived in the Mersey
for lay up in the Vittoria Dock,
Birkenhead.
12.1985: Sold to Iaco Shipping
Corporation, Monrovia, Liberia
(Kappa Maritime Ltd. (G. and P.E.
Kollakis), London).
10.12.1985: Sailed from Liverpool
renamed CASTOR under the Greek flag.

Scythia in charterer's colours in the New Waterway on 21st June 1980 (opposite page bottom) and in Cunard colours (above) received only towards the end of her time with the company. *[Opposite page bottom: Malcolm Cranfield]*

Servia in King George V Dock, Hull on 28th June 1976 in the colours of J. Lauritzen, Denmark (above) and on the New Waterway in August 1978 (below). *[Above: Michael Green collection; below: David Salisbury]*

1987: Transferred to Gold Seal Shipping Co. Ltd., Limassol, Cyprus (Kappa Maritime Ltd. (G. and P.E. Kollakis), London) and renamed KASTORA.
26.4.1989: Following an engine room fire began to take in water south east of Jamaica in position 15°08′N, 74°20′W whilst on a voyage from Puerto Limon, Costa Rica to New Orleans with a cargo of bananas.

29.4.1989: Arrived at Kingston, Jamaica under tow of the U.S. tug HARRIS B. DOUCET (98/1974) and subsequently declared a constructive total loss.
5.1989: Towed to Puerto Limon, Costa Rica.
12.9.1989: Arrived under tow at Piraeus and later sold to Pakistani breakers.
31.3.1990: Demolition at Gadani Beach began by M.H. and Company (Private) Ltd.

TUGS, TENDERS AND BARGES

Liverpool tugs, tenders and barges

The River Mersey is a tidal river and the range of the tide can be as great as 33 feet. In the early days, liners were moored in the river and passengers would embark and disembark in tenders. Passengers for the inaugural sailing of *Britannia* on July 4th 1840 were transferred to the ship by tender from the Egremont slip at the south end of Prince's Parade. The British and North American Royal Mail Steam Packet Company initially owned a series of barges and a pair of paddle tugs and tenders, *Satellite* and *Jackal*. The former operated in Liverpool for over half a century from 1848 to 1902. *Jackal* of 1853 also had an interesting pedigree, as she was the first ship built by the famous shipbuilder J. and G. Thomson, which later became John Brown & Co. Ltd. Not long after calls at Queenstown (Cobh), Ireland were introduced in 1859, *Jackal* was positioned at Queenstown and spent most of her career as the company's local tender.

With the arrival at Liverpool of increasingly larger ships in the 1880s, two new tenders were built. One was the baggage and fresh water carrier *Otter*, whilst the other was the large passenger tender *Skirmisher*, which became a familiar part of the Mersey scene until the 1940s. She also supplied fresh water to the liners. Scrapped at the age of 82 years, *Otter* was the third longest lasting Cunarder after *Hecla* (94 years) and the first *Parthia* (86 years). The first floating passenger landing stage at Liverpool was completed at St. George's Pier in 1847. However, this proved to be inadequate and in 1857 a new 1,002-feet landing stage opposite the Princes Pier was completed. In 1876 the St. George's Pier and Princes Pier portions were merged into a single 2,000-feet landing stage, the Princes Landing Stage. Tenders were also used alongside ships moored at the landing stage whilst in the early 1900s, at Rock Ferry on the Cheshire side of the River Mersey, a large buoy at the Sloyne anchorage was provided so that Cunard liners could be coaled without the need to enter the docks. In later years, the liners embarked and disembarked passengers alongside the Princes Landing Stage, which also had its own railway station. Alexandra Towing Co. Ltd., the well-known

Liverpool tug company, had a close association with Cunard. Not only did it have a tug contract at Liverpool, when Cunard moved its express liner service to Southampton in 1919, Alexandra Towing established an operation there with five tugs. Between 1911 and 1914, its passenger tenders *Herald* and *Flying Kestrel* were also sent to Monte Carlo as tenders for Cunard Mediterranean spring cruises.

Cherbourg tenders

Situated at the tip of a peninsula jutting out into the English Channel, Cherbourg is only 105 nautical miles to the south west of Southampton and is an ideal port for embarking and disembarking passengers and mail bound for Paris and the rest of Europe. Hamburg-Amerika Linie started calls for its express steamers in July 1895 in conjunction with a new fast train service between Paris and Cherbourg. The line's main German rival, Norddeutscher Lloyd, followed suit the following year, with American Line including Cherbourg on its Southampton to New York service in 1898. In 1907 White Star Line moved its main transatlantic mail service from Liverpool to Southampton and also called at Cherbourg. *Adriatic* made her maiden call on the 5th June 1907 and was met by the White Star-owned paddle-driven tender *Gallic* which was based at Cherbourg. The elderly *Gallic* was replaced in 1911 by two large tenders, *Nomadic* and *Traffic*, which had been designed to serve the company's new 45,300g *Olympic*-class trio. Because of French law, the White Star-owned tenders were registered in France and managed by a French company. Before the outbreak of the First World War, Hamburg-Amerika Linie was the largest shipping line in the world with a fleet of 190 ships whilst Norddeutscher Lloyd had 116 vessels. At the end of the war, the Treaty of Versailles imposed incredible hardship on the German nation and all vessels over 1,600-tons were handed to the victorious Allied powers whilst Hamburg-Amerika Linie and Norddeutscher Lloyd also lost all their property abroad. This provided a tremendous opportunity for Cunard Line and in 1919 the company moved its New York express liner mail service from Liverpool to Southampton. *Mauretania* inaugurated

Left: Boarding a tender at Liverpool's Princes Landing Stage in the early 1880s. Right: Passengers coming on board a Cunard steamer anchored in the River Mersey.

Skirmisher going astern from the Princes Landing Stage, Liverpool. *[B. and A. Feilden/J. and M. Clarkson]*

the new Southampton, Cherbourg to New York service on the 18th November 1919. *Imperator* (*Berengaria*) made her first call on 6th June 1920 with *Aquitania* following on the 14th August 1920. These ships were served at Cherbourg by Cunard's own tender *Satellite*, which had been a ferry on the River Mersey. Like the White Star tenders, she was French-registered and managed by a French company. In 1922 Cunard's agency in France, Cie. Nord Atlantique, took over the management of the tender. The following year, two specially-built 750 passenger-capacity tenders, *Alsatia* and *Lotharingia*, were delivered as replacements for *Satellite*. In the meantime an immense twelve-year rebuilding project was underway at Cherbourg, which included the deepening of the harbour and the construction of a new passenger terminal, the Gare Maritime, which when completed was the second largest building in France after the Palace of Versailles. The biggest passenger liners in the world could berth alongside and up to a thousand passengers an hour could be transferred to and from trains in the 305-feet wide covered railway station. At least seven trains a day whisked passengers to Paris in three and a half-hours. The Art Deco-style station building designed by René Levavasseur was opened by Albert Lebrun, President of the French Republic, on 30th July 1933.

Two ships could berth alongside the deep-water quay and as a result there was less need for tendering in the outer harbour. In 1934 Cunard sold *Alsatia* and *Lotharingia* to a local tug and tender company, La Société Cherbourgeoise de Remorquage et de Sauvetage, which had been formed in 1930. *Alsatia* was renamed *Ingénieur Cachin* whilst *Lotharingia* became *Alexis De Tocquevile*. The same company also bought White Star's *Nomadic* and *Traffic*, which were renamed *Ingénieur Minard* and *Ingénieur Reibel* respectively. *Queen Mary* called at Cherbourg on her maiden voyage to New York on 27th May 1936.

The Gare Maritime was partially destroyed by the Germans in 1944. The damage was so severe that tenders had to be used when the *Queens* returned to Cherbourg in 1948. In 1951 the Cherbourg tender fleet consisted of *Ingénieur Cachin, Ingénieur Minard*, a new *Ingénieur Reibel* ex *Sir Walter Raleigh, La Bretonnier* (originally Norddeutscher Lloyd's *Gruessgott*) and *Landemer*, a former suction dredger. Although *Queen Mary* berthed at the new Quai de France on the 8th May 1952, tendering at Cherbourg continued from time to time until the withdrawal of the *Queens* in the late 1960s.

Queen Elizabeth at the Gare Maritime with its war-damaged roof. *[Steve Booth collection]*

BARGES AT LIVERPOOL:
MONKEY (167g)
BADGER (165g)
SWAN (166g)
SQUIRREL (140g)

SATELLITE (1) 1848-1902 Iron paddle tug/tender
O.N. 23924 157g 82n
108.5 x 18.8 x 9.7 feet.
2-cyl. engine by Robert Napier, Glasgow; 80 HP.
Passengers: Board of Trade Passenger
Certificate: *1850s*: 450 to 540; *1860s*: 161 winter, 230 summer.
21.1.1848: Launched by Robert Napier, Glasgow (Yard No. 25) as SATELLITE.
17.8.1848: Registered at Glasgow under the ownership of the British and North American Royal Mail Steam Packet Company, Glasgow.
1.7.1878: Transferred to the Cunard Steamship Co. Ltd., Liverpool.
6.6.1898: Registered at Liverpool.
10.1902: Sold for demolition to A. Gordon, Newry.
26.11.1902: Register closed after being broken up.

JACKAL 1853-1893 Iron double-ended paddle tug/tender
O.N. 1334 165g 60n
125.4 x 19.5 x 9.8 feet.
2-cyl. oscillating engine by J. and G. Thomson, Govan; 86 HP.
Passengers: Board of Trade Passenger
Certificate: 161 winter, 230 summer.
18.3.1852: Launched by J. and G. Thomson, Govan (Yard No. 1) as JACKAL.
14.4.1852: Completion.
29.7.1853: Registered at Glasgow under the ownership of the British and North American Royal Mail Steam Packet Company, Glasgow. For some reason, there was a gap of over a year between completion and registration.
1859: Became the company's tender at Queenstown (Cobh), Ireland.
1.7.1878: Transferred to the Cunard Steamship Co. Ltd., Liverpool.
24.3.1887: Registered at Liverpool.
7.1893: Sold for demolition to J. Lever, Tranmere.
27.11.1893: Register closed after being broken up.

OTTER 1880-1917 Iron tender
O.N. 81390 287g 187n
142.2 x 23.2 x 10.2 feet.
C. 2-cyl. by Blackwood and Gordon, Glasgow; 40 HP.
12.8.1880: Launched by Blackwood and Gordon, Glasgow (Yard No. 160) as OTTER, a baggage and water tender.
10.9.1880: Registered at Liverpool under the ownership of the Cunard Steamship Co. Ltd., Liverpool.
26.11.1917: Sold to Rea Transport Co. Ltd., London.
3.2.1920: Sold to William Cooper and Son Ltd., Widnes as a sand carrier.
27.9.1962: Arrived at Preston for demolition by Thos. W. Ward Ltd., Sheffield.
10.3.1964: Register closed.

Satellite was Cunard's Liverpool passenger tender for over 50 years.

Jackal at Queenstown.

Otter alongside *Campania* at the Princes Landing Stage (above) and as a sand carrier at Liverpool in the late 1940s or early 1950s (below).

Skirmisher was Cunard's longest-serving ship. *[B. and A. Feilden/J. and M. Clarkson]*

SKIRMISHER 1884-1945 Twin screw tender
O.N. 87990 607g 210n
165.0 x 32.2 x 15.0 feet.
Two C. 2-cyl. by J. and G. Thomson, Clydebank; 147 HP, 10 knots.
Passengers: Board of Trade Passenger Certificate: 554 winter, 717 summer.
14.5.1884: Launched by J. and G. Thomson, Clydebank (Yard No. 221) as SKIRMISHER.
5.7.1884: Registered at Liverpool under the ownership of the Cunard Steamship Co. Ltd., Liverpool.
18.7.1934: Transferred to Cunard White Star Ltd., Liverpool.
10.1945: Withdrawn from service as the longest-serving Cunard ship.
12.2.1946: Work began on demolition at Garston by J. Routledge and Son (Liverpool) Ltd.
11.6.1952: Register closed.

SATELLITE (2) 1919-1924 Paddle tender
O.N. 106796 333g 60n
160.0 x 27.1 x 9.9 feet.
C. 2-cyl. lever engine by John Scott and Co., Kinghorn, Fife; 220 HP, 13 knots.
Passengers: 1,200.
12.6.1896: Launched by John Scott and Co., Kinghorn, Fife (Yard No. 96) as JOHN HERRON.
15.7.1896: Registered at Liverpool under the ownership of Wallasey Urban District Council, Egremont and used as a River Mersey ferry.
27.7.1910: Owners restyled Borough of Wallasey.
31.7.1919: Acquired by Cunard Steam Ship Co. Ltd., Liverpool.
10.1919: Transferred to Société Maritime de

The second *Satellite* was Cunard's first tender at Cherbourg.

Transbordements, Cherbourg (Cunard Steam Ship Co. Ltd., Liverpool) and renamed SATELLITE.
29.10.1919: Register closed.
1922: Transferred to Cie. Nord Atlantique, Cherbourg (Cunard Steam Ship Co. Ltd., Liverpool).
1924: Broken up at Cherbourg in the final quarter of 1924.

LOTHARINGIA 1923-1933 Twin screw tender
1,256g 598n
199.9 x 38.1 x 15.5 feet.
Two T.3-cyl. by David Rowan and Co. Ltd., Glasgow; 170 HP, 12 knots.
Passengers: 750.
8.3.1923: Launched by William Hamilton and Co. Ltd., Port Glasgow (Yard No.385) as LOTHARINGIA.

4.1923: Completed for Cie. Nord Atlantique, Cherbourg (Cunard Steam Ship Co. Ltd., Liverpool).
1933: Sold to La Société Cherbourgeoise de Remorquage et de Sauvetage, Cherbourg, France and renamed ALEXIS DE TOCQUEVILE.
Late 1939: Requisitioned by the French Navy, given the pendant number X 26 and reported to have been fitted as an auxiliary minelayer.
13.6.1940: Sunk (probably scuttled) at Cherbourg and subsequently refloated by German salvors.
c.1943/44: Refitted at Brest as a floating anti-aircraft battery.
26.8.1944: Sunk during a British air raid on Brest.
1945/46: Wreck raised and broken up.

ALSATIA (1) 1923-1934 Twin screw tender
O.N. 168843 1,310g 632n
199.8 x 38.1 x 15.5 feet.
Two T.3-cyl. by Wallsend Slipway and Engineering Co. Ltd., Wallsend; 164 HP, 12 knots.
Passengers: 750.
4.4.1923: Launched by Coaster Constuction Co. Ltd., Montrose (Yard No. 118) as ALSATIA.
6.1923: Completed for Cie. Nord Atlantique, Cherbourg, France (Cunard Steam Ship Co. Ltd., Liverpool).
1934: Sold to La Société Cherbourgeoise de Remorquage et de Sauvetage, Cherbourg and renamed INGÉNIEUR CACHIN.
Late 1939: Requisitioned by the French Navy, given pendant number X 24 and reported to have been fitted as an auxiliary minelayer.
6.1940: Sailed for the U.K. after the fall of France, seized at Southampton on *3.7.1940* and placed in Royal Navy custody.
1941: Assigned to the Force Naval de la France Libre (FNLN) as the depot ship VOLONTAIRE.
21.11.1942: Registered at Liverpool under the ownership of the Ministry of War Transport (London Midland and Scottish Railway, managers), London.
1946: Returned to her owners and reverted to INGÉNIEUR CACHIN.
1962: Broken up in the second quarter.

Top: *Lotharingia* was Cunard's first purpose-built Cherbourg tender.

Upper middle: *Ingénieur Cachin* ex *Alsatia*.

Lower middle: *Alsatia* (left) and *Lotharingia* (right) at Cherbourg in the late 1920s. The ferry dressed overall is Great Western Railway's *St. Julien* (1,885/1925).

Right: Cunard's Cherbourg tenders are on the right with the newly-completed Gare Maritime in the background. *[Steve Booth collection]*

BERMUDA AND ST. THOMAS.

ROYAL MAIL SERVICE.

ALPHA, BETA, DELTA,

THESE OR OTHER FIRST-CLASS STEAMERS

CARRYING HER MAJESTY'S MAILS,

WILL LEAVE

HALIFAX, NOVA SCOTIA,

FOR

BERMUDA AND ST. THOMAS,

EVERY FOURTH MONDAY,

Arriving at BERMUDA about the Fourth Day, and at ST. THOMAS about the Ninth Day, after Departure from Halifax;

Leaving ST. THOMAS for HALIFAX the Next Day, Calling at BERMUDA.

EXCELLENT ACCOMMODATION FOR PASSENGERS.

GOODS CARRIED AT MODERATE RATES OF FREIGHT.

Apply to WILLIAM CUNARD, Halifax; at the Company's Office, New York, to CHARLES G. FRANCKLYN, Agent; at the Company's Office, Boston, to JAMES ALEXANDER, Agent; in London, to **WILLIAM CUNARD**, 28, Pall Mall, S.W., and 6, St. Helen's Place, Bishopsgate Street, E.C.; in Dundee, to G. & J. BURNS, 11, Panmure Street; in Glasgow, to **G. & J. BURNS**, 267, Argyle Street; or to

D. & C. MAC IVER, 8, Water Street, LIVERPOOL.

Advertisement for the Halifax-Bermuda-St. Thomas mail service.

HALIFAX-BERMUDA MAIL SERVICE

Samuel Cunard and his family owned many ships, mainly sailing vessels (see page 291). Although Cunard had operated a winter mail service from Halifax to New York since 1815, the first mail contract with the Admiralty began in 1827, with a mail service from Halifax to Boston. In the same year, a short-lived mail route started between Bermuda and Annapolis, Maryland.

In 1833 Cunard was awarded the mail contract between Halifax and Bermuda. The success of this service, and his involvement with the British and North American Royal Mail Steam Packet Company's Liverpool-Halifax-Boston route, led to the extension of his mail contract to include Newfoundland. The Nova Scotia, Newfoundland and Bermuda Royal Mail Steam Packet Company was established in 1848 and four small screw-driven steamers were ordered for the mail service.

In the early 1860s, the Halifax-Bermuda route was extended to St. Thomas. In 1880 Kingston, Jamaica replaced St. Thomas as the southern end of the route with calls made subsequently at the Turks Island. In July 1886 the Cunard Halifax-Bermuda-West Indies mail contract was cancelled and subsequently awarded to another Halifax firm, Pickford and Black. The only Halifax-Bermuda mail ship owned by The British and North American Royal Mail Steam Packet Company was *Delta*. The rest were owned by Samuel Cunard or members of his family.

SUSAN 1823-1832 Wooden brig rigged sailing ship

107g
63.5 x 20.1 x 11 feet.
10.7.1823: Launched by W. Leppard, Halifax, Nova Scotia as SUSAN.
17.11.1823: Registered at Halifax, Nova Scotia under the ownership of Samuel Cunard, Halifax, Nova Scotia.
3.3.1827: Inaugurated Cunard mail service between Bermuda and Annapolis, Maryland.
10.1827: Placed on a new Halifax to Boston mail service.
4.1828: Replaced by LADY OGLE.
2.8.1832: Registered under the ownership of W.H.S. Neale, Halifax.
17.9.1832: Register closed after vessel lost at Jamaica.

EMILY 1827-1837 Wooden brig rigged sailing ship

89g
60.6 x 18.7 x 9.5 feet.
21.8.1826: Launched by Richard Burnett, St. Peters Bay, New Brunswick as EMILY.
16.2.1827: Registered at Halifax, Nova Scotia under the ownership of Samuel Cunard, Halifax.
1827: Placed on the mail service between Bermuda and Annapolis, Maryland and later that year was transferred to the Halifax to Boston mail service.
1835: Replaced by MARGARET.
28.7.1837: Ownership changed to J. Salter, Halifax.
36.11.1841: Registered under the ownership of H.H. Starr and J.F Nelmes, Halifax.
1843: Register closed after vessel condemned at Bermuda as unseaworthy.

MARGARET (1) 1824-1842 Wooden brig rigged sailing ship

132g
68.0 x 22.6 x 10.0 feet.
1824: Completed at Teignmouth, Devon for H.M. Revenue service as MARGARET.
31.5.1825: Sold at auction.
18.6.1825: Registered at Plymouth under the ownership of Samuel Cunard, Halifax, Nova Scotia.
5.6.1826: Registered at Halifax.

1835: Placed on the Halifax to Boston mail service.
20.4.1842: Registered under the ownership of J. Duffus*, Halifax.
2.11.1849: Registered under the ownership of J. Strachan, Halifax.
1850: Abandoned at sea whilst on a voyage from Cuba.
1852: Register closed.

LADY OGLE 1827-1842 Wooden schooner-rigged sailing ship

116g
69.9 x 19.8 x 10.8 feet.
7.8.1827: Launched by Robert Knight, Douglas, Nova Scotia as LADY OGLE.
10.9.1827: Registered at Halifax, Nova Scotia under the ownership of Samuel Cunard, Halifax, Nova Scotia.
7.1833: Inaugurated new mail service between Halifax and Bermuda.
20.4.1842: Registered under the ownership of to J. Duffus*, Halifax.
25.4.1849: Registered under the ownership of W. Baud and J. Gibson, Halifax.
13.7.1850: Registered under the ownership of L. and J. West, Halifax.
6.11.1857: Registered at Liverpool in ownership of P. Remorino, Gibraltar.
1862: Wrecked at Cadiz.
22.5.1866: Register closed.

VELOCITY 1818-1842 Wooden brig rigged sailing ship

133g
70.6 x 21.1 x 10.6 feet.
1811: Built at Bridport, Dorset as VELOCITY.
3.3.1812: Registered at London under the ownership of M. Stanton, London.
17.8.1818: Registered at Halifax, Nova Scotia under the ownership of Samuel Cunard, Halifax, Nova Scotia.
18.7.1840: Sailed from Halifax for Bermuda with the mails from BRITANNIA, which had arrived the previous day on her maiden voyage.
20.4.1842: Registered under the ownership of J. Duffus*, Halifax.
29.10.1849: Registered under the ownership of C. West, Halifax.
1856: Register closed 'vessel lost'.

* This is probably John Duffus, Samuel Cunard's brother-in-law and these ships may have been sold because Samuel Cunard was suffering from serious debt problems at that time.

OSPRAY 1848-1869 Wooden screw

O.N. 35875 274g 176n
122.0 x 22.9 x 14.0 feet.
2-cyl engine.
1848: Launched by John Wood and Co., Port Glasgow as OSPRAY.
15.6.1848: Registered at Greenock under the ownership of the Nova Scotia, Newfoundland and Bermuda Royal Mail Steam Packet Company, Greenock.
11.8.1848: Left Halifax for Bermuda as the first steamship on the Halifax to Bermuda mail service.
9.1850: Inaugurated a new New York-Bermuda-St. Thomas, Virgin Islands mail service.
14.6.1853: Transferred to Samuel Cunard, Halifax, Nova Scotia.
27.9.1853: Registered at Halifax, Nova Scotia.
1868: Trasferred to William Cunard, Halifax.
5.5.1869: Registered under the ownership of Stephen March, St. John's, Newfoundland.
7.4.1874: Abandoned at sea in a leaking condition.
13.4.1874: Register closed.

FALCON 1848-1851 Wooden screw

172n
128.8 x 23.0 x 13.9 feet.
2-cyl engine.
7.1849: Launched by Robert Steele and Company, Greenock as FALCON.
8.8.1848: Registered at Greenock under the ownership of the Nova Scotia, Newfoundland and Bermuda Royal Mail Steam Packet Company, Greenock.
27.9.1848: First voyage from Halifax to Bermuda.
8.3.1849: Inaugurated new Halifax to Newfoundland mail service.
8.5.1851: Wrecked at Cape Broyle, Newfoundland in fog.
30.9.1851: Register closed.

KESTREL 1849 Wooden screw
173n
121.1 x 23.0 x 13.8 feet.
2-cyl engine.
3.1849: Launched by Robert Steele and
Company, Greenock as KESTREL.
16.4.1849: Registered at Greenock
under the ownership of the Nova Scotia,
Newfoundland and Bermuda Royal Mail
Steam Packet Company, Greenock.
22.7.1849: Wrecked on the Avalon
Peninsula, Newfoundland whilst on
a voyage from Halifax to St. John's,
Newfoundland with passengers and mail.
9.1849: Register closed.

MERLIN 1850-1868 Wooden screw
O.N. 35793
366g 249n
140.4 x 23.0 x 14.8 feet.
2-cyl engine; 110 HP.
1850: Launched by John Wood and Co.,
Port Glasgow as MERLIN.
4.5.1850: Registered at Greenock under
the ownership of the Nova Scotia,
Newfoundland and Bermuda Royal Mail
Steam Packet Company, Greenock.
11.1850: Placed on the New York-
Bermuda-St. Thomas mail service.
14.6.1853: Transferred to Samuel Cunard,
Halifax, Nova Scotia.
12.12.1853: Registered at Halifax, Nova
Scotia.
12.1853: Transferred to Halifax to
Bermuda mail service.
1854-1855: Chartered by the British
Government as a Crimean War transport.
11.1856: Replaced by DELTA.
28.4.1865: Transferred to William Cunard,
Halifax and Edward Cunard, New York.
2.12.1868: Registered under the ownership
of W.H. Mare, St. John's, Newfoundland.
20.5.1871: Registered under the ownership
of P. Cleary, St. John's, Newfoundland.
13.10.1875: Registered under the
ownership of A.M. McKay, St. John's,
Newfoundland.
28.10.1882: Lost at Burgeo,
Newfoundland whilst on a voyage from St.
John's to Burgeo in ballast.
2.4.1883: Register closed.

LEVANTINE 1851-1853 Iron screw
190n
122.5 x 23.3 x 13.4 feet.
2-cyl engine.
6.1846: Launched by Ditchburn and Mare,
Blackwall as LEVANTINE.
20.6.1846: Registered at London under the
ownership of A. Mongredien and others,
London.
1.8.1846: Sold to J. Cunliffe, S. Brooks
and A. Easterley, London.
1.11.1851: Registered at Greenock
under the ownership of the Nova Scotia,
Newfoundland and Bermuda Royal Mail
Steam Packet Company, Greenock.
4.1853: Withdrawn from service because
of mechanical problems.
9.11.1853: Registered at Glasgow under

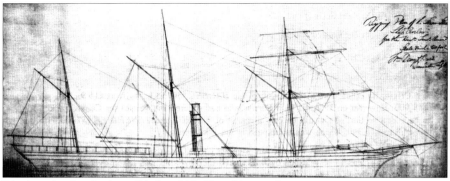

Rigging plan for *Curlew*. [National Maritime Museum]

the ownership of G. Coats, Glasgow.
15.2.1854: Register closed after being sold to
foreigners.

CURLEW 1853-1856 Iron barque rigged screw
O.N. 35848 528g 321n
128.6 x 24.2 x 14.2 feet.
2-cyl. geared engine by Tulloch and Denny,
Dumbarton.
14.9.1853: Launched by William Denny
and Brothers, Dumbarton (Yard No. 43) as
CURLEW, having been bought on the stocks.
25.11.1853: Registered at Halifax, Nova
Scotia under the ownership of Samuel
Cunard, Halifax, Nova Scotia.
12.1853: Replaced MERLIN on the New
York-Bermuda-St. Thomas mail service.
7.1854: Inaugurated the Halifax-Bermuda-St.
Thomas mail service with Halifax becoming
the northern terminus in place of New York.
1854-1855: Chartered by the British
Government as a Crimean War transport.
18.3.1856: Ran aground on a shoal near St.
George's, Bermuda whilst on a voyage from
Halifax to Bermuda, and was later declared a
constructive total loss.
1856: Register closed.

DELTA 1854-1899 Iron barque rigged screw
O.N. 1816 644g 428n
208.6 x 27.0 x 15.8 feet.
2-cyl engine; 120 HP; *1881*: C. 2-cyl by W.

King and Co., Glasgow; 120 HP.
8.1854: Launched by Robert Barclay and
Curle and Co., Stobcross, Glasgow (Yard No.
10) as DELTA.
13.10.1854: Registered at Glasgow under the
ownership of The British and North American
Royal Mail Steam Packet Company, Glasgow.
Placed on the Liverpool to Havre route.
11.1856: Transferred to the Halifax-Bermuda-
St. Thomas mail service.
7.1874: Replaced by BETA.
9.8.1875: Transferred to George Francklyn
(Samuel Cunard's grandson), Halifax, Nova
Scotia.
1881: Fitted with new compound engine.
29.8.1882: Registered at Halifax, Nova
Scotia.
16.9.1882: Registered at Glasgow.
20.9.1898: Registered at Halifax, Nova
Scotia.
13.9.1899: Wrecked at St. Mary's Bay,
Newfoundland whilst on a voyage from
Sydney, Nova Scotia to St. John's,
Newfoundland with a cargo of coal, and was
later declared a constructive total loss.
30.9.1899: Register closed.

ALPHA 1863-1888 Iron barque rigged screw
O.N. 45956 653g 514n
221.8 x 27.6 x 14.9 feet.
2-cyl engine; 112 HP; *1880*: C. 2-cyl by J.and
G. Thomson, Glasgow; 99 HP.
17.3.1863: Launched by Robert Barclay and

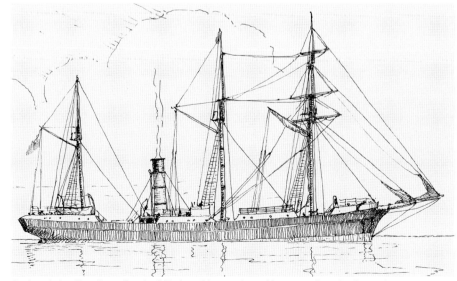

A sketch by Stephen Card of *Delta* with a reduced barquentine rig, based on a
contemporary painting.

Alpha (left) had a clipper bow whereas *Beta* (right) had a vertical stem and is shown at New York with bow damage on 4th April 1889. *[Maritime Museum of the Atlantic]*

Curle and Co., Stobcross, Glasgow (Yard No.102) as ALPHA.

14.4.1863: Registered at Glasgow under the ownership of Samuel Cunard, London.

25.6.1863: Maiden voyage Halifax-Bermuda-St. Thomas.

1880: Fitted with new compound engine.

4.1880: Kingston, Jamaica replaced St. Thomas as southern end of route with calls made subsequently at the Turks Islands.

3.6.1885: Management transferred to George Francklyn (Samuel Cunard's grandson).

7.1886: Cunard Halifax-Bermuda-West Indies mail contract cancelled

8.8.1888: Registered under the ownership of William Anderson Black (Pickford and Black), Halifax, Nova Scotia after he was awarded the Halifax-Bermuda-West Indies mail contract. She was subsequently placed on monthly Halifax to Bermuda and Turks Islands service.

1897: Transferred to Vancouver to carry freight and passengers during the Klondike gold rush.

11.4.1899: Registered at Vancouver under the ownership of Samuel Barber, Victoria, British Columbia.

15.12.1900: Wrecked in a gale at Yellow Rock (now known as Chrome Island), Gulf of Georgia, British Columbia whilst on a voyage from Vancouver to Yokohama with a cargo of salted salmon. Nine lives were lost including the owner, his brother and the captain.

15.12.1900: Register closed.

A scene at Bermuda, with a ship, believed to be *Beta*, in the background. *[Stephen Card collection]*

BETA 1874-1888 Iron barque rigged screw
O.N. 68072 1,087g 677n
235.1 x 28.5 x 14.7 feet.
C. 2-cyl by J.and G. Thomson Ltd., Clydebank; 160 HP: *1897*: T.3-cyl. by Barclay, Curle and Co. Ltd., Glasgow; 226 HP.

11.1873: Launched by Aitken and Mansell, Whiteinch (Yard No. 66) as BETA.

26.1.1874: Registered at Glasgow under the ownership of William Cunard, London.

4.1880: Kingston, Jamaica replaced St. Thomas as southern end of route with calls made subsequently at the Turks Islands.

3.6.1885: Management transferred to George Francklyn (Samuel Cunard's grandson).

7.1886: Cunard Halifax-Bermuda-West Indies mail contract cancelled

30.8.1888: Registered under the ownership of William Anderson Black (Pickford and Black), Halifax, Nova Scotia after he was awarded the Halifax-Bermuda-West Indies mail contract. She was subsequently placed on monthly Halifax to Bermuda and Turks Islands service.

1897: Fitted with a new triple expansion engine.

3.12.1898: Ownership restyled as the Halifax and West India Steamship Co. (Pickford and Black, managers), Halifax.

22.2.1908: Wrecked on the north east reef of the Grand Turk and Caicos Islands whilst on a voyage from Halifax to Jamaica, via Turks Islands, with general cargo and ten passengers. She was later declared a constructive total loss.

27.4.1908: Register closed.

WOERMANN LINE WAR PRIZE SHIPS

POLANDIA 1915-1916

O.N. 137441 2,238g 1,416n
290.4 x 38.2 x 23.6 feet.
T.3-cyl. by Blohm & Voss, Hamburg, Germany; 158 HP, 10 knots.
Passengers: 9; *1915*: Cargo only.
11.8.1898: Launched by Blohm & Voss, Hamburg (Yard No. 130) for Woermann Linie G.m.b.H., Hamburg as PAUL WOERMANN.
15.9.1898: Delivered for service between Hamburg and West Africa.
27.9.1914: Captured at Douala by the Royal Navy cruiser HMS CUMBERLAND and later handed over as a war prize to the Cunard Steam Ship Co. Ltd., Liverpool.
7.4.1915: Registered at Liverpool under the ownership of the Cunard Steam Ship Co. Ltd. (Crown nominees), Liverpool as POLANDIA.
27.9.1916: Transferred to Wm. Brown, Atkinson and Co. Ltd. (Crown nominees), Hull.
10.3.1917: Sailed from Birkenhead for Cherbourg with a cargo of government supplies but never arrived at Cherbourg, most likely because she struck a mine. 32 lives were lost.
8.5.1917: Register closed.

POLYMNIA 1915-1916

O.N. 137443 2,426g 1,530n
300.8 x 40.7 x 23.4 feet.
T.3-cyl. by Blohm & Voss, Hamburg, Germany; 157 HP, 10 knots.
Passengers: 9; *1915*: Cargo only.
25.4.1903: Launched by Blohm & Voss, Hamburg (Yard No. 166) for Woermann-Linie K.G., Hamburg as HENRIETTE WOERMANN.
28.5.1903: Delivered for service between Hamburg and West Africa.
27.9.1914: Captured at Douala by the Royal Navy cruiser HMS CUMBERLAND and handed over as a war prize to the Cunard Steam Ship Co. Ltd., Liverpool.
9.4.1915: Registered at Liverpool under the ownership of the Cunard Steam Ship Co. Ltd. (Crown nominees), Liverpool as POLYMNIA.
27.9.1916: Transferred to Kaye, Son and Co. Ltd. (Crown nominees), London.
18.10.1916: Registered at London.
15.5.1917: Torpedoed and sunk by the German submarine UC 75 fifteen miles west of the Lizard, Cornwall in position 49°54′N, 05°34′W whilst on a voyage

Paul Woermann was renamed *Polandia*. [Martin Lindenborn collection]

Huelva-Lisbon-Falmouth with a cargo of iron ore and fruit. Eight members of the crew were lost.
7.6.1917: Register closed.

POLLENTIA 1915-1916

O.N. 137444 2,229g 1,412n
290.7 x 38.1 x 23.4 feet.
T.3-cyl. by Blohm & Voss, Hamburg, Germany; 157 HP, 10 knots.
Passengers: 9; *1915*: Cargo only.
9.9.1893: Launched by Blohm & Voss, Hamburg (Yard No. 99) for Die Africanische Dampfschiffs-A.G. (Woermann-Linie), Hamburg as JEANNETTE WOERMANN.
11.10.1893: Delivered for service between Hamburg and West Africa.
5.4.1895: Owner's name altered to Woermann Linie G.m.b.H.
27.9.1914: Captured at Douala by the Royal Navy cruiser HMS CUMBERLAND. Handed over as a war prize to Cunard Steam Ship Co. Ltd., Liverpool.
9.4.1915: Registered at Liverpool under the ownership of the Cunard Steam Ship Co. Ltd. (Crown nominees), Liverpool as POLLENTIA.
23.1.1916: Sank in position 46°52′N, 28°33′W whilst on a voyage from Liverpool to Halifax in ballast, her crew was rescued by the Italian steamer GIUSEPPE VERDI (9,757/1915).
15.2.1916: Register closed.

Jeannette Woermann was one of four Woermann Line ships captured as war prizes at Douala and managed by Cunard on behalf of the Crown between 1915 and 1916. She was renamed *Pollentia*. [Martin Lindenborn collection]

POLITANIA 1915-1916

O.N. 137446 3,133g 1,845n
331.4 x 44.7 x 22.8 feet.
Q.4-cyl. by Reiherstiegwerft Schiffswerft, Hamburg, Germany; 249 HP, 10 knots.
Passengers: 9; *1915*: Cargo only.
18.5.1910: Launched by Reiherstiegwerft Schiffswerft, Hamburg (Yard No. 429) for Woermann-Linie K.G., Hamburg as ALINE WOERMANN.
23.7.1910: Delivered for service between Hamburg and West Africa.
27.9.1914: Captured at Douala by the Royal Navy cruiser HMS CUMBERLAND. Handed over as war prize to Cunard Steam Ship Co. Ltd.
14.4.1915: Registered at Liverpool under the ownership of the Cunard Steam Ship Co. Ltd. (Crown nominees), Liverpool and renamed POLITANIA.
27.9.1916: Transferred to Raeburn and Verel Ltd. (Crown nominees), Glasgow and later registered at Glasgow.
18.8.1917: Torpedoed and sunk by the German submarine UC 67 ten miles west of Cape Sigli, Algeria in position 36°56′N, 04°38′E whilst on a voyage from Tarragona to Salonica with a cargo of hay.
31.8.1917: Register closed.

UNITED STATES WARTIME STANDARD SHIPS

WAR MONARCH 1917-1918

O.N. 140361 7,887g 6,104n
410.0 x 56.0 x 29.0 feet.
Geared Steam turbines by General Electric Co., Schenectady, New York, U.S.A.; 2,500 IHP, 10.5 knots.
16.5.1917: Launched by Union Iron Works Co., Alameda, California, U.S.A. (Yard No. 133) as WAR MONARCH for The Shipping Controller, London.
17.7.1917: Completed.
29.9.1917: Registered at London under the ownership of The Shipping Controller, London.
10.7.1917-14.2.1918: Managed by the Cunard Steam Ship Co. Ltd., Liverpool.
14.2.1918: Torpedoed and sunk by the German submarine UB 57 eleven miles east of the Royal Sovereign Light Vessel (near Eastbourne, Sussex) in position 50°46′N, 00°43′E whilst on a voyage from Hull to Italy with a cargo of coal.
19.3.1918: Register closed.

WAR BARON 1917-1918

O.N. 140402 6,239g 4,677n
410.0 x 54.0 x 27.0 feet.
Geared steam turbines by General Electric Co., Schenectady, New York, U.S.A.; 2,500 IHP, 10.5 knots.
1917: Launched by Northwest Steel Co., Portland, Oregon, U.S.A. (Yard No. 1) as WAR BARON for The Shipping Controller, London.
3.8.1917: Requisitioned by the U.S. Shipping Board but subsequently released.
17.9.1917: Completed.

Aline Woermann became *Politania*. All the ex-Woermann ships were sunk by submarines in 1916 and 1917. *[Martin Lindenborn collection]*

1.11.1917: Registered at London under the ownership of The Shipping Controller, London.
21.7.1917-5.1.1918: Managed by the Cunard Steam Ship Co. Ltd., Liverpool.
5.1.1918: Torpedoed and sunk by the German submarine U 55 eight miles north east of Godrevy Lighthouse, St. Ives Bay, Cornwall in position 50°18′N, 05°35′W whilst on a voyage from Southampton to Barry Roads in ballast. Two of her crew were lost.
15.2.1918: Register closed.

WAR SWORD 1917-1919

O.N. 140413 7,950g 6,134n
410.0 x 56.0 x 29.0 feet.
T.3-cyl. by Union Iron Works Co., San Francisco, California, U.S.A.; 2,700 IHP, 10.5 knots.
Passengers: Cargo only; *1929*: 17 first, 200 third.
7.7.1917: Launched by Union Iron Works Co., Alameda, California, U.S.A. (Yard No. 142) as WAR SWORD for The Shipping Controller, London.
3.8.1917: Requisitioned by the U.S. Shipping Board but subsequently released.
14.11.1917: Registered at London under the ownership of The Shipping Controller, London.

28.8.1917-6.6.1919: Managed by the Cunard Steam Ship Co. Ltd., Liverpool.
22.7.1919: Acquired by Navigazione Generale Italiana, Genoa, Italy and later renamed CAPRERA.
24.7.1919: British register closed.
6.1929: Emigrant passenger accommodation fitted.
2.1.1932: Transferred to Italia Flotte Riunite, Genoa.
1.6.1932: Ran aground off Ilha do Pai, 15 miles north of Rio de Janeiro, and was later refloated.
1.8.1932: Arrived at Rio de Janeiro under tow.
11.2.1933: Sold to Pedro Luis Corrado e Castro, Rio de Janeiro and laid up in Rio de Janeiro.
1933: Sold to Pedro Brandão.
1940: Repaired. Passenger accommodation removed.
1941: Renamed ARABUTAN (Lloyd Nacional S.A., Rio de Janeiro, Brazil, managers).
7.3.1942: Torpedoed and sunk by the German submarine U 155, seventy miles from Newport News, Virginia in position 35°15′N, 73°55′W whilst on a voyage from New York and Hampton Roads to Rio de Janeiro via Trinidad with a cargo of coal and coke. One crew member was lost.

Two of the *War* ships survived the conflict, including *War Sword*, which was sold to Navigazione Generale Italiana. As *Caprera*, shown here at Montevideo in 1932, she became an emigrant ship. *[Raul Maya/W.A.Schell collection]*

WAR VICEROY 1917-1919
O.N. 142311 5,764g 4,226n
410.0 x 54.2 x 27.5 feet.
Geared steam turbines by General
Electric Company, Schenectady, New
York, U.S.A.; 2,500 IHP, 10.5 knots;
1925: 4-cyl 2SCSA oil engine by
FIAT, Turin, Italy; 2,800 BHP, 13
knots.
3.8.1917: Requisitioned by the U.S.
Shipping Board but subsequently
released.
9.1917: Launched by Northwest
Steel Company, Portland, Oregon,
U.S.A. (Yard No. 2) for The Shipping
Controller, London as WAR VICEROY.
17.10.1917: Completed.
22.2.1918: Registered at London under
the ownership of the The Shipping
Controller, London.
25.10.1917-16.2.1919: Managed
by the Cunard Steam Ship Co. Ltd.,
Liverpool.
16.4.1919: Acquired by Transoceanica
Società Italiana di Navigazione,
Naples, Italy and later renamed
VOLTURNO.
4.11.1919: British register closed.
20.8.1921: Transferred to Navigazione
Generale Italiana, Naples.
22.1.1925: Sold to Società
Commerciale di Navigazione (Tito
Campanella fu Pietro), Genoa, Italy.
This company was established by
Senator Giovanni Agnelli, owner of
the Italian car and motor company
FIAT, to promote the use of FIAT
marine oil engines
1925: New FIAT oil engine fitted.
3.4.1928: Sold to Angelo De Negri fu
Filippo, Genoa.
1932: Laid up in Genoa.
13.6.1933: Sold to Luigi Pittaluga
Vapori for demolition at Vado Ligure,
Italy.

War Viceroy was also purchased by Italian buyers and was renamed *Volturno*, seen here at Genoa. She was converted to a motor ship in 1925. *[Robert Moffatt Scott/W.A.Schell collection]*

RUSSIAN EAST ASIATIC QUARTET

DWINSK 1917-1918 Twin screw
O.N. 142312 8,173g 5,147n
469.5 x 53.1 x 22.3 feet.
Two T. 3-cyl by Harland and Wolff Ltd.,
Belfast; 954 HP, 14 knots.
Passengers: *1897*: 212 first, 112 second, 837
third; *later* 191 first, 90 second, 610 third.
18.2.1897: Launched by Harland and
Wolff Ltd., Belfast (Yard No. 312) for N.V.
Nederlandsche-Amerikaansche Stoomvaart
Maatschappij (Holland-Amerika Lijn),
Rotterdam, Netherlands as ROTTERDAM.
18.8.1898: Maiden voyage from Rotterdam to
New York.
5.4.1906: Sold to Det Forenede
Dampskibsselskab (DFDS), Copenhagen,
Denmark and later renamed C.F. TIETGEN.
16.12.1913: Sold to the Russian East Asiatic
Steam Ship Co. Ltd., St. Petersburg (A/S Det

Østasiatiske Kompagni, Copenhagen) and later
renamed DWINSK, she was placed on the
Libau (Latvia) to New York service.
28.12.1917: Chartered as an Expeditionary
Forces transport by The Shipping Controller,
London (Cunard Steam Ship Co. Ltd.,
Liverpool, managers).
21.2.1918: Requisitioned by the British
Government.
23.2.1918: Registered at London under the
ownership of the The Shipping Controller,
London.
18.6.1918: Torpedoed and sunk by the German
submarine U 151 about 400 miles north east of
Bermuda in position 39°10′N, 63°01′W whilst
on a voyage from Brest to Newport News. A
total of 24 lives were lost, due to accidents in
lifeboats, including one lifeboat with 22 men
aboard which was never found.
2.10.1918: Register closed.

Dwinsk was the only one of the four Russian East Asiatic liners to be sunk during the war.

KURSK 1917-1920 Twin screw

O.N. 142313 7,869g 4,637n
450.0 x 56.2 x 31.3 feet.
Two Q.4-cyl. by Barclay Curle and Co.
Ltd., Whiteinch; 1,020 HP, 15 knots.
Passengers: 120 first, 178 second, 1,268
third; *1921*: 300 cabin, 500 third.
7.7.1910: Launched by Barclay, Curle and
Co. Ltd., Whiteinch (Yard No. 482) for
the Russian East Asiatic Steam Ship Co.
Ltd., St. Petersburg (A/S Det Østasiatiske
Kompagni, Copenhagen, Denmark) as
KURSK.
2.11.1910: Maiden voyage from Libau
(Latvia) to New York.
31.12.1917: Chartered as a transport
by The Shipping Controller, London
(Cunard Steam Ship Co. Ltd., Liverpool,
managers).
31.12.1917-6.2.1918: Carried Chinese
coolies.
7.2.1918-17.6.1920: Carried Expeditionary
Forces.
21.2.1918: Requisitioned by the British
Government.
23.2.1918: Registered at London under
the ownership of The Shipping Controller,
London.
1920: Returned to A/S Det Østasiatiske
Kompagni, Copenhagen and renamed
POLONIA.
11.8.1920: British register closed.
1930: Sold to the Polish Transatlantic
Shipping Co. Ltd. (Gydnia-Amerika Line),
Gydnia, Poland.
1933: Transferred to the Constanza to
Haifa service (Palestine Line) after the
Nazi Government came to power in
Germany.
1934: Owners became Gydnia-America
Shipping Lines Ltd.
5.3.1939: Arrived at Savona for
demolition.

Top: The remaining Russian East Asiatic ships, including *Kursk*, operated in Cunard colours after the war.
Above: *Kursk* as a troopship.

Polonia in Gydnia-America colours. *[J. and M. Clarkson collection]*

CZAR 1918-1920 Twin screw

O.N. 142324 6,516g 3,812n
425.0 x 53.2 x 29.4 feet.
Two Q.4-cyl. by Barclay Curle and Co. Ltd., Whiteinch, Glasgow; 889 HP, 15.5 knots.
Passengers: 30 first, 260 second, 1,086 steerage; *1921*: 300 cabin, 500 third.
23.3.1912: Launched by Barclay, Curle and Co. Ltd., Whiteinch (Yard No. 494) for the Russian East Asiatic Steam Ship Co. Ltd., St. Petersburg (A/S Det Østasiatiske Kompagni, Copenhagen, Denmark) as CZAR.
30.5.1912: Maiden voyage from Libau to New York.
31.12.1917: Chartered as a transport by The Shipping Controller, London (Ellerman's Wilson Line Ltd., Hull, managers).
1918: Cunard Steam Ship Co. Ltd., Liverpool became managers until *8.8.1920*.
8.3.1918: Requisitioned by the British Government.
13.3.1918: Registered at London under the ownership of The Shipping Controller, London.
21.9.1920: Returned to A/S Det Østasiatiske Kompagni, Copenhagen.
1920: British register closed.
1921: Renamed ESTONIA.
1930: Sold to the Polish Transatlantic Shipping Co. Ltd. (Gydnia-Amerika Line), Gydnia, Poland and renamed PULASKI.
1934: Owners became Gydnia-America Shipping Lines Ltd.
14.8.1940: Chartered by the Ministry of War Transport, London as a troopship with Lamport and Holt Line Ltd., Liverpool, managers, she retained her Polish crew and carried a British liaison officer.
3.4.1946: Sold to the Ministry of Transport, London (Lamport and Holt Line Ltd., Liverpool, managers) and later renamed EMPIRE PENRHYN.
19.2.1949: Arrived at Blyth for demolition by Hughes, Bolckow Shipbreaking Co. Ltd.

Czar (above) and *Czaritza* were also requisitioned by the British Government during the Second World War.

CZARITZA 1918-1920 Twin screw

O.N. 142335 6,598g 4,119n
440.0 x 53.4 x 29.3 feet.
Two Q.4-cyl. by Barclay Curle and Co. Ltd., Whiteinch, Glasgow; 889 HP, 15.5 knots.
Passengers: 30 first, 242 second, 712 steerage; *1924*: 290 cabin, 500 third.
15.2.1915: Launched by Barclay, Curle and Co. Ltd., Whiteinch (Yard No. 512) for the Russian East Asiatic Steam Ship Co. Ltd., St. Petersburg (A/S Det Østasiatiske Kompagni, Copenhagen, Denmark) as CZARITZA.
6.5.1915: Maiden voyage from Glasgow to New York.
27.12.1917: Chartered as a transport by The Shipping Controller, London (Ellerman's Wilson Line Ltd., Hull, managers).
1918: Cunard Steam Ship Co. Ltd., Liverpool became managers until *23.7.1920*.
16.3.1918: Requisitioned by the British Government.
20.3.1918: Registered at London under the ownership of The Shipping Controller, London.
21.7.1920: Returned to A/S Det Østasiatiske Kompagni, Copenhagen.

1920: British register closed.
1921: Renamed LITUANIA.
1930: Sold to the Polish Transatlantic Shipping Co. Ltd. (Gydnia-Amerika Line), Gydnia, Poland and renamed KOSCIUSZKO.
1934: Owners became Gydnia-America Shipping Lines Ltd.
Late 1930s: Operated with POLONIA (ex KURSK) on the Constanza to Haifa service (Palestine Line).
10.11.1939: Requisitioned by the Polish Navy and used as a depot and accommodation ship at Devonport and renamed GDYNIA.
7.7.1941: Chartered by the Ministry of War Transport, London as a troopship with Lamport and Holt Line Ltd., Liverpool, managers, she retained her Polish crew, carried a British liaison officer and reverted to KOSCIUSZKO.
3.4.1946: Acquired by the Ministry of Transport, London (Lamport and Holt Line Ltd., Liverpool, managers), later renamed EMPIRE HELFORD and used as a troopship between Calcutta and Rangoon.
31.5.1950: Arrived under tow at Blyth for breaking up by Hughes, Bolckow Shipbreaking Co. Ltd.

Czaritza in Cunard colours.

Czaritza as Empire Helford on the landing stage at Liverpool on 28th August 1947. Astern of her is the troopship Empress of Australia (21,860/1913) completed as the Tirpitz for the Hamburg-Amerika Line. Renamed Empress of China in 1921 she was given the name Empress of Australia in 1922 following a major refit on the Clyde. In the second picture Empire Helford looks very much the worse for wear when laid-up in the Holy Loch on 2nd January 1950. Five months later she was delivered to the breakers at Blyth.

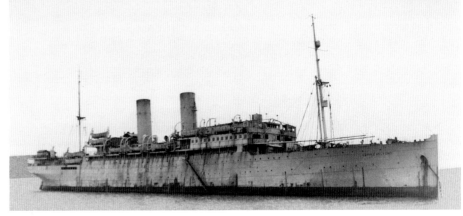

POST-WAR REPARATIONS SHIPS

ANSWALD 1919-1921
O.N. 144303 5,400g 3,435n
419.7 x 54.5 x 27.9 feet.
Q.4-cyl. by Bremer Vulkan Schiffbau & Maschinenfabrik, Vegesack, Germany; 376 HP, 11 knots.
Passengers: 5.
25.9.1909: Launched by Bremer Vulkan Schiffbau & Maschinenfabrik, Vegesack (Yard No. 520) for Hamburg-Bremer Afrika Linie A.G., Bremen, Germany as ANSWALD.
8.12.1909: Delivered.
19.8.1914: Requisitioned by the Imperial German Navy and converted to a sea plane carrier with hanger facilities constructed on deck.
17.7.1915: Commissioned as F.S.I.
15.1.1919: Released to her owners.
15.12.1919: Handed over on reparations account to The Shipping Controller and used to carry Turkish prisoners-of-war and native troops.

29.12.1919: Registered at London under the ownership of The Shipping Controller, London (Cunard Steam Ship Co. Ltd., Liverpool, managers).
7.10.1921: Registered at Bideford under the ownership of the St. Just Steamship Co. Ltd. (Sir William Reardon Smith and Sons Ltd.), Cardiff and later renamed VULCAN CITY.
24.7.1933: Arrived at Blyth for demolition by Hughes, Bolckow Shipbreaking Co. Ltd.
27.7.1933: Register closed.

SANTA ELENA 1919-1920
O.N. 143852 7,415g 4,732n
434.4 x 54.9 x 28.9 feet.
Q.4-cyl. by Blohm & Voss, Hamburg, Germany; 385 HP, 10 knots.
Passengers: 1,198 steerage.
16.11.1907: Launched by Blohm & Voss, Hamburg, Germany (Yard No. 196) for Hamburg-Südamerikanische D.G., Hamburg as SANTA ELENA.
21.12.1907: Delivered.
23.8.1914: Requisitioned by the Imperial German Navy and converted to a seaplane

carrier with hanger facilities constructed on deck
2.7.1915: Commissioned as F.S.II.
18.1.1919: Released to her owners.
26.4.1919: Delivered by a German crew to the U.S. Navy at Brest and commissioned as a troopship in the Cruiser-Transport Force, U.S. Atlantic Fleet and made two voyages carrying returning U.S. troops.
20.8.1919: Delivered to The Shipping Controller at New York and subsequently commenced service as an Expeditionary Force troopship under Cunard Steamship Co. Ltd., Liverpool, management.
19.11.1919: Registered at London under the ownership of The Shipping Controller, London (Cunard Steam Ship Co. Ltd., Liverpool, managers).
9.1.1920: Allocated to the French Government.
1920: British Register closed
2.1922: Sold to Cie. Française de Navigation à Vapeur Chargeurs Réunis, Havre, France and renamed LINOIS.
22.12.1942: Requisitioned at Marseilles

by Germany under the terms of the
Kaufmann-Laval Accord and later handed
over to Italy and renamed ORVIETO.
9.1943: Fell into German hands at
Genoa after the surrender of Italy and
after she was nominally incorporated
in the German Mittelmeer Reederei
G.m.b.H., Berlin, and her name reverted
to LINOIS.
15.2.1944: Returned to the French
flag as the German forces in the
Mediterranean had little use for large
merchant vessels.
20.6.1944: Requisitioned at Marseilles
by Germany for use as a blockship.
22.8.1944: Scuttled as a blockship at
Marseilles.
1945: Raised during port clearance and
broken up.

KAISERIN AUGUSTE VICTORIA
1920-1921 Twin screw
O.N. 144375 24,581g 14,857n
677.5 x 77.3 x 50.2 feet.
Two Q.4-cyl. by A.G. 'Vulcan', Stettin,
Germany; 17,500 IHP, 17.5 knots.
Passengers: 652 first, 286 second, 216
third, 1,842 steerage; *1921*: 459 first, 478
second, 536 third.
29.8.1905: Launched by A.G. 'Vulcan',
Stettin (Yard No. 264) for Hamburg-
Amerika Linie A.G., Hamburg, Germany
as KAISERIN AUGUSTE VICTORIA.
10.5.1906: Maiden voyage from
Hamburg to New York.
1.8.1914: Laid up in Hamburg.
27.3.1919: Handed over to U.S. Navy at
Cowes Roads and commissioned in the
Cruiser-Transport Force, U.S. Atlantic
Fleet
8.4.1919: Sailed from Brest on the first of
five voyages carrying returning American
troops.
21.8.1919: Arrived at New York on her
final voyage as a naval transport and
handed over the following day to the U.S.
Shipping Board.
23.12.1919: Formally decommissioned
by the U.S. Navy and subsequently
delivered at New York to The Shipping
Controller.
7.2.1920: Registered at London under the
ownership of The Shipping Controller,
London (Cunard Steam Ship Co. Ltd.,
Liverpool, managers).
13.5.1921: Acquired by the Canadian
Pacific Railway Co. (Canadian Pacific
Steamships Ltd.), London and later
renamed EMPRESS OF SCOTLAND.
4.12.1930: Arrived at Blyth for
demolition by Hughes, Bolckow
Shipbreaking Co. Ltd.
10.12.1930: Caught fire and sank.
5.1931: Wreck raised and broken up.

IMPERATOR 1919-1921 Quadruple
screw
See BERENGARIA page 62.
1919-1921: Managed by Cunard Steam
Ship Co. Ltd., Liverpool

Answald as *Vulcan City*.

In 1922 *Santa Elena* was sold to Chargeurs Réunis and renamed *Linois*. [*J. and M. Clarkson collection*]

Kaiserin Auguste Victoria before the outbreak of the First World War.

SHIPS MANAGED FOR THE MINISTRY OF (WAR) TRANSPORT OR SHIPPING 1940-1951

Dates under Cunard Line management are shown immediately after name

SINBAD/EMPIRE AUDACITY 1940-1941

O.N. 156145 5,925g 3,349n; *1941*: 10,231 displacement tons
450.3 x 56.3 x 23.1 feet; *1941*: 434.9 x 56.0 x 21.7 feet.
7-cyl 2SCDA oil engine by MAN-Vulkan, Vegesack; 5,200 BHP, 15 knots.
Passengers: 28
29.3.1939: Launched by Bremer Vulkan A.G., Vegesack, Germany (Yard No. 765) for Norddeutscher Lloyd, Bremen, Germany as HANNOVER.
8.3.1940: Intercepted and captured as a war prize in Mona Passage (between the islands of Hispaniola and Puerto Rico) by the Canadian destroyer HMCS ASSINIBOINE and the light cruiser HMS DUNEDIN whilst attempting to return to Germany from Willemstad, Curaçao. Crew had set fire to the ship and abandoned her.
13.3.1940: Arrived at Kingston, Jamaica.
26.4.1940: Released by the Supreme Court, Jamaica for use by the Crown.
3.5.1940: Registered at Kingston under the ownership of the Ministry of Shipping, London (Cunard White Star Line Ltd., Liverpool, managers) as SINBAD.
2.7.1940: Arrived at London.
22.7.1940: Registered at London as EMPIRE AUDACITY.
11.11.1940: Arrived at Blyth for conversion into the Royal Navy's first escort aircraft carrier by Blyth Dry Docks and Shipbuilding Co. Ltd., Blyth.
17.6.1941: Commissioned as HMS EMPIRE AUDACITY.
31.7.1941: Renamed HMS AUDACITY.
21.12.1941: Torpedoed and sunk by the German submarine U 751, 500 miles west of Cape Finisterre, Spain in position 43°55′N, 19°54′W. 73 lives were lost, including her master.
26.6.1944: Register closed.

PASTEUR 1940-1946 Quadruple screw

O.N 166305 29,523g 12,894n;
1959: 32,336g 17,025n
670.0 x 88.0 x 26.8 feet.
Four sets of geared steam turbines by Chantiers et Ateliers de St. Nazaire (Penhoët), St. Nazaire, France; 60,000 SHP, 25.6 knots.
Passengers: 287 first, 126 second, 338 third; *1959*: 216 first, 906 tourist.
15.2.1938: Launched by Chantiers et Ateliers de St. Nazaire (Penhoët), St. Nazaire (Yard No. R8) for Cie. de Navigation Sud Atlantique, Paris, France as PASTEUR.
25.8.1939: Sailed from Havre, where she had been preparing for her maiden voyage, for Brest but because of the crisis caused by German demands against Poland, her

maiden voyage from Bordeaux to Buenos Aires was deferred and, after the outbreak of war, was cancelled.
3.9.1939: Shifted to moorings at Landévennec in the inner end of the Rade de Brest.
2.6.1940: First voyage from Brest to Halifax with French gold reserve.
18.7.1940: Detained at Halifax after the fall of France.
9.8.1940: Requisitioned by the British Government.
6.9.1940: Arrived at Liverpool.
26.10.1940: Registered at Liverpool under the ownership of the Ministry of Shipping, London (Cunard White Star Line Ltd., Liverpool, managers) having been fitted out as a troopship by Cammell Laird and Co. Ltd., Birkenhead and given four-inch guns fore and aft plus two anti-aircraft guns.
30.10.1940: Sailed from Liverpool for Gibraltar via the Clyde with troops.
5.1941: Ministry of Shipping merged with the Ministry of Transport to become the Ministry of War Transport.
23.10.1945: Returned to the French flag but remained under British operational control.
6.3.1946: Released from war service.
11.4.1946: Returned to French Government control, managed by Cie. de Navigation Sud Atlantique and subsequently employed on trooping voyages, principally to French Indo-China.
2.5.1946: British register closed.
7.1956: Laid up at Brest and later used as

transport for French troops occupying the Suez Canal zone.
1.1957: Laid up at Landévennec.
18.9.1957: Sold to Norddeutscher Lloyd, Bremen.
26.9.1957: Left Brest under tow.
8.1.1958 to 6.1959: Rebuilt by Bremer Vulkan A.G., Bremen-Vegesack, renamed BREMEN and registered to Bremer Nordatlantikdienst G.m.b.H., Bremen, Germany.
9.7.1959: First voyage from Bremerhaven to New York.
1965: Transferred to Norddeutscher Lloyd, Bremen.
1.9.1970: Owner becomes Hapag-Lloyd A.G.
10.1971: Sold to International Cruises S.A., (Dimitrios J. Chandris), Piraeus, Greece.
19.1.1972: Delivered to Chandris and later renamed REGINA MAGNA and used as a cruise ship.
17.10.1974: Laid up at Eleusis, having been transferred to Armadores Regina Magna S.A. (Dimitrios J. Chandris), Piraeus.
1977: Sold to Philippine Singapore Ports Corporation, Manila, Philippines and renamed SAUDI PHIL 1 and used as an accommodation ship for workers at Jeddah, Saudi Arabia.
9.6.1980: Capsized and sank in the Indian Ocean about 400 miles south east of Socotra in position 07°35′N, 60°12′E, whilst under tow from Jeddah to Taiwan for demolition as SAUDI FILIPINAS 1.

Above and opposite page, top: *Pasteur* arriving at Cape Town on 16th April 1941 with troops bound for the Middle East. *[John Marsh]*

Below: The French liner *Pasteur* spent almost half of her career as a troopship. During her six years under Cunard White Star management, she carried many thousands of troops around the world.

EMPIRE BARRACUDA* 1941
O.N. 168073 5,735g 3,495n
391.9 x 54.2 x 28.0 feet.
Geared steam turbines by General Electric Company, Schenectady, New York, U.S.A.; 600 HP, 11.5 knots; *1932*: 13.5 knots.
29.10.1918: Launched by American International Shipbuilding Corporation, Hog Island, Philadelphia, U.S.A. (Yard No. 1494) as SACANDAGA, a U.S. Hog Island standard type design No. 1022.
22.1.1919: Delivered to the United States Shipping Board, registered at Philadelphia and allocated to Wessel, Duval and Co., New York. Following the establishment of regular services by the Shipping Board, she was subsequently placed on the American Diamond Lines' routes managed by the Black Diamond Steamship Corporation, New York.
9.1931: Acquired by American Diamond Lines Inc., New York.
1932: Rebuilding at the Federal Shipbuilding Company, Kearny, New Jersey, U.S.A. included altering the form of her stern, fitting a new rudder and propellor and modifying her engines to improve her performance. Renamed BLACK HERON, she was used on the U.S. east coast to Rotterdam and Antwerp mail service.

1938: Owners restyled as Black Diamond Lines Inc.
27.2.1941: Registered at London under the ownership of the Ministry of Shipping, London (Cunard White Star Line Ltd., Liverpool, managers) as EMPIRE BARRACUDA.
11.3.1941: Left Liverpool for Corpus Christi, Texas to load steel and scrap.
5.1941: Ministry of Shipping merged with the Ministry of Transport to become the Ministry of War Transport.
19.11.1941: Arrived at Gibraltar,

management transferred to Stanhope Steamship Co. Ltd., London.
15.12.1941: Torpedoed and sunk by the German submarine U 77, thirty four miles from Cape Trafalgar, Spain in position 35°30′N, 06°17′W whilst on a voyage Gibraltar-Cape Town-Suez with a cargo of naval and military stores, including munitions. Nine crew members and four gunners lost their lives and the survivors were rescued by HMS COLTSFOOT and landed at Gibraltar.
16.1.1942: Register closed.

Empire Barracuda, shown here as *Black Heron*, was one of a pair of Hog Island-type freighters bought from Black Diamond Lines. *[W.A. Schell collection]*

EMPIRE HAWK* 1941-1942

O.N. 168078 5,590g 3,453n
391.9 x 54.2 x 28.0 feet.
Geared steam turbines by General Electric
Company, Schenectady, New York, U.S.A.;
600 HP, 11.5 knots; *1932*: 13.5 knots.
8.10.1919: Launched by American
International Shipbuilding Corporation, Hog
Island, Philadelphia, U.S.A. (Yard No. 1489)
as COAHOMA COUNTY, a U.S. Hog Island
standard type design No. 1022. She had been
laid down as CLAUSTON.
20.11.1919: Delivered to the United States
Shipping Board, registered at Philadelphia
and allocated to the Mobile Oceanic Line,
managed by the Waterman Steamship
Corporation, Mobile, Alabama, U.S.A.
Following the establishment of regular
services by the Shipping Board, she was
subsequently placed on the American
Diamond Lines' routes managed by the Black
Diamond Steamship Corporation, New York.
9.1931: Acquired by American Diamond
Lines Inc., New York.
1932: Rebuilding at the Federal Shipbuilding
Company, Kearny, New Jersey, U.S.A.
including altering the form of her stern, fitting
a new rudder and propellor and modifiying her
engines to improve her performance. Renamed
BLACK TERN, she was used on the U.S. east
coast to Rotterdam and Antwerp mail service.
1938: Owners restyled as Black Diamond
Lines Inc.
11.3.1941: Registered at London under the
ownership of the Ministry of Shipping,
London (Cunard White Star Line Ltd.,
Liverpool, managers) as EMPIRE HAWK.
24.3.1941: Left Liverpool for New Orleans to
load sulphur.
5.1941: Ministry of Shipping merged with the
Ministry of Transport to become the Ministry
of War Transport.
12.12.1942: Torpedoed, shelled and sunk by
Italian submarine ENRICO TAZZOLI off the
coast of Brazil in position 05°56′N, 39°50′W
whilst on a voyage New York-Trinidad-Cape
Town and Alexandria with a cargo of coal and
army transport material. Her crew of 45 and
six gunners were all saved.
7.1.1943: Register closed

* In November 1940, it was reported
that Black Diamond Lines had asked the
United States Maritime Commission for
permission to sell its fleet of eight ships (all
with BLACK names) to 'British concerns'
i.e. the Ministry of Shipping: six to Cunard
and two to Cairn Line. In the end, only
two ended up in Cunard management
(BLACK HERON and BLACK TERN)
and two under Cairn Line management
(BLACK CONDOR and BLACK
OSPREY). The remaining four were sold
for further trading under the U.S. flag.

EMPIRE PORPOISE 1941-1946

O.N. 168188 7,592g 4,847n
440.0 x 56.0 x 35.2 feet.
Geared steam turbines by General Electric
Co., Schenectady, New York, U.S.A.;

Empire Porpoise on 12th March 1942. *[Ian J. Farquhar collection]*

1927: Steam turbine and electric motor by
General Electric Company, Schenectady, New
York; 637 HP, 11 knots;
1941: T.3-cyl. by Badenhausen Company,
Boundbrook, New Jersey, U.S.A.; 561 HP, 9
knots
4.8.1918: Launched by Bethlehem
Shipbuilding Corporation Ltd., Alameda,
California, U.S.A. (Yard No. 165) as
INVINCIBLE, she had been ordered as WAR
ROCK for the British Shipping Controller.
17.10.1918: Delivered to United States
Shipping Board and registered at San
Francisco, she was later requisitioned by
the U.S. Navy as a transport in the Naval
Overseas Transportation Service.
15.4.1919: Decommisioned and returned to
the United States Shipping Board.
1921: Converted to turbo-electric machinery
and used on the American Pioneer Line (Gulf
Division) service, managed for the Shipping
Board by Tampa Inter-Ocean Steamship Co.,
New Orleans, U.S.A.
26.4.1932: Arrived at New Orleans with
engine trouble and subsequently laid up there.
1937: Transferred to the United States
Maritime Commission which had been formed
to replace the United States Shipping Board.
1938: Sold to National Bulk Carriers
Inc. (Daniel K. Ludwig), New York for
conversion to a tanker but remained laid up at
New Orleans.
2 to 4.1941: Reconditioned at Mobile, fitted
with an engine built in 1920.
12.6.1941: Registered at London under
the ownership of the Ministry of War
Transport, London (Cunard White Star Line
Ltd., Liverpool, managers) as EMPIRE
PORPOISE.
16.6.1941: Left Liverpool for Baltimore to
load steel and scrap.
1943-1945: Based in Indian Ocean.
28.12.1945: Left Port Said for Alexandria
following crankshaft renewal.
31.8.1946: Renamed CHRYSANTHEMUM
following sale to Marine Enterprises Ltd.,
(Lyras Brothers), London.
1950: Transferred to Compania Maritima
Neptuno S.A., Puerto Limon, Costa Rica and
renamed CHRYSS.
31.8.1950: British Register closed.
1952: Sold to the Israel America Line Ltd,

Haifa, Israel and renamed ATHLIT.
1.10.1954: Arrived at Trieste for demolition
at the San Rocco yard of Cantieri Riuniti
dell'Adriatico.

CUBA 1941-1945 Twin screw

O.N 171463 11,337g 6,326n
476.0 x 62.3 x 35.1 feet.
Two sets of geared steam turbines by Swan,
Hunter and Wigham Richardson Ltd.,
Newcastle-upon-Tyne; 9,000 SHP, 16 knots.
Passengers: 280 first, 50 second, 76 third, 680
steerage.
20.11.1922: Launched by Swan, Hunter and
Wigham Richardson Ltd., Wallsend (Yard
No. 1108) for Cie. Générale Transatlantique,
Paris, France as CUBA.
5.5.1923: Maiden voyage St. Nazaire-West
Indies-Vera Cruz.
24.10.1940: Intercepted west of the Canaries
by the armed merchant cruiser HMS
MORETON BAY whilst on a voyage from
Martinique to Casablanca. A prize crew
was placed aboard and she was brought to
Freetown for engine repairs.
2.6.1941: Sailed to Port of Spain, Trinidad
under Elder Dempster and Co. Ltd., Liverpool
management.
16.6.1941: Registered at Port of Spain
under the ownership of the Ministry of War
Transport, London (Cunard White Star Line
Ltd., Liverpool, managers).
24.6.1941: Arrived at Boston for conversion
to a troopship.
11.2.1942: Registered at Liverpool.
14.2.1942: Left Liverpool with troops for
South Africa. Subsequently used to West and
North Africa.
3.1944 to 10.1944: Used on U.S.-Caribbean
routes.
1.1.1945: Transferred to coastal convoys from
Southampton.
6.4.1945: Torpedoed and sunk by the German
submarine U 1195 south east of the Isle of
Wight in position 50°36′N, 00°57′W whilst
on a coastal convoy (VWP-16) from Havre
to Southampton,. One crew member died
and the survivors were picked up by the
Canadian frigate HMCS NENE and landed at
Portsmouth.
19.4.1945: Register closed

Cuba at Barbados.

CAP DES PALMES 1941
O.N. 159156 3,082g 2,608n
335.6 x 44.0 x 25.6 feet.
9-cyl. 2SCSA oil engine by Burmeister &
Wain, Copenhagen; 4,500 BHP, 15 knots.
Passengers: 12.
10.8.1935: Launched by Helsingørs
Jernskibsværft og Maskinbyggeri, Helsingør,
Denmark (Yard No. 229) for Cie. de
Navigation Fraissinet, Marseilles,
France as CAP DES PALMES.
2.9.1939: Requisitioned by
the French Navy for use as an
auxiliary cruiser but later released
to her owners.
9.11.1940: Captured off Libreville
by the Free French sloop
COMMANDANT DOMINÉ
during the takeover of Gabon
from the Vichy Government.
29.3.1941: Registered at
Hamilton, Bermuda under the
ownership of the Ministry of
Shipping, London (Cunard
White Star Line Ltd., Liverpool,
managers) and later in 1941 she
was handed to the Force Naval de
la France Libre (FNFL) for use as
a fast transport/auxiliary cruiser.
5.1943: Converted at San
Francisco into an auxiliary

merchant cruiser and based in New
Caledonia..
5.7.1946: Returned to her owners.
8.1948: Resumed commercial service after
refit at Toulon.
1957: Sold to Cie. Maritime des Agrumes
(Cie. de Navigation Fruitière, managers),
Nantes, France and renamed BANORA.
11.1962: Sold to Cie. Marocaine de

Navigation Fruitière, Casablanca, Morocco
and remained under Cie. de Navigation
Fruitière management.
18.11.1965: Sprang a leak in bad weather
in position 43°04′N, 09°23′W whilst on a
voyage from Casablanca to Hamburg with a
cargo of citrus fruit.
19.11.1965: Sank under tow off Punta del
Cuerno, near Cabo Villano, Spain.

Cap Des Palmes was managed only briefly by Cunard White Star.

269

Georgic at anchor in the River Mersey in May 1948.

GEORGIC 1943-1955: see page 140.
16.3.1943: Cunard White Star Ltd. appointed managers.
1.1.1950: Managers restyled as Cunard Steam-Ship Co. Ltd., Liverpool.
19.11.1955: Laid up at Liverpool.

LIBERTY SHIPS

SAMHOLT 1943-1947
O.N. 169673 7,219g 4,380n
422.8 x 57.0 x 34.8 feet.
T.3-cyl. by Joshua Hendy Iron Works, Sunnyvale, California, U.S.A.; 574 HP, 11 knots.
3.7.1943: Launched by California Shipbuilding Corporation, Los Angeles, California, U.S.A. (Yard No. 218) as JACOB RIIS, a Liberty-type wartime standard ship built for the United States War Shipping Administration.
17.7.1943: Completed as SAMHOLT in 37 days.
17.7.1943-15.7.1947: Bareboat chartered to the Ministry of War Transport, London (Cunard White Star Ltd., Liverpool, managers).

31.7.1943: Left on maiden voyage from Los Angeles to India.
13.12.1943: Registered at London under the ownership of the Ministry of War Transport, London (Cunard White Star Ltd., Liverpool, managers).*
30.7.1947: Returned to the United States Maritime Commission and later reverted to JACOB RIIS and was laid up in the James River Reserve Fleet.
1947: Register closed.
26.10.1959: Arrived at Baltimore for demolition by the Patapsco Scrap Company.

Cunard White Star managed eight Liberty ships, including *Samholt*, seen in the West India Dock, London on 13th June 1946.

SAMSON 1943-1948

O.N. 169667 7,219g 4,380n
422.8 x 57.0 x 34.8 feet.
T.3-cyl. by Joshua Hendy Iron Works, Sunnyvale, California, U.S.A.; 574 HP, 11 knots.
8.7.1943: Launched by California Shipbuilding Corporation, Los Angeles, California, U.S.A. (Yard No. 219) as JOHN J.INGALLS, a Liberty-type wartime standard ship built for the United States War Shipping Administration.
21.7.1943: Completed as SAMSON in 38 days.
21.7.1943-18.6.1948: Bareboat chartered to the Ministry of War Transport, London (Cunard White Star Ltd., Liverpool, managers).
3.8.1943: Left on maiden voyage from Los Angeles to India.
13.12.1943: Registered at London under the ownership of the Ministry of War Transport, (Cunard White Star Ltd., Liverpool, managers) London.*
1948: Returned to the United States Maritime Commission and later reverted to JOHN J. INGALLS and was laid up in the Reserve Fleet at Beaumont, Texas, U.S.A.
22.6.1948: Register closed.
7.3.1961: Arrived at Orange, Texas for demolition by the Southern Iron and Metal Company.

SAMARITAN 1943-1947: see

VANDALIA page 207.
23.7.1943-5.6.1947: Managed by Cunard White Star Ltd., Liverpool.

SAMSURF 1943-1947

O.N. 169639 7,219g 4,380n
422.8 x 57.0 x 34.8 feet.
T.3-cyl. by Joshua Hendy Iron Works,

Samson at Malta in 1947.

Sunnyvale, California, U.S.A.; 574 HP, 11 knots.
22.7.1943: Launched by California Shipbuilding Corporation, Los Angeles, California, U.S.A. (Yard No. 228) as CORNELIUS COLE, a Liberty-type wartime standard ship built for the United States War Shipping Administration.
5.8.1943: Completed as SAMSURF in 38 days.
5.8.1943-14.5.1948: Bareboat chartered to the Ministry of War Transport, London (Cunard White Star Ltd., Liverpool, managers).
16.8.1943: Left on maiden voyage from Los Angeles to India.
20.11.1943: Registered at London under the ownership of the Ministry of War Transport, London (Cunard White Star Ltd., Liverpool, managers).*
22.8.1947: Returned to the United States Maritime Commission and later reverted to CORNELIUS COLE and laid up.
24.5.1948: Register closed.
13.2.1961: Arrived at Mobile for demolition by Pinto Island Metal Company.

SAMBRE 1943-1947

O.N. 169638 7,219g 4,380n
422.8 x 57.0 x 34.8 feet.

T.3-cyl. by Willamette Iron and Steel Corporation, Portland, Oregon, U.S.A.; 574 HP, 11 knots.
28.7.1943: Launched by Permanente Metal Corporation (Shipyard No. 2), Richmond, California, U.S.A. (Yard No. 1717) as GEORGE INNESS, a Liberty-type wartime standard ship built for the United States War Shipping Administration.
9.8.1943: Completed as SAMBRE in 34 days.
9.8.1943-22.8.1947: Bareboat chartered to the Ministry of War Transport, London (Cunard White Star Ltd., Liverpool, managers).
27.8.1943: Left on maiden voyage from San Francisco to India.
10.11.1943: Registered at London under the ownership of the Ministry of War Transport, London (Cunard White Star Ltd., Liverpool, managers).*
22.8.1947: Returned to the United States Maritime Commission and later reverted to GEORGE INNESS and laid up in the James River Reserve Fleet.
1947: Register closed.
6.10.1959: Arrived at Baltimore, Maryland, U.S.A. for demolition by the Patapsco Scrap Company.

Sambre on the Thames off Gravesend on 7th June 1946.

SAMBO 1943

7,219g 4,380n

422.8 x 57.0 x 34.8 feet.

T.3-cyl. by Joshua Hendy Iron Works, Sunnyvale, California, U.S.A.; 574 HP, 11 knots.

29.7.1943: Launched by California Shipbuilding Corporation, Los Angeles, California, U.S.A. (Yard No. 232) as EDWIN JOSEPH O'HARA, a Liberty-type wartime standard ship built for the United States War Shipping Administration.

12.8.1943: Completed as SAMBO in 35 days and bareboat chartered to the Ministry of War Transport, London (Cunard White Star Line Ltd., Liverpool, managers). She was not registered at London as she sank before reaching the United Kingdom*.

12.8.1943-10.11.1943: Managed by Cunard White Star Ltd., Liverpool.

10.11.1943: Torpedoed and sunk by the Japanese submarine I-27 in the Red Sea, south east of Hodeidah, Yemen in position 12°28′N, 43°31′E whilst on her maiden voyage from Iquique, Peru via Wellington and Aden to Suez with a cargo of nitrates and general cargo. Three crew and nine gunners lost their lives.

SAMOUSE 1944-1947

O.N. 169799 7,219g 4,380n

422.8 x 57.0 x 34.8 feet.

T.3-cyl. by General Machinery Corporation, Hamilton, Ohio, U.S.A.; 574 HP, 11 knots.

17.1.1944: Launched by Bethlehem-Fairfield Shipyard Inc., Baltimore, Maryland, U.S.A. (Yard No. 2310) as SAMOUSE, a Liberty-type wartime standard ship built for the United States War Shipping Administration.

26.1.1944: Completed in 40 days.

26.1.1944-18.4.1947: Bareboat chartered to the Ministry of War Transport, London (Cunard White Star Ltd., Liverpool, managers).

19.2.1944: Left on maiden voyage from New York to Italy.

9.3.1944: Registered at London under the ownership of the Ministry of War Transport, London (Cunard White Star Ltd., Liverpool, managers).*

14.5.1947: Sold to Bank Line Ltd. (Andrew Weir and Co. Ltd.), London and renamed MARABANK.

1960: Sold to Bertorello Febo Amedeo Societa a.s., Genoa, Italy and renamed RUSCIN.

1960: British register closed.

1962: Transferred to Seatide Shipping Co., Monrovia, Liberia (Bertorello Febo Amedeo S.a.s., Genoa, managers) and renamed WHITEHORSE.

13.6.1969: Arrived at Split for demolition by Brodospas.

SAMFOYLE 1944-1947: see VARDULIA page 206.

31.3.1944-9.7.1947: Managed by Cunard White Star Ltd., Liverpool.

* In wartime, official numbers and registration documentation were only given once the ship had reached a British port.

Sambo on her maiden voyage at Wellington on 5th October 1943. Just over a month later she was sunk with the loss of twelve lives. *[Ian J.Farquhar collection]*

Samouse in London on 6th June 1946.

Marabank ex-*Samouse* leaving Cape Town.

Ile de France leaving Cape Town in November 1945. *[John Marsh]*

ILE DE FRANCE 1944-1946 Quadruple screw

O.N 173054 43,153g 21,968n; *1949*: 44,356g 21,494n
763.7 x 92.0 x 55.9 feet.
Four sets of geared steam turbines by Chantiers et Ateliers de Saint Nazaire (Penhoët), St. Nazaire, France; 60,000 SHP, 23.5 knots.
Passengers: 537 first, 603 second, 646 third; *1933*: 537 first, 408 second, 508 tourist; *1949*: 541 first, 577 cabin, 227 tourist.
14.3.1926: Launched by Chantiers et Ateliers de Saint Nazaire (Penhoët), St. Nazaire (Yard No. R5) for Cie. Générale Transatlantique, Paris, France as ILE DE FRANCE.
22.6.1927: Maiden voyage Havre-Plymouth-New York.
11.1932-4.1933: Refit of passenger accommodation.

9.9.1939: Arrived at New York and laid up.
1.5.1940: Sailed for Marseilles.
1.6.1940; Left Marseilles for Saigon via the Cape of Good Hope.
6.7.1940 : Detained at Singapore following the fall of France.
11.8.1940: Requisitioned by the British Government.
19.9.1940: Registered at Singapore under the ownership of the Ministry of Shipping (Peninsular and Oriental Steam Navigation Company, managers), London and later used as a troopship.
5.1941: Ministry of Shipping merged with the Ministry of Transport to become the Ministry of War Transport.
10.9.1943: Registered at London.
15.9.1944-2.3.1946: Managed by Cunard White Star Ltd., Liverpool.
22.9.1945: Returned to the French flag

although remained under British control and continued trooping to Canada and the U.S. but with a French crew.
7.11.1945-5.1.1946: Repatriated troops from Southampton to Bombay via Freetown, Cape Town, Durban and Mombasa.
2.3.1946: Returned to her owners.
15.3.1946: British register closed.
4.1947-7.1949: Rebuilt at St. Nazaire by Penhoët with her funnels reduced from three to two.
11.12.1958: Sold to Okadagumi and Co., Osaka, Japan for demolition.
26.2.1959: Sailed from Havre as FURANZU MARU.
9.4.1959: Arrived at Osaka and was later sunk and refloated for the movie 'The Last Voyage' before demolition began in the third quarter of 1959.

In dry dock at Southampton in February 1946 (left) and at St. Nazaire prior to her post-war refit (right).

Ville d'Oran as a troopship.

VILLE D'ORAN 1943-1946 Twin screw
10,172g 3,811n
461.9 x 63.2 x 38.6 feet.
Two sets of geared steam turbines by
Chantiers et Ateliers de Saint Nazaire
(Penhoët), St. Nazaire, France; 20,000 SHP,
22 knots.
Passengers: 160 first, 200 second, 175 third,
400 steerage; *1949*: 188 first, 376 tourist,
671 fourth.
6.10.1935: Launched by Société Provençale
de Constructions Navales, La Ciotat, France
(Yard No. 10) for the French Government,
Ministère de la Marine Marchande,
Marseilles, France (Cie. Générale
Transatlantique, Paris, managers) as VILLE
D'ORAN.
17.10.1936: Maiden voyage from Marseilles
to Oran.
9.1939: Fitted as an French Navy auxiliary
cruiser (Pendant No. X 05) with one of her
funnels removed.
30.6.1940: Released from naval duties.
5-8.1941: Operated on Marseilles to Algiers
service and was subsequently laid up.
1.1.1943: Arrived at Gibraltar following her
seizure by the the Allies after the invasion of
North Africa.
8.1.1943: Cunard White Star appointed
temporary managers.
26.1.1943: Arrived on the Clyde for repairs.
3.3.1943: Arrived at London for conversion
into a troopship.
13.3.1943: Cunard White Star Ltd., Liverpool
appointed managers following bareboat
charter to the Ministry of War Transport.
24.3.1943: Transferred to the British flag.
1.5.1943: Arrived at Taranto, Italy and
subsequently used as a Mediterranean
troopship, mainly in North Africa and Italy.
22.3.1946: Released from war service.
12.4.1946: Returned to her owners.
12.1948-6.1949: Underwent refit at La
Seyne, France.

22.6.1949: Returned to the Marseilles to
Algiers service.
18.6.1954: Acquired by Cie. Générale
Transatlantique, Paris.
1965: Sold to Aegean Steam Navigation,
(Typaldos Brothers Ltd.), Piraeus, Greece
and renamed MOUNT OLYMPUS.
15.12.1969: Arrived at Trieste for
demolition.

EMPIRE ETTRICK 1945-1946
O.N. 180678 4,622g 2,734n
401.9 x 55.7 x 21.3 feet.
Twin 6-cyl. 2SCSA oil engines by
Maschinenfabrik Augsburg-Nürnburg,
Augsburg, Germany; 885 HP, 14.3 knots.
29.8.1939: Launched by Deutsche Werft
A.G., Hamburg-Reiherstieg, Germany (Yard
No. 226) for the Deutsche Levante-Linie
G.m.b.H., Hamburg as BUKAREST.
1940-1945: Requisitioned by the German
Navy as a training ship for Luftwaffe
torpedo aircraft pilots.

21.8.1945: Allocated to the British
Government as a war prize.
12.9.1945: Registered at London under
the ownership of the Ministry of War
Transport, London (Cunard Steam Ship
Co. Ltd., Liverpool, managers) as EMPIRE
ETTRICK.
1946: Transferred to the Norwegian
Government, Oslo, Norway and renamed
BREMNES.
13.8.1946: British register closed.
1947: Sold to Det Bergenske D/S, Bergen,
Norway and renamed CLIO.
1963: Sold to Cia Panorea S.A. (M.A.
Karageorgis, manager) Piraeus, Greece and
renamed PANOREA.
1972: Sold to United Shipowners Ltd.,
Famagusta, Cyprus (Navarino Shipping
and Transport Co. Ltd., Piraeus). The name
CHARITY was reported, but this re-naming
was not completed.
22.9.1972: Arrived Kaohsiung, Taiwan for
demolition by Yu Kuo Steel Co. Ltd.

Clio ex *Empire Ettrick*. *[J. and M. Clarkson collection]*

LARGE INFANTRY LANDING SHIPS

EMPIRE BATTLEAXE 1943-1947

O.N. 169703 7,177g 4,138n
396.5 x 60.1 x 35.0 feet.
Geared steam turbines by Westinghouse Electric and Manufacturing Company, Essington, Pennsylvania, U.S.A.; 4,400 SHP, 14 knots.
Passengers: Over 1,000 troops.
12.7.1943: Launched by Consolidated Steel Corporation Ltd., Wilmington, California, U.S.A. (Yard No. 345) for the United States War Shipping Administration as CAPE BERKELEY. She had been ordered as a dry cargo vessel but was converted into a large infantry landing ship for British use.
10.1943: Completed as EMPIRE BATTLEAXE and bareboat charterered to the Ministry of War Transport, London.
25.10.1943-22.8.1947: Managed by Cunard White Star Ltd., Liverpool.
20.12.1943: Registered at London under the ownership of the Ministry of War Transport, London (Cunard White Star Ltd., Liverpool, managers) following her first arrival at a U.K. port.
26.7.1944: Transferred to the Royal Navy as HMS DONOVAN.
19.10.1945: Reverted to the Ministry of Transport, London (Cunard White Star Ltd., Liverpool, managers) as EMPIRE BATTLEAXE
28.6.1947: Returned to the United States Maritime Commission and laid up in the Reserve Fleet.
28.8.1947: British register closed.
5.1966: Broken up at Kearny, New Jersey, U.S.A. by Union Minerals and Alloys Corporation.

EMPIRE BROADSWORD 1944

O.N. 169737 7,177g 4,823n
396.5 x 60.1 x 35.0 feet.
Geared steam turbines by Westinghouse Electric and Manufacturing Company, Essington, Pennsylvania, U.S.A.; 4,400 SHP, 14 knots
Passengers: Over 1,000 troops.
16.8.1943: Launched by Consolidated Steel Corporation Ltd., Wilmington, California, U.S.A. (Yard No. 348) for the United States War Shipping Administration as CAPE MARSHALL. She had been ordered as a dry cargo vessel but converted into a large infantry landing ship for British use.
12.1943: Completed as EMPIRE BROADSWORD and bareboat charterered to the Ministry of War Transport, London.
30.11.1943-2.7.1944: Managed by Cunard White Star Ltd., Liverpool.
19.1.1944: Arrived at Greenock.
24.1.1944: Registered at London under the ownership of the Ministry of War Transport, London (Cunard White Star Ltd., Liverpool, managers) following her first arrival at a U.K. port.
16.5.1944: Arrived at Portsmouth for Operation Overlord, the invasion of Normandy.
2.7.1944: Mined and sunk in the English Channel off the Normandy beach head in position 49°25′N, 00°54′W whilst on a voyage from Omaha Beach to the UK in ballast. One RNVR officer, two crew and five gunners lost their lives.
1944: Register closed.

Empire Battleaxe was originally used as a large infantry landing ship.

Empire Battleaxe, as a troopship, arriving at Malta after the war.

HOLLAND-AMERICA LINERS WITH DUTCH CREW

WESTERNLAND 1940-1943 and 1945-1946 Triple screw

O.N. 140596 16,479g 9,956n
574.4 x 67.8 x 40.9 feet.
Two T.4-cyl. plus a steam turbine by Harland and Wolff Ltd., Belfast (coal burning); 12,200 IHP, 15.5 knots.
Passengers: *1922*: 631 cabin, 1,824 third; *1929*: 300 cabin, 350 tourist, 800 third; *1935*: 496 tourist.
19.4.1917: Launched by Harland and Wolff Ltd., Govan, Glasgow (Yard No. 454) as the passenger liner REGINA. She had been laid down in 1913 but work was suspended on the outbreak of war.
26.10.1918: Completed as a single-funnel troopship under the ownership of the British and North Atlantic Steam Navigation Co. Ltd. (Dominion Line), London.
8.1920-1922: Rebuilt as a passenger ship by Harland and Wolff Ltd., Belfast.
16.3.1922: First voyage from Liverpool to Portland, Maine.
2.1921: Transferred to Frederick Leyland and Co. Ltd., Liverpool.
12.1925: Dominion Line taken over by the Oceanic Steam Navigation Co. Ltd. (White Star Line), Liverpool and she was transferred to the Liverpool to New York service.
12.1929: Transferred to Red Star Line's Antwerp to New York service and renamed WESTERNLAND.
2.1935: Sold to Arnold Bernstein's Red Star Linie G.m.b.H., Hamburg, Germany.
1.1937: As part of the Nazi campaign against Jewish economic interests, Arnold Bernstein was arrested on trumped-up charges of foreign currency offences and was jailed until 1939, when he was allowed to emigrate to the U.S.A.
2.1937: Red Star Linie G.m.b.H. was placed in the hands of a German Government appointed trustee and the process of liquidating the firm was subsequently put in motion
3.6.1939: Acquired with the rights to the Red Star Line name by N.V. Nederlandsche-Amerikaansche Stoomvaart Maatschappij (Holland-Amerika Lijn), Rotterdam, Netherlands and later used on the Antwerp to New York service under the banner of Holland-America Line, Red Star Line Service.
11.5.1940: Requisitioned by the Dutch Government in exile and handed over at Falmouth for use by them as temporary headquarters.
14.7.1940: Arrived at Liverpool for conversion into a troopship following time charter agreement with the Ministry of Shipping, London. Although Cunard White Star Line Ltd. were appointed managers, she continued to operate with a Dutch crew under the Dutch flag.
29.8.1940: Conversion work completed.
23.9.1940: Arrived at Dakar with General Charles de Gaulle and 1,200 Free French

Westernland in Holland-America Line colours. *[Martin Lindenborn]*

Westernland, in wartime grey, was one of four Holland-America liners time chartered to the British Government as troopships. Although managed by Cunard White Star, they retained their Dutch crew and flew the Dutch flag. *[Martin Lindenborn]*

troops. She was the flagship of a large convoy of Royal Navy ships and six troopships, including PENNLAND, formed for an abortive attempt to invade Vichy-controlled Dakar.
5.1941: Ministry of Shipping merged with the Ministry of Transport to become the Ministry of War Transport.
1941 to 1942: Trooping between Bombay and Suez.
3.1.1943: Arrived at Southend.
9.2.1943: Sold to the British Government for conversion into a naval repair ship.
7.1945: Ownership passed to the Ministry of War Transport, London (Cunard White Star Line Ltd., Liverpool, managers). Partially cut down (funnels, masts and lifeboats removed), she was laid up on the River Blackwater, Essex and was recorded as being there on *29.9.1945*.
10.1946: Sold to Christian Salvesen and Co., Leith for conversion into a whale factory ship but this was later abandoned and she remained on the River Blackwater and was subsequently sold to breakers.
15.7.1947: Acquired by the British Iron and Steel Corporation (BISCO).

1.8.1947: Arrived at Blyth for demolition by Hughes, Bolckow Shipbreaking Co. Ltd.
1947: Register closed.

PENNLAND 1940-1941 Triple screw

O.N. 145933 16,082g 9,518n
574.4 x 67.8 x 40.9 feet.
Two T.4-cyl. plus steam turbine by Harland and Wolff Ltd., Belfast; 12,200 IHP, 15.5 knots.
Passengers: 600 cabin, 1,800 third; *1929*: 300 cabin, 350 tourist, 800 third; *1935*: 550 tourist.
11.11.1920: Launched by Harland and Wolff Ltd., Govan, Glasgow (Yard No. 457) as PITTSBURGH. She had been laid down in 1913 but work was suspended with the outbreak of war.
25.5.1922: Completed and registered under the ownership of International Navigation Co. Ltd. (International Mercantile Marine Group), Liverpool.
6.6.1922: Left on maiden voyage from Liverpool to Boston.
1.1925: Transferred to Red Star Line and placed on the Antwerp to New York service.
2.1926: Renamed PENNLAND.

1927: Transferred to Frederick Leyland and Co. Ltd., Liverpool.

2.1935: Sold to Arnold Bernstein's Red Star Linie G.m.b.H., Hamburg, Germany.

1.1937: As part of the Nazi campaign against Jewish economic interests, Arnold Bernstein was arrested on trumped-up charges of foreign currency offences and was jailed until 1939, when he was allowed to emigrate to the U.S.A.

2.1937: Red Star Linie G.m.b.H. was placed in the hands of a German Government appointed trustee and the process of liquidating the firm was subsequently put in motion

3.6.1939: Acquired with the rights to the Red Star Line name by N.V. Nederlandsche-Amerikaansche Stoomvaart Maatschappij (Holland-Amerika Lijn), Rotterdam, Netherlands and later used on the Antwerp to New York service under the banner of Holland-America Line, Red Star Line Service.

16.5.1940: Requisitioned at New York by the Dutch Government in exile.

5.6.1940: Delivered at New York for time charter to the Ministry of Shipping, London. Although Cunard White Star Line Ltd. were appointed managers, she continued to operate with a Dutch crew under the Dutch flag.

13.7.1940: Arrived at Liverpool for conversion into a troopship.

28.8.1940: Conversion work completed.

23.9.1940: Arrived at Dakar as part of a large convoy of Royal Navy ships and troopships, including WESTERNLAND, formed for an abortive attempt to invade Vichy-controlled Dakar.

25.4.1941: Sunk by German aircraft in the western Aegean Sea in position 37°10′N, 23°50′E whilst on a voyage from Alexandria to Megara, Greece to evacuate troops. Four crew died and the survivors were transferred to the destroyer HMS GRIFFIN and landed at Crete.

VOLENDAM 1940-1946 Twin screw

15,434g 9,197n

550.2 x 67.3 x 32.6 feet.

Two sets of geared steam turbines by Harland and Wolff Ltd., Belfast; 8,000 SHP, 15.5 knots.

Passengers: 263 first, 436 second, 1,200 third; *1928*: 263 first, 428 second, 484 tourist; *late 1930s*: 261 first, 266 tourist, 315 third; *1941*: 3,000 troops; *1947*: 1,682 tourist.

6.7.1922: Launched by Harland and Wolff Ltd., Govan, Glasgow (Yard No. 649) for N.V. Nederlandsche-Amerikaansche Stoomvaart Maatschappj.(Holland-Amerika Lijn), Rotterdam, Netherlands as VOLENDAM.

4.11.1922: Left on maiden voyage from Rotterdam to New York.

26.5.1940: Arrived at London and requisitioned by the Dutch Government in exile.

14.8.1940: Delivered at London for time

Pennland was sunk in 1941. *[World Ship Society Ltd.]*

Volendam at Liverpool in May 1943. *[National Maritime Museum, G4048]*

Volendam arriving at Malta in her post-war guise as a troopship.

charter to the Ministry of Shipping, London. Although Cunard White Star Line Ltd. were appointed managers, she continued to operate with a Dutch crew under the Dutch flag.

31.8.1940: Torpedoed by the German submarine U 60, 200 miles west of Bloody Foreland, Ireland in position 56°04´N, 09°52´W whilst in a convoy from Liverpool to Halifax. All but one were later rescued including 335 evacuee children and she was taken in tow by the Royal Navy salvage tug HMS SALVONIA and beached on the Isle of Bute, Scotland.

12.12.1940: After discharge of cargo and dry-docking at Glasgow, towed to Cammell Laird and Co. Ltd., Birkenhead for permanent repairs and conversion to a troopship.

5.1941: Ministry of Shipping merged with the Ministry of Transport to become the Ministry of War Transport.

5.7.1941: Returned to war service.

7.1945: Returned to her owners but chartered by the Ministry of War Transport for further trooping duties.

28.5.1946: Returned to Holland-Amerika Lijn, having carrying 132,551 troops during her war service.

1947-1951: Used mainly as an emigrant ship.

2.1952: Sold for demolition to N.V. Frank Rijsdijk's Industrieele Ondernemingen, Hendrik-Ido-Ambacht, Netherlands.

17.3.1952: Arrived at Kinderdijk where her superstructure was later cut down.

6.6.1952: Towed to Hendrik-Ido-Ambacht for demolition.

NIEUW AMSTERDAM 1940-1946 Twin screw
36,287g 21,496n
713.7 x 88.3 x 50.0 feet.
Two sets of geared steam turbines by N.V. Koninklijke Maatschappij 'De Schelde', Vlissingen, Netherlands; 35,100 SHP, 20.5 knots.
Passengers: 556 cabin, 455 tourist, 209 third; *1940*: 8,000 troops; *1962*: 574 first, 583 tourist.

10.4.1937: Launched by N.V. Rotterdamsche Droogdok Maatschappij, Rotterdam, Netherlands (Yard No. 200) for N.V. Nederlandsche-Amerikaansche Stoomvaart Maatschappij (Holland-Amerika Lijn), Rotterdam as NIEUW AMSTERDAM.

10.5.1938: Left on maiden voyage from Rotterdam to New York.

14.5.1940: Arrived at New York and laid up.

12.9.1940: Sailed for Halifax, having been requisitioned at New York by the Dutch Government in exile and time chartered to the Ministry of Shipping, London.

14 to 29.9.1940: Armed at Halifax. Anti-magnetic mine degaussing strip fitted.

11.10.1940: Placed under Cunard White Star Line Ltd. management. She continued to operate with a Dutch crew under the Dutch flag.

9.11.1940: Arrived at Singapore for conversion into a troopship.

24.12.1940: Left for Sydney, Australia.

5.1941: Ministry of Shipping merged with the Ministry of Transport to become the Ministry of War Transport.

8.4.1946: Returned to Holland-Amerika Lijn.

30.4.1946: Released from war service.

22.5.1946 to 5.8.1947: Post-war refit.

Top: *Nieuw Amsterdam,* arriving Bombay, only partially repainted. *[V.H.Young and L.A.Sawyer]*
Upper middle: On the Clyde in August 1944. *[National Maritime Museum, N35944]*
Lower middle: Looking war-weary. *[Martin Lindenborn]*
Bottom: *Nieuw Amsterdam* arriving at Rotterdam 10th April 1946, having completed 530,452 nautical miles and carried 378,361 troops during the war.

29.10.1947: First post-war voyage from Rotterdam to New York.
1956: Hull painted grey.
1962: Third class removed.
1967: New boilers fitted by Wilton-Fijenoord, Rotterdam.
12.1971: Became a full-time cruise ship.
9.1972: Register changed to Willemstad, Curaçao.
25.2.1974: Arrived Kaohsiung, Taiwan for demolition by Nan Fung Steel Enterprise Ltd.

EMPIRE WAVENEY 1945-1946
Twin screw
16,754g 9,415n
546.6 x 72.4 x 42.2 feet.
Four 6-cyl. 2DA M.A.N.-type oil engines by Blohm & Voss K.a.A., Hamburg, Germany; 12,600 BHP, 16 knots.
Passengers: 270 cabin, 287 tourist, 416 third; 1936: 559 first.
20.2.1929: Launched by Blohm & Voss K.a.A., Hamburg (Yard No. 483) for Hamburg Amerika Linie, Hamburg as MILWAUKEE.
18.6.1929: Maiden voyage from Hamburg to New York.
1935-1936: Refitted as a single class cruise ship.
1940-1945: Used by the German Navy as an accommodation ship at Kiel and was damaged during an air raid.
5.1945: Taken as a war prize and allocated to the U.S. Navy. After temporary repairs she was sent to the United States for possible use as a troopship but this was later abandoned.
9.11.1945: Arrived at New York. Subsequently handed over to Ministry of War Transport, London (Cunard White Star Line Ltd., Liverpool, managers) and renamed EMPIRE WAVENEY.
1.3.1946: Caught fire in the Canada Dock, Liverpool at the end of her conversion by Harland and Wolff Ltd. into a troopship and later declared a constructive total loss. She was refloated and sold to breakers.
27.1.1947: Arrived at Dalmuir for demolition by W.H. Arnott Young and Co. Ltd., and was later stripped of her upperworks.
25.9.1947: Remains towed to Troon for demolition by Arnott Young's subsidiary, West of Scotland Shipbreaking Co. Ltd.

CARIBIA 1945-1946 Twin screw
12,049g 6,989n
497.8 x 65.8 x 27.9 feet.
Two 8-cyl. 2SCSA MAN-Vulkan type oil engines by Blohm & Voss K.a.A., Hamburg, Germany; 11,500 BHP, 17 knots.
Passengers: 203 first, 103 second.
1.3.1932: Launched by Blohm & Voss K.a.A., Hamburg, (Yard No. 493) for Hamburg Amerika Linie, Hamburg as CARIBIA.

Empire Waveney as *Milwaukee* at New York in 1945 (top) and ablaze in the Canada Dock, Liverpool in 1946 (middle). *[Top: David Whiteside collection]*

Caribia in HAPAG colours pre-war.

25.2.1933: Maiden voyage Hamburg-West Indies-Central America.
1940-1945: Used by the German Navy as an accommodation ship at Flensburg-Mürwik.
5.1945: Taken as a war prize and handed over to the British Government.
15.7.1945: Allocated to the U.S.A. but later awarded to the Soviet Union.
12.10.1945-20.2.1946: Cunard White Star Line Ltd., Liverpool, became managers.
1946: Handed over to Russia, renamed IL'ICH and placed on the Kamchatka to Vladivostok route.
1977: Hulked.

SEA PERCH 1946-1947

O.N. 180890 7,937g 4,620n
474.5 x 69.6 x 29.5 feet.
Geared steam turbines by Westinghouse Electric and Manufacturing Company, Essington, Pennsylvania, U.S.A.; 9,350 SHP, 17 knots
Troops: 2,056.
16.8.1943: Launched by Ingalls Shipbuilding Corporation, Pascagoula, Mississippi, U.S.A. (Yard No. 403) as SEA PERCH, a C3-S-A2-type wartime standard ship built for United States War Shipping Administration.
27.4.1944: Completed and was later operated for the War Shipping Administration by the United Fruit Company under the General Agency Agreement and allocated to U.S. Army control as a troopship.
20.6.1946: Registered at London under the ownership of the Ministry of Transport, London (Cunard White Star Line Ltd., Liverpool, managers) on bareboat charter from the United States Maritime Commission.
1947: Returned to the United States Maritime Commission.
16.5.1947: British register closed.
1947: Sold to the Luckenbach Steamship Co. Inc., New York, U.S.A. and renamed MATHEW LUCKENBACH.
1959: Sold to States Marine Lines Inc., New York and renamed GOPHER STATE.
1.6.1973: Arrived at Kaohsiung, Taiwan for demolition by I. Chon Steel and Iron Works.

SEA SNIPE 1946

O.N. 180897 7,994g 4,606n
468.5 x 69.6 x 29.5 feet.
Geared steam turbines by General Electric Company, Lynn, Massachusetts, U.S.A.; 9,350 SHP, 18.5 knots
Troops: 2,194.
7.12.1942: Launched by Western Pipe and Steel Co., San Francisco, California, U.S.A. (Yard No. 84) as SEA SNIPE, a C3-S-A2-type wartime standard ship built for United States

Il'ich ex-*Caribia*. *[W.A Schell collection]*

Sea Perch ended her career as *Gopher State*. *[W.A.Schell collection]*

Sea Snipe later became *Edward Luckenbach*. *[W.A.Schell collection]*

War Shipping Administration.
29.5.1943: Completed and later operated for the War Shipping Administration by American President Lines Ltd. under the General Agency Agreement and allocated to U.S. Army control as a troopship.
28.6.1946: Registered at London under the ownership of the Ministry of Transport, London (Cunard White Star Line Ltd., Liverpool, managers) on a bareboat charter from the United States Maritime Commission.

1946: Returned to the United States Maritime Commission.
19.12.1946: British register closed.
1948: Sold to the Luckenbach Steamship Co. Inc., New York, U.S.A. and renamed EDWARD LUCKENBACH.
1959: Sold to States Marine Lines Inc., New York and renamed ALOHA STATE.
21.8.1971: Arrived at Kaohsiung, Taiwan for demolition by Yi Ho Steel Co. Ltd.

CANADIAN-BUILT WAR STANDARD SHIPS

FORT SPOKANE 1946-1951
O.N 174163 7,128g 4,247n
424.6 x 57.2 x 34.9 feet.
T.3-cyl. by Dominion Engineering Works Ltd., Montreal, Canada; 505 HP, 11 knots.
13.5.1943: Launched by Burrard Dry Dock Co. Ltd., Vancouver, Canada (Yard No. 177) as MOHAWK PARK, a North Sands-type wartime standard ship, laid down as FORT NORWAY.
16.6.1943: Registered at Montreal under the ownership of the Dominion of Canada (Park Steamship Co. Ltd., managers), Ottawa, Canada.
1944: Bareboat chartered to the Ministry of War Transport, London, registered at London under the ownership of the MOWT and renamed FORT SPOKANE.
27.9.1944-22.3.1946: Managed by Watts, Watts and Co. Ltd., London.
1946: Transferred to the Ministry of Transport, London.
22.3.1946-1951: Managed by Cunard White Star Ltd., Liverpool.
1.1.1950: Managers restyled as the Cunard Steam-Ship Co. Ltd., Liverpool.
1951: Sold to Buries Markes Ltd., London and renamed LA ORILLA.
1952: Sold to Fratelli d'Amico, Rome, Italy and renamed ARIELLA.
1952: British register closed.
1965: Broken up at Trieste by Sidemar with work completed in *1.1966*.

FORT TICONDEROGA 1946-1948
O.N 169736 7,138g 4,220n
424.5 x 57.2 x 34.9 feet.
T.3-cyl. by Dominion Engineering Works Ltd., Montreal, Canada; 505 HP, 11 knots.
6.11.1943: Launched by United Shipyard, Montreal (Yard No. 22) for the Dominion of Canada, Ottawa as FORT TICONDEROGA, a North Sands-type wartime standard ship.
7.12.1943: Completed and bareboat chartered to the Ministry of War Transport, London.
21.1.1944: Registered at London under the ownership of the Ministry of War Transport, London.
7.12.1943-17.5.1946: Managed by Chellew Navigation Co. Ltd., Cardiff.
1946: Transferred to the Ministry of Transport, London.
17.5.1946-25.8.1948 Managed by Cunard White Star Ltd., Liverpool and operated in Cunard colours.
1948: Sold to Ivor Shipping Co. Ltd., (Quebec Steamship Lines Ltd.), Montreal and renamed IVOR ISOBEL.
1951: Registered in London.
1956: Transferred to Novor Shipping Co. Ltd. (Chandris (England) Ltd.), London and renamed NOVOR ISOBEL.
1958: Sold to Ocean Tramping Co. Ltd., a Hong Kong firm controlled by the People's Republic of China Government. Renamed HEREFORD.

Fort Spokane, above in New York and below in London, was one of seven Canadian-built standard ships managed by Cunard White Star between 1946 and 1951. They operated in Cunard colours. *[World Ship Society Ltd.]*

Fort Ticonderoga in New York (above) and at London in April 1948 (below).

1958: British register closed.

1959: Transferred to the People's Republic of China and renamed HO PING 51.

1967: Transferred to the Bureau of Maritime Transport Administration, Shanghai Branch and renamed ZHAN DOU 51.

1985: Reported to have been broken up in China.

SIBLEY PARK 1946-1950

O.N 175398 7,140g 4,209n
424.5 x 57.2 x 34.9 feet.
T.3-cyl. by Dominion Engineering Works Ltd., Montreal, Canada; 505 HP, 11 knots.

20.5.1944: Launched by United Shipyards Ltd., Montreal (Yard No. 31) as SIBLEY PARK, a North Sands-type wartime standard ship.

23.6.1944: Registered at Montreal under the ownership of the Dominion of Canada (Park Steamship Co. Ltd., managers), Ottawa.

1946: Bareboat chartered to the Ministry of Transport, London and registered at London under the ownership of the Ministry of Transport.

5.6.1946-30.6.1950: Managed by Cunard White Star Ltd., Liverpool and operated in Cunard colours.

1.1.1950: Managers restyled as the Cunard Steam-Ship Co. Ltd., Liverpool.

1950: Sold to Waverley Overseas Freighters Ltd., Halifax. Nova Scotia (Fafalios Ltd., London) and renamed KENILWORTH.

1956: Transferred to Cia. Filiori de Navegacion S.A. (D.J. Fafalios), Chios, Greece and renamed AEOLOS.

1956: British register closed.

1961: Sold to Speedwell Shipping Co. Ltd., Monrovia, Liberia (Southern Shipping and Finance Co., London), registered at Beirut, Lebanon and renamed ATOLOS.

1964: Sold to Prekookeanska Plovidba, Bar, Yugoslavia and renamed MOJKOVAC.

29.12.1968: Arrived at Split, Yugoslavia for demolition by Brodospas.

FORT CADOTTE 1946-1950

O.N 168448 7,128g 4,249n
424.6 x 57.2 x 34.9 feet.
T.3-cyl. by Dominion Engineering Works Ltd., Montreal, Canada; 505 HP, 11 knots.

11.2.1943: Launched by Burrard Dry Dock Co. Ltd., North Vancouver, Canada (Yard No. 159) as FORT CADOTTE, a North Sands-type wartime standard ship. Under the Lend-Lease agreement the contract was transferred to the U.S. War Shipping Administration and title subsequently transferred to the Dominion of Canada.

19.3.1943: Completed and bareboat chartered to the Ministry of War Transport, London.

2.6.1943: Registered at London under the ownership of the Ministry of War Transport, London, following her first arrival at a U.K. port.

19.3.1943-6.6.1946: Managed by Sir R. Ropner and Co. Ltd., West Hartlepool.

1946: Ownership changed to the Ministry of Transport, London.

6.6.1946-8.1950: Managed by Cunard White Star Ltd., Liverpool and operated in Cunard colours.

Sibley Park in May 1948.

Fort Cadotte at New York. *[World Ship Society Ltd.]*

Fort Musquarro in July 1947 (above) and in dry dock at Leith in March 1950 (below).

282

1.1.1950: Managers restyled as the Cunard Steam-Ship Co. Ltd., Liverpool.
1950: Sold to Nova Scotia Marine Enterprise Co. Ltd. (Counties Ship Management Co. Ltd.), London and renamed FRY HILL.
1957: Sold to Portofino Cia. Naviera S.A., Monrovia, Liberia and renamed AKTI.
1957: British register closed.
1960: Registered at Syra.
1961: Sold to A.Frangistas and E. Athanasiou, Athens, Greece, she remained registered at Syra and was renamed GLORIA.
1964: Transferred to Olistim Navigation Co. Ltd. (Franco Shipping Co.) Syra, Greece and renamed HELEN.
15.1.1967: Arrived at Kawajiri, Japan for demolition by Fujita Kaiji K.K.

FORT MUSQUARRO 1946-1949
O.N 169885 7,150g 4,227n
424.5 x 57.2 x 34.9 feet.
T.3-cyl. by Dominion Engineering Works Ltd., Montreal, Canada; 505 HP, 11 knots.
16.4.1944: Launched by Marine Industries Ltd., Sorel, Canada (Yard No. 128) for the Dominion of Canada, Ottawa as FORT MUSQUARRO, a North Sands-type wartime standard ship.
19.5.1944: Completed and bareboat charterered to the Ministry of War Transport, London
19.6.1944: Registered at London under the ownership of the Ministry of War Transport, London, following her first arrival at a U.K. port.
19.5.1944-20.6.1946: Managed by Charles Strubin and Co. Ltd., London.
1946: Ownership changed to the Ministry of Transport, London.
20.6.1946-1949: Managed by Cunard White Star Ltd., Liverpool and operated in Cunard colours.
1949: Managed by Maclay and McIntyre Ltd., Glasgow.
1950: Sold to Canadian Tramp Shipping Co. Ltd. (Counties Ship Management Co. Ltd.), London and renamed WEST HILL.
1957: Sold to Nestor Cia. Naviera S.A., Monrovia, Liberia and renamed RIO DORO.
1957: British register closed.
1960: Transferred to Monteleones Cia. Naviera S.A., Piraeus, Greece.
29.3.1963: Arrived at Hirao, Japan for demolition.

FORT MIAMI 1946-1950
O.N 173263 7,132g 4,243n
424.5 x 57.2 x 34.9 feet.
T.3-cyl. by Dominion Engineering Works Ltd., Montreal, Canada; 505 HP, 11 knots.
4.7.1942: Launched by North Vancouver Ship Repairs Ltd., Vancouver, Canada (Yard No. 107) as FORT ROUGE, a North Sands-type wartime standard ship completed as MOUNT ROBSON PARK.
13.8.1942: Registered at Montreal under the ownership of the Dominion of Canada

(Park Steamship Co. Ltd., managers), Ottawa.
1944: Bareboat chartered to the Ministry of War Transport, London, registered at London under the ownership of the Ministry of War Transport and renamed FORT MIAMI.
21.9.1944-28.6.1946: Managed by Evan Thomas Radcliffe and Co. Ltd., Cardiff.
1946: Ownership changed to the Ministry of Transport, London.
28.6.1946-1950: Managed by Cunard White Star Ltd., Liverpool and operated in Cunard colours.
1.1.1950: Managers restyled as the Cunard Steam-Ship Co. Ltd., Liverpool.
1950: Managed by George Nisbet and Co., Glasgow.
1950: Sold to Rex Shipping Co. Ltd. (Hadjilias and Co. Ltd.), London and renamed MIDHURST.
1957: Transferred to Asturias Shipping Co. S.A., Monrovia, Liberia (Hadjilias and Co., London) and renamed ANDALUSIA.
1957: British register closed.
1961: Registered at Piraeus.
1964: Sold to Cia. de Navegacion Fenix S.A., Panama (Phoenix Enterprise Co. (Chan Hoon Hi), Hong Kong) and renamed SEVILLA.
9.9.1967: Sailed from Chiba, Japan for demolition at Keelung, Taiwan.

HILLCREST PARK 1946-1950
O.N 175385 7,138g 4,221n
424.5 x 57.2 x 34.9 feet.
T.3-cyl. by Dominion Engineering Works Ltd., Montreal, Canada; 505 HP, 11 knots.

29.3.1944: Launched by United Shipyards Ltd., Montreal (Yard No. 27) as HILLCREST PARK, a North Sands-type wartime standard ship.
28.4.1944: Registered at Montreal under the ownership of the Dominion of Canada (Park Steamship Co. Ltd., managers), Ottawa.
1946: Bareboat chartered to the Ministry of Transport, London and registered at London under the ownership of the Ministry of Transport.
9.4.1946-22.10.1946: Managed by Capper Alexander and Co., London.
22.10.1946-1950: Managed by Cunard White Star Ltd., Liverpool and operated in Cunard colours.
1.1.1950: Managers restyled as the Cunard Steam-Ship Co. Ltd., Liverpool.
1950: Managed by W.H. Seager and Co. Ltd., Cardiff.
1950: Sold to Black Lion Steamship Co. Ltd. (Frinton Shipbrokers Ltd.), London and renamed BEMBRIDGE HILL.
1954: Management changed to Counties Ship Management Co. Ltd., London.
1957: Sold to Marproeza Cia. Naviera S.A., Monrovia, Liberia (B.E. Mavroleon, London) and renamed ELIMARIE.
1957: British register closed.
1965: Sold to Taiwan Maritime Transportation Co. Ltd., Keelung, Taiwan and renamed TAI FONG.
20.1.1968: Demolition commenced at Kaohsiung, Taiwan.

Fort Miami at New York. [World Ship Society Ltd.]

Hillcrest Park. [World Ship Society Ltd.]

CUNARD LAKES SERVICE 1957-1968
TRANSATLANTIC LAKES LINE
Cunard, Oranje Lijn, French Line and Fjell Line from 1968

Cunard started the Cunard Lakes Service from London to Chicago and Milwaukee in 1957, using a chartered German ship, *Erin Nübel* (827/1954). A Liverpool service commenced the following year with the chartered *Concordia* (1,367/1953) and Toronto, Hamilton, Cleveland and Detroit were later added to the schedule. The ships were painted in Cunard colours.

For most of the 1960s, chartered tonnage was used on the Cunard Lakes Service with many of the ships given well-known Cunard names ending in *ia*. This naming process continued until 1968, when the service, still with chartered ships, became the Transatlantic Lakes Line, a joint operation with Oranje Lijn, French Line and Fjell Line.

Chartered ships with Cunard names:
1960-1961 **CARIA** (ex WIEDENBORSTEL 1,380/1953)
1960-1961 **VERIA** (ex AUGUSTE SCHULTE 770/1952)
1961-1963 **MARONIA** (ex MARION 4,364/1961) New York service
1961-1964 **NORDIA** (ex NORDIC 4,560/1961) New York service
1965-1967 **ANDRIA** (ex CLIO 3,126/1958)
1966 **ALSATIA** (ex LANCASTRIAN 3,799/1956)

1966-1968 **ANTONIA** (exTHOR ODLAND 4,402/1955)
1966-1967 **ARABIA** (ex CASTILIAN 3,803/1955)
1966-1968 **ASCANIA** (ex ANATOLIAN 3,799/1955)
1966 **ASSYRIA** (ex ALMERIAN 3,649/1956)
1967 **ASIA** (ex ALMERIAN 3,649/1956)
1967-68 **ALSATIA** (ex BYSANZ 2,126/1947)
1967 **ANDRIA** (ex CARIBIA 4,524/1953)
1967-1968 **ASSYRIA** (ex AMARNA 3,422/1949)
1967 **AURANIA** (ex KYPROS 3,499/1950)
1967-1968 **ARABIA** (ex DETLEF MITTMAN 2,606/1952)

Other chartered ships and the first date ship was chartered:
1957 **ERIN NÜBEL** (827/1954)
1957 **BERNI NÜBEL** (763/1952)
1958 **CONCORDIA** (1,367/1953)
1959 **ELFRIEDE** (1,518/1950)
1961 **JOHANNA** (1,980/1953)
1964 **TAUTRA** (2,887/1957)
1965 **EVA JEANETTE** (4,415/1958) New York service
1965 **LEABETH** (2,099/1956)
1965 **RAUNI** (2,400/1950)

Caria in the Welland Canal in August 1960 (left) and *Andria* ex *Clio* on the St. Lawrence in 1967 (right). *[Malcolm Cranfield]*

Amarna, seen here as *Assyria* at Hamilton, Ontario, was one of a pair of Moss Hutchison Line ships chartered in 1967. *[Malcolm Cranfield collection]*

A number of ships, including some British Mediterranean traders, were chartered for the Cunard Lakes Service in the 1960s. These included the 1955-built Norwegian *Thor Odland* (top) seen passing Portishead 0n 21st April, 1967, Ellerman Papayanni's *Anatolian* as *Ascania* (upper middle, left) *[both; Malcolm Cranfield collection]* and *Castilian* as *Arabia* (upper middle, right) *[W.A.Schell]*. Both Ellerman ships are shown on the St. Lawrence River in 1967 and 1966 respectively. *Erin Nübel* (right) inaugurated the service and is seen is at London in April 1957. *Tautra* off Gravesend (below) in August 1965. *[Malcolm Cranfield collection]*

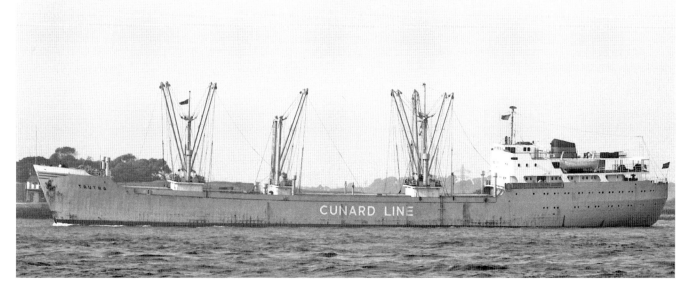

CUNARD SUBSIDIARY COMPANIES

Cunard had a number of shipping subsidiaries. As they were originally independently-run companies, they have been excluded from this fleet history. However, they were important contributors to Cunard's profitability and are featured here in brief.

Port Line Ltd.

Cunard's best-known subsidiary was Port Line, with its funnel colours similar to those of the parent company. Mainly involved in the transportation of refrigerated produce and general cargo between the United Kingdom, Australia and New Zealand, it was acquired in June 1916 as Commonwealth and Dominion Line. Although its ships had *Port* names, it was only in November 1937 that the company name was changed to Port Line Ltd. It operated as a separate business until the 1960s, when, like other traditional cargo lines, its existence was threatened by the arrival of container ships. In 1966 it became a shareholder in Associated Container Transportation Ltd., a consortium of seven shipping lines, including Port Line. The introduction of containerisation saw Port Line's fleet shrink significantly. After a short period between 1968 and 1972 when its ships were managed by Blue Star Port Line Management Ltd., the operation was transferred to Cunard Brocklebank Ltd. By 1979 its few remaining ships were transferred to Cunard Shipping Services Ltd. In 1981 the final two Port Line ships were given Brocklebank names. The best account of Port Line's history is 'The Tyser Legacy' by the New Zealand historian Ian Farquhar.

Port Line ordered a series of streamlined cargo liners in the late 1949s and early 1950s. These were among the most attractive cargo ships ever built and included the 11,945g *Port Auckland* of 1949 (top). She was converted at Singapore into the live sheep carrier *Mashaallah* in 1976 (middle). Managed by Cunard, her owners were the Kuwait-based Gulf Fisheries

W.L.L., a company in which Cunard had a 39% share. *[both: Russell Priest]*
The last two ships built for Port Line were *Port Caroline,* seen at Cape Town in 1980 (bottom), and *Port Chalmers,* both of which were transferred to Brocklebank ownership in 1981 as *Matra* and *Manaar,* respectively. *[V.H. Young and L.A. Sawyer]*

Thos. & Jno. Brocklebank Ltd.

With roots going back to 1770, Thos. & Jno. Brocklebank Ltd. was one Britain's oldest shipping lines. Trading to India and the near east, a full shareholding in the company was acquired by Cunard in 1921. Despite Indian independence in 1947, the company grew in the 1950s and by 1962 it had a fleet of 22 ships. However, during the 1960s it was badly hit by containerisation and the rise of national carriers in India and Pakistan. It acquired H.E. Moss and Co's Tankers Ltd. in 1964 and in 1968 Cunard-Brocklebank Ltd. was formed to manage all the Cunard group's cargo ships. Brocklebank's last conventional cargo ships were sold in 1983.

Top: *Mathura* seen passing Greenock in Cunard colours in March 1969. *[J.Pottinger/Malcolm Cranfield collection]*
Middle: *Port Alfred* was transferred to Brocklebanks in 1975. Renamed *Masirah* in 1978 she was photographed in the Bosphorus in April 1981. A year later she was sold to Greek buyers. *[Nigel Jones]*

Bottom: *Manaar*, formerly *Port Chalmers,* at Bluff, New Zealand on 11th March 1982. In 1983 *Manaar* and her sister *Matra* were the last Brocklebank ships to be sold. *[V.H.Young and L.A.Sawyer]*

Offshore Marine Ltd.

Founded in 1964, the Great Yarmouth-based Offshore Marine Ltd. owned the first specialised oil industry supply vessels to operate in the North Sea. Originally a subsidiary of the coaster firm London and Rochester Trading Co. Ltd., the company was bought by Cunard on 1st April 1968. Between 1969 and 1978, 22 new ships, all with *Shore*-names, were ordered and the company became the largest UK supply ship operator. *West Shore* foundered in the North Sea with no casualties on 7th January 1971. On 17th January 1974 a second ship, *East Shore* sank in the Mediterranean with the loss of her six-man crew. In 1980, Offshore Marine was sold to Zapata Offshore Services Ltd, a subsidiary of the Zapata Corporation of Houston.

Above: *East Shore* (669/1966) came to Cunard as part of the Offshore Marine fleet in 1968. *[FotoFlite incorporating Skyfotos, 332895]*
Below: *Cromarty Shore* was one of four 971g ships built for Offshore Marine during 1974 and 1975 with names of sea areas.

Flag used by A. Cunard and Son, Halifax, Nova Scotia (1809 to 1824) and S. Cunard and Company from 1824 to 1865.

1840 to c.1880
The first flags for The British and North American Royal Mail Steam Packet Company, The British and North American Steam Packet Company and The British and Foreign Steam Navigation Company were the Burns (top) and MacIver pennants (below). G. and J. Burns managed the company's finances in Glasgow, whilst D. and C. MacIver managed the ships at Liverpool. Burns and MacIver operated a joint Glasgow to Liverpool service from 1830 and its ships also flew these flags.

c.1880 to the 1990s
A crest with a lion rampant holding a globe was designed for the newly-formed Cunard Steamship Co. Ltd. and was also used for the company flag. The first chairman of the new company was John Burns and, after the dissolution of the Burns and MacIver partnership in 1881, the G. and J. Burns company used the Cunard-style flag as its house flag but with a blue background instead of red. The form of the lion has also evolved over the years.

1934 to 1950 Cunard White Star Line
On Cunard ships the Cunard flag was flown above the White Star flag. On White Star liners, the flags were reversed. These flags continued to be flown until the late 1960s by passenger liners to New York.

1990s to the present
A new flag was introduced which reflected a ship's officer's cap badge.

1840 to the present
Originally, the number of black bands on the funnel varied depending on the number of funnel sections. Some later ships had an additional black band whilst the current fleet has two bands.

1969 to 1982
The white and back funnel colours of *Queen Elizabeth 2* were also used initially for *Cunard Adventurer* and *Cunard Ambassador*.

**Cunard-Brocklebank Bulkers Ltd.
and Cunard-Brocklebank Ltd.**
These companies used the colours of
T. and J. Brocklebank Ltd., Liverpool.

Moss Tankers Ltd.

Atlantic Container Line
1970-1976.

Atlantic Container Line
1976 onwards.

Cunard Ellerman Shipping Services Ltd.

HULL COLOURS OF CUNARD PASSENGER LINERS, CRUISE SHIPS, TENDERS AND CARGO SHIPS
1840 to early 1890s Black with red boot topping.
Early 1890s to 1971 Black with red boot topping and thin white stripe for most services.
1969 to present Federal grey with red boot topping and thin white stripe for *Queen Elizabeth 2* and the three current Queens.
Queen Elizabeth 2 also had light blue boot topping from 1979 to 1980, a light pebble grey hull with no white stripe from 1982 to 1983 and a navy blue hull with red, gold and blue stripes halfway up the superstructure from 1994 to 1999.
Cunard cruise ships 1920s to 1996
1920s to 1996 White with red boot topping. Some of the white hull ships of the 1920s and 1930s had green boot topping. The cruise ships built in the 1970s also had a red stripe below the main deck.
1948 to 1973 'Cruising green' i.e. four shades of green was used for *Caronia*, *Mauretania*, *Carmania* and *Franconia*.
Illustrations by Stephen Card

S. CUNARD AND COMPANY

Samuel Cunard's ancestors were German Quakers who had emigrated to Pennsylvania in the 17th century. After the American War of Independence, Robert Cunard, Samuel's grandfather, who was a loyalist, fled with his family to the British colony of New Brunswick. In 1783 Robert's son, Abraham, settled in Halifax, Nova Scotia where he worked as a master carpenter for the Royal Engineers. Samuel, the second of nine children, was born in 1787. His father, Abraham, was an astute businessman who bought water rights in Halifax harbour in order to build trading wharves. In 1809 Abraham and Samuel founded the firm A. Cunard and Son.

     With its knowledge of shipbuilding and timber, the new company was initially involved in the timber trade. It bought forest land in Nova Scotia and exported timber, mainly to Britain. With its own warehouse and wharf, it also imported sugar, molasses, coffee and spirits from the West Indies and became a shipping agency. The first of many ships owned was the locally-built schooner *Margaret*, which was constructed in the early 1810s. She was also the first of a number of vessels featuring the name of Abraham's wife. In 1815, A. Cunard and Son won a government contract to supply an armed trade and fisheries protection vessel, which was also used to carry the Lieutenant-Governor on his official duties and the mails to New York in winter. This small sloop *Earl Bathurst* was replaced in 1817 by a larger ship, the brig *Chebucto*. Ten years later, the

Cunard company was awarded the first of many mail contracts by the Admiralty (see page 256).

     After the death of Abraham in 1824, the company was renamed S. Cunard and Co. By then it had become one of Halifax's leading trading companies. Samuel's brother Joseph set up his own firm, Joseph Cunard and Co., in Chatham on the River Miramichi, New Brunswick. Here he owned forestry land and his shipyards built many ships. Up to the mid-1840s almost a hundred ships were registered in Joseph's name. However, in 1848 his company failed and he had to flee his creditors, leaving S. Cunard and Co. burdened with his debt. Meanwhile, Samuel had diversified his business significantly. Not only was he the agent for the East India Company and the General Mining Association, he also bought considerable tracts of land on Prince Edward Island. His shipping interests were also extensive and it is estimated that over 75 ships were registered in his name at Halifax - some of the keys ships are listed below.

     The story of the Cunard family has been superbly written up by three Canadian historians. Louise Manny's 'Ships of Miramichi' includes the story of Joseph Cunard, whilst Phyllis Ruth Blakeley's coverage of Samuel Cunard in the 'Dictionary of Canadian Biography' is very well researched. Kay Grant's 'Samuel Cunard Pioneer of the Atlantic Steamship' is not only enjoyable to read, it offers the best insight into Samuel Cunard's character.

Some of the ships owned by Samuel Cunard and S. Cunard and Co.

Name	Type/rig	Tonnage	Service	Name	Type/rig	Tonnage	Service
				JANET	Brig	280	1826-7
COUNTESS DALHOUSIE	Schooner	91	1817-?	ADVENTURE	Brig	266	1826-7
ECLIPSE	Sloop	95	1817-?	PACIFIC	Ship	402	1827-35
REBECCA	Schooner	29	1818-22	MARGARET	Brig	261	1827-32
ACTIVE	Schooner	47	1819-20	GEORGE CANNING	Brig	265	1827-29
CHANCE	Brig	144	1819-25	SAMUEL CUNARD	Ship	303	1827-34
HIBERNIA	Schooner	58	1819-25	CLARENCE	Brig	255	1827-28
PRINCE OF WATERLOO	Brig	143	1819-24	SUSAN & SARAH	Brig	329	1827-39
THORNLEY	Brigantine	164	1819-23	LADY STRANGE	Schooner	118	1828
CHERUB	Schooner	79	1821-22	GEORGE	Schooner	114	1828-30
DESIREO	Schooner	76	1821-?	JOHN	Schooner	91	1828
MARY ANN	Brig	98	1821-24	SOPHIA	Brig	107	1828
JANE	Brig	84	1822-?	WILLIAM	Brig	268	1828-29
QUEEN	Schooner	67	1823-26	JANE	Brig	268	1828-37
ELIZA	Brig	201	1824	CATHERINE	Brig	146	1828-32
ELIZA	Schooner	52	1824-32	LADY SARAH MAITLAND	Schooner	139	1828-32
ATALANTE	Schooner	31	1824-26	SYLPH	Brig	156	1829-31
LONDON	Brig	203	1825-?	SYBYLLA	Ship	375	1829-35
SHUBENACADIE	Brig	179	1825-27	ROSE	Ship	416	1829-42
BRAZILIAN PATRIOT	Schooner	70	1825-27	JANE	Brig	143	1830-33
SIR WALTER SCOTT	Brig	219	1826-27	ANN	Brig	91	1830
BAINBRIDGE	Ship	429	1831-35	TRIAL	Schooner	75	1830
EARL DALHOUSIE	Brig	314	1826-27	SARAH	Schooner	151	1832
JOHN BAINBRIDGE	Barque	366	1826-27	JAMES	Barque	359	1832-34
MARGARET	Brig	134	1824-27	KATE	Brig	141	1832-37
HENRIETTA	Schooner	154	1826-30	WILLIAM THE FOURTH	Brig	130	1833-38
TAY	Brig	300	1826-27	MARIA	Brig	171	1833-?
TRUE BLUE	Brigantine	101	1826-27	MARGARET	Barque	627	1836-38
EUTERPE	Schooner	77	1826-28	LADY PAGET	Barque	500	1837-38
FAME	Schooner	124	1826-28	LADY LILFORD	Ship	596	1838-39
JESSIE	Brig	345	1826-27	SUSAN	Brig	163	1843-46
ADMIRAL LAKE	Brig	155	1826-31	ROSE	Paddle	73	1853
MARMION	Brigantine	136	1827-28	PASHA	Screw	179	1859-87

Campania's first class dining saloon could accommodate all first class passengers and, with its long tables, was typical of the liners of the late 19th century. Diners sat on revolving chairs with the Cunard rampant lion carved on the back.

The drawing room on *Campania* was very opulent with thick curtains, velvet-covered ottoman settees and richly-carved panelling.

On *Mauretania* Victorian excess gave way to more refined interiors. They were also designed by an architect, Harold Peto, instead of the shipyard. The comfortable first class lounge had a pink and green Wilton carpet, Aubusson wall tapestries and French-style settees and chairs.

Aquitania was Cunard's answer to White Star Line's *Olympic* class. Although the rooms were elegant, they had none of the stylish and original features of *Mauretania*. *Aquitania*'s classical-style first class lounge with its fluted columns and painted ceilings was reminiscent of an English 18th century country house.

Although *Scythia* (2) was Cunard's first passenger liner to be delivered after the First World War, her first class accommodation was rather uninspiring. Whilst the style of the first class dining saloon, with its pierced dome ceiling, still harked back to an earlier era, there was a distinct lack of decoration, certainly in comparison with the pre-war Cunarders.

The panelled first class smoking-room was situated at the aft end of A-deck.

Scythia also had two garden lounges in first class, where passengers could relax, have tea and watch the sea go by. Note the exposed bulkheads.

A comfortable first class cabin on *Scythia*.

Queen Mary was Cunard's first liner to do away with period decoration. However, unlike French Line's *Normandie*, she did not totally embrace modern contemporary design. Her interiors were a mixture of British conservatism and American Art Deco. This can be seen in the panelling and lighting of the first class lounge and ballroom (above) and the forward-facing, semi-circular observation lounge and cocktail bar (below).

Queen Elizabeth dispensed with Art Deco and her interiors had an understated British modern style. No doubt influenced by Orient Line's iconic *Orion*, her public rooms, such as the first class salon (above), were elegant but not brash, with soft colour schemes and hidden lighting. The difference between *Queen Elizabeth*'s design and *Queen Mary*'s can be seen in her more restrained observation lounge and cocktail bar (below).

The interior décor of its first two post-war Canadian liners, *Saxonia* and *Ivernia*, reflected the optimistic colours and designs of the 1950s. With its windows overlooking the bow, *Saxonia*'s first class 'Chintz Lounge' had pink sheet-plastic wall panel studded with painted mirrors and fan-shaped ceiling lighting.

For the second pair of Canadian liners, Cunard returned to more traditional designs. The result was a mish-mash of styles, clearly illustrated by the classical columns and pilasters and 18th century-style chairs in *Sylvania*'s first class restaurant. On *Carinthia*, the rosewood dining room chairs came from the pre-First World War liner *Aquitania*.

The interiors of *Queen Elizabeth 2* were conceived by a team of Britain's most talented designers. The most successful public room was undoubtedly the Queen's Room, which was designed by Michael Inchbald. With its space-age ceiling and columns reminiscent of Stanley Kubrick's 1968 film '2001 A Space Odyssey', the Queen's Room remained virtually unchanged throughout *Queen Elizabeth 2*'s thirty-nine-year career with Cunard.

A standard cabin on *Queen Elizabeth 2*. In 1969, the quality of *Queen Elizabeth 2*'s cabins was superior to those of most British liners of that time and all had en-suite toilets and showers or baths.

INDEX OF SHIPS

All ships mentioned are indexed. Names in capitals are those carried whilst in Cunard company ownership or management, and for these ships, the page numbers of fleet list entries are in **bold type**. Chartered ships with Cunard names are in upper and lower case. Proposed names are shown in brackets.

Aurania (1) as the Boer War Transport No.20. *[Thomas Stanley]*

Fred Olsen's *Bysanz* (2,126/1947) ran for Cunard in 1967 and 1968 as *Alsatia*. *[V.H. Young and L.A. Sawyer]*

The German *Bilbao* (2,250/1953) at Montreal in August, 1962 in Cunard colours on their Lakes service.   *[Marc Piché]*

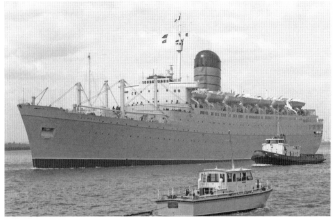

Saxonia was converted in 1963 into a dual-purpose cruise and transatlantic liner, painted in 'cruising green' and renamed *Carmania*. She was fitted with a large lido deck, heated pool, sports deck and four 60-passenger launches.

Cunard Countess nearing completion at Copenhagen, alongside *Cunard Conquest*, which entered service a year later as *Cunard Princess*.

302

Lycia in 1965. *[V.H.Young and L.A. Sawyer]*

The undignified end of a great liner. With a crane alongside and her hull buckled from the intense heat of the fire, *Seawise Universtity*, the former *Queen Elizabeth*, awaits her final fate Hong Kong harbour. *[William H. Miller]*

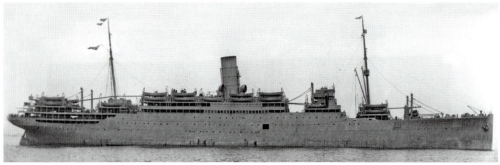

This photo of *Samaria* (2), in wartime colours was published in a US newspaper after she struck the aircraft carrier HMS *Furious* on 17th December 1939. At the time she was bound for the United States and was passing through a blacked-out convoy. None of her passengers, many of whom were American, were reported to have been injured and she returned to Liverpool. *[Baltimore Sun/J. and M. Clarkson collection]*